"Kaplan's biography masterfully depicts the life of Abraham Joshua Heschel, showing us how Heschel became the great moral and spiritual genius of the mid-twentieth century. We are all in Kaplan's debt."
—REUVEN KIMELMAN, professor of classical Judaica, Brandeis University

"As one blessed to have sat at the feet of Abraham Joshua Heschel, I enthusiastically endorse my fellow student Edward Kaplan's biography of our teacher and master. Kaplan's intimate understanding of Heschel's great life, work, and thought enables a new generation to at least meet in print what we encountered in person."
—DAVID NOVAK, professor of Jewish studies and philosophy, University of Toronto and author of *Jewish Justice*

"Abraham Heschel is one of the most significant American religious thinkers of the past century whose message remains pertinent today not only for contemporary Judaism but also for followers of other faiths, and even for those of no specific faith but who nonetheless search for the meaning of human life in our chaotic world. Professor Kaplan is to be congratulated for summarizing in a single volume his decades of scholarly research into the life and works of Heschel, this unique Jewish thinker who was at once a metaphysician, theologian, spiritual observer, and acute commentator of the human condition as well as a social and political activist."
—SEYYED HOSSEIN NASR, University Professor of Islamic Studies, George Washington University

"Edward K. Kaplan's magisterial biography of the greatest Jewish prophetic figure of the barbaric twentieth century is a masterpiece! It is also incredibly timely. We need the wisdom, courage, and compassion of the inimitable Rabbi Abraham Joshua Heschel. The very future of our world depends, in part, on the legacy of Heschel's prophetic witness."
—CORNEL WEST, Professor of the Practice of Public Philosophy, Harvard University

"Rabbi Abraham Joshua Heschel was many things: an inspired and visionary theologian, an immensely learned and wide-ranging scholar, an impassioned and courageous activist, and a powerfully eloquent moral voice. It is tempting (and understandable) to mythologize a man who accomplished so much,

but it is also easy to lose sight of the real person behind the myth. In this wonderful distillation of many years of painstaking research, Ed Kaplan presents us with Heschel the man. Kaplan's love for his subject is so clear, I anticipate readers will find the love contagious."
—RABBI SHAI HELD, author of *The Heart of Torah: Essays on the Weekly Torah Portion*

"Edward Kaplan's lucid biography of Rabbi Abraham Joshua Heschel illuminates the profound contributions of one of the most outstanding religious figures of the twentieth century. Kaplan chronicles the development of this exceptional scholar whose academic career flourished in America not only because of his brilliance but also because he embodied the qualities of one of his principal subjects of study: the prophets. Heschel's commitment to civil rights, opposition to the Vietnam War, and interreligious relations show us what inspired religious leadership looks like—leadership our world today desperately needs."
—MARY C. BOYS, Dean Skinner and McAlpin Professor of Practical Theology, Union Theological Seminary in the City of New York

"I loved this book. Kaplan's engaging, incisive biography brings alive Heschel's extraordinary personality, theology, prophetic voice, and monumental contributions to Jewish thought, interfaith understanding, and the moral soul of America. *Abraham Joshua Heschel: Mind, Heart, Soul* evokes a much richer and deeper understanding of this spiritual giant as it simultaneously rekindles the reader's passion for the work of Jewish social justice."
—RABBI DAVID SAPERSTEIN, director emeritus, Religious Action Center of Reform Judaism

"Kaplan offers a close reading into the complex emotional, intellectual, and cultural experiences that shaped Heschel's depth theology, radical mysticism, and social activism and catapulted him into becoming a fearless champion of human rights. Scholars and concerned citizens everywhere will benefit from the needed reminder that indeed 'the earth is the Lord's.'"
—WALTER EARL FLUKER, Martin Luther King Jr. Professor of Ethical Leadership, Boston University School of Theology

ABRAHAM JOSHUA HESCHEL

UNIVERSITY OF NEBRASKA PRESS · LINCOLN

Abraham Joshua Heschel
Mind, Heart, Soul

EDWARD K. KAPLAN

THE JEWISH PUBLICATION SOCIETY · PHILADELPHIA

Adapted from *Abraham Joshua Heschel: Prophetic Witness* by Edward K. Kaplan and Samuel H. Dresner (Yale University Press, 1998) and *Spiritual Radical: Abraham Joshua Heschel in America, 1940–1972* by Edward K. Kaplan (Yale University Press, 2007)

Library of Congress Cataloging-
    in-Publication Data
Names: Kaplan, Edward K., 1942–, author.
Title: Abraham Joshua Heschel: mind,
    heart, soul / Edward K. Kaplan.
Description: Lincoln: University of
    Nebraska Press, [2019] | Includes
    bibliographical references and index.
Identifiers: LCCN 2019004040
    ISBN 9780827614741 (pbk.: alk. paper)
    ISBN 9780827618275 (epub)
    ISBN 9780827618282 (mobi)
    ISBN 9780827618299 (pdf)
Subjects: LCSH: Heschel, Abraham
    Joshua, 1907–1972. | Rabbis—
    United States—Biography.
Classification: LCC BM755.H34 K369
    2019 | DDC 296.3092 [B]—dc23
LC record available at https://
    lccn.loc.gov/2019004040
Set in Ehrhardt by Mikala R. Kolander.
Designed by N. Putens.

To my father, Kivie Kaplan (1904–1975), and his generation
of people committed to social justice.

To my students from Amherst College (in consortium with
Smith College, University of Massachusetts Amherst, Mount
Holyoke College, Hampshire College) and Brandeis University,
who transformed my academic course "Mysticism and the
Moral Life" into a spiritual and intellectual partnership.

CONTENTS

PHOTOGRAPHS

Following page 206

1. Heschel's father, Rabbi Moshe Mordecai Heschel

2. Heschel's mother, Rivka Reizel Perlow Heschel

3. Abraham Joshua Heschel, age seventeen, in Warsaw

4. Abraham Joshua Heschel at Hebrew
   Union College in Cincinnati, ca. 1940

5. Abraham Heszel (Heschel)'s Declaration of Intention
   to become a U.S. citizen, dated May 29, 1940

6. Seymour Siegel (*left*), Abraham Joshua
   Heschel, and Samuel H. Dresner, ca. 1949

7. Sylvia Straus Heschel, ca. 1949

8. Abraham Joshua Heschel and daughter,
   Susannah, born May 15, 1952

PREFACE

Heschel's story is the story of the twentieth century: its horrors and its marvels.

Abraham Joshua Heschel (1907–1972) lived his first thirty-three years in Europe and his final thirty-two in the United States. This biography grapples with an enigma: how does Heschel's devotion to the living God of justice and compassion, his faith, remain intact (though often anguished) before and after the Holocaust?

Heschel reflected upon the meaning of existence with the all-embracing knowledge of a highly educated Jew who had mastered the classic texts of traditional Judaism and the full curriculum of twentieth-century European humanism. In March 1940 he stepped off the boat in New York City, a penniless refugee from Hitler's Germany. Speaking as "a brand plucked from the fire of an altar to Satan on which millions of human lives were exterminated," as he memorably proclaimed, Heschel became one of America's foremost theologians and activist public intellectuals.

Heschel's models were the Hebrew prophets who spoke for God, demanding absolute truth and righteousness in everyday life. As a learned scholar, he embodied several Jewish cultures that thrived in Europe before the Holocaust: strict Talmudic learning and Hasidic spirituality, Yiddish and Hebrew secularism, German Liberal Judaism and Modern Orthodoxy. Heschel famously asserted that "God is in search of mankind" and that each and every human being is an image of the Divine. As a naturalized American citizen, he developed a vivid, contemporary Jewish theology and confronted problems that still continue to plague us: poverty, war, racism, and the necessity of truth and compassion in American democracy and the State of Israel. And as a philosopher and literary virtuoso, Heschel developed a rhetoric aimed to transform the reader's manner of thinking, appealing to our intuitive as well as rational sensitivities. He was convinced that every thoughtful person was capable of achieving certainty in the reality of God through prayer, study, and moral sensitivity. For Heschel, there is continuity between the inwardness of worship and active commitment to social justice.

Such was my hope personally. As a secularized intellectual stirred by expressions of religious faith and its elusive certainties, I sought to understand how a traditional Jewish scholar, poet, teacher, and writer, ordained as a Hasidic rabbi in Warsaw, had earned a PhD in philosophy from the University in Berlin during the rise of Hitler. Heschel's doctoral thesis, "Prophetic Consciousness" (published in 1936), indeed prepared him to become a dissident in America during the turbulent 1960s, until his untimely death in December 1972, during the "Christmas bombings" of America's Vietnam War he so vehemently denounced.

For my entire academic life, I have remained fascinated with the analogies between poetry, prayer, and social action. Careful, meditative reading and interpretation of French poetry and thought, among other literatures, have aroused in me the (vaguely understood) "feeling" of what it must be like to be a "mystic," to love God at the heights of ecstasy, to achieve union with the Godhead. Mystics are convinced that they have experienced the living God, beyond images, beyond ideas; Heschel was steadfast in his trust in the God of justice and compassion. How can many of us who do not share that certainty live and think in accord with foundational religious teachings, Jewish or otherwise? My strategy has been to study the mystic's life.

To further my own quest for certainty and share it with students, I developed an undergraduate course entitled "Mysticism and the Moral Life," which I taught, in various permutations, first at Amherst College and then at Brandeis University, for about forty years. We studied the lives and works of writers who testified to their mystical faith, or its insufficiency, and validated their experiences by their efforts to lead moral lives. These creative writers lived in harmony with poetry, compassion, and faith. While the course evolved over time, I kept returning to three exemplars: Thomas Merton, the Trappist monk; Howard Thurman, the African American teacher of spiritual disciplines; and Abraham Joshua Heschel.

One more autobiographical fact may help explain my passionate quest to understand Abraham Joshua Heschel. Early in 1966 during my second year of graduate school at Columbia University, as I prepared for a PhD in French literature, I was introduced to Heschel through my father, Kivie Kaplan, an idealistic businessman, and the Reverend Martin Luther King Jr., who was close to Heschel. My father, who did not have a college education, devoted his busy life to the social justice missions of the Union of American Hebrew Congregations (the UAHC, now the Union for Reform Judaism, or URJ) and the NAACP (National Association for the Advancement of Colored People). He served as national president of the NAACP from 1966 until his death in 1975, in a telephone booth at La Guardia Airport between board meetings of these two organizations. As my father's son, I had the immense privilege of meeting and speaking with scores of human rights activists, primarily white Jewish liberals and African Americans at all levels of involvement. Dr. King was just one of those NAACP members (before the Southern Christian Leadership Conference [SCLC]) I grew up with. I inherited my father's legacy of idealism, although, I admit, I resisted the pull of activism.

Apart from my training in French literature and thought, since college I had become immersed in Hindu philosophy. I criticized as "boring" the hyper-rationalistic Reform Judaism of the 1950s in which I was raised. Fearing I would jump ship, Dr. King somehow informed my father about Rabbi Abraham Heschel, who was reputed to be a mystic. Dad wrote to Heschel, who admired my father's dedication as a Jew to civil rights, asking him to send me some of his books. Heschel obliged. For the first time in my life, I read a "Jewish book" that convincingly evoked the reality of God. (It was *Man Is Not Alone*, 1951.) When I later met Rabbi Heschel (as I called him) in his Jewish Theological Seminary office, we spent two hours discussing my graduate studies of French literature, and especially poetry, which Heschel deemed to be "important work." The bond was sealed. I chose to work out my perplexities through Judaism. Heschel's life and writings became my guide.

ACKNOWLEDGMENTS

My gratitude to the Jewish Publication Society (JPS), its director, Rabbi Barry Schwartz, and managing editor, Joy Weinberg, and Leif Milliken of the University of Nebraska Press (UNP), for their professionalism, support, and devotion to bringing this biography of Abraham Joshua Heschel to fruition. JPS and UNP together cement an admirable team. Thank you to Rabbi Barry Schwartz for advancing the essential relationship of Abraham Heschel to the Jewish Publication Society, from the era of Solomon Grayzel to the present, and for your clear and rapid communication, which enhanced our work together. To Leif Milliken, my gratitude for your highest publication standards, rigorous defense of scholarly integrity, and diplomatic skills in the service of excellence.

Thank you, Joy Weinberg, for consistently upholding the highest standards of scholarly publication, in your attention to details as well as larger issues of intelligibility. Your demands for improvement have challenged and inspired me, reminding me of the Brandeis University slogan, "Truth unto its innermost parts."

My profound gratitude to Hadassah Margolis, for providing sensitive and intrepid editing and a humane intelligence that gave me confidence, enriching my lifelong dialogue with Abraham Joshua Heschel.

Writing a biography, especially, involves a world of human contact, which I treasure. Words are not adequate to thank the numerous people who shared their experiences and insights during the two decades of research and writing the original Yale University Press volumes—where they are named to the best of my ability. Through conversations, letters, the documentation and translations they provided, visits in their homes, and so much more, they have elevated my sense of responsibility, as a biographer and as a Jew, to retrieve their silenced voices.

Yale University Press must equally be thanked for the outstanding production and marketing of the two-volume biography over a long period of time and for their permission to publish an abridgment of the two-volume biography under their copyright.

Writing, even scholarly writing, can become a vehicle of friendship. My gratitude to members of Heschel's family, particularly to his widow, the late Sylvia Straus Heschel; his daughter, Susannah Heschel; the late Thena Heshel Kendall (Heschel's niece, his brother Jacob's daughter); and Yitzchak Meyer Twersky (son of Pearl Heschel Twersky, Heschel's first cousin). I am forever grateful to Abraham Joshua Heschel himself, for believing in me, for his warmth and generosity, and for opening our minds to "radical amazement" and "holiness in words."

I am deeply grateful to my children, Jeremy Joshua Kaplan, Aaron Emmanuel Kaplan, and Sima Chava Kaplan, as well as their partners and families, who give us hope for the future and joys in the present.

My wife, my life partner, Janna Kaplan, deserves a singular recognition. Together, we share Heschel's presence in our lives, as well as we delight and anguish in being Jewish. Janna's insights and skills played a crucial role in the preparation of this book for publication.

It is a special pleasure to acknowledge the essential contribution of the late Rabbi Samuel H. Dresner, lifetime disciple of Abraham Joshua Heschel, who initiated the original biography more than forty years ago. In 1942 Dresner met Heschel at the Hebrew Union College in Cincinnati, wrote his dissertation on the *zaddik* under Heschel's direction, spent ten years translating Heschel's Hasidic essays, and edited an anthology of Heschel's works. To quote Dresner's words in a 1995 letter to me, "I alone was at Heschel's side since I first met him in 1942. For a long time, his voice cried in the wilderness. In those days and for a considerable time afterward, I and a very few others alone recognized who he was and what he could mean to Jews and non-Jews alike."

Rabbi Dresner worked for over a decade to establish a Heschel archive, housed at the Jewish Theological Seminary, which includes his own diary of classes and conversations with Heschel, invaluable interviews, rare bibliographical sources, and otherwise unknown biographical facts that partly grew out of the copious notes he made of his conversations, classes, and seminars with Heschel. Also included are recordings of roundtable discussions of Heschel's work by colleagues and former students of Heschel, organized by Jack Wertheimer and Dresner, which display candor, good humor, and love for Heschel. Dresner secured generous grants from the National Endowment for the Humanities and from Menachem Riklis of Chicago to prepare a biography of Heschel. I was honored when in 1989 he invited me to collaborate on the biography of his master, his own fragile health preventing him from pursuing this alone. *Abraham Joshua Heschel: Prophetic Witness* (Yale University Press, 1998) was the outcome of that collaboration. Sadly, Rabbi Dresner passed away in 2000 before we could begin work together on the second part of the biography, chronicling Heschel's life in the United States, beginning in 1940.

I also wish to acknowledge two important repositories of Abraham Joshua Heschel's archives and personal papers.

After Heschel's untimely death in December 1972, Heschel's papers were deemed "personal possession of the family," his widow Sylvia Straus Heschel and daughter Susannah Heschel. The papers remained in their New York apartment and inaccessible to scholars. In 2012, several years after the death of Mrs. Heschel, Susannah sold her father's personal papers to the Duke University Library Special Collections. The Heschel Archive at Duke became officially available for use in July 2014, long after Yale University Press had published the two-volume Heschel biography (1998, 2007).

Duke University's Heschel Archive website is expertly catalogued and easy to use. I especially value the correspondence—letters in German, Hebrew, Yiddish, and English—and manuscripts, page proofs of books, information on publications, and reviews. I chose not to supplement with this newly available material for the current one-volume adapted biography of Heschel, judging the Duke Archive would not present significant surprises to me, but rather additional depth and confirmation of my insights. That said, these documents may indeed encourage readers to follow the suggestions embedded in my narrative and provide pleasant discoveries for those who enjoy exploration in depth and detail.

I have been assembling my own personal Heschel archive starting with the time I first met Heschel in 1966. Over the years, this collection has been further augmented by vast amounts of primary and other sources relating to my work on the biography. When Rabbi Dresner and I began working together, he gave me a copy of all his materials. My own research took me to Europe, Israel, New York, and other centers of intellectual or cultural activity connected to Heschel's life. To ensure the continuity of Heschel studies, in 2018 I donated my Heschel archive to the Jewish Theological Seminary. The AJH/JTS Archive has been thus enriched by many more interviews, photographs, previously unknown primary documents, my copious research notes and travel logs, recorded interviews, and earlier drafts of the Yale University Press two-volume biography. Dresner's and my collections, combined together now at the Jewish Theological Seminary, make available to scholars and seekers primary and secondary sources documenting Heschel's life and legacy, thoughts and actions, personal and professional relationships, as well as the joys and sorrows of his broken heart.

To future scholars, writers, and admirers of Heschel: you now have access to an ethical and spiritual gold mine, which awaits your curiosity, and ours.

NOTES ON THIS VOLUME

This biography is the fruit of several metamorphoses. The basic narrative of *Abraham Joshua Heschel: Mind, Heart, Soul* remains true to my original two-volume biography, presented in succeeding editions: first, *Abraham Joshua Heschel: Prophetic Witness* (Yale University Press, 1998), co-authored with the late Rabbi Samuel H. Dresner; and then *Spiritual Radical: Abraham Joshua Heschel in America, 1940–1972* (Yale University Press, 2007). Together, these books constitute the most thorough account of Heschel's life and works and their personal and cultural settings. Both volumes received National Jewish Book Awards.

Some years later, a request for a one-volume abridgment in French translation came to me from Daniel Tollet, a historian of Poland and editor of a series on Jewish studies at the firm of Honoré Champion in Paris. As a professor of French literature, I had published two books on Heschel in French, *La sainteté en paroles: Abraham Heschel; Piété, poétique, action* (Paris: Le Cerf, 1999; the original, *Holiness in Words*, published by SUNY Press in 1996) and *Abraham Heschel, un prophète pour notre temps* (Albin Michel, 2008). Dr. Tollet's idea inspired me to condense and programmatically rework the two substantial volumes. An outstanding former student of mine from Brandeis University, Hadassah Margolis, who had worked with me before, helped me sift through the more than one thousand pages and remove large chunks of information and loving detail to consolidate the core material. Subsequently, the translator of the French abridgment, John E. Jackson, an eminent literary scholar from the University of Berne, Switzerland, and a friend, produced a lucid French version of our typescript, published as *Abraham Joshua Heschel: Une biographie* (Honoré Champion, 2016).

The volume you now hold in your hands preserves the substance of the two originals, but with a crisper style and far fewer details. Heschel's inner struggles come into clearer focus. The depiction of Heschel's emotional life complements his intellectual and cultural experiences. For example, we follow Heschel's development as a young poet, writing in Yiddish, and as a graduate student of philosophy in Berlin, writing in German, during the rise of Hitler. That Heschel became a religious and social activist in the United States during the civil rights movement, the Cold War, the Vietnam War, and other turbulent events of post–World War II America cannot be truly understood without this connection to his formative past.

Readers will appreciate the attention paid to Heschel's remarkable command of literary English, as even before his immigration he wrote eloquently in Yiddish, Hebrew, and German. Slow, meditative reading of Heschel's own writings is imperative, and careful, patient reading of the biography is similarly rewarding. This one-volume biography also benefited from further improvements in style and updates that did not appear in the earlier volumes.

This book will reward us with a sense of empathy with Heschel's powerful emotions. The God of pathos, the living God of feeling and compassion, is truly the companion of Heschel's engagement in the world at large. Mysticism and the moral life are joined in his sensibility.

This biography also serves as an introduction to all forms of Jewish life in Europe before the Holocaust. The larger questions concern us all: How did Heschel preserve his faith in the God of justice and love for humankind after the Holocaust? Heschel's postwar years in the United States develop a critique of war, economic and spiritual poverty, political corruption, the terrible ambiguities of religious faith, and the fragility of truth.

In the United States Heschel developed a sort of neo-Hasidism that inspired Jewish renewal in worship, both within and beyond the synagogues and denominations. The interfaith consequences of Heschel's own trajectory provide models for our search for meaning.

A few other technical matters to guide you, the reader:

- The present book is fully documented with an updated bibliography and revised notes.
- Occasionally italics appear in quotations from Heschel. Unless otherwise specified, the italics are Heschel's own.
- Almost all referenced books appear in the bibliography; if a given work does not appear there, the full citation can be found in the notes.

My hope is that appreciative readers of this comprehensive one-volume biography will be inspired to share it widely with others and to read, and reread, Heschel's own vivid writings, a living source of insight, research, and reflection.

ABRAHAM JOSHUA HESCHEL

PART I

From Hasidism to Modernity

CHAPTER 1

Hasidic Warsaw, 1907–1925

Born in Warsaw, Abraham Joshua Heschel embodied several Jewish cultures that flourished there before World War II. This center of Congress Poland, which from 1815 to 1915 belonged to the Russian Empire, enjoyed the fullest autonomy of any province controlled by the tsarist regime. Its Jewish population steadily became the largest and most influential in Europe. By 1917, when Heschel was ten years old, Jews comprised 41 percent of the city's population. Jewish culture, secular and religious, was thriving. There were Zionist organizations, youth movements, labor unions of various political tenor, and numerous Hebrew and Yiddish newspapers and periodicals. The legacy of the Haskalah (Jewish Enlightenment) favored translations of European masterpieces into Yiddish or Modern Hebrew.

The Warsaw community was traditionally religious, and Hasidism the largest grouping among observant Jews, inspired in the eighteenth century by Rabbi Israel Eliezer, the Baal Shem Tov (the Master of the Good Name). In 1880 two-thirds of the three hundred officially sanctioned synagogues in Warsaw were Hasidic, as were many small *shteibls* (houses of prayer and study). Heschel was born into this pietistic movement.

Despite his insular community, Heschel received a complex political education. Absorbing the instability of a turbulent world, East

European Jews were devastated by the First World War, caught in the crossfire of national and regional interests over which they had no control. Local pogroms, the Russian Revolution, and the ensuing civil war forced Jews to migrate. Jewish soldiers in the opposing camps were drafted to the slaughter. Ancestral towns were decimated. Thousands chose to flee. Large numbers of *Mitnagdim* (opponents), traditional Jews suspicious of Hasidic exaggerations of prayer and ecstasy, arrived from various parts of Eastern Europe. Cities such as Warsaw, Berlin, and Vienna provided safe havens for the survivors.

As a result, the traditional religious life that had flourished now became precarious. As refugees came to Warsaw, some maintained their essentially medieval way of life, but others brought worldly trends and radical fervor. Many yeshivot (academies of Torah and Talmud study) closed. Sacred learning declined, while socialism, communism, Zionism, and other movements captivated young Jews. Believers feared that such freedom would threaten faith and destroy communities.

As a precocious child, Heschel felt the power of these competitions in which the soul of Jewishness was at stake.

HESCHEL'S SPIRITUAL FOUNDATION

Heschel's Hasidic identity included both legend and harsh historical events. He was the scion of a spiritually regal tradition, which he had been trained to embody. He could proudly trace his pedigree (in Yiddish, *yichus*) back to the fifteenth century. Later, in fact, in the United States, he would consecrate his ancestors by drawing up, probably from memory, a list of 250 family members, going back several centuries.[1]

His dynastic prototype (and namesake) was Rabbi Abraham Yehoshua Heschel (1748–1825) of Apt (in Polish, Opatow). Five generations separated the boy from this ancestor, known by the title of his book, *Ohev Yisrael* (Lover of the Jewish people). This "grandfather" (as Jews refer even to distant predecessors) was also known as the Apter Rav (the latter word meaning "rabbi") because he exercised the legal authority of a community rabbi. Venerated for his diplomatic as well as spiritual skills, the Apter Rav mediated disputes among Hasidic leaders during a period of extreme factionalism. After the death of Hasidism's founder, the Baal Shem Tov, the Apter Rav became a spokesman for the third Hasidic generation.

Heschel's paternal ancestors came from Medzibozh (in Polish, Miedzyborz), where the Apter Rav was buried next to the Baal Shem Tov. In the autobiographical preface to his final book, *A Passion for Truth* (published posthumously in 1973), Heschel recalls his father's stories as his earliest sources of inner identity: "That little town so distant from Warsaw and yet so near was the place to which my childish imagination went on many journeys. . . . For most of the wondrous deeds my father told about either happened in Medzibozh or were inspired by those mysterious men who lived there."[2]

These mythic origins became concrete. Heschel's grandfather— also named Abraham Joshua Heschel (1832–1881)—established his family in Medzibozh, where he became rebbe, the charismatic leader of the community. Heschel's father, Moshe Mordecai Heschel (1873–1916), was born there, as were his uncles and aunts.[3]

Heschel's father received his vocation from the noble Hasidic dynasty of Rabbi Israel Friedman (1797–1850), rebbe of Ruzhin (in Polish, Radzyn). The Ruzhiner rebbe, Heschel's father's great-grandfather, traced *his* ancestry back to the biblical King David; some devotees even considered him to be a reincarnation of the Baal Shem Tov.[4]

Yet Israel of Ruzhin was an ambiguous figure, because of his wealth and the luxuriousness of his Hasidic court. Adversaries decried its opulence; followers revered the rebbe's hidden piety and appreciated his compassion. His influence was undeniable. Five of his sons married daughters of other Hasidic dynasties and established their own courts in Sadagora, Zinkov, Husyatin, and Tchortkov.

Heschel's father was about eight years old when they moved to the Hasidic court of Rabbi Dovid Moshe Friedman (1828–1904) in Tchortkov. Dovid Moshe's palace was indeed sumptuous, but he himself led an ascetic life of prayer and study. Heschel's father encouraged his precocious son to emulate a regal attitude that was both compassionate and spiritually elevated.

From his mother, Rivka Reizel Perlow (1874–1942), Heschel inherited the Lithuanian Hasidic tradition. Her father, Rabbi Jacob Perlow (1843–1902), born in Poland, was brought up in the home of her grandfather, Shlomo Hayim of Koidanov (1797–1862), an eminent Lithuanian rebbe.[5] Shlomo Hayim married a descendant of Rabbi Levi Yitzhak of Berditchev (1740–1810), a mystic, Talmud scholar, and compassionate friend of ordinary people.[6]

The young Heschel was especially attracted to Rabbi Levi Yitzhak of Berditchev, who defended suffering Jews against God's strict judgment. Renowned for his humility, Levi Yitzhak would intercede to God for mercy on behalf of even the most ignorant Jew. And he spoke directly to God using the Yiddish vernacular of the people, rather than Hebrew, the sacred language favored by the learned spiritual elite.

Heschel's maternal grandparents, Jacob and Chaya Perlow, eventually settled in Minsk-Mazowiecki (known among Jews as Novominsk), an industrial town located about twenty miles from Warsaw. Chaya Perlow gave birth to twins, a boy and a girl, Alter Israel Shimon and Rivka Reizel; they were Heschel's uncle and mother.

We now enter the modern history of Heschel's parents, Rabbi Moshe Mordecai Heschel and Rivka Reizel Perlow. Married around 1890 in Novominsk, they remained for ten years at the Hasidic court of the bride's father. It was a vibrant traditional environment. Rabbi Perlow built a large yeshiva, the first Hasidic school of higher Torah learning in Poland, where hundreds of students came to live and study. A remarkable spiritual personality, the rebbe of Novominsk combined devotion to Torah study, talmudic learning, and inner piety. He was reputed to inspire *teshuvah* ("turning" or repentance) by the very sound of his voice.

In 1902, after Rabbi Jacob Perlow died, Rivka Reizel's twenty-eight-year-old twin brother, Alter Israel Shimon, became the rebbe of Novominsk. By then the "old Tchortkover rebbe" (as Dovid Moshe was known) advised his stepson Moshe Mordecai to relocate closer to Warsaw.

So, around 1904, Moshe Mordecai and Rivka Reizel, with their five children—Heschel's four sisters, Sarah Brakha, Esther Sima, Gittel, and Devorah Miriam, and his brother, Jacob (Heschel was not yet born)—settled in Warsaw's Pelzovizna district, a poor, predominantly Jewish area on the right bank of the Vistula River. Heschel's father functioned as a *vinkl rebbe* (a neighborhood or "corner rebbe").

Their next move decided Heschel's future. His father, known as the Pelzovizna rebbe, established his modest Hasidic court at 40 Muranowska Street, in the thriving center of Warsaw's Jewish district. In this new, large apartment building of gray stone blocks where he and his family lived, Moshe Mordecai worked, studied, and prayed.

On January 11, 1907, Abraham Joshua Heschel was born. To honor his father's line, he was given the complete name of Abraham Joshua Heschel Heschel. (Hasidim often place a full name before the family name.) That designation paid homage to the Apter Rav and his grandfather Rabbi Abraham Joshua Heschel of Medzibozh. As the youngest child, "Avrumele" (little Abraham, in Yiddish) soon became the family's most favored member.

Heschel was trained to become a rebbe. In the family apartment, Hasidic protocol governed domestic relationships by formal but loving rules. When the rebbe entered a room, everyone stood up. Jacob, the eldest son (called Yankele), would later recall that he had rarely remained seated in his father's presence. The children addressed their father in the third person.[7]

Yet Avrumele enjoyed special status. His father recognized him as an *illui* (prodigy), a precocious and superior intellect, and often spoke with him, sometimes confiding personal thoughts. In turn, Heschel internalized Hasidism by observing his father. Correct behavior was crucial, since a zaddik (a righteous or holy person) had to embody Torah. One's father's entire physical bearing might shape a child's inward self.

Reb Moyshele, as Heschel's father was affectionately called, was fairly tall, and he conducted himself with a noble and gentle demeanor. His aristocratic manners reflected his Ruzhin upbringing; his gestures were as exquisite as his apparel. According to Hasidic standards, every Jew was considered a "prince." So as not to demean himself while eating, Reb Moyshele would not bend to reach his food, but lift it to his mouth. Throughout his life, Heschel would later reflect his father's erect posture and deliberate motions.

Moshe Mordecai's loyalty to ancestral values required courage, for his family lived in bitter privation. He was not a practical man and had very little money. His small and mostly poor following provided modest fees for his advice and blessings. Moreover, he never kept money in his house overnight. At the end of each day, he distributed any remaining cash to the needy.

Heschel's closest childhood friend from Warsaw, Yehiel Hofer, was sensitive to this contrast. He wrote that in Warsaw, "Moshe Mordecai became acquainted with Jewish poverty"; it was said that at the Ruzhiner rebbe's home there were "golden knobs on the doors, the food was brought to the table on golden vessels, and the family rode in coaches drawn by three horses."[8] Even so, Heschel remembered that despite lacking adequate nourishment, his father always had a flower placed on his desk.

GROOMING A HASIDIC PRINCE

Heschel's nascent social conscience and "religion of sympathy" with God in exile emerged. As he saw it, all Jews were exiles. Certainly,

Heschel wrote, his father in cosmopolitan Warsaw considered himself to be in exile from Medzibozh, where his holy ancestors were buried: "He confided in me, 'For I was indeed stolen out of the land of the Hebrews' (Genesis 40:15)."[9]

Yehiel Hofer recalls a childhood scene that Heschel must have witnessed countless times: "The rebbe trembled uncontrollably when poor women burst into the prayerhouse, would fall in front of the Holy Ark, pull the curtain aside, open the doors and, weeping and wailing, grab the Torah scrolls, begging mercy for a desperately ill husband or sick child, or sometimes for a mother of children who was on the verge of leaving this world. He could find no rest."[10] Years later, Heschel recalled a similar story about the Apter Rav: "He was asked by many other rebbes, 'Why are your prayers always accepted and not ours?' He gave the following answer: 'You see, whenever a Jew comes to me and pours out his heart and tells me of his misery and suffering, I have such compassion that a little hole is created in my heart. Since I have heard and listened to a great many Jews with their problems and anguish, there are a great many holes in my heart. . . . [God] sees this broken heart . . . so He has compassion for my heart and that is why He listens to me.'"[11]

Everyday realities entered Heschel's home by virtue of its urban location. Political conflicts were summoned up by the songs of workers in the tin button factory within the apartment complex. And just a few blocks away from Heschel's home was the street life that epitomized Jewish Warsaw's contradictions, as evoked by Isaac Bashevis Singer: "Here, a bearded Jew with earlocks walked by in a fur-lined hat and satin gabardine . . . and soon a dandy came by in modern clothes . . . [who] smoked openly on the Sabbath demonstrating his lack of faith in the Torah. Now came a pious young matron with a bonnet on her shaven head, to be closely followed by a girl with rouged cheeks, a kind of blue eye shadow, and a short-sleeved blouse that revealed her bare arms."[12]

For the most part, however, Avrumele's religious education remained insulated from Warsaw's pluralistic society. By age three he entered the male universe of study. Childhood was serious but happy: prayer, learning sacred texts, seeking holiness everywhere. From an early age, he began to closely study Bible, Mishnah (the oral law, the foundational book of Talmud), and the religious codes, as preludes to entering the "sea of Talmud." At home, the cute and lively boy became a star performer in Jewish texts. Notably, he displayed not only a prodigious memory, but also precocious charm and wit. Family members enjoyed it when Avrumele, scarcely more than a toddler, would recite the *Kiddush* (sanctification over wine) when placed on a table or chair.[13]

As a child of rabbinical aristocracy, Heschel was not sent to *heder* (religious elementary school). Rather, he began formal studies with tutors by age three or four, when most other boys entered *heder*. Avrumele had a preceptor (teacher or instructor) who directed his study of texts, accompanied him on walks and visits, and might have even slept in his room. Above all, the little rebbe's character was being formed to announce piety by his very presence.

As an adult, Heschel would offer insight into the cultivation of the rebbe he was meant to become by sharing this anecdote with American readers: "'Why do you go to see the rebbe?' someone asked an eminent rabbi who, although his time was precious, would trudge for days to visit his master on the Sabbath. 'To stand near him and watch him lace his shoes,' he answered."[14]

A TEXTUAL FOUNDATION

The pedagogical method was medieval, the content ancient; the entire day was given over to study and prayer. First, boys memorized the basic Hebrew texts: siddur (prayer book) and Torah (the Five Books of Moses). They recited the weekly Torah selection, translating it into Yiddish. Ideally, teacher and pupil discussed the text's meaning as applied to human situations and spiritual issues. Typically, rote memory was the rule.

The next stage involved *Humash mit Rashi*, the Pentateuch with the classic interpretations of Rashi (acronym of Rabbi Shlomo Itzhaki, 1040–1105), which Heschel also learned by heart. Along with Bible were elements of the *Shulchan Arukh*, the standard code of Jewish law compiled by the great Talmud teacher Joseph Caro (1488–1575). Traditional rabbis had to master the codes to justify legal decisions and proffer advice.

By age eight Heschel had begun Talmud study, the communal, spiritual, and personal foundation of Jewish life. This text study was a physical and social process. The boys "learned" with a partner, a *haver* (in Hebrew, "comrade"). One of them recited the text, swaying, or chanted a *nigun* (wordless melody). Pondering a sacred text was a form of physical prayer; the boys, imitating their fathers and teachers, rocked back and forth (a movement called *shucklin*), while their singsong voices rose and fell.

Talmud study could later include midrash, theological and creative Rabbinic commentaries on the Bible. As for Hasidic texts, these were written but mostly conveyed orally, accompanying followers of Hasidism throughout their lifetime.

Heschel entered Warsaw's larger Hasidic community at one of the *shteibls* (home or room for study and prayer that approximated the Hasidic customs of the ancestral villages) associated with the dynasty of Ger. Heschel's Gerer *shteibl* was near his house, on his street, at 17 Muranowska Street.[15]

The *shteibl*'s rigorous daily schedule typified the regimen of Heschel's childhood and early adolescence. Living at home, the boys woke at five, walked to the *shteibl*, where they sat at long wooden benches and tables, and began to recite text. From seven to eight they prayed the *Shacharit* (morning) service with fervor. After prayers the boys returned to their families for breakfast. By ten they headed back to the *shteibl*, where they studied at their tables until noon. Students used the time between sessions to study non-talmudic subjects, such as the Torah portion, midrash, and Hasidic books recommended by their rebbes. Each day ended with *Mincha*, the afternoon service, although often the boys returned after dinner to study well into the evening.

The liturgical calendar governed their lives. Heschel's lifelong abhorrence of "killing time" (in Hebrew, *bitul z'man*, "nullification of time") originated in this period.[16] Students were expected to spend most of their waking hours studying or praying; losing just one precious moment in frivolity or laziness was considered a sin. Jewish spirituality was engraved daily in the boys' consciousness. The holy Sabbath was its weekly culmination.

Years later, in the United States, Heschel, now an author and professor, conceived his mission to convey this spiritual atmosphere to modern, even assimilated English-speaking readers. Sabbath observance was the crown. Indeed, the Sabbath was holiness in time—a major spiritual opportunity for all Jews. Recounting his family's fervent preparations for the ceremonial Friday evening meal, he would remind secularized readers that the Sabbath could help them "strive for spiritual integrity . . . [a daily life of] inwardness, compassion, justice and holiness."[17]

HUMILITY AND INTELLECTUAL PRIDE

The forming of Heschel's inner integrity as zaddik was as deliberate as mastering texts. Intellectual skill seemed to be the precocious boy's dominant quality. Gifted with an eidetic (visual) memory, around age seven he could scan books quickly, remembering their contents. Driven by a desire for knowledge—and perhaps a budding ambitiousness—Heschel at nine or ten began to consume the books in his father's library.

Heschel also applied his mental energies to amuse himself during

the few moments outside of study. For the sheer challenge, he catalogued and learned by heart all the products in the millinery store
of his friend Yehiel's father. Early on, he relished the intricacies of
chess, one of the few amusements Hasidim favored.

A bridge was forming, perhaps, to secular curiosity. Many religiously educated Jewish boys developed an extraordinary mental
discipline, due in large part to Talmud study and *pilpul*, a deft method
of talmudic dialectic analysis originating among East European Jews.
In addition to enhancing analytical skills, Talmud study advanced
Heschel's unusual ability to retain large amounts of reading matter.
He claimed that his book on theology in the Talmud, published in
Rabbinic Hebrew from 1962 to 1965, drew heavily upon his memory
of sources.

Even as a boy, Heschel was treated like a rebbe, with deference.
Expecting wise answers to their questions, people rose to greet him
when he entered a room.[18] Some even brought him *kvitlakh* (peti-
tions), joking that if he became a rebbe, all the other rebbes would
lose their followers.

At the same time, the family worried at early signs of Heschel's
pride. He claimed to have read most of—if not all—his father's
books by age twelve. His elder brother, Jacob, remembers being
shocked at Avrumele's boast that he could write better ones himself. A scion of generations of Hasidic rebbes who were believed to
possess supernatural qualities, perhaps Heschel could not help but
feel some sense of entitlement. Still, the boy was reprimanded for
his excessive self-regard.

FAMILY EMIGRATIONS

Heschel's political awareness was often dramatic. In 1914 the seven-
year-old's relatively secure existence was disrupted as the Russian
and Austro-Hungarian empires were preparing for war. Yehiel Hofer
describes how Moshe Mordecai's "court on Muranowska Street was

filled with Jews drafted for the Russian army and about to be sent to the front. Their pleas and those of their families that the rebbe should pray for them . . . gave him no rest."[19]

Heschel's far-flung clan, as well, was uprooted, eventually bringing the generations closer geographically. While the Russian military was expelling Jews from villages near the front, Rabbi Yitzhak Meir Heschel (Heschel's uncle) fled by way of Vizhnitz to Vienna, arriving in September 1914 with his family, including his son, also named Abraham Joshua Heschel (1888–1967), and Abraham's wife (and cousin), Sarah (Avrumele's eldest sister).

Along with tens of thousands of others, the Heschel and the Friedman clans—the rebbes of Tchortkov, Husyatin, Sadagora, and Boyan—also took refuge in Austria's capital. In Vienna they maintained regular contact with the Warsaw relatives and participated in all significant decisions relative to family, education, marriage, and religious politics.

Vienna became the vital center of Heschel's paternal branch. The Kopitzhinitzer rebbe established his court at 9 Ruepp Gasse, in Vienna's predominantly Jewish Second District. His thriving community became the Warsaw relatives' second home. Eventually, Heschel's sister Devorah Miriam married and moved to Vienna. His sister Gittel went there for a short time before returning to Warsaw. His brother Jacob married a Viennese cousin, Sarah Friedman, and the couple settled in Vienna.

The Vienna clan exerted a strong conservative influence on Heschel. The Heschels and the Friedmans, connected by marriage with the Ruzhin dynasty, were prominent leaders of the Agudat Israel, the Orthodox Jewish umbrella organization that had been established to combat the increasing assimilation and secularization of European Jews. This coalition became an authoritative force during the 1915 German occupation of Poland, joining representatives from the academic, political, and religious worlds. The Agudah (as it was also known) then consolidated its political force at the two "Great Assemblies" held in Vienna, in 1923 and 1929.

The Heschel clan thrived in Warsaw, reuniting Heschel's mother and uncle, the Novominsker rebbe Alter Israel Shimon Perlow (1874–1933), her twin brother. Despite the German invasion of 1914 menacing his Hasidic court, the rebbe refused to abandon his followers—that is, until Hanukkah 1915, when a German-born Russian official told him that "an order had been issued to arrest him and bring him to Russia," and the rebbe left Novominsk secretly.[20] By then, most of his community had already reached Warsaw. With his wife and eight children (there would eventually be twelve), Rabbi Perlow became the Heschels' neighbor, establishing his Hasidic court at 10 Franciszkanska Street, one long block away.

Heschel increased the intensity of his early Hasidic education at age eight, when he initiated regular visits to his maternal uncle, the Novominsker rebbe, who in turn made Talmud study and contemplative prayer the focus of Heschel's existence. Rabbi Perlow was revered as "a rebbe's rebbe" whose constant recitation of the Mishnah by heart became legendary. The young Heschel was lifted to another level by Rabbi Perlow's piety. Almost every day, accompanied by a tutor, he visited his uncle to study and converse, internalizing the Novominsker rebbe's utmost purity.

By 1916 Warsaw was occupied by the German army, and a typhus epidemic spread throughout the city, aggravated by the British blockade.[21] Then, on November 16, six weeks before Avrumele's tenth birthday, Heschel's father, Moshe Mordecai Heschel, died suddenly at age forty-three.

His death was a traumatic loss for Heschel and his family. Their lives became increasingly precarious, dogged by poverty. Heschel's mother heroically maintained her husband's *shteibl*. Her brother in Warsaw and the Heschels in Vienna provided some financial support, but they were constrained by their own lack of resources for their large families. Sometimes Heschel's mother had to send Yankele and Avrumele into the street to sell matches or other small items.[22]

Heschel veiled his grief. He referred to his father's early death only in the preface to his final book, *A Passion for Truth*, and even then, the mention was simply factual. The boy's shock and sorrow, mixed with the effects of the German occupation, the family's poverty, and disease, cannot be gauged. But it was certain that his childhood had come to a close.

PARAGONS OF PIETY

Soon after Heschel turned ten on January 11, 1917, his uncle, the Novominsker rebbe, then around forty-four years of age, took charge of his education. Unlike Heschel's father, the rebbe was small in stature—about five feet tall—and patently frail of health. Yet his home was welcoming and lively; the Perlows had eight daughters and four sons. Their nine rooms on Franciszkanska Street consisted of two adjoining apartments with a separate entrance for the rebbe. The family lived in the rear unit; the *shteibl* entrance was at the front.[23]

Rabbi Perlow complemented his nephew's spiritual education by familiarizing Heschel with the influential Hasidism of Ger (in Polish, Gora Kalwaria), headed by Rabbi Abraham Mordecai Alter (1864–1948), Polish leader of the Agudat Israel. (Rabbi Alter's father, Rabbi Yehudah Leib Alter, revered as the *Sfat Emet*, was Poland's most prominent Jewish religious representative.) What Heschel's uncle may not have anticipated was the radical influence of the original founder of the dynasty, Rabbi Menahem Mendl Morgenstern of Kotzk (1787–1859), whom many Gerer Hasidim revered. Indirectly but decisively, Rabbi Perlow proceeded to introduce Heschel to the harshly critical perspective of the Kotzker rebbe, which clashed with the optimistic traditions that had shaped Heschel's identity until then.

The Kotzker rebbe was an extremist. Unlike the generous Baal Shem Tov, who taught compassion out of respect for human limitations, the Kotzker rebbe was dismayed at human mediocrity and militantly, sometimes cruelly, upheld absolute standards. For the last twenty years of his life, he withdrew from his community. It was believed that the Kotzker was pathologically depressed.

As Heschel would later describe it, his own sensibility became torn between polar opposites, "the joy of Medzibozh [the home of the Baal Shem Tov] and the anxiety of Kotzk,"[24] for even then he recognized that the Kotzker's "passion for truth" could be destructive. Heschel's mature modern temperament would emerge from this tension.

Heschel took on this radical sensibility more fully when his uncle selected a new tutor for him, Bezalel Levy, a Gerer Hasid who followed the way of Kotzk. Reb Bezalel lived in Heschel's apartment building on Muranowska Street. A short man with fierce eyes and unusually long *payot* (sidelocks), he accompanied Avrumele everywhere, teaching and interrogating him. His influence was decisive—psychologically damaging in some ways, but also reinforcing the boy's drive for spiritual integrity.

Above all, Reb Bezalel assaulted Heschel's pride. Systematically and relentlessly, Bezalel instilled the Kotzker's lofty standards, the futility of human efforts, the foolishness of pride. Nothing less than extreme humility would make true piety possible. As Heschel recalled, "His one aim was to plant in my heart the feeling of contrition, of repentance, the danger of being a rebbe's son. He would constantly break down my ego, my self-confidence. To such an extent that whatever inferiority complexes I have . . ."[25] Heschel did not complete the sentence.

Years later in the United States, Heschel would confront not only his own fragile self-esteem, but also that of Saul Lieberman, the revered master scholar of Talmud who had memorized both Talmuds and their variants; Lieberman became Heschel's nemesis at the Jewish Theological Seminary in New York. Like Heschel, Lieberman had been a child prodigy and a product of the same harsh East European Jewish pedagogical tradition. In this case, Lieberman's father, a learned rabbi, had attacked his son's pride, calling him "idiot" and other humiliating names. This brutality was reinforced when Lieberman began training in *musar* (ethics) yeshivot, where the harsh discipline sometimes led to pathological self-loathing in the students, who reciprocated by censuring others.[26] Later, when both men would become professors at the Jewish Theological Seminary, the Jewish culture wars of the eighteenth century persisted—Heschel was the Hasid and Lieberman the *Mitnagid*. The inwardness of prayer, for Heschel, was the ideal; for Lieberman, the correct details of the Talmud were paramount. The ancient clash of cultures would be aggravated by both men's craving for approval, and even adulation, from colleagues and students.

In the end, though, Bezalel's challenges also strengthened Heschel's confidence. The young man took charge of his own discipline. He sought books that could transform him, some of which his family judged to be dangerous, including works by Rabbi Nahman of Bratslav (1772–1810), the Baal Shem Tov's great-grandson, a "tormented master" whose often pessimistic writings voiced anguish at God's remoteness.

In retrospect, Heschel would admit that he was a person divided, plagued by contradictory perceptions of himself. In his autobiographical preface to *A Passion for Truth*, he explained, "The Baal Shem gave me wings; the Kotzker encircled me with chains. . . . I owe intoxication to the Baal Shem, to the Kotzker the blessings of humiliation."[27]

Adjusting inwardly to Reb Bezalel's ruthless supervision, his father's death, and poverty at home, Heschel reached religious maturity under the guidance of Warsaw's distinguished Torah and Talmud scholars. The Novominsker rebbe gave substance to his nephew's piety by placing him within his rabbinical network. Heschel was mastering the textual foundations of traditional Jewish life, as well as Hasidic, kabbalistic, and aggadic literature.

Heschel turned thirteen on January 11, 1920, becoming an adult with full religious responsibilities. His bar mitzvah (literally, "son of the commandments"), three years after his father's death, was a significant dynastic event. He was especially honored that his grand-uncle Rabbi Yitzhak Meir Heschel, the old Kopitzhinitzer rebbe of Vienna, risked his fragile health to attend. Other rabbinical scholars, known as "leaders of the generation," were also present. Heschel had the extraordinary distinction of putting on the tefillin of Rabbi Levi Yitzhak of Berditchev, his maternal ancestor.[28] A festive meal with invited guests was held after the morning service.

Rabbinical ordination (*semikhah*) was the next stage. Heschel was qualified to become a practicing rabbi, as he had mastered the relevant sections of Talmud and all four parts of the *Shulchan Arukh*. Although Hasidic rebbes were not required to be ordained, the family felt that Heschel should. Yet, he was advised to wait a few years, to increase his competence in Talmud.

Heschel's advanced mentor, chosen by the Novominsker rebbe, was the prominent Talmud scholar Rabbi Menahem Zemba (1883–1943), a member of the Warsaw Rabbinical Council, active in the Agudat Israel political party, and a follower of the Gerer rebbe.[29] An extraordinary teacher, Zemba combined intelligence, prodigious learning, and simplicity.

Heschel was about sixteen years old when Rabbi Zemba ordained him. Reb Bezalel recognized his former pupil's authority by inviting Heschel to officiate at his marriage.

During this time, Heschel also studied at the Mesivta Yeshiva, the foremost Hasidic institution of traditional learning, which his brother, Jacob, was already attending.[30] (Zemba was one of its leading teachers.) Founded in 1919 by rabbinical authorities and the Agudat Israel community, it added spiritual enthusiasm and Hasidic customs to analytical rigor. The rebbe of Ger, as president of the Agudah, became the honorary head of the institute.

Paradoxically, this urban Hasidic academy may have kindled Heschel's drive for secular knowledge. The Polish Ministry of Education required all schools, even religious seminaries, to offer secular subjects. The Mesivta complied by establishing a separate program with its own director and teachers, offering courses on the Polish language, mathematics, history, literature, and science. This two-hour-a-day modern curriculum prepared advanced students to enter a *Gymnasium* (a secular government high school), from which they were required to graduate before matriculating at a Polish university. Studying the dual curriculum would complete Heschel's metamorphosis from budding Talmud scholar to modern European intellectual. For its part, talmudic study "stimulated ingenuity and independence of mind," Heschel would later write. "[My] thinking became full of vigor, charged with passion."[31]

FIRST PUBLICATIONS

In 1922, when Heschel was fifteen, he submitted his first commentaries on Talmud and later Rabbinic works to the Hebrew-language Warsaw monthly *Sha'arey Torah: Kovetz rabbani hodshi* (Gates of Torah: Monthly rabbinic journal), whose editorial office was located at 4 Muranowska Street, near his home. His first essay appeared in the fall in a special student supplement, *Bet Midrash*. Two more studies followed, published in winter and spring 1923.[32]

Heschel's primarily judicial analyses meticulously adhered to ancient procedure: he quoted a problem from the Talmud, then assessed commentaries from classic Jewish sources, and subsequently offered a tentative conclusion. A close look at these talmudic *novellae* (new interpretive insights), or points of Rabbinic law, reveals young Heschel's focus on the relationship between *halakhah* (religious law) and inner intention. Such a hierarchy among the laws to follow might require decisions of major consequence. Here the precocious neophyte was already flexing his dialectical muscles.

He began by publishing *hidushei Torah* (new interpretations on Torah texts or Rabbinic law), short, elliptical pieces written in concise Rabbinic Hebrew, some not more than ten lines long. He skillfully clarified difficult passages and detected minute distinctions.

In publishing these works, Heschel entered a community of Talmud scholars that included both Hasidic and non-Hasidic rabbis from Poland and Russia. Young Heschel had thus solidified his identity. With the full name of the Apter Rav as his own, he dedicated his first published words to his deceased father: "Avraham Yehoshua Heschel, son of my teacher Moshe Mordecai, May His Memory Be Blessed."

TRANSITION TO JEWISH MODERNITY

Heschel soon reached another decisive milestone. The Novominsker rebbe wanted him to be betrothed, as were most Hasidic boys of his station. His uncle proposed a *shiddush* (a match) with one of his eight daughters, Gittel Tova (1908–1956), considered to be the brightest and the most beautiful.[33] Were Avrumele to marry Gittel Perlow, he would receive *kest* (dowry or financial support) from her family and reside with them for several years before establishing his own Hasidic court. Warsaw's leading rebbes, as well as venerated elders of the family, encouraged this excellent prospect. We have no evidence of Heschel's view of the matter.

Heschel's mother, Rivka Reizel, made a heroic decision. She understood Avrumele, his exceptional mind and spirit. Now she felt compelled to safeguard his independence. Although she revered the Novominsker way of life, she refused to place her gifted son prematurely under her brother's total authority. Perhaps in this she was influenced by a family friend, Fishl Schneersohn, a modern Jew who was also close to her brother, the Novominsker rebbe. In short, she lovingly rejected the match, saying that her son was too young.

Around 1923, in fact, Heschel met this man who would transform him yet again. Fishl Schneersohn (1887–1958), a regular visitor to the Novominsker rebbe's ceremonial *tish* (literally, "table") during the third meal on Sabbath afternoons, securely bridged traditional Hasidism and modern thought. A physician, psychiatrist (director of a "psychological-hygiene" clinic in Warsaw), writer, acclaimed public speaker, and descendant of the founders of Lubavitch (Chabad) Hasidism (the family name was unmistakable), Schneersohn was a modern observant Jew working to develop a "science of mankind" adapted from Hasidic practice. He sought to integrate the physical, intellectual, and religious dimensions of human experience, a process he called "psycho-expedition."

Visiting Heschel's home, Schneersohn helped wean him from the tyrannical Reb Bezalel and from his family's authority.[34] "The Professor," as the family called Schneersohn, persuaded Rivka Reizel to let her son add secular studies to religious learning. She, too, realized that Heschel's intellectual needs surpassed traditional boundaries. And she could trust the Professor, a scientist who kept the mitzvot. Schneersohn became Heschel's first modern mentor.

The Professor had himself completed the journey on which Heschel was now embarked, from *heder* to the university. Born into a Hasidic family in Kamenetz-Podolsk (in Polish, Kamieniec Podolski), Schneersohn was an ordained rabbi by age sixteen. He went on to earn a medical degree from the University of Berlin and in 1920 became professor of "curative-pedagogy" at the University of Kiev.

Schneersohn's synthesis of psychoanalysis, mysticism, art, and social science was just the right mix to inspire Heschel's quest for an appropriate medium for his religious and intellectual yearnings. To Schneersohn, a psychotherapist was also a spiritual guide who helped patients utilize systematic self-discipline to reach the equivalent of "'Hasidic ecstasy' (*dveikut*), an intimate ecstatic concentration" (or, cleaving to God).[35] Schneersohn was preparing modern Jews to integrate these diverse energies.

Heschel had now entered the secular world. Venturing beyond the house of prayer without relinquishing his faith, he read current periodicals, newspapers, and books—in Hebrew and Yiddish translation—to supplement his voluminous religious inquiries. His independence was noticed by some acquaintances who saw him reading at a café table for several hours. (Jews were forbidden to enter the municipal library dressed in Hasidic garb.)

Heschel's encounter with modern Jewishness was taking place within a European crisis of ideologies. Zionist and socialist organizations possessed effective vehicles of education and propaganda, and schools trained children according to their secular norms. In Poland, young Jews from traditional families were stirred by the free-thinking and intellectual audacity brought to Warsaw by Russian and Lithuanian refugees. An increasing number of devout youths were abandoning the way of *halakhah*, the divine laws of religious behavior. Furthermore, Poland's Hasidim were themselves beginning to challenge the strict boundaries between Torah Judaism and the cosmopolitan world. Many Hasidim became worldly in their outward appearance, while remaining loyal to rabbinical authority. Family photographs show Heschel and his brother, Jacob, then around sixteen to eighteen years of age, already without beards and sidelocks.

LIBERATION THROUGH POETRY

Following the Europe-wide wave of emigration, especially among Jews from Poland, tsarist Russia, and Lithuania, several of Heschel's strictly devout relatives began to settle in Vienna and New York City. The first to leave was Heschel's uncle, Rabbi Yehuda Aryeh Leib Perlow (1877–1960), one of his mother's brothers. He arrived in the United States in 1924, settling in Brooklyn.[36] Two years later, Heschel's first cousin, Rabbi Nahum Mordecai Perlow (1896–1976), a son of the Novominsker rebbe, also settled in Brooklyn.[37] Heschel's older brother, Jacob, had once dreamed of becoming a religious *halutz* (pioneer) in Palestine[38] but decided instead to move in 1926 with his wife Sarah to Vienna, where several of the Heschel cousins had already settled. (Jacob and Sarah immigrated to London in 1939.)

In 1924, at age seventeen, Heschel still planned to advance his education, religious or otherwise, in Poland (or Lithuania). The Heschels in Vienna maintained their traditional communities, while Heschel by now was writing poetry in Yiddish and reading what was available in Yiddish and Modern Hebrew, practically everything. The cultural trajectory from shtetl to university was launched.

Heschel appreciated the works of Hillel Zeitlin (1872–1943), the Warsaw writer, philosopher, and mystic who, like Fishl Schneersohn, bridged Hasidic spirituality and contemporary values. Zeitlin was a conspicuous visitor to Heschel's uncle's Sabbath discourses.[39]

Zeitlin's dynamic identity was another prototype of Heschel's own journey. At the time Heschel probably met him, Zeitlin was translating the Zohar from the original Aramaic-Hebrew dialect into Yiddish. Everyone in Warsaw recognized Zeitlin, who since 1908 had presided over his own *tish* at 60 Shliska Street.[40] Heschel also knew Zeitlin's son Aaron, himself a poet and writer (they would renew their friendship after World War II in the United States).

A need for self-expression drew Heschel to the center of modern Jewish culture, within walking distance from his home on Muranowska Street. Heschel would continue down Nalewki to 13 Tlomackie Street, headquarters of the Yiddish Writers and Journalists Association (later to become the PEN club). These men and women communicated in Yiddish, idiom of the majority of Jews in Poland, Lithuania, and Russia. Together they would create a modern literature and integrate *Yiddishkeit* (Jewishness or Jewish culture) with European civilization.

In 1925 Heschel took a decisive step: he submitted some of his personal writings for publication. A recently established Yiddish paper, *Literarishe Bleter* (Literary pages—an illustrated weekly of literature, theater, and art), announced that Melekh Ravitch, its literary editor, was preparing another collection of writings. Ravitch, who was also secretary of the Yiddish Writers Association, was open to receiving manuscripts for consideration at the organization's Tlomackie Street headquarters.

Favorably impressed with Heschel's writings, Ravitch chose some prose pieces and several poems. Heschel's first known literary act, entitled "Der Zaddik fun Freyd" (The zaddik of joy), appeared in the May 21, 1925, issue of the weekly *Illustrirte Vokh*.[41] The author now called himself Avruhum Heschel.

Heschel unveiled another, bolder, aspect of his sensibility a year later, in Ravitch's 1926 anthology *Varshever Shriftn* (Warsaw writings): a poem about yearning for sensual love. His untitled *lied* (in Yiddish, "song" or "poem") was completely secular. Its two final lines evoked a troubled ambivalence toward freedom: "Hearts can only tremble, tremble / And not be joyful."[42]

Literature became Heschel's vehicle of self-liberation. Within two years, the Yiddish Writers Association began to provide him with support—financial, emotional, and professional.

Now Heschel envisaged a university education. But his proficiency in Jewish texts did not qualify him for admission to a university in Poland or Germany. Candidates were required to earn a diploma from a government-certified *Gymnasium*, capped normally by the *Abitur* examination, which included Latin and modern languages (especially Polish and German), history, literature, and mathematics. The limited nonreligious program at the Mesivta Yeshiva would not suffice; Heschel had to find a secular high school.

His desire not to embarrass his traditional family led him to choose Vilna, Lithuania, where Schneersohn knew he would find a supportive and stimulating community. Meanwhile, Warsaw was home to various progressive Jewish schools unified under the Central Yiddish School Organization, a non-Zionist international movement promoting

Yiddish-language culture. With encouragement, and some money, from Schneersohn and other Yiddish writers, Heschel hired tutors to teach him Polish and Latin, and later, German, before leaving for Vilna. (He already knew Modern Hebrew.)

One incident during these secular studies brought Heschel an extraordinary insight into Hasidic radicalism.[43] Always a meticulously observant Jew, Heschel concealed this story for years, speaking of it confidentially, to my knowledge, only with Samuel Dresner, a student of Heschel's at the Hebrew Union College in Cincinnati and the Jewish Theological Seminary in New York in the 1940s. "Consider the paradox," Heschel told Dresner. "This event represents the true greatness of Hasidism, yet I cannot tell it. People would not understand."

Young Heschel had run out of money, forcing him to stop modern language lessons. His friend Yitzhak Meir Levin, a merchant who prayed every Sabbath at Heschel's father's *shteibl* and a follower of Kotzk Hasidism, knew that about the stoppage of lessons and noticed that the young man was despondent. One late Friday afternoon, Levin arrived before the *Mincha* service to greet the Sabbath. Heschel wanted to talk with him; however, Levin was preoccupied, fortifying his emotions for the holy day's arrival. They then spoke after the evening Sabbath service, but Heschel refused to explain why he was upset. So, to change the subject, Levin told him about a new edition of sayings by Rabbi Pinhas of Koretz, Heschel's ancestor and a friend of the Baal Shem Tov. Heschel was very interested.

The next morning, on the Sabbath, Heschel was sitting in his father's chair before the *Shacharit* service when in came Levin with the precious book. (There was an *eruv* in Warsaw, a demarcation defining the area within which observant Jews are permitted to carry objects on the Sabbath.) Heschel opened it with anticipation. To his horror, he saw it contained money, which Jews were forbidden to touch on the Sabbath. He dropped the book at once. Noting the boy's astonishment, Levin responded with a story from Kotzk about how one may violate a lesser rule pertaining to the Sabbath in order to remove depression—the most perilous sin according to Hasidism. This was a shocking but precarious lesson, profoundly helpful to Heschel in his struggle for spiritual integrity. Sadness contained no holy spark. The young man's Sabbath *atzvut* (melancholy) placed him at greater spiritual risk.

Yitzhak Levin's act of generosity taught Heschel the value in certain crises of spiritual audacity, without which, Heschel asserted, Judaism could not survive in the modern world. Already during his Hasidic adolescence, Heschel was distressed with the rigidity of Jewish Orthodoxy. Yet Levin's Kotzk radicalism helped Heschel to remain observant.[44] Kotzk Hasidism fortified Heschel's faith by reminding him that the mitzvot are meant to hallow the person and fulfill God's will.

In 1925, after much discussion, the Novominsker rebbe released Heschel to go to Vilna and attend a Yiddish-language *Gymnasium* there: "You can go, but *only* you. . . . You, you are holy flesh, do not become polluted from the world!"[45]

Heschel left Warsaw, the city of his birth, on a Saturday night after the Sabbath. Fishl Schneersohn gave the young man his coat, for he possessed practically nothing. Heschel exchanged his velvet Sabbath cap for an ordinary weekday cap, and accompanied by his cousin Aaron Perlow, a son of the Novominsker rebbe, he boarded the train to Vilna.

The destiny of Aaron's sister (Heschel's first cousin and almost fiancée), Gittel Perlow (who now took the Hebrew form of her name, Tova), provides a significant counterpoint to Heschel's brand of loyalty to tradition and to family. When Heschel left Jewish Warsaw for Jewish Vilna, Gittel Perlow went to Palestine with the socialist labor Zionist movement. She then entered the secular world, first studying pedagogy at the University of Brussels, then completing a doctoral dissertation, on Jewish education in the talmudic period, at the Sorbonne.[46] She published her thesis as a book and dedicated it to her father and mother. Repudiated by her family for marrying a non-Jew, she believed she had remained loyal.

Heschel's new surroundings in Vilna did not keep him from remaining in close touch with his family. He became a regular on the eight-hour rail connection between Vilna and Warsaw. On the Vilna train, Heschel would put on a modern suit; returning to Warsaw, he would restore his Hasidic garb. Avrum Yehoshua, as his companions knew him, thus effected his transition into the modern world on a round-trip ticket.[47]

CHAPTER 2

Vilna and Berlin, 1925–1931

When Heschel reached Vilna at age eighteen, he looked like a European student: clean-shaven, without sidelocks or a beard. The new look was appropriate for Vilna, where he would encounter a modern pluralistic Jewish world—a culture of coexistence.

Vilna (Yiddish for Vilnius) was known as the "Jerusalem of Lithuania." It was the five-hundred-year-old capital of Lithuania, and Jews comprised about 36 percent of its population. That said, since May 1922, after Poland became a republic, the city had been incorporated into Poland.

A great variety of Jewish cultures had thrived in that small area some eight hundred miles northeast of Warsaw. By the seventeenth century, Vilna had consolidated its reputation for sacred learning, particularly Talmud. In the late nineteenth century, it also became the birthplace of the Jewish socialist labor movement, the Bund, and other nonreligious groups. In 1925, the year Heschel arrived, the Yidisher Visnshaftlekher Institut (YIVO, Jewish Scientific Institute) was founded there to document Yiddish-speaking East European Jewry. And in Vilna, there were young, active Zionists and Hebrew-speaking modern intellectuals known as *maskilim*, with whom Heschel relished conversations.

He had rented a cheap room on Poplawes Street in the home of a simple, very devout old Jewish man. Far from the city center, the Poplawes district was sparsely populated by poverty-stricken Jews.[1] Heschel's room contained only a drab iron bed.

His street led into town toward the west; toward the east, beyond the Poplawes district, was the Belmont Forest, a favorite recreation and walking spot. Parallel to Poplawes Street was Subocz, where poor Jews also lived. Heschel often walked through this large expanse of subsidized housing, the center of Bund activity where socialists, communists, and other leftist groups held celebrations and meetings.

At the public Strashun Library downtown, Heschel could find books in German, as well as all the Jewish classic texts, rare editions, and manuscripts. All at once he was exposed to a profusion of current Yiddish literature, Hebrew and Yiddish translations of European masterpieces, and Jewish newspapers and periodicals from around the world!

Religious observance was, of course, readily available. Near the library, about thirty small places of worship, including a Hasidic *shteibl*, were operating around the synagogue courtyard.

A SECULAR JEWISH UTOPIA

It was probably Fishl Schneersohn, an advocate for pedagogical reform, who judged that a secular, Yiddish-language *Gymnasium* would best prepare Heschel for his major transition to the University of Berlin. The then seven-year-old Mathematics-Natural Science Gymnasium (in Polish, Matematyczno-Przyrodnicze Gymnazjum; known as the Real-Gymnasium of Vilna), founded in 1918 by the Vilna Jewish Central Education Committee (TsBK), was a modern coeducational school offering the entire Polish curriculum in Yiddish. Although the sciences were emphasized (hence the German term *Real*, "concrete reality"), its humanities classes were of the highest quality. Its nonreligious Jewish environment was also rich in social and intellectual opportunities. Sunday through Friday, student activities were divided between the academic curriculum and extracurricular clubs.

It was a new world for Heschel. His classmates recalled him as being shy and quiet, a somewhat withdrawn person, a loner who had few friends.[2] His immediate educational goals were pragmatic: to gain knowledge and earn academic certification.

It isn't surprising that he remained somewhat apart. Having studied alone or under Hasidic tutors before entering the Mesivta Yeshiva, Heschel had grown up with limited school experience. Infrequent and formalized social contact with girls or women would have ill-prepared him for coeducation. Lacking basic cultural upbringing, he would have to exert tremendous efforts to master subjects for which other students had been preparing for years.

He remained on the periphery of a group of classmates consisting of Nahum (Nakhte) Faynshtayn, Benjamin Wojczyk, and Abram (Abrashke) Lewin, whose parents lived in Vilna and were Bundists. Wojczyk remembers Heschel with perhaps only one true confidant. Independent, Heschel spent most of his time with writers and artists not associated with his classes.

Nonetheless, at the *Gymnasium* Heschel absorbed the uplifting atmosphere of Yiddish secularism. Academic excellence and enthusiasm for Jewishness comprised the essence of the Real-Gymnasium, which was much more than a school; it was a community, almost a family, another reason Schneersohn had directed Heschel there in the first place. Teachers and students shared an intimate, imponderable love of being Jewish, an idealistic sense of self and peoplehood encompassed in the term *Yiddishkeit*. They were the vanguard of a humanistic Jewish utopia.

The teacher who dominated all memories and impressed Heschel most profoundly was Moyshe Kulbak. A poet, playwright, novelist, political idealist, and Yiddishist who also wrote in Hebrew, he was politically left-wing and artistically avant-garde. In class, Kulbak proved to be a marvelous communicator, masterfully provoking students' spontaneous reflections. Other instructors typically assigned passages of text to memorize and recite the next day, without discussion. Instead, Kulbak and his students shared ideas. He inspired collaboration and personal involvement with the text—precisely what Heschel in his later years would expect of his own students and readers.

Outside of school, Heschel joined a group of innovative Yiddish-speaking writers and artists—men with left-wing ideals, who later became known collectively as Young Vilna (in Yiddish, Yung Vilne). In this environment, Avrum Yehoshua, as he was known, was a compelling presence, both appealing and out of place. Shlomo Beilis, a poet and journalist born in Vilna and a firm communist, described Heschel as "[a] person of an entirely different type than we. . . . Very solid, and not loose in any way. . . . He looked like a rabbi, a genuine rabbi. Medium height, broad shoulders, thick-set, with very deep-set, beautiful eyes. And he looked like a religious scholar." Heschel's charisma was "the silk and satin he possessed in his soul."[3]

Beilis depicted the group members' relations with him as "proper, but distant." The men never addressed Heschel directly with the familiar *du* (thou), but with the formal *ihr*, in the third person, just as Heschel's father had been addressed. "With him we couldn't make jokes, and he wasn't, as they say, *anshei shloymaynu*, not one of our crowd. He was from another world. We respected him." Heschel's lifelong cultural alienation had begun.

What was the source of the (perhaps mutual) social discomfort? Was Heschel tense? Haughty? Reserved? Modest? Or simply shy?

He certainly was not an introvert. Rather, he favored long, meaningful conversations—though these were not completely intimate, as Beilis explained: "We used to walk together and talk, but we never asked each other about our *yichus*, our ancestors."

Yet Heschel did not disguise his piety, his sense of closeness to

FROM HASIDISM TO MODERNITY

God. One day, upon entering the Zakreta Forest about two miles from town, Heschel suddenly put on his hat. Surprised, Beilis asked him why. "Avrum Yehoshua replied graciously, 'It would be hard for you to understand. For me a forest is a holy place [in Hebrew, *makom kadosh*]. And a Jew, when he walks into a holy place, covers his head.'"

When Heschel shared his literary efforts with avant-garde companions, the group appreciated his poems but found their form outdated. "They were very fine, intelligently written poems . . . in a very old style," Beilis wrote. "They didn't possess a drop of irony; they were dead serious. As a person he was 'dead pious' so to speak, as were his poems. . . . But they possessed density, mass. Every feeling was enveloped in an idea." At the same time, these secularists "marveled at how such a zaddik came to write such erotic poems. It was a wonder."

For Heschel, however, there was no inherent contradiction between piety and sensual yearnings. His sensibility embraced both restraint and aspiration.

This was the time, late in 1926, when Heschel's first published (and untitled) *lied* was prominently published on the last page in the second poetry issue of the *Varshaver Shriftn*.[4] This internationally circulated book of more than a thousand pages, dated 1926–1927, marked an era. Would Heschel take his place alongside Sholem Asch, Yitzhak Bashevis (pen name of I. B. Singer), Moyshe Kulbak, and Melekh Ravitch, who were also included in the anthology?

On June 3, 1927, Heschel's second poem appeared in Warsaw's *Literarishe Bleter* (Literary pages), a recently established Yiddish weekly, which Ravitch served as literary editor.[5] Heschel, then twenty, was possibly considering a career as a writer.

Heschel sought Kulbak's advice. The master read some of Heschel's poems. "You will never be a great poet," Kulbak told him frankly, "but you will become an excellent philosopher."[6]

Kulbak's mixed message eventually proved to be prophetic. Heschel continued to write poetry, improving greatly, and his first book (in 1933) was a collection of his Yiddish verses. Later, in the United States, he would be acclaimed as a religious philosopher but criticized (by rationalistic Americans) for his "poetic" style.

By the end of the academic year, students at the Real-Gymnasium were required to pass oral and written tests sent from Di Tsentrale Yidishe Shul-organizatsye (Central Yiddish School Organization) headquarters in Warsaw. On June 24, 1927, Heschel successfully completed his final examinations—the last hurdle before seeking entrance to the University of Berlin.[7] In a matter of months he would be making his way to the German capital.

Heschel's Vilna experience had decisively advanced his pluralism. Thirty years later, when invited to contribute a preface in Yiddish to the historian and archivist Leyzer Ran's "memory book," *Jerusalem of Lithuania* (1974), Heschel would hallow Vilna for transmuting secular virtues into spiritual gold: "Jewish Vilna was an environment whose walls, corners and cellars breathed memories of gigantic intellects, reminiscences of self-sacrifice for Jewishness, of reverence of God and man, of charity and the thirst for knowledge."[8] He had reconciled his Hasidic spirituality with ethical activism: "The readiness of self-sacrifice for justice and the dignity of man, inherited from many holy generations, was also glowing in the modern Jews. So many secularist Jews who lived the life of saints and did not know it!"

Vilna thus also set in motion Heschel's lifelong mission to unveil the world's holy dimension.

STUDENT IN BERLIN

When the twenty-year-old Heschel arrived in Berlin in the fall of 1927, Germany's intellectual giants were still present. During the Weimar Republic (1919–1933), the sciences, philosophy, and the arts were flourishing as never before. In the 1920s Berlin had also became a center of Yiddish culture as East European Jews fled there to escape virulent Russian antisemitism, pogroms, the Bolshevik revolution, civil war, and extreme poverty.

Heschel did not rent rooms in Berlin's predominantly East European Jewish section, known as the Scheunenviertel. This area of East Berlin, not far from the university and near the Alexanderplatz, was populated by Jewish immigrants who preserved the dress and customs of their shtetls. Instead, Heschel took rooms (which he frequently changed for financial reasons) near the university or in the Charlottenburg section to the west. He remained in close touch with his mother and sisters and sent them whatever money he could spare from his meager earnings at odd jobs.

Heschel's university career officially began on April 27, 1928, when he registered at the Philosophical Faculty of the University of Berlin with a *kleine Matrikel* (partial or provisional matriculation) contingent upon passing the general entrance examinations.[9] As a foreign student he was required to take special tests before being allowed "full" matriculation at the university. His diploma from the Vilna Real-Gymnasium was not accredited abroad, nor were Polish graduation certificates considered equivalent to the German *Abitur*. So he enrolled at the Deutsches Institut für Ausländer (German Institute for Foreigners).

A modern Judaic education remained imperative to him as well. Heschel also enrolled in the Hochschule für die Wissenschaft des Judentums (Academy of Scientific Jewish Scholarship), which trained Liberal (not the same as American Reform) rabbis and scholars. Founded in 1872, the Hochschule stimulated Heschel's curiosity about "higher criticism," an objective method of Bible analysis based on examination of the text's historical strata. Liberal thinkers considered Judaism to be the product of complex cultural developments, rather than of divine revelation—the supernatural event at Mount Sinai. The Hochschule admitted nontheological students, including women and some non-Jews. Graduates became scholars and teachers as well as rabbis.

Meanwhile, Heschel maintained informal ties with the Modern Orthodox seminary, the Rabbiner-Seminar für das Orthodoxe Judentum. Both the Rabbiner-Seminar and the Hochschule were on the same street, Artilleriestrasse. Rabbi Azriel Hildesheimer had founded the Orthodox seminary in 1873 to combat Liberal and Reform Judaism for undermining the divine authority of biblical and Rabbinic texts.[10] Hildesheimer applied the knowledge he had gained from the study of mathematics, astronomy, and Semitic languages at the Universities of Berlin and Halle to justify *halakhah*, the foundation of Orthodoxy. Post Hildesheimer, the seminary's second period was dominated by David Hoffmann, who exercised a unique combination of talmudic and secular scholarship.[11] Hoffmann defended the faith by publishing a book faulting the historical method of the Protestant biblical scholar Julius Wellhausen, the authority for the majority of university scholars.

The Orthodox seminary thus provided a sophisticated academic environment for traditionalists. At the time, its leading intellectual figure, Joseph Wohlgemuth, taught courses on Jewish philosophy, theology, and practical *halakhah*.[12] As editor of the scholarly Orthodox monthly *Jeschurun*, he published his own study of *teshuvah* (repentance) in Max Scheler's philosophy of religion, helping to disseminate Scheler's thought in Jewish circles—which may have influenced Heschel's future choice of a dissertation topic.[13]

Heschel had already studied most of what the Orthodox seminary could teach him about Talmud. Now he wanted to understand the biblical criticism and theology provided by the Liberal Hochschule. He did not intend to become a Liberal or Reform rabbi, and the Hochschule did not threaten his faith.

The University of Berlin (officially the Königliche Friedrich-Wilhelms-Universität) provided the foundation of his humanistic education. This outstanding research and teaching institution attracted students from all over Europe.[14] By 1928 there were about twenty thousand matriculated students, 10 percent of whom were women.

After considering several fields of specialization, Heschel constructed a compatible array of courses. As his "major" focus, he settled upon philosophy, perhaps the broadest and most rigorous discipline. For his two minor concentrations, he hesitated between psychology and art, deciding upon art history and Semitic philology. The study of esthetics sustained his passion for beauty, while ancient Near Eastern languages gave scientific grounding to his pietistic mastery of religious texts.

Yet the intellectually omnivorous Heschel's fundamental commitment was to the study of religion: the human experience of the Divine. He enrolled in both the Faculty of Philosophy and the Faculty of Theology, the latter defined by modern Protestant biblical scholarship.

Here, Heschel did not subordinate his love for the Bible to his professors' "objective" methods. For the first time in his life, he was compelled to integrate religious and secular standards, which he did by translating spiritual intuitions into a philosophical idiom. At the university, he focused on the Hebrew prophets. At the Hochschule, he also focused on the Bible, using critical methods opposed by the Orthodox Rabbiner-Seminar.

In his personal life, Heschel remained observant, seeking out Orthodox homes where he could share a Sabbath meal. He was frequently invited by Rabbi Jakob Freimann, who had come from Frankfurt to Berlin in 1928 to head the Rabbinical Court and also lectured at the Orthodox seminary.[15] Some of Heschel's family members believed that he had continued his traditional religious studies in Berlin and perhaps associated with students such as Joseph Baer Soloveitchik and Menahem Mendel Schneerson who were gathering around the revered talmudic scholar Rabbi Haim Heller. Yet no direct evidence of these affiliations has been found.

For Heschel, cultural life beyond the academic institutions was equally compelling. He visited Berlin's museums, concert halls, and galleries. Heschel recalled, "There were concerts, theatres, and lectures by famous scholars about the latest theories and inventions, and I was pondering whether to go to the new Max Reinhardt play or to a lecture about the theory of relativity."[16] The electric tramway and omnibus allowed for convenient access to the underground railway system, and one could easily reach other parts of the city and the suburbs via the Stadtbahn (city railway) and Ringbahn (circular railway through the city's center). Further, Heschel's reading and research opportunities were nearly limitless. The University Library, reserved for professors and students, contained 678,000 volumes, and everyone could use the much larger Staatsbibliotek (Prussian State Library).

Yet, within himself, Heschel harbored discontent. Although his basic certainty of God's concern for humankind remained firm, he hoped to reconcile his faith with Western categories of thought. Heschel's university professors emulated the ambition of the philosopher and historian of ideas Wilhelm Dilthey (1833–1911) to establish a "philosophical anthropology," a science of humanity in which all realms of activity were grasped as a whole. Eventually, Heschel would subordinate their hypotheses, including Dilthey's, based on psychology and critical philosophy, to his own (Hasidic) convictions. He would apply the university's philosophical discourse to his biblical standard of ethics, prophetic inspiration, and prayer.

Heschel studied with Heinrich Maier, chair of the philosophy department and historian of systems. Maier represented neo-Kantianism, the reigning intellectual ideology of the time. This school held that knowledge is constrained by the limits of reason. By describing the logical functions of the emotional imagination, Maier sought to determine the essence of thought by means of psychological and philosophical analysis.[17] Heschel would not accept Maier's scientific criteria.

But it was the versatile professor Max Dessoir who provided the most productive mediation for Heschel's pursuit of a modern religious vocabulary. Dessoir combined psychology, philosophy, esthetics, and analysis of occult phenomena—a mixture congruent with Heschel's eclectic skills. (Heschel eventually chose Dessoir as co-director of his doctoral dissertation.)

At the university's Theological Faculty Heschel concentrated on Bible. He worked closely with the Swiss-born Alfred Bertholet, who had arrived at the university during Heschel's second year. An ordained Protestant pastor, Bertholet helped renew the study of Old Testament narrative through his mastery of the several civilizations of the ancient Near East.

To fulfill his secondary concentration in Semitic philology, Heschel studied with Eugen Mittwoch, co-director of the university's Institute for Semitic and Islamic Studies from 1920 to 1933 (when the Nazis removed him from the position). With Mittwoch, Heschel advanced his scholarly knowledge of biblical Hebrew and Arabic, required for research in medieval Jewish philosophy.[18] Heschel's first academic publications would develop directly from this field.

Heschel broadened his humanistic education with art history, his other secondary specialization. He felt fortunate to attend lectures by the innovative Swiss art historian Heinrich Wölfflin (who had also studied with Dilthey), then a visiting professor in Berlin.[19] Heschel's sponsor of his secondary concentration, Albert Erich Brinckmann, did not arrive until the fall of 1931, during Heschel's third year at the university. Although Heschel was considering a concentration in esthetics or psychology, he remained faithful to his commitment to apply the standards of philosophy to the study of religious cognition.

THE HOCHSCHULE'S MODERN JEWISH CURRICULUM

The Hochschule's small but distinguished faculty, some members concurrently associated with the university, gave Heschel an overview of contemporary Jewish scholarship. Ismar Elbogen, an authority on worship, author of the major work *The Jewish Liturgy in Its Historical Development*, and the school's dominant personality, used historical criticism, the philological examination of texts, to sustain his belief that an evolved Judaism was testimony to the reality of God.[20]

Heschel was especially drawn to the Hochschule by the prospect of studying with Julius Guttmann, a professor of Jewish philosophy who placed mitzvot—which he called "this worldly miracle"—at the center of Judaism, while developing a critical approach to philosophical systems.[21] Guttmann held that modern Jewish thinkers should establish the validity of religion either "ideationally," by rational argument, or by appealing to a reader's inner life. In this, Guttmann may have helped Heschel through his own struggles to reconcile critical philosophy and spiritual insight—to approach this problem with a sympathy for inwardness coupled with severe objectivity.

Heschel and Guttmann, in fact, had several intellectual affinities in common. For one, Heschel shared Guttmann's neo-Kantian belief in a priori cognitive categories, for Heschel possessed a "certainty" about the living God. Guttmann's serious consideration of phenomenology also reinforced Heschel's work with Dessoir. On a personal level, Heschel and Guttmann often took walks together, and Heschel, along with other students, enjoyed visiting Guttmann and his wife, Grete, on Sabbath afternoons. Possibly Guttmann may have also influenced Heschel to choose a university thesis in philosophy based on interpreting the Hebrew Bible.

Above all, Heschel admired the scholar, rabbi, and philosopher Leo Baeck, the Hochschule's most prominent teacher. Heschel declared that Baeck was "the most *educated* man" he had ever met.[22] A quintessential German Jew, Baeck combined piety, intellectual sophistication, and skilled community leadership; he was unofficially thought of as chief rabbi of Berlin. Although Heschel did not assent to Baeck's rationalism, through him Heschel continued to draw upon the legacy of Dilthey, Baeck's professor at the University of Berlin, in maintaining a passionate interest in a variety of cultural manifestations.

Heschel's intense studies during his first two years in Berlin brought success. On April 24, 1929, he passed the supplementary government examinations for foreigners in German language, history, and literature, as well as in Latin and mathematics.[23] Possessing unusual competence in the basic curriculum of the Hochschule, he also mastered medieval philosophy and historical Bible criticism. In December 1929 he completed the Hochschule's intermediate examinations.

Heschel's third academic year at the Hochschule (1929–1930) brought him further recognition, with some chastening of his pride. The school's ruling spirits, including Guttmann and Baeck, proposed a competitive essay on "Prophetic Visions of the Bible," expecting Heschel to win; this topic was related to the doctoral dissertation he had begun to prepare. As it turned out, the first prize went to another outstanding student, Moses Sister. Heschel took second place.[24]

The Hochschule acknowledged the excellence of both students by according them teaching positions. For his part, Heschel became an assistant to Hanoch Albeck, a specialist in talmudic philology and midrash. Heschel's remarkable competence in this field, a by-product of his Warsaw studies, was sorely needed.

A JEWISH PHILOSOPHICAL MENTOR

Helping Heschel integrate his diverse worlds—and rise above them—was a mentor outside his academic institutions: David Koigen (1879–1933), one of Fishl Schneersohn's closest associates. Born and raised in a rural Hasidic community in Ukraine, Koigen was a philosopher of history and culture (an early sociologist) trained in Europe's leading universities (he too had studied with Dilthey, among others). He exercised his calling privately, for he did not belong to any school faculty.

Heschel befriended Koigen in 1928, soon after Koigen lectured at the Hochschule. The following year Heschel was often welcomed at the Koigens' apartment, and by 1930 Heschel moved into a room just two blocks away. He shared Koigen's noble ambition to rescue the Jewish soul from indifference, assimilation, or alienation.

Koigen's East European Jewish odyssey anticipated Heschel's own journey into modernity. His intellectual passion helped shape Heschel's responses to contemporary conditions and values, in essence connecting Warsaw to Berlin. In fact, his two mentors from these two cities knew each other in depth. Koigen and Schneersohn, both secularly educated Jews of Hasidic background, had met at the University of Kiev in 1920, when Schneersohn was teaching pedagogy and medicine and Koigen was professor of social philosophy. Koigen described Schneersohn as a "descendant of the founding family of Habad" and "a man in whom Hasidism and secular culture carry on a symbolic battle."[25] With his warmth and fervent intellect, Koigen became Heschel's model of the modern Jewish thinker.[26]

Koigen's vivid historical autobiography, *Apokalyptische Reiter* (*Apocalyptic Horsemen*; Berlin, 1925), demonstrated how a traditional religious upbringing helped shape his revolutionary ideals and, ultimately, his innovative manner of Jewish thinking. Koigen believed that an updated interpretation of Hasidism could provide a forceful model for contemporary Jews to emulate. A truly religious humanism would preserve faith while fostering a strong sense of moral freedom and responsibility. While he admired the role of rebbe or zaddik, the charismatic leader who could impart self-confidence to his followers, Koigen believed that every person, educated or not, was capable of approaching God.

Koigen formulated a Jewish anthropology, a neo–Hasidic definition of being human, which Heschel would soon develop on his own terms. Its common foundation was the holiness of each and every person as an image of God. The two men founded a sociological journal,

Ethos; vierteljahrsschrift für Soziologie, Geschichts und Kulturphilosophie
[Ethos: Quarterly for sociology, history and cultural philosophy], to help effect a "profound transformation" of "philosophy and religion, scientific consciousness, pedagogy, state, and political parties."[27]

Heschel joined Koigen's personal seminar during his third academic year in Berlin. Meeting weekly at the family apartment, this intimate study group (called a Philosophische Arbeitsgemeinschaft) focused on contemporary Jewish issues. The Koigen Circle (as it was also called) provided common discussion topics for degree candidates at several academic institutions—the university, the Hochschule, and the Rabbiner-Seminar—as well as for people who had already earned their doctorate. (Mrs. Helena Koigen and the Koigens' son Georg often participated in these discussions.) The conversationalists engaged in what we would call today "Jewish renewal," interpreting religious tradition in order to highlight its relevance in one's own time.

Participating critically in these discussions, Heschel came to realize that even among these highly educated Jews, most of whom were East Europeans like himself, he was a misfit. They were rationalist philosophers; he was a religious thinker. Nonetheless, Heschel became the circle's most prominent member (other than the leader himself). He did not speak most often; rather, he deftly clarified issues and fortified his own approach. Among his peers, he was the least deferential to Koigen, even as he respected his master's standing.

Heschel drew upon Hasidic sources. And despite his recognition of Koigen's authentic understanding of Hasidic piety, he began to dissociate himself from his teacher's sociological emphasis: that the culture of an individual was primary. Instead, Heschel concentrated on the person who relates to God.

Through debate in Koigen's Circle in 1930, Heschel developed a method that would appeal to those without traditional faith. Interpreting the subtle modalities of emotion and intuition in his presentation of the American philosopher of religion William James, Heschel insisted that Judaism must not be limited to ritual, law, or secular nationalism. Judaism could be renewed by facing the living God.

HESCHEL'S POETIC VISION

While maturing as a German-speaking academic, Heschel preserved his inner Hasidic identity. Writing Yiddish poetry remained a personal necessity. He joined Berlin's Organization of East European Jewish Students Living in Germany and kept in touch with Melekh Ravitch and other poets in Warsaw.

By this time, Heschel had accumulated a body of work of which he was proud. His lyrical pieces not only expressed his innermost struggles; they evoked his hypersensitive moral conscience and his steadfast, independent relationship with God. Furthermore, there had been a significant expansion in substance as well as innovations in form.

Desirous of recognition and money (the latter an urgent need), in July 1929 he mailed five new poems to *Zukunft* (Future), the influential Yiddish monthly run by the Forward Association of New York. This was an ambitious move, for the work of almost every significant Yiddish writer appeared in the progressive journal, which reached Poland, Russia, South America, and Palestine, as well as North America—a veritable worldwide Yiddish-speaking community.

Four months passed without even an acknowledgment. Then he learned that the December 1929 issue of *Zukunft* had launched his literary career, including four poems that exemplified his unique amalgam of ardent moral sensitivity and thirst for God.

The opening poem, "God Follows Me Everywhere," evoked the intuition at the foundation of his biblical theology, anticipating his doctoral dissertation on prophetic consciousness. Within the secular city of Berlin, the poet senses how the Almighty takes the initiative. As set forth in Heschel's American theological summa, *God in Search of Man* (1955), the Divine constantly seeks the righteous person, who becomes an *object* of God's awareness: "God follows me everywhere—Spinning a web around me . . . / Blinding my sightless back like a sun."

This inaugural poem also defined the paradox of Heschel's verbal art. Poets readily understand that ordinary words can barely convey insights and feelings, while some metaphors have the power, at least suggestively, to overcome the dilemma. Heschel's instruments were his "speechless lips forever astonished." In the United States, he would develop the category of the "ineffable" while striving, in rhythmic, ornate prose, to evoke God's presence. Heschel's God is alive, concrete, available, but the essential, mystical reality—what he called God's "faceless face"—defies human understanding.

Heschel's final poem, the Yiddish "Ikh un Du" ("I and Thou"), expressed his exceptional intermingling of self and God (in contrast to Martin Buber's famous 1923 book of the same title, widely appreciated as the "I and Thou" relation or dialogue between the person and God): "Messages proceed from your heart to mine . . . / Exchanging and blending my pain with Yours . . . / Am I not— You? Are You not—I?" Heschel boldly implied that God lives within him (anticipating his later analysis of the prophet's sympathy with "God's pathos," the divine "emotions" responding to human events). Whereas Buber envisaged "dialogue" between a human "I" and a divine "Thou" as an existential remedy for the alienation that followed the First World War, as it gave priority to human efforts to communicate, Heschel stressed the priority of the divine "I," insisting that the person responds to God's initiative. God is the prototype of human compassion. Both "I and Thou" and "God Follows Me Everywhere . . ." summarized Heschel's spiritual personality.[28]

After these poems appeared, a letter finally arrived from the editor of *Zukunft*, Abraham Liessen, along with a much-needed honorarium for the four accepted poems. Liessen also asked Heschel if he had been influenced by Rainer Maria Rilke, the German-speaking poet from Prague. In his response, on February 24, 1930, the now more assertive twenty-three-year-old Hasidic poet maintained that his religious poems were not inspired by literature, but from original experience: "I didn't have to study in Rilke's *heder* to recognize that there is a God in the world. I had other teachers, other paths, other images." Heschel's message was prophetic: "There is a God in the world."[29]

Liessen then featured four of the poems Heschel had sent him in February 1930 in *Zukunft*'s August issue, at the conclusion of its literary section. These pieces dwelled upon forms of ecstasy related more to the body than to a sober religious-ethical conscience. Here Heschel revealed his more conventionally artistic, though sincerely lyrical sensibility: fantasy, humor, and a playful desire for love.

A different heartening message arrived from Tel Aviv in Palestine. Heschel had mailed the first set of poems from *Zukunft*, with some new pieces, to Haim Nahman Bialik, the celebrated Hebrew poet (who also wrote in Yiddish), whom he had met earlier in Berlin. On March 18, 1930, Bialik answered to congratulate Heschel for "the first fruits of your poems presented before the public." Reacting frankly to the manuscript samples, he gently urged Heschel to "correct their minor blemishes. . . . After all, you are still a beginner. Sharpen and sharpen your pen until you sharpen it more than enough, until it breaks. . . . I believe in you." Heschel was proud of this sensitive support from the master.[30]

On April 25, 1930, another major poem of Heschel's appeared in the widely circulated *Naye Folks-Tzaytung* (New people's newspaper), the organ of Warsaw's Jewish Bund. This poem of ethical commitment, entitled "I will give you—O world," ends with his ultimate pledge to redeem the imperfect world: "Take me as your friend! / Take me as your serf." This secular pledge rings with a tone of sanctity.

Heschel proved to be a proficient multitasker. During the eight months between this publication in Warsaw and his repeated requests to publish his already submitted poems to *Zukunft* in New York, he completed his university course requirements to qualify for the doctoral dissertation. All the while, he made connections with other expatriates. Along with A. N. Stencl, a Yiddish writer born in Poland, who participated in Germany's Yiddish expressionist movement, Heschel co-founded an avant-garde Yiddish periodical, *Berliner Bleter far dikhtung un kunst* (Berlin pages of poetry and art), associated with the Organization of East European Jewish Students Living in Germany.

Heschel now consolidated his poetic vision. He placed a sequence of six of his poems (some of them published for the second time) in the inaugural November 1931 issue of *Berliner Bleter.* Their ruling theme was the poet as witness to God. God, Heschel pronounced, is both near and far; above all, God is real. Such was the foundation of Heschel's wisdom and experience.

CHAPTER 3

Prophetic Inspiration and Hitler's Rise, *1929–1935*

At the University of Berlin where Heschel studied, the neo-Kantian theory of knowledge was the accepted standard: thinkers examined only what could be derived from sense data as processed by structures of the mind (the "categories"). Heschel defended his vocation as philosopher of religion against the backdrop of his professors' doxa of neo-Kantian rationalism. "To them," he wrote, "religion was a feeling. To me, religion included the insights of the Torah which is a vision of man from the point of view of God. They spoke of God from the point of view of man. To them God was an idea. . . . But to assume that He had existence would have been a crime against epistemology."[1]

Nonetheless, an inchoate disquiet was driving him to justify his Hasidic faith. At first, he placed great hopes in his humanistic studies: "How can I rationally find a way where ultimate meaning lies . . . ? Why am I here at all, and what is my purpose? I did not even know how to phrase my concern. But to my teachers that was a question unworthy of philosophical analysis."

Heschel's piety appeared to be foreign to contemporary thought. His professors refused to address religious questions, and Heschel judged that the objectivity of German academia distorted their conception of reality: "My teachers were prisoners of a Greek–German way of thinking. They were fettered in categories which presupposed certain metaphysical assumptions which could never be proved. The questions I was moved by could not even be adequately phrased in categories of their thinking."

Heschel challenged their sanctioned neo-Kantian theory of knowledge as he sought common ground with modern religion: Was God real, as he believed, beyond rational knowledge, or a mental and social construct? He strove to reconcile philosophical idealism with convictions that flowed from sacred sources. "Man's dignity consists in his having been created in the likeness of God" was Heschel's irreducible premise.

Thus, in Berlin, he remained profoundly apart. The university neither valued his piety nor welcomed him as a Polish Jew. The Hochschule, which deemed sacred texts to be historically derived, did not encompass his loyalty to revelation. And while the Rabbiner-Seminar utilized philosophy and scientific methods, it did not provide a spiritual community. Heschel went beyond these sectarian ideologies, without rejecting them entirely. Each institution was, at best, a halfway home.

A PARADIGM SHIFT

As a doctoral candidate in philosophy, Heschel pondered the sources of religion and ethics. Ernst Cassirer's philosophical anthropology may have helped him in bridging the abyss between philosophy and Judaism.[2] In the 1920s, as Wilhelm Dilthey's student, Cassirer had synthesized disparate disciplinary realms to develop his own neo-Kantian philosophy of "symbolic forms." Cassirer aspired to embrace all forms of culture—including metaphysics, theology, mathematics, biology, and physics—within one system. By examining the symbol-producing powers of the mind, Cassirer justified a rational (what he also called a "spiritual") principle of human freedom and creativity, an impulse toward meaning, each discipline developing its standards of interpretation. He elaborated upon his theories in a three-volume magnum opus of extraordinary scope. Heschel dreamed of attending the University of Hamburg, where he could study with Cassirer.

The son of a wealthy Jewish tradesman, Ernst Cassirer was an exemplary modern intellectual. Though not observant, he never denied his Jewishness; he contributed essays to Jewish periodicals and served on the Hochschule's board of governors. Heschel filled notebooks with quotations from Cassirer's works, hoping that Cassirer would supplement the guidance of David Koigen. Cassirer shared Koigen's ambition to coalesce all forms of culture and had studied with many of the same professors. Heschel was not able to study with Cassirer, but he retained his admiration for Cassirer's elegant opus—from a distance.

That said, even Cassirer's philosophy of symbolic forms did not welcome the holy dimension. Symbolic knowledge, in Cassirer's view, remained exclusively a product of the mind. And so, when he needed to choose a dissertation topic, Heschel went beyond Cassirer and formulated an alternative paradigm for religious cognition: God's concern for humankind. "We do not suffer symbolically," he avowed. "We suffer literally, truly, deeply. Symbolic remedies are quackery. The will of God is either real or a delusion."[3]

Heschel had found a fulcrum to highlight God's perspective. To dislodge philosophical idealism, relativism, or philosophy of mind, he adapted Albert Einstein's theory of relativity, which asserted that scientific judgment can be conditioned by the observer's location. He focused on the Hebrew prophetic consciousness: the appreciation of God as source of revelation.

Heschel adapted his method from phenomenology, the study of consciousness and its contents. In structural terms, Heschel as phenomenologist elucidated his conviction that God is the *Subject*, while human beings are *objects* of divine awareness. Internally, Heschel did not need to justify his faith. Yet his method of analyzing the prophets' awareness of God would allow him to communicate his faith to those outside the sanctuary.

These intellectual contradictions made Heschel miserable, almost depressed. In 1953, thirteen years after his immigration to the United States, he explained those circumstances to a group of American Reform rabbis. To this progressive rabbinical audience, Heschel defined himself as a modern: "Your problems are not alien to me. I, too, have wrestled with the difficulties inherent in our faith as Jews."[4] In a rare autobiographical parable that summarized months of inner conflict, he described his cognitive breakthrough on one afternoon in Berlin, when he was suddenly reminded that he was still, essentially, a pious Jew bereft of his liturgical community:

> In those months in Berlin I went through moments of profound bitterness. I felt very much alone with my own problems and anxieties. I walked alone in the evenings through the magnificent streets of Berlin. I admired the solidity of its architecture, the overwhelming drive and power of a dynamic civilization. . . .
>
> Suddenly I noticed the sun had gone down, evening had arrived.
> *From what time may one recite the Shema in the evening?*
> I had forgotten God—I had forgotten Sinai—I had forgotten that sunset is my business—that my task is [quoted in Hebrew] "*to restore the world to the kingship of the Lord.*"
> So I began to utter the words of the evening prayer.
>
> *Blessed art Thou, Lord our God,*
> *King of the universe,*
> *who by His word brings on the evenings. . . .*

And Goethe's famous poem rang in my ear:

Ueber allen Gipfeln ist Ruh'
O'er all the hilltops is quiet now.

No, that was pagan thinking. To the pagan eye the mystery of life is *Ruh'*, death, oblivion.

To us Jews, there is meaning beyond the mystery. We should say

O'er all the hilltops is the word of God.

Ueber allen Gipfeln ist Gottes Wort. . . . How grateful I am to God that there is a duty to worship, a law to remind my distraught mind that it is time to think of God, time to disregard my ego for at least a moment! It is such happiness to belong to an order of the divine will.

Heschel had "forgotten God." This was a common condition for the secularized majority, but astounding for a scion of Apt, Medzibozh, Ruzhin, and Novominsk. Heschel was enthralled with German culture (symbolized by Goethe's well-known poem), but this epiphany did not harmonize these two cultures, secular German and ancient Jewish.

As Heschel explained to the Reform rabbis, he had almost been seduced by Berlin's cultural treasures, but his memory of Goethe's poem had awakened his dormant loyalty to *halakhah*. The ingrained ritual obligations of Heschel's first twenty years of life filled the emptiness behind nature's exterior beauty and the cultural splendors of Berlin. His spiritual recollection had triumphed over anguish: "On that evening, in the streets of Berlin, I was not in a mood to pray. My heart was heavy, my soul was sad. It was difficult for the lofty words of prayer to break through the dark clouds of my inner life. But how would I dare not to *daven* [pray]? How would I dare to miss a *Ma'ariv?*" "Fear of God"—a visceral emotion of reverence—what Kierkegaard called "fear and trembling"—had reawakened his religious obligation to pray three services each day. What Heschel later called "awe" or "radical amazement," an intuitive reverence before the very miracle of daily existence, brought him back to the Jewish way of life.

This had not been a crisis of faith but a crisis of attentiveness, an ideological clash. *Halakhah* now helped Heschel to refine his studies. The analysis of religious intuition, not philosophy, became his priority. "As you cannot study philosophy through praying," he realized, "so you cannot study prayer through philosophizing." If there was a battle to be fought between philosophy and piety, he would "give the weaker rival a chance: to pray first, to fight later."[5]

HEBREW PROPHETIC CONSCIOUSNESS

Heschel's rigorous doctoral dissertation, entitled *Das prophetische Bewußtsein* (Prophetic consciousness), became the foundation of his mature religious philosophy. Speaking years later to an assembly of Jewish day school principals, Heschel asserted that the dissertation had inaugurated his life's mission "to maintain a Jewish way of thinking."[6] Written between 1930 and 1932, during the rise of Hitler, this academic analysis succeeded in translating Heschel's own prophetic vision within the boundaries of rational discourse.

This tour de force was almost an announcement of Heschel's future American mission. Parts 1 and 2 analyze the pre-exilic prophets: Amos, Hosea, Isaiah, and Jeremiah. Heschel took particular care to refute psychological explanations of prophetic insight as forms of temporary psychosis, ecstasy, or poetic inspiration. Part 3's two chapters comprised his conclusion, "Theology of Pathos" and "Religion of Sympathy." Such was the doctoral candidate's real agenda: interpret the Hebrew Bible as the divine source of human piety.

Heschel's dissertation was multivalent. It was a notable intellectual achievement to study the ancient Israelite prophets within the framework of neutral academia; it was also a prime autobiographical document. Just as Heschel's Yiddish poetry unveiled his feelings of intimacy with the Divine, so too his sympathetic analysis of prophetic consciousness suggested that he identified with those men summoned by God. His intellectual agenda was ambitious: apply philosophical terms to describe the components of divine inspiration. His prophetic goal was to convey the reality of God.[7]

Pragmatically, since doctoral candidates had to pass judgment on previous scholars, Heschel duly cited or alluded to authorities within and beyond his field, painting his interpretation on the canvas provided by Alfred Bertholet, Martin Buber, Max Dessoir, Wilhelm Dilthey, Hugo Gressmann, Julius Guttmann, David Koigen, Max Scheler, and Ernst Sellin. (Koigen was cited six times, exceeded only by Bertholet, cited seven times.) Contemporary philosophy supplied the "scientific" language.

Heschel's immediate target was Martin Buber's broadly disseminated theory of "dialogue." Heschel acutely sensed the secularizing potentials of Buber's insistence that God can be spoken about only in the "betweenness" ("das Zwischenmenschliche") of human and divine. Heschel understood that the "biblical humanism" favored by many of Buber's followers might subtly displace the overwhelming reality of God. For Heschel, divine revelation validated *halakhah*, the practical foundation of Jewish life.

In his preface, Heschel explained how he analyzed the dynamics of the prophet's primal intuition: the certainty of being addressed by God. He believed that his alternative theory of prophetic insight would dislodge the prevailing rationalism. To justify the cognitive value of certain emotions, he applied the thought of Max Scheler, a moral philosopher and phenomenologist who had developed analyses of religious experience.[8] Heschel, like Scheler, also applied Dilthey's theory of Verstehen (understanding or comprehension) to religious knowledge. More than academic philosophy, the integrity of Jewish tradition was at stake.

Heschel's eclectic method was compatible with his certainties. While respecting academic discourse, he firmly implied that a transcendent God, a real God, is the source of prophetic insight. Phenomenology (or "systematization," as he called it) allowed him to preserve, with an apparent objectivity, the real power of divine inspiration.[9]

Heschel also significantly readjusted Buber's terminology. Without citing Buber, Heschel reinterpreted the vocabulary of "dialogical structure" to validate his own belief in divine revelation: God is active while the prophet remains autonomous; their "meeting" contains "a subject-subject-structure: the self-conscious I, the prophet's active I, encounters the subjective reality of Him who inspires [the prophet]. A dialogue between God and the prophet takes place."[10]

Furthermore, Heschel firmly rejected the then current theories of altered consciousness. Returning to the structure of ecstasy, he closed part 1 of the dissertation by re-centering the event from the person to God: "The authentic reality of revelation occurs beyond prophetic consciousness. The prophet experiences, as it were, that transcendent action as an 'ecstasy of God' Who emerges from the distance and inaccessibility of His person, to reveal Himself to the prophet."[11] God needs persons; divine communication is fulfilled only when the prophet proclaims it to God's people.

In part 2, Heschel uplifted the intuition of "I and Thou" (as expressed in his Yiddish poem) to a theological level: God's active concern for humankind is the content of prophetic sympathy with the "divine *pathos*" (the Greek word for emotions). God is not aloof from the consequences of human decisions. Theology is inseparable from ethics.

Aided by some neologisms, Heschel then embarked on a potentially devastating critique of institutional religion. Hebrew prophecy is the opposite of "theotropism," the human need to seek God; in priestly religion, people systematically seek closeness to God. God's turning toward the human—what Heschel calls the divine "anthropotropism"—is a fuller path to redemption.

Heschel's personality emerges most compellingly in "Pathos as Category *sui generis*" (part 3, section 14). This argument seems to paraphrase sources from Kabbalah and Hasidic literature, which elsewhere he located in the Zohar: "Every event within the world brings with it an event within God."[12] Countering the secular humanistic projects of his time, Heschel reiterated his ambition to establish a "theomorphic anthropology" or "religious anthropology, as a specific discipline alongside theology." Such was Heschel's answer to the generation of Dilthey-inspired humanists.

Heschel asserted his personal judgment most explicitly in the final chapter, "Religion of Sympathy." Emotions have both cognitive and spiritual force: "For the biblical person who understands the unity of psychological life, in which passions are, as well, an integral part of the spiritual, a cold objective attitude cannot form a religious life. It is an emotional religion of sympathy [with God's pathos], not the practical ritual fulfilled, that corresponds to its psychological structure."[13] The same was true of the author, for whom ritual observance was a means to a higher end: attachment to God.

This would have been a rousing finale for a theological essay but was not appropriate for a rigorous university treatise. And so, the dissertation did not stop there. Toward its very end, the candidate declared his own prophetic passion without abandoning his scholarly detachment. In lyrical and intense prose, the scholastic discourse gave way to a pledge:

> We understand the person enflamed with prophetic zeal, who knows himself to be in emotional agreement and harmony with God. We understand the power of Him enflamed with anger and who turns away from His people . . . and that suffering is of such power, of such

obvious value, so unique, that still today a calling remains inherent in its idea, that of being present to demonstrate it [sympathy with the divine pathos] as a form or as a possibility. Perhaps that is the final meaning, the ultimate value, and the ultimate dignity of an emotional religion. The depths of the personal soul thus become the place where the comprehension of God [*Verständnis für Gott*] flowers, the harmony of agreement [*Einverständnis*] with the transcendent pathos.

Heschel's final sentence thus returned to his "religious anthropology." He reasserted the sacred character of humankind, teaching: "In that experience [of becoming the object of God's concern] in which [the human] experiences transcendent attention, the awareness of God is awareness of self." Thirty years later, Heschel would close *The Prophets* (1962), his expanded translation of the thesis, with this paraphrase: "'Know thy God' (1 Chron. 28:9) rather than 'Know thyself' is the categorical imperative of the biblical man. There is no self-understanding without God-understanding."[14]

When his dissertation was nearly finished, Heschel efficiently coordinated his personal and academic lives. On November 10, 1932, he wrote Dean Hartung of the Philosophical Faculty to declare Professors Dessoir's and Bertholet's willingness to serve as the co-directors of his doctoral dissertation; he completed the typescript less than a month later. Then, on December 5, 1932, Heschel used wit to prod his New York editor, Abraham Liessen, about his still unacknowledged submissions: "I am very surprised that my things [poems] have not, for such a long time, found a future in 'The Future' [*Zukunft*]."[15]

A mere four days later, on December 9, Heschel submitted a typescript of his *Inaugural-Dissertation* to Dessoir. Within two weeks, Dessoir had read it. On December 21, Dessoir wrote his evaluation and passed the dissertation on to Bertholet, who completed his own reading on January 5, 1933. The two sponsors then agreed upon a grade and sent individual reports to the philosophy department, which voted and remanded their decision to the dean. The comments, although confidential, were conveyed in some way to Heschel as he revised his thesis for publication.

Dessoir, reacting as a psychologist and a philosopher of esthetics, challenged Heschel's method: "To begin an assessment of this study with its external form, I have to say that it is written in faulty German and contains a great number of newly invented, yet quite superfluous technical terms. Much of this will have to be remedied before publication."[16] Nonetheless Dessoir appreciated the candidate's "independence[,] particularly laudable in a beginner." All in all, Dessoir's conclusion was positive: "The analyses are executed in a clear and consistent manner, so that at least a most appreciable preliminary task has been accomplished in this dissertation, which could be the basis for further study."

Bertholet, an Old Testament scholar in the university's Theological Faculty, concentrated on Heschel's textual exegesis. Like Dessoir, he appreciated the candidate's insights but not his pedantic style. While recognizing Heschel's global theory of prophetic inspiration, he pointed to some counter-evidence. He also objected to the limits imposed by Heschel's overly systematic strategy of phenomenology. He regretted that Heschel examined only the pre-exilic prophets. And, again like Dessoir, he wanted Heschel to pay "more attention to prophetic phenomena *outside* the Old Testament" and "to translate into the language of modern psychology processes experienced in more primitive states of consciousness"—exactly what Heschel had categorically refused to do. Chapters of his dissertation explicitly reject the standard, though reductive norms of anthropology, poetic inspiration, ecstasy, and psychosis.

Dessoir represented an appropriately generous view. The candidate and his professors did not have to agree. Heschel's covert defense of prophetic consciousness thus initiated his lifelong oppositional, even polemical, approach to theoretical debate. Deftly, his tactic was to revise *terminology* in order to discredit his opponent's basic notions. At the same time, phenomenology and its focus on cognitive emotions might bridge scientific and religious perceptions of the world.

1933: YEAR OF GRIEF AND RAGE

These academic tensions were accompanied by catastrophic personal and historical events. As Heschel prepared for his general examinations, he learned that his beloved uncle, Rabbi Alter Israel Shimon Perlow, had suddenly died. The fifty-eight-year-old Novominsker rebbe, known to have heart disease, unexpectedly succumbed to a stroke on January 3, 1933. Heschel had lost the sponsor of his inmost identity.

Less than a week later, Heschel received permission from the dean of the Philosophical Faculty to schedule his oral examinations. He was expected to answer questions about everything he had studied at the university during the previous five years.

Then history provided a challenge of worldwide consequence. On January 30, 1933, a political calamity transformed Heschel's future and that of the Jewish people: Adolf Hitler was appointed chancellor of the German Republic. In a stately ceremony, the aged president, Paul von Hindenburg, administered the oath of office. Hitler and the Nazi Party swiftly consolidated their power. Within six weeks, at the beginning of March, elections ratified their dictatorship, and the German legal system became an instrument of oppression. Heschel's doctorate, required to secure an academic post, was also in jeopardy.

Under increasingly stressful conditions Heschel took his oral examinations on February 23. He answered rigorous questions about his several areas of concentration from Max Dessoir, Heinrich Maier, Eugen Mittwoch, and Albert Brinckmann. This examining committee passed Heschel with the overall grade of *Sustinuit* (Sufficient), a respectable but undistinguished ranking. As Dessoir reminded his colleagues, he knew the candidate to be superior to his performance, for this audit was primarily a public display of knowledge under pressure.

To receive the doctorate, only one step remained: submit two hundred published copies of his dissertation (most to be distributed to libraries). It would not be easy. Although candidates could usually find funding to subsidize their first academic book, Heschel possessed meager financial resources. Moreover, the situation for Jews in Germany was worsening as Hitler rapidly imposed his authority. Four days after Heschel's examinations, on February 27, the Reichstag building was set on fire. A Dutch Communist was blamed, and Hitler used flimsy evidence to pass a series of emergency decrees that undermined civil liberties and basic protections for all Germans. Then came the National Socialists' victory in the March 5 elections—an ominous outcome for Germany and for the world.

It hit Heschel's mentor, David Koigen, to the quick. In January, Koigen had lost his pension from the Prussian Education Ministry. As someone who responded passionately to political events, Koigen was overcome with anxiety.[17] Two days after the elections, David Koigen died of a heart attack. He was fifty-four.

And so, within just two months of his uncle's passing, Heschel sadly contemplated the black-framed photograph of his Berlin mentor on the front page of the March 10 issue of the *Jüdische Rundschau*, Germany's leading Zionist newspaper.

Koigen's effect on Heschel would remain indelible. In the United States, Heschel would always allude to his "teacher, David Koigen" with utmost reverence, a tone he reserved for few other persons. Three photographs would grace the walls of Heschel's book-lined study in his New York apartment: portraits of his mother and his father and a photograph of David Koigen.

In Germany, on March 21, Hitler ceremonially opened the Reichstag at the Potsdam Garrison Church, where Frederick the Great was enshrined. Two days later, the deputies passed the Enabling Act, which legally gave Hitler dictatorial powers. Articles of the Constitution guaranteeing civil and political equality, regardless of race or creed, were suspended. Within days, thousands of people, mostly Jews, were taken into "protective custody."

In these appalling circumstances, Heschel urgently continued to seek a publisher for his dissertation, without which the university could not award his degree. He submitted his typescript to the Berlin firm of Salman Schocken, but it was rejected. Later, he was astounded to learn that one person had blocked this opportunity: Schocken's good friend Martin Buber.[18] This was a severe blow; by 1933 very few German firms were allowed to produce and market books by Jewish authors.

Unsuccessful in Germany, Heschel thought of Poland, and he planned a trip home. A generous March 31 letter from the sympathetic Dean Hartung to the Polish consular authorities quickly helped Heschel obtain travel documents.

This was not a minute too soon. The very next day—Saturday, April 1—a government-sponsored anti-Jewish boycott inaugurated a methodical persecution. Nazi supporters intimidated citizens who tried to enter Jewish-owned stores and professional offices. The store and office owners were instructed to place a yellow star with the word "Jude" (Jew) on their windows and doors by ten o'clock Saturday morning at the latest.[19] Storm troopers, carrying inflammatory placards in German and English, were then posted in front of these establishments to warn "Aryan" Germans not to enter. Many citizens, to their credit, refused to obey the Nazis, but most yielded. It was Germany's first large-scale anti-Jewish attack, and its intent was as much to humiliate the Jews as to undermine their economic stability.

Heschel had to publish his thesis soon, lest the university deny him his diploma. Nazis were quickly taking control of Germany's academic institutions, beginning with the law of April 26, 1933, against the "alienization of German high schools, colleges, and universities."[20] After arriving in Poland, Heschel contacted the Polish Academy of Sciences in Kraków to ask if its Oriental Studies Division might consider publishing his dissertation.[21] He had a long wait for the answer.

Meanwhile, Heschel, under the guise of anonymity, challenged the Nazis with an explosive poem entitled "In tog fun has" ("On the day of hate").[22] While in Warsaw, he arranged for its publication in the Yiddish daily *Haynt*; it appeared on May 10, 1933, the very day the Nazis planned to publicly burn Jewish books. A note accompanying the poem informed readers that the author "Itzik" (a derogatory nickname for "Jew") was "a world-famous German-Jewish writer whose books found a 'place of honor' in a bonfire, which burned in the German State."[23]

This dramatic poem, Heschel's longest (forty-six lines), was energized by a frightful contradiction: a clash of holiness and abomination. It opened with bitter sarcasm: "On the Sabbath day / At ten o'clock, a filthy-brown mass of people / Sat on shoulders, on doorsteps, on thresholds. . . . / *Gut yontif* [happy holiday], pure-bred Germans!"

As a poet, Heschel passionately wielded his one weapon: irony. So he taunted the "master race," who desecrated the holy Sabbath and God's people at one and the same time: "On every window pane, / the hand spits a burning Star of David. / . . . Gleaming on the entrances of Jewish homes————/ *The Ineffable Name of God*, light and dark / ITZIK—burns in every window!"

Heschel was asserting that human sanctity rose above evil. With sustained anger, he identified the accursed "Jew" (*Itzik*, or "kike") with the sacred Hebrew term *Shem Hameforash*, "the Ineffable Name of God." Thus emerged the positive affirmation: Jewish and divine were one.

Writing was indeed Heschel's Golden Bough, shielding him on his descent into the abyss. Still in Warsaw seeking a publisher for his dissertation, Heschel arranged for a Jewish press in Warsaw (Indzl Ferlag) to publish his first book: *Der Shem Hameforash: Mentsh. Lider* (*God's Ineffable Name: Man; Poems*), a collection of sixty-six Yiddish poems that consecrated his life's first cycle, from childhood to maturity, from Hasidism into modernity. Heschel dedicated the volume to his deceased father "of blessed memory" as he addressed Yiddish speakers who could understand his struggles (we remember that Heschel dedicated his first talmudic publications to his father, his "teacher").

The book's title proclaims Heschel's guiding precept: the divine value of humankind. The Hebrew term *Shem Hameforash* refers to the Tetragrammaton, YHVH: the ineffable name of God, which could only be pronounced by the High Priest at the Jerusalem Temple during the Day of Atonement. The biblical book of Genesis asserted that all human beings are holy, created in God's image.[24] The book's epigraph—"I asked for wonder instead of happiness, and you gave them to me"—reflects the poet's modernity, creative energy arising from *tensions* between awe ("wonder"), closeness to God, and an inescapable alienation. Heschel understood that he himself was a mixture of positive and negative energies. As he said, thanking God, "You gave *them* to me."

In retrospect, Heschel's poetic book anticipates his mature theology. Each of its six sections defines a different, though equally authentic sphere. Section 1, "Human Is Holy," establishes the intimacy of the poet and God. Its opening poem, "I and You," previously published, marks Heschel as Buber's successor, for whom God's "emotions" are intertwined with his: "Am I not—You? / Are you not—I?"[25] Heschel dedicated the next poem, "Help," to his friend Yitzhak Levin, who supported his humanistic education. Other pieces in this opening section deal with suicide and "God's tears," divine compassion, while rejecting the confusion of worldly power. As "God's Tears" concludes, "The sins of the poor are more beautiful / than the good deeds of the rich."

The poet's independent relationship with God expands in section 2, "Bearing Witness," in which he implores the Divine to reveal its presence further. The subsequent sections dramatize the poet's joy as well his troubles. The "love poetry" of the third section, "To a Woman in a Dream" (in Yiddish, "Tsu a froy in kholom"), provides the only hint of Heschel's love life. While there is no evidence of actual romantic involvements, the sensual aspect of his poetry has ripened. The adolescent fear of physical intimacy is surpassed by the older poet's expressed excitement—though this remains characteristically chaste. "Between Me and the World" returns to the ethical quandaries of city life. "Nature-Pantomimes" finds ecstasy in landscapes that welcome the Jewish imagination.

Heschel's most subtle confession, however, occurs in the book's structural center. The nine poems of section 4, entitled "Between Me and the World" ("Tsvishn mir un velt"), portray the writer's irremediable contradiction: his closeness to God estranges him from the world. The poem entitled "Lonely" juxtaposes two key words, *eynzam* (lonely) and *keynzam* (undefined). As for many mystics or people of prayer, such was Heschel's lifelong paradox.

The last section, "Redemptions" (or "Repairing the World"), highlights once again Heschel's pledge: "My Song," first published in 1930 in Warsaw's *Naye Folks-Tsaytung*, states simply that he would become the world's servant, its slave. Neither God nor humankind could ask for a greater commitment.

Heschel's Yiddish poetry constituted an act of prophetic judgment: confronting the enormity of selfishness, evil, and injustice in the contemporary world. Heschel urged God to lift the veil of inscrutability and to help the poor, the downtrodden, those who endured disease, criminals—they, too, needed to be redeemed.

Yet, Heschel also recognized that the Divine ultimately remains unknowable, and as such, we cannot blame God; we must act.

Once again, as he would do throughout his life, Heschel was multitasking. He sought a publisher for his doctoral dissertation, kept at bay the university's Nazified administration, published his first book in Warsaw, and submitted the typescript of his dissertation to the Polish Academy of Sciences in Kraków.

In August 1933 he returned to Berlin and rented a new room. By then, some of his teachers and acquaintances were deliberately preparing to leave Germany. All the while, the fate of his dissertation remained uncertain. Without the degree in hand, Heschel could not qualify either for academic employment or for a visa to another country.

In these precarious times, writing became Heschel's instrument of spiritual survival. His first published essay in German, "David Koigen," printed in the February 27 issue of the *Jüdische Rundschau*, memorialized his mentor. He signed it "Dr. Abraham Heschel." To his mind, the still unpublished dissertation was completed.

Heschel's obituary of Koigen defined his own ideals. He probed his teacher's internal contradictions as he interpreted "the exceptional character of [Koigen's] appearance."[26] Due to some nerve damage, one side of his face was immobile, a condition Koigen himself interpreted as representing two sides of his nature. Heschel stated that his teacher "lived within a curiously tense dialectics of spirit and being, of idea and matter." For Heschel, Koigen was an ideal "philosophic personality." He averred that Koigen "never suppressed within himself the 'situational thinker' [*Gelegenheitsdenker*]." This sensitivity to contemporary events, a sort of applied ethics, would become Heschel's own hallmark as a religious philosopher in the United States.[27]

In July 1934, about sixteen months after his oral examinations for the doctorate at the University of Berlin, Heschel completed his degree at the Hochschule, easily passing the Talmud and Rabbinics examination. The new Talmud professor, Alexander Guttmann, ordained him (since Hanoch Albeck had recently immigrated to Palestine).[28] To complete certification, Heschel wrote a paper entitled "Apocrypha, Pseudo-epigraphic Writings and the *Halakhah*."[29]

Heschel now possessed the diploma of an ordained Liberal rabbi trained in historical textual analysis. But he did not intend to practice as a clergyman, modern or otherwise. Heschel's Jewish academic certification, in any case, was not useful in Nazi Germany, and his goals were broader. He hoped this Jewish diploma and his doctorate in philosophy would qualify him for an academic position in another country.

Meanwhile, the fate of Heschel's doctorate hung in the balance. His thesis had not yet been accepted for publication. On March 8, 1934, the Oriental Studies Committee of the Polish Academy considered *Das prophetische Bewußtsein* with misgivings, "because it is mainly a psychological-philosophical work." Despite this gross misunderstanding of his method, the committee sent the manuscript to outside experts for their evaluation.[30] What conclusion those experts reached is unknown, but after several months the committee returned the thesis to Heschel, not yet rejected but accompanied by a letter stating that "the question of costs is also not unimportant." Clearly, the academy needed a subsidy to publish the work. Asking an author to so contribute was common practice—except that Heschel had no money.

Heschel continued to seek other sources of income. During his early years in Berlin, from 1927 on, he earned money from menial labor of an intellectual sort. In addition to tutoring assimilated Jews in Hebrew, one such task was to establish an index for an edition of the *Tsena Urena*, a Yiddish-German commentary on the Torah intended for women, which the prominent social worker Bertha Pappenheim, who founded the Jüdische Frauenbund, the Jewish Women's Movement (and was also Freud's patient known as Anna O.), was editing in Roman alphabet letters.[31]

Meanwhile, the academic deliberation might have dire

consequences. The slogan "publish or perish" was literally true. Political developments made it clear that a Jew could no longer teach in Germany. The law of April 1933 had established stringent quotas in all academic institutions. Acts of violence against Jews were increasingly common, and the professional activities of German citizens of Jewish descent were severely limited or even halted. He needed time. And money.

By February 1935 Heschel located the necessary financial support. The previous year he had met Erich Reiss, editor of the refined German Jewish publisher Erich Reiss Verlag, which specialized in German literature, translations, books on theater and acting, works of history, children's books, the fine arts, and some books of Jewish interest. Reiss had published David Koigen's autobiography, *Apocalyptic Horsemen*, in 1925.

Reiss was charmed by Heschel. He invited Heschel to edit a series entitled "Judaism Past and Present," solicit manuscripts, and evaluate proposals. This position furthered Heschel's contacts in the intellectual world. Of more immediate importance, Reiss agreed to subsidize publication of Heschel's dissertation.

SAVED BY MAIMONIDES

Now the viability of Heschel's doctorate depended upon his skill in writing letters in two borrowed languages. In German, Heschel continued to solicit the Berlin University authorities for extensions, and he began intricate consultations with the Academy of Sciences in Kraków in a Polish idiom that he seemed to have learned primarily from books.[32] Heschel's sympathetic sponsor in Poland was Tadeusz Kowalski, professor at the liberal Jagiellonian University, a specialist in Muslim languages and cultures, and the recently appointed chair of the Oriental Studies Committee. With Kowalski's patient support, Heschel began—painstakingly—to revise his thesis for publication.

Meanwhile, at the University of Berlin, the Nazis replaced the anti-Nazi Dean Hartung, who respected Jewish students, with a staunch Nazi sympathizer, Ludwig Bieberbach. The Nazis had so centralized their control that all academic transactions were regulated by the highest political authorities.

The ironies of history were both harsh and hopeful. During this period, Nazi racism stimulated Jewish creativity. Most German Jews possessed little traditional learning, and even those who had participated in Jewish affairs tended to identify as Germans. Now, forced to rely only upon themselves, and yearning to recover their heritage, Jews flocked to synagogues, studied Jewish texts, and began publishing books and periodicals. As an editor for Reiss, Heschel contributed to this Jewish renaissance. He gave lectures to adults from Berlin's Jewish community, among whom East European Jews played a considerable role. Heschel became an interpreter of tradition.

In this realm too, Reiss was helpful. Late in 1934, anticipating the eight hundredth birth anniversary of the great medieval philosopher Moses Maimonides (1135–1204), Reiss invited Heschel to write an accessible, popular, and inspiring biography of this thinker whom assimilated German Jews might admire. Heschel's biography of the Rambam (as Maimonides was also called), a religious scholar, philosopher, medical doctor, and social authority, spoke to Jews constrained to live in Nazi Germany but bereft of their religious culture. In Heschel's hands, this life story was also a precocious autobiography of sorts, portraying a religious and philosophical sage whom Heschel was striving to emulate.

Against the common view of Maimonides as a pure rationalist, Heschel emphasized the philosopher's yearning for contact with God. Part 1, "Development and Maturity," traced the Rambam's astounding intellectual skills and spiritual insight. Part 2, "Renunciation and Fulfillment," explained how the pure scholar, preferring contemplation to action, transformed himself and his life after his beloved brother David unexpectedly died. The unspoken mysteries of

Heschel's own bereavements enriched his rendition of Maimonides's depression following David's death. "Seeing him [David] was my only joy." The Rambam fell into a pathological melancholy. Eventually, his vision of reality ripened, "provoking in his soul a decisive crisis."[33] By age forty, Maimonides "had mastered the difficult art of patience and forgiveness."

Heschel was only twenty-eight when he wrote these words, but for several years he had already endured extraordinary stress, losses, and dislocations. Yet there is no evidence in Heschel's life of either reduced capacity for work, psychosomatic illness, or clinical depression; quite the opposite. In contrast to Maimonides's temporarily reduced "intellectual activity" during his melancholy, Heschel dramatically increased his research and writing.

Still, the medieval philosopher was yearning to receive divine inspiration. And in the end, Heschel's Maimonides became an ethical hero, in addition to an intellectual, psychological, or even spiritual genius. The final chapter, "Imitation of God"—the only part of the book that Heschel himself, years later, adapted and translated into English—celebrated the Rambam's medical service during the last fifteen years of his life.[34] Heschel aptly summarized the journey: "Maimonides's final transformation: from contemplation to action, from the knowledge of to imitation of God. God was no longer an object of his understanding: He became the model to follow." Worship, thought, and action became one.[35]

Heschel would also insist upon Maimonides's deeper, prophetic goal: to make his God-consciousness available to everyone, to sanctify the everyday. Years later, Heschel's English version would add, "Thought itself is holy. Thought itself is the presence of God."[36] No clearer statement of Heschel's future goal as philosopher of religion can be found.

Soon after it appeared in May 1935, *Maimonides: Eine Biographie* was praised as an accessible resource with a scholarly foundation.

Reviewers appreciated the lively narrative as "a work of art that combines scientific strictness and noble popular appeal." Reading it was "a thorough delight."[37]

A French translation by Germaine Bernard appeared the following year in Paris, published by Payot as part of its distinguished historical series. A preface by Bernard Chapira of the École pratique des Hautes études praised the biographer's originality "as an act of revenge for the past and a sort of compensation for today's persecutions."[38] Speaking boldly in a manner forbidden in Germany, Chapira stressed how Heschel's story of Maimonides could help fortify European Jews menaced by assimilation or tyranny.

Heschel himself became an object of German Jewish identity. As an editor at the Erich Reiss Verlag, a degree holder from the Hochschule, and author of a popular biography of Maimonides, Heschel was praised in the intellectual periodical *Der Morgen*. Founded in 1925 and published in Berlin, *Der Morgen* had begun as a bi-monthly, with articles about history, philosophy, religion, psychology, literature, and other topics of Jewish interest. Most of its contributors were Jews associated with the Hochschule, the Rabbiner-Seminar, or the Berlin Lehrhaus. The journal's most dynamic period coincided with Hitler's rise after the Reichstag arson of February 1933.[39]

By this time, most German Jews had become what was known as *seelischer Luftmensch* (a spiritually empty person)—in other words, alienated from their Jewish selves.[40] Meanwhile, since the 1920s, a number of relatively assimilated German-speaking Jews—such as Franz Rosenzweig, Franz Kafka, and Buber—were attracted to Hasidism and other forms of traditional religious culture. That idealized image of East European Jewry still engaged them.[41]

Heschel, meanwhile, was appreciated as a rare composite Jewish identity. He was an East European representing authentic Jewishness: a scion of noble Hasidic dynasties (both Polish and Lithuanian), the holder of a diploma from the Liberal Hochschule, and far along in completing a doctorate in philosophy from the University of Berlin. Moreover, like Maimonides and Abravanel, he was equally at ease in *halakhah* and *aggadah*, nourished uniquely by Hasidic stories and texts. This was a chance for Heschel to help German Jews reshape their identities.

The *Der Morgen* editors recognized that Heschel's pluralistic vision might provide a much needed and welcomed alternative to Jewish alienation. In the March 1935 issue, Heschel's book of Yiddish poems, *Der Schem-hameforasch—Mentsch* (as it was spelled in German), was commended as "modern poems from a Polish Jew."[42] The reviewer praised Heschel as a former Hasid, educated in Germany, and able to communicate religious insight in a pertinent idiom. Heschel attuned tradition with modernity without losing their spirit.

In the June 1935 issue of *Der Morgen*, Leo Hirsch, a poet, playwright, and essayist, published a German translation of Heschel's Yiddish poem "Ikh un Du," preparing the way for Heschel to meet Martin Buber and contribute to the German Jewish renaissance.[43]

A DOCTORATE AT LAST

Finally, three years after his oral examination and defending his PhD dissertation, Heschel received his doctorate. Considering the Nazi domination, somehow the university administration allowed this Polish citizen (i.e., not a German Jew) to submit unbound page proofs that were printed in Kraków and Berlin, rather than bound volumes, as originally stipulated. The Latin diploma in the name of "Abraham Heschel Varsoviano" (of Warsaw) was dated December 11, 1935, and signed by Ludwig Bieberbach and the university rector, Wilhelm Krueger, a Nazi stooge. Why these two Nazis would have helped Heschel by spurring the decision to allow him to submit unbound copies is unknown. While Heschel was still expected to submit two hundred bound books (such copies were widely distributed to journals for review), he officially became Dr. Abraham Heschel.

CHAPTER 4

Symbolic or Sacred Religion, 1935–1939

Heschel, at age twenty-seven and with no prospect of employment, faced the precarious start of his career. His "teacher" and rival, Martin Buber, already a venerable elder at age fifty-two, was an internationally acclaimed author and lecturer, stabilized by inherited wealth. The two had first met in Berlin during the 1929–1930 academic year, perhaps through David Koigen, who had known Buber since their student years. Heschel spoke several times with Buber during the latter's lectures at the Hochschule and the Berlin Lehrhaus.

Heschel felt ambivalence toward his elder, both affinity and rivalry. He admired Buber's enormous learning in a myriad of fields, praising him "as the most *erudite* man he ever met."[1] Moreover, he valued Buber's efforts to render the spirit of Hasidism in a humanistic literary idiom. At the same time, he felt angry and hurt at Buber's almost catastrophic dismissal of his dissertation submitted two years before to Schocken. This rejection had jeopardized Heschel's doctorate, forcing him to seek publication abroad.

Now that the book was—finally!—soon to be published in Poland, Heschel felt fortified to receive Buber's opinion of his foundational work, now titled *Die Prophetie* (On prophecy). Better still, Buber might enlist him in his movement of Jewish renewal—and, on an even more practical level, maybe help him to secure an academic position.

Heschel recognized it would be a delicate task to foster an alliance with Buber while preserving his independence. On June 18, 1935, while correcting galley proofs of *Die Prophetie*, he overcame months, even years of inhibition. He initiated a bold exchange with this hero of Jewish cultural renewal in Germany.[2]

Heschel asked his senior if he would be willing to examine his doctoral dissertation nearing publication. The young man's request was tactically astute. While soliciting Buber's evaluation, he mentioned his recent biography of Maimonides, proof of his prowess as a scholar and writer. Heschel was attempting to establish a completely honest relationship with Buber and resolve his own conflicting attitudes toward his elder. His comprehensive letter of July 24, 1935, concluded by alluding to Buber's initial opposition to his manuscript, which caused him an "everlasting grief" ("unvergänglicher Schmerz"). Heschel thus disclosed a heady stew of contradictory attitudes: hope, flattery, anger, sadness, respect, veneration, and affection. And he enclosed proof of his accomplishments: his book of Yiddish poetry, his most intimate self-expression.

Apparently, Buber understood that Heschel's letter was deeply personal. Answering Heschel immediately, Buber accepted the offer. Buber's letter included a reprint of a paper he had originally delivered to a high-level colloquium at Davos, Switzerland: "Symbolic and Sacramental Existence in Judaism," a comparative analysis of prophetic inspiration and Hasidic spirituality.[3] In this somewhat indirect manner, the philosopher of dialogue addressed the substance of Heschel's dissertation—the primacy of divine revelation, God's initiative, the very foundation of Heschel's theology.

Was Buber thus proposing that the two men analyze each other's works in which they covered similar terrain very differently? Not exactly. This debate was more than a wrestling match of two fervent intellectuals. At stake was the soul of contemporary religion.

Heschel wrote again to oppose Buber's dialogical methodology, which contradicted Heschel's God-centered perspective. His second letter to Buber constituted the clearest rebuttal to what Heschel regarded as his era's theological compromises—briefly put, symbolic versus transcendent religion. Heschel rejected Buber's interpretation of the Bible in which the prophet is primarily a living "symbol" of the covenant between persons and God. For Heschel, God's "behavior" and "emotions" were more than symbolic. Heschel feared that Buber's view of prophecy as "symbolic action" might be used to justify a purely humanistic religion, a philosophical anthropology without God.

Biblical exegesis carried grave theological implications. Heschel warned Buber that he, as a Jewish thinker, perilously associated his theory of symbolic "incarnation" with a Christian typology whereby the Hebrew text could be read as predicting the coming of Christ. Meanwhile, Heschel himself was walking a tightrope, since his own Yiddish poetry expressed an "intermingling" of God's emotions with his. Also, Heschel's Hasidic piety seemed in practice (if not in theory) to be "incarnational," for he believed the community's rebbe or zaddik had to be a living symbol of Torah.

Heschel's dissertation pointed repeatedly to the God of pathos and systematically refuted anthropological or psychological accounts. For Heschel, the Bible was the original witness to the living God. Claiming that Buber substituted a "symbol" for God the transcendent Subject, Heschel concluded, "I feel free to carry forward these questions but ask for confirmation if I have misinterpreted your words."[4]

There is no further evidence of a continuing conversation; the gulf between Hasidic Warsaw and academic Frankfurt could not be bridged, only recognized. (Heschel eventually sent Buber the revised dissertation, published as a book in 1936. Only later, when the Nazis increased their persecutions, did Buber ever do any of the things Heschel had hoped he might: involve him in the Jewish renewal movement or help him secure an academic position.)

Nor would either thinker make any adjustments to his faith (or a priori judgments). In fact, in Buber's 1942 book, *The Prophetic Faith*, he explicitly rejected Heschel's witness to God's pathos: "And Hosea does as he is bidden. But this does not at all mean that he 'feels with God,' as some think* [*from a note referring to *Die Prophetie*]."[5] The battle was over, now reduced to a footnote.

We should not lose sight, however, of the spiritual gravity of their debate, which never ended. Each thinker misread the other for a noble cause. For Buber, Heschel's implicit claim to "know" divine "emotions" from the God-side was perilous. Buber refused to assume that human beings can experience God's "feelings," just as he refused to consider the mitzvot to be prescriptive expressions of God's will. Buber did not feel called by *halakhah* (and did not attend synagogue). For Heschel, the sacred origin of the mitzvot justified their legal and ritual authority in religious life. This hermeneutical conflict carried immense implications for Jewish continuity.

Heschel correctly trusted Buber to accept their differences, which remained unresolved. Yet the paucity of references to Buber in Heschel's books and essays is surprising, despite many parallels in terminology and ideas. One explanation is that Heschel, on principle, rarely criticized "one of his teachers" publicly or even privately. Instead of systematically refuting opposing views with carefully documented argumentation as would a disinterested academic, Heschel became an "irenic polemicist" who transformed the terminology of opposing thinkers (usually without naming them), so as not to impugn their positive contributions.[6] In this way he disputed their ideas while advancing his perspective.

There is an intriguing biographical substratum to Heschel's and Buber's mutual ambivalence. Buber "discovered" Hasidism as a child, before Heschel was born, but from a skeptical viewpoint. In his widely read essay of 1918, "My Way to Hasidism," Buber explained how he was raised in Lemberg (Lwow) and Galicia by his grandfather, a wealthy businessman and modern but observant Jew who edited a critical edition of the midrash. The boy spent summers at his father's estate in the Bukovina, where he visited, as he wrote, "the dirty village of Sadagora."[7] The coincidence is amazing, for this "decadent Hasidic court"—as Buber called it—was the home of Heschel's paternal grandmother, whose father, Sholem Joseph, was the rebbe of Sadagora. Somewhat later, young Buber visited the town of Tchortkov, where "there still lives today the direct recollection of [the Ruzhiner's] son, Dovid Moshe. Unfortunately I received nothing of him at that time."[8] Heschel's father was raised in Tchortkov, at the Hasidic court of his stepfather, Rabbi Dovid Moshe Friedman. Unconsciously, Buber retained raw, mostly negative associations of Heschel's deepest spiritual roots.

Later in life, Buber became immersed in Hasidic spirituality through philosophy, literature, and European cultural politics. Yet Heschel averred that Buber was "not at home in rabbinic literature," particularly Talmud, which even contemporary Judaism had to integrate.[9] Such were the seeds of a divergence that made their spiritual brotherhood a sibling rivalry as well.

AN ALLY IN KOWALSKI

As 1935 ended, Heschel was still struggling to fulfill the university's demand to deliver two hundred bound copies of his dissertation. The pressures were increasing. He had no steady job and virtually no money; he could barely meet payments to the Polish Academy of Sciences to print his book.[10] The political crisis magnified the stress.

Bereft of a national identity, Heschel was fortunate to have a supportive ally in Kraków, Tadeusz Kowalski, professor of Islamic studies at the liberal Jagiellonian University. Their professional correspondence, in Polish, brought Heschel's anxiety to the surface. Yet Kowalski proved to be, at the very least, a noble professional. He and Heschel worked together to produce a well-edited book.

The process had begun on February 3, 1936, when Heschel wrote Kowalski that he would mail his Polish abstract soon (the dissertation, written in German, required an abstract in Polish). More urgently, Heschel shared his difficulty in finding an "Aryan bookstore" in Germany to carry the work. Heschel proposed a workaround: could Kowalski obtain from the Polish Consular mission an affidavit to allow his book to be printed in Poland or even Germany? "It can be granted," Heschel said, "if the Polish consulate certifies that sale of this book published by the Polish Academy of Sciences . . . will add to the 'betterment' of relations between Polish and German scholars." And Heschel added, "(The above phrase is not the best one)."

There was no time to lose. Kowalski managed to obtain the official statement from the Polish consulate; he sent it to Heschel, who rushed it to the Polish officials. Somehow it worked: the cover page of one copy of the thesis gives Kraków as a place of printing, and the other, the Erich Reiss Verlag of Berlin!

Other problems remained, however. On February 21 Heschel asked Kowalski to correct grammatical or idiomatic errors in his Polish abstract. Now his objective in reaching out to Kowalski extended beyond that of a scholar who knew that Polish was not his native language and wanted his work to be impeccable. Heschel also confided in this Polish professor his Jewish homelessness—his political, cultural, and spiritual exile.

In March 1936 Kraków Polska Akademja Umiejetnosci (the Polish Academy of Sciences) finally delivered bound copies of his dissertation. Heschel was euphoric. On March 23 he sent Kowalski this succinct note of appreciation: "I received today the first copies of my book about prophecy. I remember very clearly your careful attention to my case. The mere words 'thank you' do injustice to my true feelings." Heschel's diploma, and perhaps his life, was saved. Beyond this, his credentials as a biblical interpreter and theologian of "divine pathos" were secured.

In the marketing of *Die Prophetie*, Heschel proved to be a keen publicist. He provided names and addresses of learned journals as well as Jewish community newspapers and periodicals to receive review copies and closely monitored the book's distribution.

THE ORBIT OF HENRY CORBIN

Heschel was already working on a new research project: applying his mastery of Maimonides's philosophy to an intricate study of Solomon Ibn Gabirol (ca. 1021–1058), a controversial eleventh-century metaphysician also appreciated as a poet and mystic. Gabirol's central work was available only in Latin translation (the *Fons vitae*), with renditions into Hebrew and German. Scrupulously following the rules of academic diligence, Heschel began with the problem of determining which versions would be considered valid.

Gabirol himself reflected Heschel's many interests: philosophy, theology, poetry, prophecy, and prayer. Yet Heschel did not treat Gabirol as another historical alter ego, as he had with Maimonides. Instead of biography, Heschel mapped out Gabirol's system, his philosophical vocabulary. There is scant evidence of personal identification in the dry monographs Heschel produced on Gabirol's neo-Platonic sources and metaphysics. Yet, it was clear he found medieval philosophy to be intellectually stimulating, inspiring, and gratifying his need for rigor. Was Heschel inspired by the Golden Age among Muslims, Jews, and Christians?

Heschel's commitment to sacred values in an age of crisis, the 1930s, impressed Henry Corbin, a French Islamic expert impassioned with spirituality and German existential philosophy. At the time, Corbin was pursuing research in Berlin. He read Heschel's *Die Prophetie* as soon as it appeared, and with tremendous excitement: Heschel's phenomenology of Hebrew prophetic inspiration confirmed Corbin's fascination with Islamic mysticism and the centrality of the Prophet. Corbin immediately asked Henri Jourdan, director of the

French Institute in Berlin, to arrange a meeting with the author. On May 5, 1936, Jourdan wrote to invite Heschel and Corbin to his home, since the Nazi authorities forbade professional contacts with Jews.[11]

These two young scholars, meeting in Berlin that Sunday afternoon, formed a spiritual alliance and a warm, substantial friendship. They met again two days later, when the first review of *Die Prophetie* appeared, and Heschel gave Corbin an inscribed copy of his book.[12] They discussed Corbin's translations of Heidegger (the first in French), new editions of Kant's works, and the French translation of Heschel's *Maimonides*, soon to appear in Paris. It was a pleasant personal encounter as well, for Corbin was a dynamic personality, and his wife, Stella, extremely bright and vivacious.

There were deeper, unspoken affinities as well. Corbin, like Heschel, experienced early bereavement; his mother had died when he was ten years old. Corbin began seminary studies, intending to become a priest, but his interests were broader. In 1925, with a diploma in Catholic theology and medieval philosophy in hand, he began learning Arabic at the École des Langues Orientales in Paris, working closely with Georges Vajda, a Hungarian-born Jew who specialized in medieval Jewish spirituality. Corbin became an authority in Persian texts—interpreting them using phenomenological methods inspired by Max Scheler, Edmund Husserl, and Wilhelm Dilthey. Heschel, too, was inspired by the generation of his teachers—all of them, in one way or another, disciples of Wilhelm Dilthey, who, like Heschel, was ever in search of a more inclusive humanism.

SPIRITUAL AND CULTURAL RESISTANCE

As Berlin prepared to host the Olympic Games of 1936, Heschel developed a less scholarly, but no less inspirational, livelihood: writing essays and book reviews for the *Gemeindeblatt der jüdischen Gemeinde zu Berlin*, the widely circulated newspaper of the city's Jewish community.[13] He inaugurated his journalistic activity with a series of brief essays on Rabbinic leaders of talmudic times. These sketches, appearing from February to August 1936 under the general title "Personalities of Jewish History," were acts of "spiritual resistance to the Nazis," implicitly addressing the situation of Jews in Germany.[14]

During the following month, as the High Holy Days approached, Heschel took on the role of prophetic witness, a voice for God's perspective, both admonishing and inspiring his community. His two theological essays, also printed in the *Gemeindeblatt*, welcomed readers to the solemn ten-day period of self-examination and repentance beginning on the eve of Rosh Hashanah. Heschel probed the spiritual condition of German Jews, whom he considered to be handicapped by assimilation, ignorance of tradition, or indifference.

"The Power of Repentance" ("Die Kraft der Buße"), which appeared in the September 13 issue, was a forthright call to God in a secular age. Instead of consoling victims, Heschel challenged Jews to look within and root out self-deception. He insisted that the Jewish people had to stand ready before the living God in order to be redeemed.

"The Marranos of Today" ("Die Marranen von Heute") appeared on September 16, the first night of Rosh Hashanah. Heschel considered his German brethren, forced by the Nazis to acknowledge their origins, to be a new breed of Marranos: Jews on the outside, spiritually empty within. Heschel pushed them toward theological thinking: "The world has fallen away from God. The decision of each individual and of the many stands in opposition to God. . . . But still, we ache when we see God betrayed and abandoned." Human feelings of vulnerability and sorrow, he believed, could not be compared with those of the God of pathos.

Despite the Jews' painful situation, Heschel asserted that God is present and must be allowed to enter human awareness: "There is no return to Judaism without repentance before God." He prophetically proclaimed "utmost readiness" before God as the "fundamental idea of Jewish education."

With these essays, he advanced his life's mission. Heschel was becoming a rebbe for the modern world, even a prophet to the perplexed, to those culturally assimilated Jews in search of a solid identity.

A personal loss also marked the holy season. On Rosh Hashanah (September 17), the day after "The Marranos of Today" appeared in the *Gemeindeblatt*, Heschel's uncle Rabbi Yitzhak Meir Heschel, the rebbe of Kopitzhinitz in Vienna, died. The rebbe's son and Heschel's first cousin, Abraham Joshua Heschel (also husband of Heschel's sister Sarah), assumed dynastic leadership.[15]

Heschel continued to transmit his family's Hasidic legacy through his writings and teaching in Berlin. He hoped Buber would invite him to Frankfurt-am-Main, Germany's second largest Jewish community. In this diverse community, traditionalists struggled with reformers. Jewish educational renewal as practiced by Buber and Franz Rosenzweig—reaching out to those without religious knowledge, who constituted the majority—had become the dominant force. In 1920 Rosenzweig had established the Jüdisches Lehrhaus, and its adult education program launched a Jewish cultural revolution—a dynamic, interactive pedagogy countering the German standard of aloof, scientific, specialist lecturers. Buber joined Rosenzweig the following year. Together, they engagingly introduced assimilated Jews to the classical texts: Bible, the prayer book, midrash, and Jewish literature and philosophy.

After Rosenzweig's untimely death in 1929, the Frankfurt Lehrhaus ceased operation. In November 1933, however, Buber reopened the school under the auspices of the Center for Jewish Adult Education (Mittelstelle für jüdische Erwachsenenbildung bei der Reichsvertretung der Juden in Deutschland), an umbrella organization. His collaborator was Ernst Kantorowicz, an assimilated sociologist who had returned to Judaism.[16]

But Buber had long planned to immigrate to Palestine. In early 1937, after ten years of uncertain negotiations, he prepared to establish himself in Jerusalem. Around that time Buber decided to offer Heschel a responsible position at the Frankfurt Lehrhaus.

Heschel embraced Buber's mission to preserve and enhance Judaism in a state of emergency. Buber valued Heschel's mastery of classical Jewish sources, his training in European philosophy, and his authentic Hasidic piety. Kantorowicz, who continued as co-director of the Mittelstelle and supervised its pedagogical program, lacked knowledge of Judaism.[17] Heschel was the perfect associate, and as an observant Jew, he could better provide for the community's religious needs.

Heschel was thirty years old when he moved to Frankfurt on March 1, 1937. He was steadfast in his new responsibilities. He had barely placed his baggage in his rented room when he consulted with Kantorowicz at the Mittelstelle. The very next day, he wrote to Buber that at Kantorowicz's suggestion, he had agreed to "draft a circular about the prayer book."[18]

Heschel was at ease in this open-minded environment, where people shared their ideas honestly and with passion. He was delighted to "develop a friendship" with Ludwig Feuchtwanger (brother of the novelist Lion), as Heschel put it, "a very spiritual man" associated with the Frankfurt Lehrhaus and professor in Munich, who was the first reviewer of *Die Prophetie*.[19]

Heschel also began to tutor Buber, "his teacher," in Modern Hebrew, the language in which Buber was expected to lecture in Jerusalem. Of course Buber knew biblical, Rabbinic, and Hasidic Hebrew, but he could not yet speak and write the current idiom. Heschel was fluent in Hebrew, and he could speak and write the everyday language. The sixty-year-old Buber, with his extraordinary linguistic gifts, made rapid progress under Heschel's guidance.[20]

Heschel's unique personality impressed the Modern Orthodox

Simon family in whose Frankfurt home Heschel rented a room. He was perceived as an unusually congenial and discrete presence.[21] Rosie, the Simons's fifteen-year-old daughter, astutely observed this quiet boarder as a private, controlled person who, nonetheless, was warm and generous. She remembered him as a "God-fearing man so Orthodox that he referred everything to the One above us, even when he relished . . . a good piece of cake." At the same time, she felt Heschel's emotional distance. He was an attractive, eligible, polite bachelor, but he seemed to have no friends. He never brought anyone home.

Heschel enthusiastically embraced the Mittelstelle's pedagogical outreach. He prepared curricular materials under Buber's directives and took trains to small towns around Frankfurt or beyond, giving lectures of general interest, such as how to interpret the Bible, Jewish philosophy, or Talmud. Typically, he lectured informally at the local Jewish community center (*Gemeindehaus*). In town, he offered courses under the auspices of the Frankfurt Lehrhaus, usually at the Westend Synagogue, the Unterlindau Synagogue, or the Haupt Synagogue.[22]

Heschel the pedagogue sought to arouse personal involvement with the sacred text. This was also Rosenzweig and Buber's intent for the Frankfurt Lehrhaus, where classes took the form of seminars rather than lectures. The new education avoided the formal, hierarchical relations of the typical German system in which students listened passively, taking notes, while the professor sat at the desk or podium and read a prepared lecture, without looking up. Modern teachers cultivated a warm group atmosphere and appealed to the inner life. Heschel communicated his love of Judaism, inspiring listeners to take the Bible seriously from his own reverence for the text.

Germany was now a frightful place for Jews. Living under the pall of disaster, the enormity of which was not yet to be imagined, Heschel joined the multitudes who pursued opportunities to leave

Germany. He began to study English, assisted by his landlord, Jacob Simon, who knew five languages, having been a foreign representative for a metal firm.

Heschel studied English newspapers with horror. He was shocked by a report in the *Times* of London extolling the 1937 Annual Nazi Congress in Nuremberg. As he later recalled sardonically, "I rarely read anything so glowing, so beautiful, so enthusiastic as about this marvelous meeting of the Nazis."[23] People were blind to the evil in these grand spectacles. Fascism had perilous esthetic appeal.

It was in this state of mind that Heschel wrote another biography to elevate Jewish self-esteem. The occasion was the five hundredth birth anniversary of Don Isaac Abravanel (1437–1509), the Jewish Portuguese and Spanish statesman, financier of kings, biblical exegete, and theologian. Heschel thought an uplifting interpretation of the 1492 expulsion of Jews from the Iberian Peninsula might hearten German Jews on the brink of their own mass exodus. In the biography, Heschel stressed the theological significance of the Jews' history: "History is the encounter of eternity and temporality. Just as the word is the cloak of revelation and a testimony of prayer, so history forms a vehicle for God's actions in the world."[24] He stressed, using italicized type, "*The Jewish question is a question of God to us.*"[25]

For Heschel, Abravanel was an exemplary modern thinker: "He was at home in the fields of Jewish literature, in *Halakhah* and *Aggadah*, in religious philosophy and exegesis, but also in Christian theology and Islamic philosophy."[26]

The book's concluding sentences prepared readers for the contemporary expulsion of Germany's Jews. With forceful irony, Heschel explained how, from a moral perspective, the dreadful destiny of Spanish Jewry might provide some consolation:

> The Jews, who had played a leading role in the politics, economics and social affairs of their country, had to leave their Spanish homeland.

The conquest of the New World was achieved without them. Had they remained on the Iberian peninsula, they would surely have participated in the deeds of the Conquistadores. When the latter arrived in Haiti, they found over one million inhabitants. Twenty years later only one thousand remained.

The desperate Jews of 1492 could not know what they were spared.[27]

Readers were deeply stirred by Heschel's penetration of history's incongruities.[28] By implication, at the very least, victims of Nazism would not share responsibility for Spain's colonialist barbarities. And Heschel's sardonic suggestion that moral rectitude might emerge from persecution would prove to be appallingly correct.

The Prussian Jewish Community commissioned and subsidized Heschel's lucid essay on Abravanel (thirty-two pages, including copious source notes), among the final works Erich Reiss managed to publish in Berlin before the Nazis liquidated his company. The following year, Heschel's small volume was translated into Polish, subsidized by the Friends of the Hebrew University, perhaps due to Buber's support.[29] Jews in Poland were beginning to foresee another inquisition. Heschel's Abravanel might provide them all with a grim but abiding hope.

SACRED TRADITION FOR MODERNS

In December 1937 Heschel renewed contact with Henry Corbin. The philosopher and Islamic scholar welcomed Heschel's insights on the Hebrew prophets into his wide sphere, which included philosophers and scholars of mysticism in France, Germany, and Palestine.[30] In Paris, Corbin had developed interpretations of Persian mysticism, published translations of Heidegger and Karl Jaspers, and begun teaching at the École pratique des Hautes études. Corbin wrote Heschel to confirm his intention to translate selections from *Die Prophetie* into French. Heschel was delighted.

At the same time, Heschel's letter to Corbin dated January 18, 1938, revealed the melancholy beneath his aspirations. Addressing Corbin as "Lieber Freund" ("Dear Friend"), Heschel confided his sense of isolation, concealed from his Frankfurt acquaintances: "It is depressing and quite a drawback that spiritually one has to fend for oneself here, that there is no company which could inspire and enrich one spiritually. I don't know how long I will stay here."[31]

Was this the same existential loneliness Heschel expressed in his Yiddish poetry? In Frankfurt, where he had hoped to combine his spiritual and intellectual pedagogy, conditions apparently were not propitious for developing personal intimacy. Most of his collaborators had emigrated or were preparing to do so. Heschel had many reasons, known to him alone, to keep his feelings to himself.

Heschel's letter to Corbin did disclose a new project, one closest to his heart. He was preparing essays on prayer that would mature into a book-length study of spiritual consciousness. Two months earlier, Heschel had begun to write an essay on "the nature and the reality" of prayer. His spiritually audacious goal was to establish piety (in Hebrew, *hasidut*) as the foundation of a living Judaism. "Piety," as he understood the term, was a distinctively Jewish form of consciousness, transforming both the inner life and behavior. Piety combined faith, belief, attachment to God, observance of the mitzvot, and loyalty to the Jewish people; all would inspire action in the world. At this early stage, Heschel named his study of piety, his phenomenology of spiritual insight, a "systematology."[32]

Heschel's immediate, most urgent task was to impart the spirit of the Hebrew prophets. His letter to Corbin listed the chapters of *Die Prophetie* he should translate for a special issue of *Hermès*, a journal of religion and philosophy Corbin was editing, published in Brussels and distributed in Paris. Heschel ended by sealing their spiritual alliance: "The whole time I have thought with pleasure of our meeting in summer 1936 and, again and again, I wanted to continue contact at least by writing. Maybe now this correspondence will make a good start."[33] Sadly, their conversations on philosophy, Jewish and Islamic mysticism, and beauty would be interrupted by world strife.

In February 1938, in a speech to Quaker leaders, Heschel judged the significance of the impending war. Initially, the German Quaker and pacifist Rudolf Schlosser had invited Buber to address the group, but Buber was ill and had designated Heschel to take his place.[34] "Buber's assistant"—as Heschel was described—impressed the audience as "a very serious young man, with strong inner concentration, [who] attempted to fathom the meaning of this new persecution of the Jewish people."[35]

To this predominantly non-Jewish audience, Heschel interpreted the crisis in theological terms. Applying his prophetic perspective, he formulated a call to action. Just as his Abravanel biography sought theodicy in Spain's expulsion of the Jews, so too Heschel found a sacred message in Germany's campaigns of terror. He opened his "Search for a Meaning" ("Versuch einer Deutung") speech dramatically, with a symbolic scene:[36]

Carved over the gates of the world in which we live is the escutcheon of the demons. It happens in our time that the peoples are forging their sickles into swords and their scythes into spears. And by completely inverting the prophetic words, the peoples turn away from the words that come from Zion. Our lot is that we must face that world.

Heschel's judgments were bold and confident. He felt connected to his audience, some Jews but primarily Quakers who had heroically saved Jews and others from the ravages of disease, poverty, and persecution in Germany, Austria, and England. Speaking in solemn biblical cadences, he highlighted humanity's inescapable responsibility to take action in response to evil. He cited a dictum of

"Rabbi Baal Shem, the founder of Hasidism," to explain how Nazi evil serves a judgment on both Christians and Jews: "If a person sees something evil, he should know that it is shown to him so that he may realize his own guilt—repent for what he has seen." People of conscience, he avowed, can recognize radical evil within everyone (including themselves) and oppose the torturers more vigorously.[37]

With this, Heschel was judging contemporary civilization as a whole. He was not targeting secularization, nor religion as such, but rather the failures of institutional religion: the trivialization of belief in God and a diminished moral courage. People had lost contact with the ultimate; indifference could even inhibit the Divine.

For a believer, this was a grim diagnosis. God was in exile, imprisoned even "in the temples." The present was no different than in biblical times, when the God of pathos had hid the Divine Face and withdrew compassion from the people.

That evening, with his distinctive blend of faith and ethical audacity, Heschel defined a model of prophetic religion. His historical assessment was sound: Jews must leave Germany. Furthermore, his listeners could emulate his faith even at the brink of despair: "Perhaps we are all now going into exile. It is our fate to live in exile, but HE has said to those who suffer: 'I am with them in their oppression.'"

Heschel's talk so heartened Rudolf Schlosser that, at great personal risk, the Quaker leader distributed hundreds of mimeographed copies of Heschel's speech. Later in the United States, Heschel would translate and revise the speech and, in 1943, announce to American readers, still relatively unresponsive to the catastrophe, "the meaning of this war."

SEEKING A SAFE HAVEN

Heschel further intensified his efforts to find an academic appointment outside Germany. After making extensive inquiries, he realized virtually no positions were available. Yet, soon after his speech to the Quakers, he mailed a copy of *Die Prophetie* to Louis Finkelstein, president of the Jewish Theological Seminary of America, the Conservative rabbinical school in New York City, in the hope that the seminary might sponsor an invitation. That same month, Heschel was invited to join the faculty of a rabbinical academy that the Jewish community in Prague, Czechoslovakia, was attempting to establish.[38] He answered immediately to express interest.

Then, in one horrifying week, any sense of security that Heschel, or any European Jew, might still have possessed was shattered. On March 12, 1938, the Germans invaded Austria. The very next day, the Anschluss (annexation) was completed: all Austrian citizens, including Heschel's relatives in Vienna, became "Germans" subject to Nazi control. That very day as well, Martin Buber and his wife left Frankfurt for Palestine.[39]

The following week Heschel received two hopeful responses. Louis Finkelstein's letter, dated March 16, 1938, cordially acknowledged receiving his book "of which I have read several reviews. . . . I hope to read it in the course of the next few weeks," he promised.[40] On March 17 the Prague Jewish community wrote to thank Heschel for his "expression of willingness to enter into negotiations" for a position in their school.[41]

Heschel maintained himself in two discordant spheres. Intellectually, his life was flourishing. He pursued teaching, research, and publication, promoting *Die Prophetie* with Tadeusz Kowalski's help, eagerly awaiting reviews from around the world. In Frankfurt he and Ernst Kantorowicz supervised the work of the Mittelstelle and kept Buber informed by mail. All the while, however, Heschel remained acutely distressed by the suffering his extended family in Warsaw and Vienna had to endure. Jews in the Austrian capital were being systematically terrorized. Among them were Heschel's sister Sarah, her husband, Rabbi Abraham Joshua Heschel (now rebbe of Kopitzhinitz), and their ten children. Also living in Vienna were

Heschel's sister Devorah Miriam Dermer and her husband; and his brother, Jacob, with his wife, Sarah, and three-year-old daughter, Thena. There were also Friedman cousins, the rebbes of Boyan and Tchortkov and their families. Where could they or he go? The American quotas were filled. At this point, only clergymen and certain professionals were eligible for the few remaining non-quota visas.

Acts of violence increased. Thousands of Jews escaped or were deported. The German SS and Gestapo did not spare Heschel's pious family: Nazis and other hoodlums badly beat up his brother-in-law, the rebbe of Kopitzhinitz, and his cousin Israel. Despite it all, the rebbe refused to emigrate, insisting on his duty to remain with his Hasidim.

The rebbe's heroic defense of Jewish law, the obligation not to shave, probably saved the family's lives. Since the rebbe was one of the few bearded Jews left in Vienna, the Nazis routinely photographed him to depict a typical Jewish man. His youngest son, Meshullam Zusya, remembered that "nearly every day my father was dragged out of the house and forced to march in front of the jeering Austrian Nazis and made to mop up a freshly painted swastika on the street."[42]

The Heschels were not able to emigrate until almost a year after annexation. In February 1939 Rabbi Abraham Joshua Heschel of Kopitzhinitz, his wife, Sarah, and several of their children left for the United States. In the same month Jacob managed to reach London with his family, sharing an apartment with relatives who had also escaped. Eventually nine of the Kopitzhinitzer rebbe's children settled in America. Only one daughter, Leah Rachel, died in the Holocaust with her husband, Ephraim Fischel. The Friedmans of Vienna, the Tchortkover rebbe and his family (Jacob's in-laws), immigrated to Palestine, settling in Tel Aviv.[43] Dozens of other relatives would later perish.

Without an invitation from abroad or any money, Heschel had no choice but to remain in Frankfurt and seek help from contacts in the community. He was frequently invited to the home of Leni Rapp, the wife of a prominent doctor and a daughter of a Frankfurt Jewish community leader. Heschel also enjoyed many Sabbath evenings at the home of Rapp's uncle Rabbi Jacob Horovitz, who also taught courses on Maimonides at the Lehrhaus and in whose synagogue he worshiped.

Meanwhile, Heschel remained in close touch with his mother and sisters as well as writers and academic colleagues in Warsaw. In Poland there was relatively less foreboding about the future. He thought about returning there if a teaching position was offered. Despite growing tensions between Poland and Germany, one could travel between Warsaw and Frankfurt with the appropriate documents. The letters to and from his mother and sister in Warsaw helped all of them maintain some hope. As his sister Gittel wrote, "Each day that we receive a letter from you is a holiday for us."[44]

CHAPTER 5

Struggling to Escape, 1938–1940

During these excruciating months, Heschel's exchange of letters with Martin Buber in Jerusalem provided a lifeline. It is remarkable how closely they kept in touch, despite the formality Heschel fittingly maintained with his elder. Buber provided crucial stability as Heschel endured horrendous insecurity. The support was mutual. Buber in fact wrote Heschel about his installation as professor of social philosophy at the Hebrew University in Jerusalem, sending him the text of his inaugural lecture, "The Demand of the Spirit and Historical Reality," which declared the primacy of activism over allegedly academic scholarship.[1]

When Heschel briefly went home to Warsaw, he could hardly bear what he saw. In a letter to Buber on April 25, 1938, he poured out his anguish, explaining that Poland was in the grip of an "epidemic of despair." The country was becoming hazardous because of nationalist, anti-Jewish politics, while economic conditions were desperate. Heschel did not anticipate being able to undertake "anything durable here within the near future."[2]

Heschel was gloomy but he advanced his projects. He apprised Buber of his teaching, reassured him that Heschel's mother's condition was relatively good ("the same"), and said he expected to begin his Lehrhaus lectures immediately upon his arrival in Berlin the next day.

His letter to Buber continued by explaining, as he had to Henry Corbin, that his "Wissenschaft" ("academic") monographs—as he put it, "works in the style of my Gabirol studies"—were nothing more "than a preparation."[3] Heschel intended to apply elements of medieval thought (Jewish, Islamic, and Christian) as groundwork for his future philosophy of religion.

Heschel's letters to Buber became even more frequent, for mail could travel rapidly between Frankfurt and Jerusalem. On May 22 he added a long postscript response to Buber's suggestion that Heschel return to Warsaw. "[When at home] I saw that there cannot be any inner development in that dreary environment, full of resignation and depression." Heschel now made an explicit request to the well-connected Buber: "I would certainly consider the possibility for scholarly work in Jerusalem as *the* way for me."[4]

While Heschel was attracted to Palestine, his immediate interest was prompted more by his predicament than by a commitment to political or religious Zionism. Unlike Buber, Gershom Scholem, and other intellectuals of Buber's circle, he had not planned long in advance to settle in the Holy Land. Heschel also knew that Buber himself had experienced years of frustration before his attempts to obtain a post there proved successful. Nevertheless, Heschel asked Buber for help.

More realistically, Heschel placed his hopes in American Jewish institutions, about which he was well informed. Identifying himself as a "modern" candidate, he lucidly assessed job possibilities at the (Reform) Hebrew Union College in Cincinnati, the (unaffiliated, community-sponsored) Dropsie College in Philadelphia, the (Conservative) Jewish Theological Seminary, and the (Orthodox) Yeshiva University (Rabbi Isaac Elhanan Theological Seminary) in New York.

But Heschel did not remain preoccupied with himself. Under these harsh conditions, he was mapping out a curriculum that might enrich, and even save, Jewish civilization. While maneuvering for emigration, he drafted a booklet on studying the Bible. And with Ludwig Feuchtwanger and Erich Guttmann, he advanced work on a practical bibliography of Jewish sources that Buber had begun to compose, a "Catalog of Books for Jewish Youth."

Nonetheless, Heschel was anxious and disappointed about not having received an invitation from abroad or an immigrant visa. He thought a tourist visa might be obtainable instead. The next letter Heschel wrote to Buber, his last from Frankfurt, dated October 24, 1938, was factual and terse. His situation was unchanged. Concluding with an allusion to Buber's supportive advice, Heschel hinted at his own efforts to overcome despair: "Only Psalm 2:4 gives me comfort" ("He that sitteth in the heavens shall laugh: the Lord shall have them in derision").[5] When Buber opened this letter in Jerusalem, about a week later, Heschel, along with thousands of other Polish Jews, had been expelled from Germany.[6]

SAVED BY EXPULSION

On October 28 two Gestapo agents arrested Heschel in his Frankfurt room and ordered him to pack two bags. He took clothing and manuscripts, abandoning most of his books and papers. With exquisite contempt couched in politeness, the agents made Heschel carry his heavy luggage. Together they slowly walked to the police station, where he was held overnight.[7]

Heschel was one among thousands of Jews with Polish passports forced into trains and transported to the border between Germany and Poland. All over Germany, Hitler's police carried out an expulsion that, despite the panic, still did not hint at the possible destruction of European Jewry.

This crisis was hard to imagine, but not entirely unexpected. On March 31, 1938, the Polish government passed a law requiring all its Jewish citizens residing abroad for more than five years to renew their passports by the end of October or lose their right to return to

Poland. Very few of the approximately seventy thousand "Polish" Jews living in Germany and Austria, many of whom were born there and did not even speak Polish, actually completed the forms.

As the October 31 deadline approached, the Germans found a legal pretext to dispose of these "foreigners." Before dawn on October 28, German police agents entered the apartments of Jews in several cities and put them on trains to the German-Polish border. Most of these refugees were refused entrance into Poland, but they were allowed to communicate with the outside. Those who could secure official invitations might leave.

We do not know the details of Heschel's temporary confinement, but he did not remain long at the no-man's land border between the two countries. Contacts in Warsaw helped Heschel return home by the first week of November. He found shelter with his mother and sisters on Dzika Street, near the neighborhood where he had grown up.

He was thirty-one years old. Now in Warsaw, "Abraham Heszel" (as his Polish documents read) was seeking a job and a visa as he continued to teach, write, ponder, and pray. Antisemitism was increasing in Poland, yet many Jews still perceived no grave peril.

On November 9, 1938, Heschel wrote Buber about the mass expulsions that suspended his career in Germany. The following day, one week after the deportation of Polish Jews, Hitler sent a forthright message to the world. An unprecedented wave of anti-Jewish violence, arson, looting, desecration, and destruction broke out all over Greater Germany.

These atrocities reached the wider world. In New York the American Jewish Committee reported the following in its *Contemporary Jewish Record* (a monthly digest culled from European sources):

> Beginning in the early hours of the morning, in Berlin at 2 a.m., and continuing through the entire day, wrecking crews of Storm Troopers and Nazi Party members in uniform, in many cases under police

protection, carried on a systematic and thorough campaign of pillage and destruction of Jewish-owned stores and synagogues in virtually every town and city in the country. . . . The destruction of stores and shops was accompanied by the burning of synagogues throughout the country, while fire-fighting units took precautions only to prevent the fires from spreading to neighboring buildings.[8]

In Vienna, all of the twenty-one synagogues were attacked, and eighteen were wholly or partly destroyed. Torah scrolls were dragged from the synagogues and desecrated in the streets.[9] Jews were arrested, beaten, and sent to concentration camps. Many Jews committed suicide. The pogrom of November 9–10—called "Bloody Thursday" at the time—was vigorously condemned in Britain, France, and the United States.

Ironically it was fortunate that Heschel had been expelled from Germany, as he was spared this barbarism. The aggression coordinated by Joseph Goebbels, subsequently known as the Kristallnacht pogrom (Night of the Broken Glass), was far more sinister and destructive than the sanitized image of crystal suggests. This well-orchestrated violence ended the German policy of deporting Jews or pressuring them to leave. It anticipated the policy of extermination.

This was one of the most harrowing weeks of Heschel's life. Four days after Bloody Thursday, his friend and benefactor Erich Reiss was arrested in Berlin and dispatched to the Oranienburg concentration camp.[10] That was only the beginning.

Soon, however, Heschel received lifesaving support. Three weeks after his expulsion from Germany, he was invited to join the faculty of the Warsaw Institute for Jewish Science (Instytut Nauk Judaistycznych), a modern academic institution located in the neighborhood of the Yiddish Writers and Journalists Association, where the adolescent Heschel had submitted his first poems to Melekh Ravitch. Associated with the University of Warsaw, the Warsaw Institute for

Jewish Studies was similar to the Hochschule in Berlin in its scholarly outlook, except it specialized in cultural and historical research about Polish Jewry. Founded in 1928 by the rabbi and historian Moses Schorr and the historian Mayer Balaban, among others, the institute combined scientific research, a broad conception of Judaic studies, and openness to spiritual issues.[11] Its four-year program had two divisions: one preparing teachers of Hebrew language and Judaic subjects, the other training rabbis in advanced critical methods. Had there not been a war, it might have become Heschel's most compatible academic community.

Substituting for Moses Schorr (who was now expending his energies protecting Jewish rights in the political arena), Heschel was hired as a lecturer (*Dozent*) to teach Bible and Jewish philosophy.[12] In his native city, benefiting from the opening of a teaching slot, Heschel received a faculty position not available in Berlin, and one well-suited for his eclectic skills.

Meanwhile, Heschel the philosopher and theologian realized that the German outrages against humanity provided an opportunity to repudiate moral relativism. Europe could not survive if all ethical systems were deemed to be equally valid. Heschel's theocentric view of the Hebrew prophets provided a radical antidote: the living God as the source of an absolute moral standard. Each and every human individual was an image of the Divine.

This became Heschel's theological goal. Helpless before military force, as a thinker he might liberate people's ideas. As he had mentioned earlier to Henry Corbin, he was constructing a "systematology," a phenomenology of prayer. Now he began to publish exploratory essays on the inner life of piety.[13]

Practical considerations remained. Heschel again advanced the possibility of a job at the Cincinnati-based Reform seminary, Hebrew Union College. For several years already, its president, Julian Morgenstern, backed by his Board of Governors, had dedicated himself to saving as many European Jewish scholars as possible. He called this notable group his "College in Exile."[14] Heschel did not yet know that Morgenstern was already engaged in intricate negotiations with the U.S. State Department to invite Heschel and several others to the school.

When Heschel learned that Buber would soon be visiting Poland, his joy knew no bonds. On March 20 Heschel responded to Buber's recent letter: "My heart is overflowing. It is easier to remain silent than to speak appropriately. It is good for me to be thinking of the reunion with you."[15] Before Heschel sealed the envelope, however, even more lifesaving news arrived: a formal appointment from President Morgenstern for Heschel to serve as a research fellow in Bible and Jewish philosophy at the Hebrew Union College. His proposed salary would be $500 a year, in addition to board and lodging in the college dormitory. Finally Heschel could justify his application for immigration to the United States.[16] He shared the delightful news with Buber.

Yet Heschel received some frustrating news as well. In a memorandum to Polish officials written in both English and Polish, dated April 18, 1938, American vice consul William H. Cordell explained that Heschel, who was registered in the Warsaw Consulate office as "a non privileged immigrant in the Quota," had to wait an additional nine months before his documents could even be examined. The line in front of him was long.

Heschel responded to Morgenstern on April 30 from his mother's Dzika Street address. For the first time writing in English, he communicated awkwardly but with considerable tact: "It was very kind of you to think of me and to help in this sorrowful time." He went on to explain the "enormous difficulties" he was encountering in getting a visa: "As there are nearly no prospects here, I intend leaving for another country to try and get a visa there."[17]

London became Heschel's immediate target destination. He

remained in touch with his brother, but Jacob had no money and no civil status in England. Tragically Heschel's mother and sisters in Warsaw were not qualified for a visa. Only if Heschel settled in another country was there any hope to get them out of Poland as well.

Connections were crucial. Through Ruth Horovitz (daughter of Rabbi Jacob Horovitz, whose home he had often visited in Frankfurt), Heschel negotiated with the Religious Emergency Council of Great Britain. Ruth prevailed upon Judith Hertz, the eldest daughter of the chief rabbi of the United Hebrew Congregation of the British Commonwealth, who in turn consulted with her fiancé, Rabbi Solomon Schonfeld, who was principal of the Jewish secondary schools movement, rabbi of the Orthodox Adath Yisrael Synagogue, and a German member of the Agudat Israel directing the Emergency Council's day-to-day operations. Thanks to their repeated efforts, the Home Office approved Heschel's transit visa to London on June 20, 1939.

Heschel decided to leap. Even without a visa to the United States, he would embark for London and there continue his efforts. Seeking help for himself, though, Heschel was afflicted by an unhealable wound: his mother and sisters must be left behind in Warsaw. Exit permits for them were impossible to obtain.

Heschel, now a thirty-two-year-old refugee, reached London on July 13, 1939. His brother, Jacob Heshel, who had settled there with his wife and daughter (and Anglicized the family name), welcomed him. Without delay Heschel mailed a note to Jerusalem, sharing with Buber yet another defining moment: "A few hours ago I arrived here, and I feel the need to connect with you in my thoughts. The first impression is already a gain. It has style, this city. Whatever is behind it remains to be looked at more closely." Rhapsodic, Heschel nevertheless remained suspicious of appearances. Amid overwhelming uncertainties, his mission remained intact: "Prospects for work here are rather gloomy. But I am glad finally to be here."[18]

Heschel first stayed in his brother's small apartment. "Uncle

Avrumele" (as Jacob's young daughter, Thena, called him) brought cheer to his hosts, his playful sense of humor lightening their distress. Together the brothers easily created a happy atmosphere, joking and laughing. At Sabbath meals, they sang *zemirot*, Jewish table hymns cherished by tradition. Once little Thena locked herself in the sitting room and wouldn't get out, refusing to slip the key under the door. Uncle Avrumele saved the day when, with great merriment, he crawled into the room from a small window on the porch.[19]

In London, Heschel met with prominent Jews, among them Rabbi Joseph Hertz, the chief rabbi. Heschel also spoke with Leo Baeck, his former teacher from the Berlin Hochschule, who was temporarily in England. Like many others, Heschel attempted to convince Baeck to remain in safe territory, but the revered rabbi insisted upon returning to Berlin to care for his flock. (Baeck remained there until deported in January 1943 to the Theresienstadt concentration camp. He survived and was liberated in 1945.)

By mail, Heschel maintained close communication with Morgenstern and Buber. His increasingly frequent letters to them shared details of the complex bureaucratic hurdles. The two elders sustained his hopes.

Then came the inevitable war. On September 1, 1939, German forces invaded Poland. Hitler's true intentions could no longer be denied. Two days later, on September 3, Britain declared war on Germany, and a few hours later so did France.

London was in turmoil. Thousands of Jewish children—including Thena Heshel and her Jewish school classmates—were evacuated to the countryside, where they roomed with local families and attended classes. Thena returned home within six weeks; most of the others stayed away.

Heschel had escaped from Warsaw just in time. As he would proclaim twenty-five years later, evoking an image from Zechariah (3:2), he felt like "a brand plucked from the fire of an altar of Satan on which my people was burned to death."[20] Reaching London "just six weeks before the disaster began" was his second deliverance. The first had been his expulsion from Germany and resettling in Poland one week before the Kristallnacht pogrom. Now it was no longer safe in Poland; the German bombardment was destroying his native Warsaw.

We cannot fathom Heschel's excruciating feelings of helplessness, moral responsibility, and desolation. He was cut off from his family. There were no possible sponsors who could rescue his mother and sisters. Heschel himself was not yet authorized for any destination and risked deportation from London.

Henceforth, inseparable in Heschel's consciousness were two irreducible, contradictory realities: the destruction of the cultures that nurtured his spirit and trained his thinking versus his loyalty to the God of pathos. Heschel's American mission would emerge from that contradiction. "This is the task," he wrote years later, "in the darkest night to be certain of the dawn, certain of the power to turn a curse into a blessing, agony into a song."[21]

While the world anticipated even greater devastation during the following weeks, President Morgenstern, patient but unswerving, lobbied for his stranded "College in Exile." He visited Washington DC several times to obtain visas to rescue these scholars.

More than two months passed before Morgenstern was able to rectify Heschel's visa predicament. In September the Hebrew Union College president informed the American consul general in Dublin, Henry H. Balch, that full-time teaching positions were extended to Heschel and another German Jewish scholar, Franz Rosenthal, both of whom were temporarily residing in London. (Morgenstern had already reached out to the American consul general in London without success.) Balch answered on October 13, stating that he had referred the cases back to London, since the Dublin office did not possess a record of their applications. In his response, Morgenstern skillfully mentioned his personal conversations with the "Hon. A. M. Warren, Chief of the Visa Division, Department of State, Washington DC," to whom Balch ultimately reported.[22]

Meanwhile, the Nazi occupation of Poland brought disease, starvation, looting, and systematic persecutions. In November widespread epidemics were reported. On December 13, 1939, Heschel confided in a letter to Buber the agony of his first intimate, war-related loss: his sister Esther Sima was killed in a bombing raid.[23]

Now Jews were being murdered, imprisoned, or herded into walled districts in cities controlled by the Germans. By the year's end, the neighborhood where Heschel had spent his childhood and youth became enclosed in the Muranow Ghetto. In New York the American Jewish Committee's *Contemporary Jewish Record* reported, "Cruelties inflicted upon the Jews of Warsaw assumed unbelievable proportions. After driving Jewish residents into a ghetto early in November, the area was barricaded from the rest of the city. . . . Refugees from the city revealed (Dec. 17) that an average of 500 Jews died each day as a result of disease and starvation."[24]

The *White Book* issued by the World Jewish Congress on December 17, 1939, presented an even grimmer report. An estimated 250,000 Jews had been killed by disease, starvation, and Nazi firing squads. Some 30,000 Warsaw Jews had perished, and a majority of the 40,000 Jews who attempted to escape during the bombardment were also killed.

A subsequent Paris dispatch of January 7, 1940, disclosed that more than 2,500 Jews were reported to have committed suicide. About 17,000 Jews and Poles had been executed by order of German military courts, and 23,000 had been arrested in the period between the war's outbreak and the first week of December.

How could a bystander remain sane? How could Heschel continue his religious teaching? Could he justify his faith that God cares about humankind?

By his thirty-third birthday, January 11, 1940, Abraham Heschel, profoundly alone, faced personal peril and inconceivable loss. Nevertheless, while awaiting final word on his visa, he succeeded in initiating, if not establishing, an adult education program in London. The purpose of his "Institute for Jewish Learning," as announced in the leading community newspaper, the *Jewish Chronicle*, was "to introduce all ages and classes of Jew to the history and tradition of their forebears, by means of a cultural approach through lectures by reputed scholars."[25] Heschel's organizing abilities seemed to be at their peak.

The Institute for Jewish Learning opened on January 30, 1940, and Heschel inaugurated his program with a lecture entitled "The Idea of Jewish Education."[26] The next day, on January 31, the American Consulate in London granted Heschel a non-quota visa, and he immediately declared his intention to become a U.S. citizen. That very day, he joyfully informed Morgenstern: "I will lose no time in arranging my journey and I will see to start as soon as possible."[27]

Heschel further determined that this was a propitious time to reconfirm his now warm relationship with his mentor, Martin Buber. The following week (February 7) Heschel sent Buber his final letter from Europe.[28] When looking back on their original discussion on the prophets, between December 1934 and February 1935, Heschel had pointed to his elder's sometimes severe difficulty in achieving clarity of expression and urged Buber to improve the style of his new book. Now Heschel realized that his collegial advice might have been received as patronizing (in today's lingo, passive-aggressive). So in the interest of dialogue, Heschel took this opportunity to confess his own feelings of vulnerability. He thanked Buber for his support, all the more appreciated because of his own self-doubt.

Heschel then returned to their common task of spiritual renewal. Enclosing a list of lectures planned for his London Institute for

Jewish Learning, Heschel deplored some negative reactions to his religious point of view:

My opening lecture, "The Idea of Jewish Education" (which I myself consider to be very good!), caused indignation, because I supported an inherently Jewish-spiritual concept of education. Those standing on the "left" found [this] "reactionary thinking." For me, the ignorance and blindness of these people is the wonder of the century. I was a bit angry. Others understood the implications.

Like his Rosh Hashanah sermons from Berlin that had challenged German Jewish "Marranos" to fortify Jewish integrity, Heschel's spiritual perspective had offended some listeners. He hoped that his program would survive his departure: "If I were an *erlikher yid* [in Yiddish, an honest or genuine Jew], I would stay here to preserve this important institution in the mental desert of London."[29]

But the institute ceased to exist after Heschel's departure. The first series of lectures was to end on March 20. By then Heschel had already boarded his ship.

Heschel's London lecture, "The Idea of Jewish Education," was one crucial part of his European legacy of spiritual renewal. In November 1939 Henry Corbin's French translations from *Die Prophetie* appeared in a special issue of *Hermès* devoted to Islamic mysticism.[30] Corbin's preface, dated October (barely a month after the Nazi invasion of Poland), proclaimed the need to "unveil" the transcendent Source of ultimate meaning, challenging "the abyss, where one might be annihilated." As guest editor of this journal, Corbin enlisted Heschel and others to discredit nihilism by reconciling the Abrahamic religions: Judaism, Christianity, and Islam. Toward this aim, Corbin translated large extracts of Heschel's Berlin dissertation on Hebrew prophetic inspiration.

Spirituality was indeed Heschel's primary focus. Heschel

consolidated his German and Polish legacy by preparing two other invited essays, on prayer, that combined academic analysis and personal testimony. His "Das Gebet als Äusserung und Einfühlung" ("Prayer as Expression and Empathy" in German), published in the prestigious academic journal *Monatsschrift für die Wissenchaft des Judentums*, delimited the "essence" of spiritual consciousness (as did his doctoral dissertation). A second essay, "Al Mahut Hatefillah" ("The Essence of Prayer" in Hebrew), prepared for a volume honoring Mayer Balaban, co-founder of the Warsaw Institute of Jewish Studies, justified the power of piety as a metaphysical "event" transforming the human vision of the world.[31] As Heschel explained, the praying person is "heroic," for "intentionally or not, he puts his life in danger. He surrenders himself to the One to whom his being and essence belong; he makes a decision, he accuses God, gives notice, confesses himself, makes a vow, accepts the yoke of His rule, pawns his soul, accepts an acquisition, and seals a covenant."[32] Thus, prayer is a total commitment, and reciprocal, affecting God as it affects the person.

Such was Heschel's testimony to a shattered world. He remained confident that prayer can connect us with God, the ultimate source of human energy.

The Nazis would confiscate both publications—the swan song of his teachers' generation.

ENTERING THE UNITED STATES

On March 9, 1940, "Abraham Heszel" boarded the Cunard White Star liner *Lancastria* at Liverpool, England.[33] Among the 480 passengers, approximately 360 were classified as German Jewish refugees. The ship's manifest outlined Heschel's tangible identity: "Occupation—professor; Nationality—Polish; Race or people—Hebrew; Complexion—dark; Hair—black; Eyes—brown; Height—5ft 6in; Final destination—Cincinnati, Ohio."

During the twelve-day crossing of the Atlantic at the cusp of an impending world war, there were many terrifying moments. Violent storms battered the vessel. When waves smashed with tremendous blasts through several portholes, crew and passengers feared that a torpedo had hit their ship.

On March 21 the *Lancastria* docked in New York. Upon disembarking the boat, Heschel was startled to see an African American man kneeling to polish the shoes of a white man. Like many Europeans, he had never before seen a Negro, as black persons were then called. Heschel was shocked by this view of America's racial hierarchy, a segmentation to which he remained particularly alert.[34]

His old, Hasidic world was still available, in part. Heschel was met by his cousin, Rabbi Moshe Friedman, the Boyaner rebbe who had emigrated from Vienna, and his son Israel, now a social worker in Harlem. Also, a year before, his sister Sarah and her husband, Rabbi Abraham Joshua Heschel, the rebbe of Kopitzhinitz, had arrived from Vienna. For nearly three weeks Heschel would reside with his sister and brother-in-law at 132 Henry Street on New York's Lower East Side.

First, within hours of landing in New York City, Heschel wrote to Morgenstern at Hebrew Union College. Using the ship's stationery, he informed his benefactor, "I have just arrived in New York! *Baruch ha-Shem*! [in Hebrew: Thank God!] I would like to make my respects to you. Thank you very much."[35] He could scarcely find words to acknowledge his deliverer.

The festival of Purim began two days later. For Heschel and many other Hasidic refugees, joy at the Persian Jews' deliverance from Haman—and their own deliverance from the Nazis—was intermixed with grief for their loved ones who had recently died in Europe and anguish for those left behind. Heschel's sister Esther Sima had perished in Warsaw. His mother and sister Gittel remained in the city's ghetto. Another sister, Devorah Miriam Dermer, and her husband still lived in Nazi-dominated Vienna. Heschel was incapable of helping his remaining family in Europe.

The new immigrant began to reinvent himself as a future American citizen. First he assembled a professional network. He received mail at the American Express office on Fifth Avenue, explored libraries, and contacted prominent figures, among them the biblical scholar William Foxwell Albright of the Johns Hopkins University and Louis Finkelstein, president of the Jewish Theological Seminary. The latter contact would eventually prove to be most fruitful. In fact, with HUC president Morgenstern's approval, Heschel met with faculty of the Jewish Theological Seminary and gave a lecture in Hebrew to the rabbinical students.

Shortly before midnight on April 9, 1940, Heschel boarded an all-night train to Cincinnati. Arriving at Hebrew Union College the next afternoon, he settled in a dormitory room, as Morgenstern had promised. Sheltered in the heartland, he was now "Abraham Heschel, Instructor in Bible," rebuilding a life and a career.

EPITAPHS

As a bitter epilogue to Heschel's escape, the Cunard liner *Lancastria*, which had carried him and thousands of others to safety, returned to Europe, where it was rededicated as a troop transport. On June 17, 1940, as the British Expeditionary Force was being evacuated from France, German and Italian planes bombarded and sunk the ship. As the *New York Times* announced much later on page one, more than twenty-five hundred British soldiers, women, and children went down aboard the *Lancastria* to die in a blazing sea of oil, singing "There'll Always Be an England."[36]

The bare facts of Heschel's losses point to his heavy burden of good luck. From 1940 on, as he pieced together his new life in the United States, he learned of the deaths of many people he loved. Moyshe Kulbak: after immigrating to Minsk in 1928 and becoming an official "Soviet" writer, he was arrested in 1937 and perished in a prison camp soon after. Hillel Zeitlin: on the eve of Rosh Hashanah, wrapped in his tallit and tefillin and clutching his copy of the Zohar while preparing for deportation to Treblinka, the Nazis shot him. Menahem Zemba: the heroic rabbi of the Warsaw Ghetto and supporter of the uprising against the Nazis was shot and killed while leading his five-year-old grandson by the hand across the street.[37]

Heschel rarely spoke publicly of his immense bereavements. He did acknowledge his intimate sorrow, however, in dedications to some of his books. He dedicated the epigraph of his biblical masterpiece, *The Prophets* (an expanded translation of his Berlin doctoral dissertation), "to the martyrs of 1940–45" and cited Psalm 44 ("Why dost Thou hide Thy face?"). He also dedicated his 1962 study of Talmud, *Torah Min Ha-shamayim* (*Heavenly Torah as Refracted through the Generations*), to his martyred family: "To the memory of my saintly mother, Rivka Reizel, and to the memory of my sisters, Devorah Miriam, Esther Sima, and Gittel, who died in the Holocaust, May Their Souls Be Kept Among the Immortals."[38]

All the while, Heschel's internal battle, commenced at least at his father's early death, never ceased. In the confessional preface to his final book, *A Passion for Truth*, he defined himself as divided, torn between faith and anguish, between love of God and abhorrence of human apathy, moral weakness, and deliberate evil. Heschel found raging within himself the compassion of the Baal Shem Tov of Medzibozh and the opposing cruel demands of Truth of the Kotzker rebbe: "To live both in awe and consternation, in fervor and horror, with my conscience on mercy and my eyes on Auschwitz, wavering between exaltation and dismay? I had no choice: my heart was in Medzibozh, my mind in Kotzk."[39]

What was subsequently called the Holocaust would only magnify Heschel's fervor for social justice and his reverence for the divine human image.

PART II

*Theological Foundations
in America*

CHAPTER 6

Becoming an American, 1940–1945

Alone, poor, the immigrant entered a strange, unfamiliar world. Heschel settled in Cincinnati eight months after war had been declared in Europe. In the 1940s it was a typical American city with a large, mostly German Jewish population dating from before the Civil War. This majority had established the Reform movement in North America, whose academic center was Hebrew Union College (HUC), founded by Rabbi Isaac Mayer Wise in 1875. Now, American Judaism was divided into three "denominations"—Orthodox, Conservative, and Reform—with Reform Judaism the most populous and best organized. Significant cultural differences existed among Cincinnati's Jews.

Heschel lived in the Americanized, predominantly German Jewish Clifton neighborhood. He felt more comfortable, however, among the traditional Jews of the Avondale area, known humorously as the Gilded Ghetto. That community of about twenty thousand fostered Jewish culture through Zionist groups, meetings led by Hebrew speakers, theater activities, and religious schools for children from Orthodox and Conservative congregations (which did not have Sunday schools, unlike their Reform counterparts).

Heschel's new home was a small suite, with one bedroom and a living room, in the Hebrew Union College student dormitory.

Even with free room and board, his material needs were barely met by his yearly salary of $1,500 (the original offer of $500 had been increased). He took meals with the young rabbinical students in the dining room, which was not kosher, and ate only vegetarian and dairy foods, including eggs and cheese, unless kosher Osherwitz salami was available to purchase (an unhealthy diet for a man with incipient heart disease, as he would later discover).

As war and persecutions continued in Europe, Heschel closely followed events in Hebrew, Yiddish, German, and English newspapers (including the *New York Times* and the *Contemporary Jewish Record*), all readily available in Cincinnati. Without civil status or money, Heschel could not sponsor visas for family or friends stranded in Europe. In any case, U.S. immigrant quotas were filled. Heschel rarely referred to his family's peril, but students noticed that he sometimes sighed deeply in distress.[1]

Heschel attempted to preserve his alliance with Martin Buber. Soon after arriving at HUC, he wrote Buber in Jerusalem to describe his discouragement.[2] But there was no answer, and Heschel did not write again for almost two years.

As if to compensate for Buber's silence, Heschel renewed his warm friendship with Eduard Strauss, a confidant from Frankfurt who had escaped from Germany and was now living in Manhattan. A biochemist by training, Strauss had been a popular Bible teacher at the Frankfurt Lehrhaus. Strauss was one of the few people Heschel addressed in German with the familiar *du* (thou) instead of the formal *Sie* (you).

Hebrew Union College was a foreign environment for Heschel. The academic community was small, American, and tightly knit. The 1940–1941 catalog listed twelve professors, one professor emeritus, two visiting professors, and one "research professor" (not based on campus). The student body consisted of about sixty young men, most of them around eighteen years old, insulated by age and experience from life's concerns. Heschel and the other refugee scholars—Samuel Atlas, Alfred Gottschalk, Alexander Guttmann, Franz Landsberger, Franz Rosenthal, Isaiah Sonne, Eugen Täubler, Eric Werner, and Michael Wilensky—were surprised that some students lacked the most basic Judaic knowledge. The curriculum assumed minimal Hebrew. Most students entered the Preparatory Department (the remedial level), which included four levels of Hebrew-language instruction and introductory courses on Bible, liturgy, Mishnah, and midrash, as well as public speaking. There were also advanced courses that reflected the Reform emphasis on the ancient world and the history of Judaism as a culture and civilization.

Meanwhile, social graces were considered indispensable to these future Reform leaders, expected to minister to affluent, culturally assimilated, predominantly German Jewish congregations. Students received training in deportment, and most of them needed it; the majority came from western or midwestern lower- or middle-class families, often of East European origin. A dormitory matron provided gentility and order. In keeping with Cincinnati's southern culture, African American help made the beds daily, did the students' laundry, and, dressed in white coats, served meals in the dining room at tables spread with formal cloths.

Spiritually, too, Heschel was out of his element at HUC, where religious observance was even more removed from tradition than German Liberal Judaism. What Hebrew Union College called "divine services" followed classical Reform style, itself modeled after Protestant ceremonies, and performed mostly in English, led by a "reader." The Hebrew texts of the Torah and haftarah were spoken, not chanted. A student choir was accompanied by an organ (traditional Jews are forbidden to enrich services with instrumental music). The centerpiece of this ceremony was a sermon (not the Torah reading), often delivered as a pedagogical exercise by a rabbinical student. Decorum was crucial.

Furthermore, while observance of the Sabbath, the holiest day of the week, was respected at Hebrew Union College, the manner of observance was also far from traditional. Students were required to attend chapel services Friday evenings at 5:30 and Saturday mornings at 10:00, but the community largely disregarded Sabbath prohibitions of work, travel, and the use of electricity. Indeed, for most students, the week's highlight was Friday night, for off-campus dates. Weekday worship at 3:50 p.m. was optional, and there were no *Mincha* or *Ma'ariv* services.

Similarly, in the Cincinnati Reform synagogues (called temples), an organ was played on the Sabbath. A choir, often comprised of non-Jews, provided a backdrop to the service. The rabbi and cantor, rather than the congregation, performed the ritual. Men did not cover their heads with a *kippah* or wear a tallit.

In principle, American Reform called for preserving Judaism by modifying tradition. The Pittsburgh Platform of 1885, which Cincinnati rabbi David Philipson had helped draft, directly challenged Orthodox beliefs. The classical Reformers of the period dismissed the possibility of divine revelation, rejected the authority of the mitzvot, and abrogated the laws governing kosher food. In addition, prayers and holidays judged to be obsolete were removed.

Instead, proponents of classical Reform advocated for "ethical monotheism." Reform Jews were to pursue social action (or social justice) and replace parochial conceptions of Jewish peoplehood with universal values. Along those lines, the Pittsburgh Platform opposed the establishment of a Jewish homeland in Palestine, arguing that Jews were citizens of the countries in which they lived.

Nevertheless, at the time Heschel entered the scene, American Reform Jews were becoming more receptive to traditional practices, as the generations of predominantly German Jews committed to assimilation were being replaced by East European immigrants who maintained the ancestral religion. Thus, in 1937 the Central

Conference of American Rabbis, the professional association of Reform spiritual leaders, promulgated a new policy, called the Columbus Platform, which stated, "Judaism as a way of life requires, in addition to its moral and spiritual demands, the preservation of the Sabbath, festivals and Holy Days, the retention and development of such customs, symbols and ceremonies as possess inspirational value, the cultivation of distinctive forms of religious art and music and the use of Hebrew, together with the vernacular, in our worship and instruction."[3]

A gulf nonetheless remained between American Reform Judaism and Heschel's vision. The updated Reform still emphasized a nontheological approach that reduced acts of holiness to "customs, symbols, and ceremonies" with "inspirational value." For Heschel, observance of the mitzvot required that Jews respond to God's will; the Torah was divinely revealed, not a social artifact. Hebrew Union College rescued Heschel from the catastrophe in Europe, but it could not provide him with a spiritual home.

Heschel thus attempted to live in two worlds, maintaining his public observance in awkward ways. He did not wear a *kippah* while eating, as would Orthodox men and even some Reform rabbinical students; they noticed that when he said the *Motzi* (the blessing over bread at the beginning of the meal) he covered his head swiftly with a handkerchief. They wondered whether he chose not to wear a yarmulke to avoid ridicule or whether he was just trying to fit in.

Privately, Heschel fulfilled his devotions with fervor, a fact appreciated by some students. Alone in his room, after (or before) chapel, Heschel would perform all three prayer services required by sacred law. In his room he wore the tallit and *kippah*, and every weekday morning he wrapped tefillin around his head and arm. When praying he would *shuckle* (sway), with eyes tightly shut, or pace around with his tallit covering his head.

Heschel enthusiastically set out to master the English language.

Among the books in his dormitory rooms were Shakespeare's complete works, an unabridged English dictionary, and *Roget's Thesaurus*, replaced several times as it became thumbed and tattered beyond use.[4] He delighted in learning new words, even remembering the circumstances of each acquisition.

Heschel's intellectual sanctuary was the HUC library. One of the great Judaica resources in the world, it housed several important collections and more than twenty-five hundred manuscripts. There he continued his research in medieval Jewish philosophy, a foundational academic field that helped him refine his own theological system. More significant, he found rare Hasidic manuscripts and conceived a new, deeply meaningful project: a history of the Baal Shem Tov.[5]

To seal his commitment to his new country, two months after settling in Cincinnati, before summer recess, Heschel began the process of naturalization. He obtained a certificate of arrival at the United States District Court. His declaration of intention, dated May 29, 1940, in the name of "ABRAHAM HESZEL (known as Heschel)," summarized his civic identity and physical features: age, 33; eyes, brown; complexion, dark; height, 5ft 7in; weight, 160 pounds; nationality, Polish; religion, Hebrew; born, Warsaw, Poland, on January 11, 1907.[6]

CONFRONTING ALBERT EINSTEIN

After the first few months at Hebrew Union College, Heschel inaugurated the practice of spending the long summer recess, from June through September, in New York City. This time, rather than lodge with his sister's family in Lower Manhattan, he rented a room at 362 Riverside Drive on the Upper West Side, near the Jewish Theological Seminary and Columbia University. He conducted research in the schools' libraries, met with academics, and fostered contacts with other immigrant groups.

The nearly four months Heschel spent in New York that summer opened important opportunities. Several European institutions had relocated in New York City. There was YIVO, the secular research institute familiar to him from his Warsaw and Vilna days. Founded in Vilna in 1925 to preserve East European culture—including Hasidic material—YIVO moved to 123rd Street in New York, which became its center in 1940. Respected as a published Yiddish poet, Heschel joined the organization's board of directors; he may have been YIVO's only religiously committed board member.

That summer Heschel made two momentous decisions that advanced his sense of personal security and his sacred mission. First, he strengthened his ties with the Jewish Theological Seminary president Louis Finkelstein, a scholar of the talmudic period and a canny administrator who had enlisted influential figures from the realms of science, the humanities, and different faiths for a think tank. Finkelstein's dream was to reconcile science and faith. To this end, he inaugurated the "Conference on Science, Philosophy, and Religion in Their Relation to the Democratic Way of Life," to be held at the Jewish Theological Seminary in September.

At that conference, Albert Einstein, America's most prestigious Jew, was a central figure. Einstein did not present his talk in person at the opening session on the natural sciences (September 11, 1940), but his paper "Science and Religion" was read, distributed, and hotly debated. The Nobel laureate resolutely opposed the idea of a personal God, Heschel's primal certainty as a Jew. The interfaith, interdisciplinary audience was polarized, despite Einstein's diplomatic suggestion that scientific curiosity included a spiritual motive.[7]

Heschel, for his part, made a bold move, astounding for a recent immigrant. Though not a speaker at the conference, Heschel had arranged, through the Jewish Theological Seminary and the German Jewish refugee community, to publish "Answer to Einstein" ("Antwort an Einstein") in *Aufbau* (Reconstruction), a German-language newspaper dedicated to the "Americanization" of immigrants, with a readership of about thirty thousand. Its September 13 issue head-lined the controversy: "Einstein's Dismissal of Any Kind of Belief in a Personal God." Heschel's "detailed response" was announced for the following week.[8]

The editors of *Aufbau* abridged Einstein's original paper (which they translated into German) in a manner that heightened the polemic. Entitled "God's Religion or Religion of the Good?" it began dramatically by blaming "all the present conflicts between the spheres of religion and science" on the concept of a personal God "who interferes with natural events." Decrying the "juvenile period of man-kind's spiritual development," Einstein called on religious teachers to "have the courage to give up [this] teaching" and instead cultivate the humanistic triad of "the Good, the True, and the Beautiful."[9]

The following week, Heschel defended the reality and moral neces-sity of a personal God. Boldly, he derided Einstein's naturalistic faith as "a magical resurrection rite," while prudently noting that he was responding to "Einstein's communication to the Conference . . . as printed in *Aufbau*." He satirized Einstein as "a missionary for a forgotten confession" and rejected Einstein's premise that only "natural events" could appropriately be discussed. Heschel asserted that Einstein, as a Jew, should not revert to an outmoded paganism. With shaky logic, he associated the physicist's scientism with Nazi racial theories that led directly to "the view that all life and action are determined by natural factors, blood, soil, and race."

Heschel's model for the sanctity of human life was the Hebrew Bible, not biology. Pointing to the dangers of deifying reason, he claimed that a morally neutral science "cannot be prevented from creating poisonous gas or dive-bombers; and rationalism is powerless once 'the magnificent blond beast' . . . takes arms in order to sub-jugate inferior races." He concluded that religion bounded by the limits of science could not guarantee morality. Spiritually speaking, pride or hubris was the greatest peril facing modern civilization.

Heschel's audacious "Answer to Einstein" advanced his lifelong campaign against secularized religion, anticipated by his debate with Martin Buber. In it Heschel upheld his faith in the living God as essential to ethical sensitivity. Religion, not science, must clarify "why there is a world in the first place" and interpret "the meaning of life and death, the meaning of being and of history."

JEWISH DIVERSITY IN CINCINNATI

Heschel's first full academic year at Hebrew Union College began on October 19, 1940, following the High Holy Days, a month after his rejoinder to Einstein appeared in *Aufbau*. His faculty title remained the same, the lowest position open to the refugee scholars: fellow in Jewish philosophy.

Heschel's teaching, for the most part, was limited to basic courses. A specialist in medieval Jewish philosophy, he offered an introductory course and an advanced seminar on Hasdai Crescas's *Or Adonai* (*Light of the lord*, a major synthesis of Jewish beliefs and dogmas). He also taught elementary Hebrew.

Heschel found the classroom stultifying, and he was not alone. The refugee professors were welcomed sympathetically, but it was no secret that they did not fit in. Their standards remained far higher than the curriculum could offer, even as they struggled to teach in English. Both the refugee scholars and their American students tended to perform poorly in class.[10]

On campus, Heschel was perceived as quiet and shy. He rarely spoke his mind, always listening, usually asking questions. He developed an irenic personality, a diplomatic reserve, emphasizing the positive. Above all, he maintained a dignified, deeply respectful loyalty to President Morgenstern, who had saved his life. And yet, some skeptics like Jacob Rader Marcus, HUC's American-born history professor, considered Heschel to be a fraud who exaggerated his "reverent obligation" toward Hebrew Union College.[11] Perhaps, simply, Heschel could not find an idiom adequate to communicate his strong emotions.

Music afforded Heschel some opportunities to connect with the Americans. Heschel gladly accepted invitations from Rabbi David Philipson, militant anti-Zionist and classical Reform leader, to ride in his chauffeur-driven car to the Cincinnati Symphony. He confided to one of his students that music was essential to his being and competed with prayer as his greatest joy. As an adolescent in Warsaw and a student at the University of Berlin, he had decided that the arts were the ally, not the foe, of religion.

Despite Jacob Marcus's criticism, he formed a tie with Heschel through music. Marcus's wife, Antoinette, was a concert pianist and singer, and after some time Heschel was invited to the Marcus home for a private recital. There he was introduced to Sylvia Straus, a talented pianist from Cleveland. Exactly six years younger than Heschel (both were born on January 11), Straus was studying in Cincinnati with the eminent pianist, composer, and teacher Severin Eisenberger. Her musical performance that evening enchanted Heschel.[12] They would marry four years later.

Less advantageous to Heschel's career, but congruent with his deepest values, was his admiration for the most radical member of the HUC faculty: Abraham Cronbach, the founder of the Social Studies Department. On the surface, theirs was a most unlikely alliance. Cronbach was an ethical extremist who sought to Americanize Judaism far beyond classical Reform. Cronbach opposed Zionism and the use of Hebrew in religious services and Jewish life. He was a pacifist during the First and Second World Wars and spoke at the funeral of Julius and Ethel Rosenberg, who were executed for treason.[13] But Cronbach appealed to Heschel as a mensch, a human being of unusually strong character, an uncompromising dissenter. For Cronbach, anything in the Jewish tradition that did not meet his standards was not Jewish, while anything outside the tradition that was ethical was. Perhaps Cronbach appealed to Heschel's own spiritual radicalism, vividly expressed in his Yiddish poetry of the early 1930s.

Through Cronbach, Heschel learned about American civil rights struggles. At the Cronbach home, Heschel and HUC students met ministers, social workers, local Jews and Christians, and members of the African American community. One day Heschel complimented Maurice Davis, a rabbinical student (who would later marry Cronbach's daughter, Marion), for befriending one of the black men on the janitorial staff without talking about it. Emotionally Heschel told Davis, "I want you to know that is what Judaism is all about."[14]

In his free time, Heschel often walked the two or three miles from the Clifton area, where he lived and worked, to the Jewish neighborhoods of the Avondale section, where he bought kosher food and met people who shared his learning, observance, and support for Jewish Palestine and modern Hebrew culture. Heschel became closest to Rabbi Louis Feinberg, a self-effacing Conservative rabbi who integrated Orthodoxy and modernity into his life and ministry.[15] Feinberg's family had emigrated from Lithuania, and from the 1920s to 1950 he was rabbi of the Avondale synagogue Adath Israel, the leading Conservative congregation in Cincinnati, whose worship services were congenial to Heschel.

Heschel's other spiritual resource was a prominent Orthodox rabbi, Eliezer Silver, the forceful and flamboyant leader of the Kneseth Israel synagogue. Born and reared in the Kovno province of Lithuania, Silver immigrated to the United States in 1907 and became the founding president of the American branch of Agudat Israel, which by 1939 had consolidated into an international organization of Orthodox rabbis opposed to Zionism and other forms of modernity. Several of Heschel's close relatives were among its leaders. Heschel admired Silver and worshiped in his synagogue, despite the latter's uncompromising view of Reform Judaism as a blasphemous source of assimilation. Silver visited the HUC campus only once: to place the institution in *herem* (excommunication).

That being said, spirit was more consoling than ideology. Both Rabbis Feinberg and Silver offered safe havens for Heschel's devotions: Feinberg embodied the traditional wellsprings of American Conservative Judaism, and Silver the zeal of Lithuanian Orthodoxy.

But the most valuable support for Heschel's emotional life during those difficult years in Cincinnati was his Sabbath afternoon *midrashah* (study group), organized by the nondenominational Cincinnati Bureau of Jewish Education. Each Shabbat afternoon Heschel walked to Bureau headquarters on Rockdale Avenue. Waiting for him were eight to ten young Hebrew speakers, high school or college students. Most of them had received scholarships for a year at the excellent Hertzlia Gymnasium in the Jewish city of Tel Aviv and had returned fluent in Hebrew. Heschel was a cultural Zionist, committed to a Jewish state in Palestine and the practice of Hebrew in the Diaspora. He and his students spoke impeccable Modern Hebrew with the Sephardic accent of the Zionist pioneers.

For those precious hours of text study and personal communication in Hebrew, Heschel was freed from the tensions of teaching at HUC. With these students he could behave naturally and became an effective pedagogue who instilled critical thinking. Most students would later remember with nostalgia chanting Hasidic melodies at sunset for the *Havdalah* service separating the Holy Day from the rest of the week. As the room darkened, Heschel taught them wordless songs (*nigunim*) from his past. The mood was melancholy and peaceful.

Heschel also joined the Ivriah Society. Founded in 1911, this group was associated with the Cincinnati branch of Poale Zion (Labor Zionists), organized to counteract the anti-Zionism at Hebrew Union College. For decades the society sponsored lectures and welcomed prominent Hebrew writers, poets, educators, and scholars to their monthly forums. For Heschel, the Hebrew language itself unified the multitude of Jewish sects scattered or destroyed by the war.

ARCHITECTURE OF A NEW THEOLOGY

All the while, destruction continued to rage in Europe. As Hebrew Union College's second term began on January 6, 1941, Heschel was dismayed at most Americans' apparent indifference to the situation abroad; while newspapers such as the *Cincinnati Post* and *New York Times* reported war news in detail, it was usually relegated to their inside pages. Heschel expressed his pessimism in a letter to his friend Eduard Strauss: "The good is not pleasant and 'the beautiful is nothing but the beginning of the horrible.'" Heschel still affirmed his faith in God: "I think that, despite everything, we are not at all deserted. And this is what counts!"[16]

Work helped Heschel overcome his gloom. He carried on his research on medieval Jewish philosophy while reviving his personal, theological project: essays (now in English) on piety and holiness. He began by translating and revising his earlier articles written in German or Hebrew.[17]

That summer Heschel returned to New York and continued to make significant professional inroads. Now a master of English literary prose, he saw his first major article in English, "An Analysis of Piety," printed in the March 1942 edition of the *Review of Religion*, published by Columbia University's Department of Philosophy and Religion. The editors also invited him to review a book edited by the eminent historian Salo Wittmayer Baron to celebrate the eight hundredth anniversary of Maimonides's birth. Heschel was being recognized by academic specialists.[18]

"An Analysis of Piety" contained the kernel of Heschel's entire mystical and prophetic theology. Intended for a general audience, it described Hasidic spirituality in modern terms. Without focusing on Judaism as such, Heschel extended his phenomenology of prophetic inspiration to rescue the old notion of "piety" from its negative connotations. He analyzed "the inner life of a pious man," and it is said that he drew his ideal portrait of that "pious man" from his uncle, Rabbi Alter Israel Shimon Perlow, the Novominsker rebbe.

The work displayed an unusual, and perilous, style of writing: rhythmical, concise, harmonious, with a penchant for aphorisms and literary devices such as antithesis and alliteration. Heschel's amalgam of analytic and poetic prose, however, had a pragmatic as well as esthetic function: to transmit his germinal insight, namely *the re-centering of the self to God.* The pious person, he wrote, "is not aiming to penetrate into the sacred. Rather, he is striving to be himself penetrated and actuated by the sacred, eager to yield to its force, to identify himself with every trend in the world which is toward the divine." He envisioned a "ladder leading to the ultimate," ascending from the ethical to the holy. In other words, awareness of God was inseparable from ethics.

"An Analysis of Piety" concluded by recognizing the holiness of life itself—and specifically by defining death as "the ultimate self-dedication to the divine." The last sentence would become one of Heschel's boldest formulations: "For the pious man it is a privilege to die."[19]

Writing again had brought Heschel freedom. Now, barely two years after arriving in the United States, he felt confident to announce publicly his grand design: the construction of a modern theology inspired by his studies of Solomon Ibn Gabirol. He dared name this ambitious goal in the March 1942 *Hebrew Union College Bulletin*—the creation of his "systematology," a philosophical rendition of spiritual insight and Jewish living.

And, once again, Heschel decided to pursue his relationship with Martin Buber. Heschel knew that the previous year Buber had submitted the manuscript of a historical novel, *Gog and Magog*, to the Jewish Publication Society (JPS) in Philadelphia and was awaiting a response. Buber, still in Palestine, wanted more American readers; in part because of financial difficulties, he could no longer furnish the needed subsidy for a publisher to print his books in their original German. Heschel believed he could help in securing JPS publication of the novel.

Writing to Buber, Heschel took it upon himself to explain his own twenty months of silence, while emphasizing their shared ideals: "I miss your wisdom and friendship. But it is impossible to write. To experience the atrocious at a distance makes me mute."[20] He added in Hebrew, "May it be His will to see each other in times of consolation." Heschel also told Buber that he could exert some influence at the Jewish Publication Society (how, we do not know, but this would turn out to be a useful rehearsal for Heschel in submitting his own future books to JPS). Perhaps most significantly, Heschel informed Buber that he was advancing his own "systematic study of religion." Concluding on a personal note, he sent regards to Buber's wife. Buber answered almost immediately, restoring their collegial communication for their mutual benefit.

Heschel had discovered that in the United States scholarly publishing in particular was a bleak business, restricted by financial considerations, perhaps to an even greater extent than in Europe. He wrote Buber that even William Foxwell Albright, the preeminent archaeologist at Johns Hopkins, had to print his major books at his own expense.[21] This situation may have encouraged Heschel to elaborate his religious philosophy in a less technical style, so as to avoid having to fund his own book-length works.

In 1943 the prestigious scholarly *Jewish Quarterly Review* published part 1 of Heschel's monograph on reason and faith in the work of Saadia Gaon (882–942), considered the founder of Judeo-Arabic literature, for a special issue commemorating the millennium of the thinker's death. Part 2 of Heschel's study then appeared in the journal in 1944.

Heschel went on to reprint the two parts together as a pamphlet of sixty-seven pages with the Jewish publisher Philip Feldheim. Entitled *The Quest for Certainty in Saadia's Philosophy*, it became Heschel's first "book" in English. Part 1 recapitulated Saadia's efforts to define faith as compatible with reason. Although reason and "critical examination" served as guarantors, Saadia taught that intuition or insight was the true mode of religious knowledge. Part 2, "Reason and Revelation," was quite relevant to modern theology. According to Heschel, Saadia's masterwork repudiated complacent Orthodoxy's shallow rationalism and empiricism or pragmatism, the reigning American educational ideology.

Saadia's sophisticated apologetics, *The Book of Belief and Opinions*, would provide a conceptual model for Heschel's *Man Is Not Alone* (1951). Separated by centuries, the two men shared the same goal: to achieve certainty in religious faith. Almost instinctively, Heschel was constructing a treatise on piety, spirituality, and ethics—a modern and devout philosophy of religion.

THE NEW GENERATION

How could Heschel communicate this mystical theology to others? In addition to writing, the thinker, to survive, had to teach.

For his third academic year (1942–1943), Hebrew Union College promoted Heschel to instructor in Jewish philosophy and rabbinics, thus acknowledging his expertise in Talmud and medieval thought. His assigned courses, however, remained elementary: liturgy (in the Preparatory Department), Rashi's commentaries (for the lower and medium levels), and intermediate Hebrew.[22]

Heschel's pedagogical hopes were rekindled by a group of twenty-two freshmen, the largest class ever to enter Hebrew Union College. These candidates were in many ways a typical band of young American males. Eighteen came from large cities, mostly in the Midwest and the East; nine were college graduates, one had a PhD, while thirteen were still undergraduates and required to matriculate simultaneously at the University of Cincinnati. These young Reform Jews, many of whom would become prominent rabbis or religious thinkers, presented Heschel with both challenges and opportunities.

Heschel's first American follower was Samuel Dresner, an intense young rabbinical student from a moderately observant Reform family in Chicago. In high school, Dresner's encounter with a homeless woman in downtown Chicago had transformed his preoccupation with sports and girls to questions of evil, God, and moral responsibility.[23] Now ready to be inspired, Dresner was ignited by Heschel's chance remark from Pirkei Avot (Ethics of the Fathers): "The shy person cannot learn and the impatient person cannot teach, so you don't be shy and I won't be angry."[24] After several conversations outside of class, Dresner became convinced that Heschel was "the greatest Jew of his time," the zaddik of his generation. He became Heschel's lifelong disciple.

Sadly, many students remained unimpressed. An aloof Heschel would sit at a desk and lecture from notes. His classroom pedagogy would almost destroy his reputation and his morale.

Cultural differences were largely responsible for this mutual misunderstanding. In European universities, students would rise when the professor entered. American students, however, closer to the ideals of the Frankfurt Lehrhaus, expected to interact with their teachers and expressed themselves freely. Heschel presented his lessons methodically, but he usually proceeded by digression, a style more appropriate to a yeshiva than to an American college. Most frustrating for his students, he referred to so many unfamiliar works that most of them got lost and were able to grasp only bits of the lesson. To some of them, Heschel appeared to be badly prepared, distant, sometimes defensive.

As he began to publish essays in English, students took their revenge with parodies of his opulent literary style. During one

Purim-spiel, the comical play that celebrates the raucous holiday, some students took aim at the aphoristic final sentence of "An Analysis of Piety"— "For a pious man it is a privilege to die"—chanting a series of parodies: "For a pious man it is a privilege to eat," ". . . it is a privilege to drink," ". . . it is a privilege to piss," and so on.

And yet, Heschel's charisma was appreciated. His classes on liturgy were well received. Many students had never seen a traditional weekday morning service. Heschel conveyed his love of worship, sometimes by taking his class to an Orthodox synagogue or to Rabbi Feinberg's service at the Conservative synagogue Adath Israel. Traditional prayer could create common ground.

Outside of class, Heschel counseled students. He listened to them, encouraged them, and often even confided in them. Unlike most of the other professors, American or European, he called students by their first names, establishing a mutual bond.

American culture also fascinated Heschel. Some evenings he exercised in the HUC gymnasium, and he went regularly to the corner theater on the hill down Clifton Avenue, where the feature film changed twice a week. Movies helped Heschel to increase his proficiency in English, and they were relaxing, though he felt guilty about spending his time this way. After one late show he lamented to a student, Arnie Wolf, who often accompanied him, "When my grandfather was tired, he used to read Kabbalah; when I'm tired, I go to the movies."[25]

COPING WITH CATASTROPHE

Refugees endured bitter estrangement from the American Jewish community. For twenty years Heschel would remain silent about his experience of these war years. In 1963 though, as Gershon Jacobson, a Jewish refugee from the Soviet Union, interviewed him in Yiddish, that conversation in Heschel's mother tongue released an emotional flood.

Heschel began with his failure, in 1941, to make American Jews understand the gravity of the suffering of Jews in Europe. He then witnessed a massive public failure of American Jewry. On July 21, 1942, a huge rally to support European Jews took place at Madison Square Garden in New York City, organized jointly by the American Jewish Congress, the Jewish Labor Committee, and B'nai B'rith. Reports had come from Poland that the Nazis had murdered seven hundred thousand to a million Jews. British prime minister Winston Churchill and the American president Franklin Roosevelt sent statements condemning the atrocities. The Synagogue Council of America urged rabbis and their congregations to dedicate the fast of Tisha b'Av to the victims. These spiritual acts did not have pragmatic consequences. Few concrete measures were taken to rescue or even aid Polish Jews. The American Jewish organizations battled over differences of policy. No concrete programs emerged from these disastrous competitions. Heschel was among thousands of other Jews, refugees or native born, aghast at this disunity.[26]

The facts were readily available. Less than a week after the rally fiasco, prime evidence of what the writer Hayim Greenberg denounced as the moral "bankruptcy" of American Jewry, the Jewish Telegraphic Agency transmitted the first news of widespread expulsions from the Warsaw Ghetto. By mid-August, reliable sources were reporting that "3,600 men, women, and children had been brutally deported in trains to internment camps in unoccupied southern France and sent off to an 'unknown destination' eastward, these representing the first contingent of a total of 10,000 Jewish refugees" who were being sent to their deaths.[27]

Heschel hoped that Reform Jews, whose rabbinic institution had saved him, might be more committed than other agencies. He attended the annual meeting of the Central Conference of American Rabbis, where a Quaker leader was unable to persuade Jewish groups to send food packages to Jews in ghettos and concentration camps.

Heschel summarized, "The Rabbis declared that this could not be done officially because it would help the Germans if food was sent to the territories they controlled."[28]

Heschel was crushed, irremediably wounded in his Jewishness. Prayer was his only recourse, as he later admitted to Jacobson in 1963: "I went to Rabbi Eliezer Silver's synagogue in Cincinnati, recited Psalms, fasted, and cried myself out. I was a stranger in this country. My opinion had no impact. When I did speak, they shouted me down. They called me a mystic, not a realist. I had no influence on the Jewish leaders."[29]

By calling him a "mystic," Heschel's critics were expressing bias against emotion in Judaism. True, for Heschel, the very existence of Judaism's spiritual treasures hung in the impassioned balance. Heschel needed to find more effective ways to reach into the heart and mind and spirit of American Jews.

During his December 1942 vacation in New York, he spent a Shabbat evening at the home of Mordecai Kaplan, dean of the Teachers Institute at the Jewish Theological Seminary and editor of *The Reconstructionist*, a widely read periodical whose masthead proclaimed its humanistic goals: "the advancement of Judaism as a civilization, . . . the upbuilding of Israel's ancient homeland, and . . . the furtherance of universal freedom, justice and peace." Although Heschel's reverence for the living God contradicted Kaplan's view of God as "an idea" serving human needs and aspirations, Kaplan had been deeply moved by Heschel's "Analysis of Piety" essay. In his diary, Kaplan the inveterate rationalist had composed a long poem inspired by a Heschel passage, which he now planned to include it in his new prayer book.[30]

After their Shabbat together in New York, Heschel wrote a note of thanks to Kaplan: "I have often thought of our talk and felt like saying that the community of *kavanah* [inner devotion] is more decisive than the difference of *nusach* [custom]."[31] Despite Kaplan's aversion to "supernaturalism," he was open-minded, even attracted to Heschel's piety.

Heschel began to write and speak with a prophetic judgment of the unfolding European catastrophe. In full control of literary English, he translated and adapted his 1938 talk to the Quaker group in Frankfurt, "Versuch einer Deutung" ("Search for a Meaning"), for publication in the March 1943 *Hebrew Union College Bulletin*. Retitled "The Meaning of This War," his first such printed statement in America opened dramatically: "Emblazoned over the gates of the world in which we live is the escutcheon of the demons. The mark of Cain in the face of man has come to overshadow the likeness of God. There have never been so much guilt and distress, agony and terror. At no time has the earth been so soaked with blood."[32]

Heschel put forth his prophetic challenge: we must not blame God for these lethal persecutions; rather, God holds us accountable for our lack of moral courage: "Let Fascism not serve as an alibi for our conscience. We have failed to fight for right, for justice, for goodness; as a result we fight against wrong, against injustice, against evil." Heschel also disparaged the nonetheless necessary war against Germany as its own evil: a consequence of social wrongs, weakened democracies, and the trivialization of religion. For Heschel, authentic religious commitment was the most abiding "action."

With a characteristic antithesis, Heschel concluded by reminding Jewish readers that they were "either slaves of evil or ministers of the sacred." Citing a midrash on the covenant at Sinai, he summarized the present challenge: "Israel [the Jewish people] did not accept the Torah of their own free will. When Israel approached Sinai, God lifted up the mountain and held it over their heads saying, 'Either you accept the Torah or be crushed beneath the mountain.' The mountain of history is over our heads again. Shall we renew the covenant with God?"

Heschel had found his militant voice. The following February

(1944), his essay, strengthened by his addition of new powerful phrases, was republished in *Liberal Judaism*, the organ of the Union of American Hebrew Congregations (the national organization of Reform synagogues). More directly than ever, Heschel chastised America's largest Jewish denomination as he urged them to act: "A messenger recently came and conveyed the following message from all the European Jews who are being slaughtered in the hell of Poland: 'We, Jews, despise all those who live in safety and do nothing to save us.'"[33]

Heschel was ceaselessly aware that in April 1943 German soldiers had begun to liquidate the Warsaw Ghetto. Heschel's mother and sister Gittel were among the seven hundred thousand Jews remaining in the district where he grew up. At 6:00 a.m. on April 19, the day of the first Passover seder, German troops entered the ghetto walls, where they were challenged by the heroic Jewish uprising. In early May the Germans assaulted the Jewish resistance command post; several Jewish leaders committed suicide to avoid capture. On May 16 the Nazi commander General Jürgen Stroop reported that "the Jewish section of Warsaw no longer exists."[34] Meanwhile, Heschel saw American Jewry persisting in its contemptible evasiveness.

In Cincinnati, Heschel was on the verge of collapse. He couldn't sleep; he could hardly speak; he spent his days just walking in the Burnett Woods across the street from the college. By telegram or telephone, he learned that his mother had died of a heart attack when German soldiers stormed their apartment. He responded to the news as would any traditional Jew: gathering a minyan together to hold a service in his dormitory room to honor her. Later he was informed that his surviving sister, Gittel Heszel, had been deported to Treblinka, where she was murdered.[35]

SPIRITUAL RESCUE OF AMERICAN JUDAISM

Heschel's writings advanced his resistance. While the Warsaw Ghetto uprising was under way across the Atlantic, his second essay on spirituality, "The Holy Dimension," appeared in the University of Chicago's *Journal of Religion*.

The article introduced Heschel's foundational notion of "radical amazement": a mental shock that initiates a transformation of religious thinking; here he called it "wonder and awe." Heschel explained that a phenomenology of wonder and awe could persuade us that God was near: "While penetrating the consciousness of the pious man, we may conceive the reality behind it."[36]

Heschel insisted that free human beings had to attune their actions to God's pathos: "Man is an animal at heart, carnal, covetous, selfish, and vain; yet spiritual in his destiny: a vision beheld by God in the darkness of flesh and blood. Only eyes vigilant and fortified against the glaring and superficial can still perceive God's vision in the soul's horror-stricken night of falsehood, hatred, and malice."

Heschel lived in two worlds. Faculty meetings at HUC reflected little of the global calamity. On April 11, 1943, a week before the Warsaw uprising, the faculty discussed alumni responses to a questionnaire on curriculum and decided to make changes in the Department of Rabbinics. On April 23 a motion to approve Heschel's promotion to a full faculty position with the title of instructor was debated. Jacob Marcus was the only person to vote against it; he submitted a memorandum to justify his view that "no recommendations for appointments be made for the duration of the war, or until the financial future of the College is assured."[37] However, at that meeting, Heschel was highly praised. The motion to promote him was carried by four to one, and the following month the HUC Board of Governors, headed by David Philipson, approved the promotion. A new era seemed ready to open for Heschel at Hebrew Union College.

In the summer of 1943 Heschel was heartened by the aggressive campaign of Rabbi Eliezer Silver's emergency rescue committee (the Va'ad Hatzalah) to save Jews in Poland and Germany. Now that the full extent of Hitler's so-called final solution was widely acknowledged, Silver sought to rescue every Jew possible. Motivated by the sacred imperative of *pikuach nefesh* (saving human life), the Va'ad supported controversial policies such as ransoming Jews and cooperating with Revisionist Zionists (the nonreligious political extreme right), the terrorist Irgun organization, and other groups antagonistic to their spiritual values. Rescuing as many Jews as possible, not just Orthodox rabbis and yeshiva students, was paramount.[38]

At this moment, Heschel, not yet a naturalized citizen, became a political dissident. He joined Rabbi Silver, Heschel's cousin Mordecai Shlomo Friedman (the Boyaner rebbe), and other strictly Orthodox rabbis in a public protest aimed at securing a meeting with President Roosevelt at the White House. On October 6, 1943, three days before Yom Kippur, four hundred rabbis, most of them formed in European yeshivas, bearded and dressed in traditional garb, marched down Pennsylvania Avenue, accompanied by the Jewish War Veterans of America. This Jewish "March on Washington" was the only rally in America's capital to save European Jews.[39]

The president of the United States did not receive the protestors, because Roosevelt's Jewish advisers had told him that these immigrants were not official community leaders. Instead they were greeted on the Capitol steps by an uncomfortable Henry Wallace, the vice president. Rabbi Silver intoned their petition in Hebrew, after which Rabbi David Burrack translated it into English. The protesters urged the U.S. government to deliver "the remnants of the people of the Book" and to open Palestine and other nations to Jewish refugees. Wallace responded with vague expressions of sorrow but no plans to rescue the remaining victims. The rabbis returned home discouraged. Yom Kippur that year was especially grim.

Despite a description of this dramatic event in the *New York Times*, the established Jewish organizations did not support the protesters with specific acts. To Heschel, this was yet more evidence of moral bankruptcy.

After the holidays, Heschel, now as associate professor of Jewish philosophy and rabbinics, began his fifth and final academic year at Hebrew Union College, 1944–1945. Despite his promotion, his course offerings remained elementary: he taught liturgy and Rashi in the Preparatory Department and a class on medieval exegesis of the Torah in the Collegiate Department.

Heschel's scholarship, on the other hand, was momentous in both quantity and quality. His distinction as a leading Judaic scholar was confirmed by invitations to contribute to multiple commemorative volumes.

His longstanding efforts to obtain a position at the Conservative movement's Jewish Theological Seminary of America (JTS) in New York seemed likely to be gratified. Heschel had been regularly sending reprints of his articles to Finkelstein. The JTS president appreciated Heschel's distinctive qualities. In thanking Heschel for a copy of "An Analysis of Piety," Finkelstein recalled "with a great deal of pleasure" Heschel's lecture at JTS during his first week in New York, adding this forecast: "It seems to me that your coming to this country may help greatly in stimulating Jewish religious thought." The following year (1943), Finkelstein wrote that Heschel's "The Holy Dimension" might provide an antidote to "the confusion of our day."[40]

In January 1944 Heschel announced in the *Hebrew Union College Bulletin* that he had completed a monograph in Hebrew, "Did Maimonides Strive for Prophetic Inspiration?," for the *Louis Ginzberg Jubilee Volume* honoring the seventieth birthday of the Jewish Theological Seminary's most prestigious faculty member. The following summer Heschel completed a second monograph in Hebrew on divine inspiration, "Prophecy after the Cessation of Prophecy," a companion to the Maimonides piece, to be printed five years later in the *Alexander Marx Jubilee Volume*.[41] The esoteric Heschel had spoken.

The personal thrust of these foundational studies of divine inspiration—or *ruach ha-kodesh* (the Holy Spirit)—cannot be overstated.

Heschel's exhaustively documented monographs deployed the academic neutrality of Wissenschaft des Judentums in the service of faith. Hundreds of citations to rare and classical sources testified to the living reality of God and the continuing ability of human beings to receive divine inspiration.

Heschel again asserted his spiritual agenda in another scholarly collection, this one memorializing Moses Schorr, the rabbi, scholar, and member of the Polish Parliament whom Heschel had replaced at the Warsaw Institute of Jewish Studies in 1938–1939. (Deported by the Russians, Schorr died in a prison camp in Central Asia.) In contrast to the academic luminaries from New York, Cincinnati, and Jerusalem who contributed articles on Mishnah and Talmud, Heschel chose to present an anonymous kabbalistic commentary on the prayer book, a thirteenth-century manuscript that he edited and introduced with a short bibliography. In addition to its value as a previously unknown historical document, it illuminated the manner by which *kavanah*, associated with ancient sacrifices after the destruction of the Temple, was transferred to prayers.[42]

It was then that Louis Finkelstein recognized Heschel as an authority on Jewish mysticism. In 1944 the JTS president invited Heschel to contribute a chapter to a reference book he was editing, *The Jews: Their History, Culture, and Religion*. Around the same time, the editors of the *Journal of Religion* asked Heschel to review *Major Trends in Jewish Mysticism* by Gershom Scholem, the world expert in that neglected academic field. Heschel's synopsis was surprisingly neutral: "Scholem, who labored for more than twenty years in the field . . . has proved a master of philological analysis and historical synthesis alike."[43] In contrast, Heschel favored a personal approach to Jewish mysticism.

Heschel's scholarly writings advanced his esoteric agenda: to demonstrate that classic Jewish authorities validated his conviction that God's voice did not cease after the prophets. Heschel implied that divine revelation remained available. That way, indirectly, he justified his own elevated discourse poised to initiate a mode of thinking centered on God.[44]

Above all, Heschel's writings in English challenged conventional views of Judaism. A prime example is his far-reaching essay "Faith," which Mordecai Kaplan had solicited for *The Reconstructionist*. Heschel firmly contradicted the editor's dogmatic rationalism with this bold assertion: "Faith is a force in man, lying deeper than the stratum of reason[,] and its nature cannot be defined in abstract, static terms."[45] True to the phenomenology he had developed at the University of Berlin, Heschel gave precedence to intuition, not reason, in religious cognition. He posited a universally shared sense of the holy, an a priori structure of consciousness: "Each of us has at least once in his life experienced the momentous reality of God. . . . Jewish faith is recollection of that which occurred to our ancestors."

Heschel concluded the essay with his foundational principle: God is in search of man. He assumed that readers could ultimately perceive themselves as *objects* of God's concern. His final phrases pulsed with a sacramental fervor: "Faith does not spring out of nothing. It comes with the discovery of the holy dimension of our existence. Suddenly we become aware that our lips touch the veil that hangs before the Holy of Holies. Our face is lit up for a time with the light behind the veil. Faith opens our hearts for the entrance of the Holy. It is almost as though God were thinking for us."

It is a tribute to Mordecai Kaplan's open-mindedness that he requested and published this essay. By now, Heschel had positioned his Trojan horse of spirit within the fortress of social science.

FINDING AN INSTITUTIONAL HOME

Heschel continued this research and writing amid agonizing world events. During his customary summer in New York, from June to October 1944, the war took a decisive turn. The *New York Times* headlines of June 6 announced: "D-Day, Allied Invasion of Normandy: Allied Armies Land in France in the Havre-Cherbourg Area; Great Invasion Is Under Way."

Heschel went back to Cincinnati for the fall semester, but when it ended he returned to New York. He remained in the city beyond the opening of HUC's spring semester in order to deliver a speech that would turn out to mark a crucial turning point in his public career. At the final session of YIVO's nineteenth annual meeting, Heschel spoke in Yiddish on "The East European Era in Jewish History" ("Di mizrekh-eyropeishe tkufe in der yidisher geshikhte"). The event took place on Sunday afternoon, January 7, 1945.[46] (Heschel was originally scheduled to address the opening session on Friday evening at Hunter College, but he postponed his talk until after the Sabbath.)

That afternoon Heschel became an epoch-defining orator for Americans, just as he had for Quaker leaders in 1938 Frankfurt, when he had blamed human indifference, not God, for the increasing persecutions of Jews. Now in New York, he took an oppositional stance, countering the strict empirical methods of Max Weinreich, YIVO's notable research director and a firm secularist (whom Heschel frequently consulted by telephone from Cincinnati).

Heschel subsumed Jewish secularism into a religious process. Judging that the very existence of Judaism was at stake, Heschel distilled the "essence" of East European Jewish culture as sanctification. To his fellow speakers of Yiddish he issued a prophetic challenge: "Shall we, Heaven forbid, be subject to the fate of Sephardic Jewry after the catastrophe of 1492: fragmented groups in Turkey and Morocco, stray individuals in Amsterdam, magnificent synagogues and fossilized Jewishness?"[47] Insisting upon the "hidden light" of Jewish piety, he concluded, "This era was the Song of Songs (which, according to the Rabbis, is the holiest of Holy Scripture) of Jewish history in the last two thousand years. If the other eras were holy, this one is the holy of holies."

Religious and secular listeners were divided over Heschel's rousing speech, which quickly became legendary. The historical record soon became exaggerated. Heschel was credited with inspiring the audience "of several thousands" attending the conference's opening session to rise spontaneously in prayer.[48] In reality, he spoke at the final session to an audience of hundreds. Regardless, Heschel's YIVO speech defied the Shoah (the word "Holocaust" was not yet used) by absorbing both secular and religious Yiddish cultures into his holy history.

Also in January 1945 Heschel's essay "Prayer" appeared in the *Review of Religion*. Once again Heschel brought his analysis of the inner life to an English-speaking general readership, but this time his presentation was explicitly Jewish, even as his goals remained universal. He introduced the "essence" of worship with a story about the Gerer rebbe, Rabbi Isaac Meir Alter, who cherished the sigh of a shoemaker who had bewailed his lack of time to make his morning prayers. Heschel suggested, "Perhaps that sigh is worth more than prayer itself."[49] Then, without mentioning the Hebrew terms, he examined the classic problem of law (*halakhah*), or outward acts, versus intention (*kavanah*), emotion, and inner awareness. Of the two, he asserted, foremost is the desire to pray.

Heschel also clarified his other key notion, that of the "ineffable," the impossibility of finding words to adequately describe spiritual reality. Drawing upon his 1939 German-language essay, "Prayer as Expression and Empathy" ("Das Gebet als Äusserung und Einfühlung"), he delimited "two main types of prayer": the prayer of self-expression, which comes from the heart; and the prayer of empathy, in which we humans project ourselves into prescribed words. "A certain passage in the morning prayer was interpreted by the Kotzker Rabbi to mean that God loves what is left over at the bottom of the heart and cannot be expressed in words. It is the ineffable feeling which reaches God rather than the expressed feeling."

Characteristically, Heschel ended on a practical, even edifying note. He urged readers to imitate the Divine, to the point of transforming the world: "To pray is to dream in league with God, to envision His holy visions." And, he taught, prayer must be fulfilled in action.

While pursuing contacts at the Jewish Theological Seminary, Heschel was negotiating for a position at Yeshiva University, the preeminent Modern Orthodox institution in New York City. The previous summer he had proposed some courses to Jacob I. Hartstein, Yeshiva's academic director, and they exchanged letters in February. By late March Heschel was settling on a teaching schedule, including Jewish mysticism and the history of Jewish philosophy.[50] On April 10 Hartstein tentatively offered Heschel two courses in the college and perhaps a seminar in the graduate school. Then the correspondence stopped; it continued only after Heschel received an offer from the Jewish Theological Seminary. Did Rabbi Joseph Soloveitchik, the guiding light at Yeshiva University, play a discrete role in keeping Heschel at a distance? No documents provide an answer.

Heschel spent the Passover recess in New York, at the beginning of a period of extraordinary international turmoil that began with President Roosevelt's death on April 12. Three weeks later, on May 7, 1945, the war in Europe was over. Amid these events, Heschel's courtship of the Jewish Theological Seminary neared its consummation.

Decisive support for Heschel's transfer to JTS came from Louis Ginzberg, a founding father of the seminary and Finkelstein's teacher and closest adviser. Ginzberg was the first professor Solomon Schechter had hired when he assumed the presidency of the Jewish Theological Seminary in 1902; subsequently, Ginzberg had helped Schechter recruit the seminary's top scholars.

It might seem surprising that Ginzberg appreciated Heschel's talents. After all, despite his expertise in Jewish legends, Ginzberg believed that *halakhah* was the essence of Judaism, and he was not interested in the dynamics of religious belief. By origin and temperament, he was a *Mitnagid* (an opponent of Hasidism). Born in Kovno, Lithuania, in 1873, he had received advanced training in the yeshivot of Kovno, Telz, and Slobodka. Like Heschel, he took pride in his *yichus* (pedigree): he was the great-grandnephew of the Vilna Gaon, Rabbi Elijah ben Solomon Zalman, a talmudic genius and fierce adversary of the Hasidic movement.[51]

But Ginzberg was a modern Jew—open-minded, highly educated, cosmopolitan. From the University of Berlin, he had transferred to Strasbourg, earning a doctorate at the University of Heidelberg with a dissertation on *aggadot* (Rabbinic stories and legends) in the writings of the church fathers. His vast erudition had led to his *Legends of the Jews* (7 volumes, 1909–1938). As a master of Talmud and authority on *halakhah*, he became an unofficial *posek* (authoritative legal decider) for the Conservative movement, writing many responsa on problems of contemporary Jewish practice.

Furthermore, Ginzberg was proficient in Kabbalah, Hellenism, and several modern European languages and literatures. He recognized Heschel as an authentic Jew who, like himself, possessed wide erudition and an intelligence sharpened by European culture. Heschel, he decided, should be invited to join the Jewish Theological Seminary faculty.

On May 24 Finkelstein sent Heschel an official letter of appointment as associate professor of Jewish ethics and mysticism in both the Rabbinical School and the Teachers Institute. This title fit Heschel perfectly.

While negotiations with JTS continued, Heschel tactfully kept President Morgenstern apprised of his approaching decision to leave Hebrew Union College. Three weeks before receiving Finkelstein's letter of appointment, Heschel sent his official letter of resignation to Morgenstern. Heschel declared his respect for the institution and alluded to his efforts on its behalf; he then candidly admitted his reservations: "While I find that there are ideals and obligations which I whole-heartedly share, I do not feel that my own interpretation of Judaism is in full accord with the teachings of the College."[52] He concluded by expressing his loyalty to the school. Nonetheless, some of his fellow HUC colleagues, such as Marcus, perceived his departure as abrupt.

Heschel's most positive closure to his Cincinnati years was to complete his naturalization as an American citizen. He had signed his declaration of intention on May 29, 1940. Five years later, almost to the day, on May 28, 1945, "Abraham Heschel" certified his oath of allegiance to the United States of America.[53]

CHAPTER 7

Rescuing the American Soul,
1945–1951

Heschel expected to find a spiritual and intellectual home at the Jewish Theological Seminary in New York. Founded in 1886 to counteract the effects of American Reform, this Conservative academy had reached national prominence under Solomon Schechter, who served as president from 1902 to 1915, and his successor, Cyrus Adler. Louis Finkelstein had assumed the presidency in 1940, after Adler retired.[1]

When Heschel joined the faculty in the fall of 1945, JTS was championing Schechter's ideals of Wissenschaft des Judentums: history-based criticism of classic texts. Its religious standards were traditional and largely compatible with those of Orthodoxy. Worship at the seminary chapel followed patriarchal lines: women and men sat on opposite sides of the aisle, although no *mechitzah* (partition) separated them.

Heschel took meals at the Jewish Theological Seminary's kosher cafeteria, developed ties with students, and took full advantage of the library's outstanding collection of books and manuscripts.

In the meantime, the war in the Pacific was coming to an end with unequaled brutality and destruction of human life:

New York Times, August 7, 1945: "First Atomic Bomb Dropped on Japan; Missile Is Equal to 20,000 Tons of TNT; Truman Warns Foe of a 'Rain of Ruin'"

New York Times, August 9, 1945: "Soviets Declare War on Japan; Attack Manchuria, Tokyo Says; Atom Bomb Loosed on Nagasaki."

Soon, the threat of nuclear annihilation and the Nazi Holocaust would become indelibly associated in Heschel's mind.

THE FINKELSTEIN ACADEMY

The JTS faculty was predominantly European by birth and training. All faculty members were observant Jews, but eschewing spiritually committed approaches, they engaged almost exclusively in meticulous historical and textual research. Talmud was the most valued subject matter.

Unlike their counterparts at Hebrew Union College, most JTS rabbinical students were well prepared in Judaic studies. More than a third had studied in yeshivot or Yeshiva University's high school. A great many had entered the Conservative seminary to escape the narrowness of Orthodoxy and experience a distinctly American practice of Judaism.

President Finkelstein seemed an ideal figure to help provide an answer. Born in Cincinnati of immigrant Lithuanian Jews, he grew up studying with his father, an Orthodox rabbi; by age sixteen he had mastered the Bible and several tractates of the Babylonian Talmud. After public high school, he earned degrees at both the City College of New York and the Jewish Theological Seminary, where he studied Talmud under Louis Ginzberg. In 1918 he earned a PhD in religion from Columbia University, and the following year he received an advanced rabbinical degree from JTS that gave him authority to make decisions on Jewish law. He became the rabbi of an Orthodox congregation in the Bronx while teaching Talmud at JTS, to which he soon returned full time.

Attentive to national politics, in 1940 Finkelstein became President Roosevelt's adviser on Judaism and its application to world peace. Finkelstein often said that Judaism was "the least-known religion" (an expression Heschel would later use). To remedy the general ignorance, he organized educational projects, including the multivolume reference *The Jews: Their History, Culture and Religion* (1949), to which Heschel contributed his essay on Jewish mysticism (completed in June 1945, at the very beginning of his first year at JTS).

Finkelstein had what might appear to be conflicting goals for the Jewish Theological Seminary. He envisioned it as a world-class academic institution that generated important scholarship and also trained rabbis for the pulpit. In point of fact, JTS professors were rewarded for publishing technical monographs or critical editions of classic texts, but not for their ability to inspire students.

Finkelstein expected Heschel, who combined spirituality with modern thought, to be a role model for the future rabbis. His first decision, however, was to place Heschel in the Teachers Institute (TI), the more democratic (open to students of both sexes) and practical curriculum, which trained instructors of Hebrew and Jewish culture. The Rabbinical School was the more prestigious and authoritative program. By positioning Heschel at the TI, Finkelstein hoped to counteract the influence of Mordecai Kaplan, JTS's most impressive classroom personality,[2] who had become founding dean of the Teachers Institute in 1909 (he also taught at the Rabbinical School). Unlike most JTS professors, Kaplan enjoyed engaging students in discussion, and he prepared his lessons carefully. An intellectual adventurer, he invariably challenged students' belief in miracles and a personal God, which he derisively termed "supernaturalism."

Meanwhile, Kaplan felt marginalized at JTS. Traditionalists worried that he was undermining the faith of the rabbinical students. His foundational work, *Judaism as a Civilization: Toward a Reconstruction of American Jewish Life* (1934), furnished pragmatic rather than metaphysical explanations for Jewish customs, ceremonies, and beliefs. His movement, the Society for the Advancement of Judaism (later called Reconstructionism), promulgated a sociological view of religion that, from Heschel's viewpoint, allowed nonbelievers to feel comfortable about their Jewishness. God was an "idea," or a cosmic "process," not a transcendent entity revealing the divine will to Moses on Mount Sinai. The joke circulated: "There is no God and Kaplan is His prophet."

Although seminary authorities isolated Kaplan, his central principle, that Judaism was a civilization, was widely accepted. Since he was a fervent Zionist, the Teachers Institute espoused Jewish nationalism and the Hebrew language. The arts also flourished, with courses and performances of dance, theater, and music. Under his energetic leadership, TI became a model for Hebrew high schools, colleges, and Jewish day schools throughout the country.

Heschel, expecting to divide his teaching evenly between the Rabbinical School and the Teachers Institute, was severely disappointed with his assignments. Finkelstein allocated him eight to ten hours a week in the Teachers Institute, including elementary courses on medieval Jewish philosophy and *Humash* (Five Books of Moses), much the same as he had taught at Hebrew Union College. Since he was given only one required course in the Rabbinical School, which alternated between Maimonides and Yehuda Halevi, for just one hour a week, Heschel had limited access to rabbinical students, and his courses remained basic.

Nevertheless, Heschel presented himself as a spiritual advocate. He gave his inaugural lecture at the Jewish Theological Seminary, "A Jewish Philosophy in a Time of Crisis," on Monday, April 1, 1946. Strangely, the seminary did not preserve copies or accounts of this lecture, but it has been reconstructed with a degree of plausibility from a typewritten draft of a working draft on the postwar revival of Judaism known to have been prepared around that time by the JTS faculty. (It was never completed.) The typescript included some corrections in Heschel's handwriting, and many passages echo "The

Meaning of This War" and other Heschel essays, recent or yet to come.

Heschel (presumably) opened it with a characteristic flourish: "The horrors of the second World War have filled the hearts of all upright men with reproach and shame. Never has there been so much guilt and distress on this earth. The catastrophe has left its indelible mark on the soul and body of many peoples. Israel [the Jewish people], however, has been most grievously wounded. One-third of its members were exterminated and many of the survivors impoverished, facing starvation, disease, and even persecution."[3]

Practical recommendations followed. The Jewish Theological Seminary should send a study commission to Europe, improve religious education in the United States, support scholarly research projects and adult education, strive for a Jewish homeland in Palestine, and generally broaden its concerns: "There can be no religious piety without social justice, no lasting economic prosperity without the sense for the spiritual." Heschel's unique idiom appears to emerge most strongly at the end, with the focus on holiness: "Let us never forget that the sense for the sacred is as vital to us as the light of the sun. There can be no nature without the Torah, no brotherhood without a father, no humanity without God."[4]

REMNANTS OF EUROPEAN COMMUNITY

In New York, Heschel was able, through immigrant friends and acquaintances, to re-create a community that incorporated some of the varied Jewish cultures from Europe he had lost. He retrieved a connection with literary Warsaw with his friend Aaron Zeitlin (the son of Hillel), a Yiddish writer whose wife and children had died in Auschwitz. Zeitlin now published poems that forcefully evoked the Shoah. Heschel also saw several friends from Germany.

By mail Heschel communicated with others who had immigrated to Palestine, especially Yehiel Hofer, the closest confidant of his youth in Warsaw. Hofer's wife and children had been murdered by the Nazis; then the Russian "liberators" deported him to a work camp in Siberia. After the war, Hofer reached Tel Aviv, where he remarried, practiced medicine, and became a writer in Hebrew and Yiddish. Despite Heschel's own financial limits, he periodically sent Hofer money. Heschel also kept in touch with his elders, including Fishl Schneersohn, who now worked in the Ministry of Education, developing principles of ethical training in Tel Aviv. And of course, Martin Buber, who remained a strong presence for Heschel.

Furthermore, Heschel remained close to his extended Hasidic family now living in the New York area. They included the Perlows on his mother's side, Hasidim from Novominsk, who were skeptical of him. Although they respected his learning in Talmud, they faulted him for teaching at a non-Orthodox institution, which they saw as undermining the Torah-true religion. They judged that his writings did not adequately emphasize the demands of *halakhah*.

Among the Perlows, Heschel was closest to Aaron, a first cousin with whom he had grown up in Warsaw. (Aaron was brother to Tova, now living in Paris.) In 1930 Aaron and his wife, Malka Twersky (from another Hasidic dynasty), had settled in Brooklyn; six years later, after he became a naturalized U.S. citizen, Aaron had helped Heschel emigrate and adjust to America's many demands. Now, renewing their friendship in New York, Aaron and Heschel enjoyed long conversations together. Perlow was strictly Orthodox but modern, "a shaven man" with an established position in the diamond trade. He worked in the early morning so he could study in the New York Public Library's Judaica section from 11:00 a.m. to 8:00 p.m. every day.[5]

Heschel reserved his deepest feelings, however, for his paternal cousins, by whom he was more readily accepted. They were descendants of the rebbe of Ruzhin. Heschel cherished his visits to the *shteibl* (house of prayer and study) of his first cousin and namesake, Rabbi

Abraham Joshua Heschel, the rebbe of Kopitzhinitz and husband of his oldest sister, Sarah.[6] The Kopitzhinitzer possessed exceptional warmth and lovingkindness (*hesed*); for him, ethics was inseparable from the ritual commandments. The rebbe, Sarah, and their ten children (Heschel's cousins, nieces, and nephews) welcomed "Professor Heschel," as he was known in their community. While they profoundly disagreed with the tenets of Conservative Judaism, their love for him, and for all Jewish people (*ahavat Yisrael*), was central to their observance, as was the commandment of hospitality (one meaning of the name "Heschel").

Heschel spoke with his brother-in-law on the telephone almost every weekday, usually between 1:00 and 2:00 p.m., using the Warsaw dialect of their native Yiddish. People who observed these conversations said they had never seen Heschel so relaxed and natural as he was at those times.

Just as Heschel's traditionalist connections in North America were wont to test and judge him, so did his secularist connections. Melekh Ravitch, Heschel's editor in Warsaw, was keen to understand how his former protégé had remained devout. In March 1946 Heschel traveled to Montreal to lecture at Ravitch's Yiddish Folk School. After Heschel's presentation, they sat together and discussed fundamental issues of Judaism, especially the Holocaust and faith in a living God. Ravitch rejected Heschel's "stubborn piety," which he insisted did not give meaning to the suffering and death of innocent people.[7] For his part, Heschel persistently maintained that compassion for God's suffering (his theology of God in exile) could incite responsible citizens to act and thus avoid another Holocaust.

Years later Ravitch would describe this encounter in light of his first (1925) meeting with the adolescent Heschel: "Everything about his face is as it was twenty-one years ago," Ravitch wrote in his Yiddish-language memoirs. "With the exception of the beard which he shaved smooth with an electric apparatus. Also the cigar, brown and fragrant, which the guest smokes from time to time, in rabbinic fashion, even *rebbe*-like."[8]

Their deliberations continued for several hours. It was Purim, when Jews are commanded to hear the reading of Megillat Ester (the Scroll of Esther). Heschel excused himself in order to complete this mitzvah, but Ravitch asked him to remain. Heschel then "put on a yarmulke and read the Megillah with a cantillation and Warsaw accent to the well-known tune which I [hadn't] heard in nearly half a century." Then they returned to their debate, which was never resolved.

HESCHEL IN LOVE

In the summer of 1946, following his first academic year at JTS, amid unceasing professional activity and anguish about the war, Heschel met up again with Sylvia Straus. She had come to New York for an audition with the virtuoso pianist Arthur Rubinstein; the maestro appreciated her talent and advised her to remain in the city to study with the composer and pianist Edward Steuermann. Rubinstein promised to assess her progress the following year. Straus consequently moved to New York, where she continued to study piano and took courses in philosophy at Columbia University. (Perhaps she and Heschel had remained in touch since their first meeting at the home of Jacob and Antoinette Marcus.)[9]

Straus was lovely, with deep dark eyes, lush hair, and a classic Semitic nose. Spirited and clever, she was interested in ideas, and Heschel found her enthusiasm quite appealing. He was also fascinated by her artistry and her happy, Americanized family. Sylvia's parents were immigrants; her father, Samuel, came from Russia, and her mother, Anna, from Poland. Sylvia's three brothers doted on her.

Otherwise, Heschel and Sylvia came from very different backgrounds. While Sylvia's family spoke some Yiddish at home, they were minimally observant. Her mother did light the Shabbat candles on Friday nights, but her father was a secular socialist. Sylvia herself was unfamiliar with Orthodox Judaism and did not know Hebrew. Later Heschel would teach her Jewish laws and customs, the halakhic way of life that was second nature to him. Sylvia found Heschel handsome, and she enjoyed his playful sense of humor, a quality he readily shared with close friends and relatives. She was also attracted to his European culture and Jewish piety.

When Heschel was thirty-nine and Sylvia thirty-three, both primed for marriage, Heschel proposed to her and she accepted. Then they went together to ask Heschel's ally Louis Ginzberg and his wife for their endorsement. Thus they received a JTS blessing.

They looked forward to a wedding in Los Angeles, where the Straus family had moved. Sadly, after the wedding was arranged, Sylvia's mother Anna suddenly passed away; the couple postponed the ceremony in observance of the initial mourning period. They were married in an Orthodox ceremony on December 10, 1946.[10] There was no honeymoon. Afterward, the couple began renting an apartment on New York's Riverside Drive.

Each of them had serious professional goals. They agreed that Sylvia would continue to pursue her performance career, which demanded long hours of practice, while Heschel would remain in his Jewish Theological Seminary study late into the night to continue his research and writing. Like many two-career couples, each supported the other's autonomy. With his marriage, Heschel also recognized, and accepted, the gulf between himself and his wife— their two fundamentally different Jewish identities.

CONFRONTING THE HOLOCAUST

On January 18, 1947, a month after Heschel and Sylvia married, Heschel gave a second major address in Yiddish at YIVO. The topic of the twenty-first annual conference was the revival of Judaism and the Jewish people after the war. Owing to the dramatic effect of his first appearance two years earlier, Heschel was featured at this larger convocation. Nearly three thousand people packed the Hunter College assembly hall to hear him speak on "The Meaning of Jewish Existence." In contrast to the other predominantly historical papers, Heschel focused on the spiritual dimension—this time even more forcefully than in his previous address.

Using this speech as a springboard, Heschel began developing essays for publication. "To Be a Jew: What Is It?" appeared in September 1947 in the Yiddish-language *Yidisher Kemfer*, the Labor Zionist newspaper edited by the prominent Jewish writer and activist Hayim Greenberg. Heschel warned the Labor Zionists, "We are the only channel of Jewish tradition, those who must save Judaism from oblivion, those who must hand over the entire past to the generations to come."[11]

Soon Heschel exposed his personal vulnerability as a Jew who had survived the genocide. Reading Yiddish poetry opened up his heart to express this sensitivity. While reviewing his friend Aaron Zeitlin's two substantial volumes of Yiddish verse for *Yidisher Kemfer*, Heschel proclaimed that the Jewish people were enduring a mourning process. First came shock: "We still feel the blow to our heads. It feels like the heavens above have dropped in chunks. We have not yet grasped the disaster that has befallen us. We are still before the funeral—ready to sit shivah, bewildered, confused and petrified." Then a glimmer of self-awareness, anxiety, questioning, intense mental suffering followed: "When I think of my people, burned in the crematoria of Poland, a shudder begins to course through my veins. I feel the claws of insanity." Such agony isolated Heschel in America. Only poetry like Zeitlin's could hint at the magnitude of his grief.

In the same review essay, with bitterness, he denounced assimilation—the antireligious cult of the Jewish Enlightenment with its celebration of worldly values, "the plate-lickers of non-Jewish culture."[12] Heschel agreed with Zeitlin that one way forward was to integrate modern and mystical thought, including Kabbalah and Hasidism.

Heschel concluded by citing a terrifying poem of Zeitlin's that depicted "a large gloomy rat" inspecting a ruined world, "a world without God and without Jews." Yet another Catastrophe was possible.

Heschel could not share these emotions with American students. Teaching was not as intimate as writing. His classroom demeanor at the Jewish Theological Seminary mirrored that at Hebrew Union College. Dissatisfied with his assigned courses, he withdrew his interest from formal classes. He deserved his poor reputation. Heschel's required philosophy course at the Rabbinical School was the worst. It met at 9:00 a.m. on Mondays, too early for most students. Heschel would begin by calling the roll, so the class would start ten minutes late, and he usually finished before 10:00. Sometimes he would stop his lecture in mid-sentence when the bell rang.[13]

It was obvious that Heschel cared most for his writing. He often brought in galley proofs of articles or books and read them to the class, sometimes penning in corrections while he talked. Many students felt insulted. Others, however, considered themselves honored to be among the first to hear his words. To some students Heschel was disorganized; to others he taught the way a Hasidic rebbe would: telling stories aimed at producing dramatic insights.

Still, he could be extremely generous to receptive students, to whom he gave hours of his time, inviting them to his office for probing conversations, advising them on personal problems, and nurturing their spiritual growth. The younger students at the Teachers Institute, in particular, who were less burdened with required courses, appreciated Heschel's lessons on Rashi, which helped them understand this classic commentator for the first time.

Although Heschel was not allowed to teach courses on Hasidism, he tried to create special worship opportunities, one of which was a 10:00 p.m. weekday evening service, a *Ma'ariv* minyan. His most successful prayer project was the late Shabbat afternoon *seudah she-lishit* (third meal) in the cafeteria, modeled after the Hasidic *sholosh seudos*. At sundown, with lights extinguished, students would sit around the rebbe's table in silence, then begin chanting *nigunim*.

Although Heschel was generally a failure in the classroom, he did fulfill Finkelstein's expectations in one important respect. Most rabbinical students were followers of Mordecai Kaplan; they felt comfortable with his sociological approach to religion and were enamored by his fervent proselytizing. Heschel, with his opposed views and his own followers, was able to reinvigorate serious theological debate among the students, as Kaplanians and Heschelians vied with one another in the cafeteria and dormitories. And so it was that Heschel acquired a devoted student following.

He formed a lifelong tie with Wolfe Kelman, a rabbinical student who came from distinguished Hasidic stock.[14] Born in Vienna in 1923, Kelman had grown up in a thriving Orthodox community in Toronto. He was unhappy at JTS. He found the courses elementary and the professors aloof. He wanted to quit, but his classmate Samuel Dresner (who had transferred from Hebrew Union College to follow his revered teacher) insisted, "You have to meet Heschel." "What do I have to do with some little Hasidic rebbe from Poland," Kelman answered. But Dresner set up his appointment with Heschel for the next day.

Kelman knocked on the door and Heschel ushered him into his small office, filled with cigar smoke. While Heschel continued a telephone conversation, Kelman picked up a *sefer* (religious book in Hebrew) and started to read it, absorbed. A few minutes later, Heschel put down the telephone and asked, "So you know that book?" Kelman smiled, "I know that book very well. My grandfather wrote it." Heschel looked at him. "Excuse me, young man, what is the grandson of the Dinover Rav doing at the Jewish Theological Seminary?" Kelman answered, "I will tell you, if you tell me what the grandson of the Ohev Yisrael [the Lover of Jews, Heschel's ancestor the Apter Rav] is doing at the Seminary." Heschel jumped up from his desk and hugged Kelman, an embrace that inaugurated Heschel's closest American friendship.

The two men had much in common, despite their differences in age. Both had descended from Hasidic dynasties and chose to leave their loving but restrictive Orthodox families for the larger Jewish world and beyond. They shared the trauma of having abdicated their ancestral charge while remaining Hasidic in spirit. And they had an easy rapport, for both enjoyed telling stories. For Kelman, Heschel was "a friend, a helper, a shoulder to lean on."

Kelman was ordained in 1950. But instead of taking a pulpit, he became executive vice president of the Rabbinical Assembly, the professional body of Conservative rabbis, which gave him access to the wider Jewish world and interfaith Christian organizations. His office was housed in one of the JTS buildings, and he and Heschel would spend time together daily.

Even though their friendship was close, they both preferred to maintain a certain formality. Kelman never called Heschel by his first name. In fact, only acquaintances and a few Christian friends called him Abraham. Even his wife, Sylvia, called him Heschel, from his full first name, Abraham Joshua *Heschel* Heschel. Heschel's usual mode of relating to people, including intimates, was to guard his inner self, maintaining his dignity as he perceived it.

Also closer than most to Heschel was Marc Herman Tanenbaum, Kelman's dear friend and JTS roommate, who came from a Yiddish-speaking Orthodox family in Baltimore. Tanenbaum's mother welcomed Christian neighbors into their home, and early on Tanenbaum became comfortable with people of other faiths and ethnicities. Precocious, he entered Yeshiva University at age fourteen and graduated in 1945. He then entered the Jewish Theological Seminary, seeking a less restrictive but still devout Judaism.

During Tanenbaum's last year at JTS, he and Heschel formed a lifelong bond, almost accidentally. One day Tanenbaum found himself in the elevator with Heschel, who noticed the student seemed worried. In his instinctively warm way, Heschel made it safe for Tanenbaum to admit to having family problems. Heschel then invited him to his office, where they sat for two hours while Tanenbaum poured out his distress. He felt guilty at leaving his mother alone after her husband's death. Suddenly Heschel picked up the telephone, placed a call to Marc's mother, and spoke with her gently in Yiddish: "Be strong, and you will be strong." Tanenbaum understood that Heschel was giving his mother *nechamah*, Jewish consolation. From that moment, he developed a reverence for Heschel as the embodiment of Jewish life.[15]

Ordained at the same time as Kelman, Tanenbaum never became a pulpit rabbi. First, he returned to New York and worked in public relations at *Time* magazine. Then he joined the small publishing house of Henry Schuman, where he would soon help Heschel launch his American literary career.

Another student, from an entirely different cultural background, provided Heschel with a more critical perspective. Born in 1919 in Bad Homburg, Germany, Fritz A. Rothschild grew up in a middle-class Orthodox family. As a rebellious young man, he joined the Religious Zionists (Mizrahi), learning Hebrew so he could become a typesetter in Palestine. Germany's anti-Jewish laws prevented Rothschild from completing a *Gymnasium* degree, the *Abitur*, without which he could not enter a university. So instead this venturesome thinker attended classes taught by Martin Buber and others at the Jüdisches Lehrhaus in Frankfurt.

One day Rothschild heard a young Lehrhaus professor named Abraham Heschel lecture on the Bible at a conference for Jewish youth leaders. He was quite taken with Heschel, who spoke German elegantly (though with a marked Yiddish accent) and took the Bible seriously, arousing respect in his skeptical audience.

In November 1938 Rothschild was arrested and confined for seven weeks in Buchenwald, but he managed to get a visa to Northern Rhodesia to work in an uncle's business. In 1943, while in Africa, Rothschild wrote a long letter to Martin Buber, asking about the future of Jewish culture and inquiring whether "Dr. Abraham Heschel is still alive and how he is." Buber informed Rothschild that Heschel was "a lecturer at Hebrew Union College in Cincinnati."[16]

Five years later, Rothschild arrived in New York alone, without any means of support, hoping to study at the Jewish Theological Seminary. After failing an informal entrance examination, Rothschild secured a job with a Hebrew publisher on Delancey Street. Later he learned that Heschel was now at JTS. He visited Heschel at his office, and Heschel took the initiative to support Rothschild's candidacy for a Jewish Theological Seminary degree.

Rothschild qualified to enter the Teachers Institute as a third-year student in the five-year degree program. Eventually, Finkelstein allowed Rothschild to enroll in text courses at the Rabbinical School, along with a number of intellectuals interested in graduate work, university teaching, and research. The "Institute for Theology," as the special group was called, included Arthur Cohen, Moshe Greenberg, David Winston, and Arthur Hyman. They studied with Saul Lieberman and other JTS luminaries, including Heschel.

In 1951 Rothschild entered Columbia University's graduate program in philosophy, hoping to write his doctoral dissertation on Heschel's religious thought. Later Rothschild joined the Teachers Institute faculty. He and Heschel developed a salutary working relationship: Heschel would show manuscripts to this brilliant, strong-willed German Jew, who in turn, with respectful chutzpah, would debate with his teacher and help him clarify his ideas. Eventually Rothschild became Heschel's closest colleague and interpreter of his thought.

While forging new ties, Heschel continued to reconnect with figures from his past, as if to recover his destroyed community. One day

Heschel heard that Leo Baeck, the revered leader of Berlin's former Jewish community, who had managed to survive the Holocaust, was visiting New York, staying at the Biltmore Hotel. Anxious to see Baeck again, Heschel telephoned the hotel. Baeck picked up, answering in German, "Ja, Baeck hier." Heschel was so overcome with emotion, he couldn't speak. Baeck waited; then, thinking it must be a wrong number, he began to hang up. Finally, Heschel stammered, "Dr. Baeck, I'm coming down to see you at the hotel." When he entered, there stood Rabbi Baeck with his cane, dignified as ever, stiff as a ramrod. Baeck immediately went to Heschel, grasped his hand, and said, "Heschel, in the last issue of the *Monatsschrift* there was your article on the essence of prayer. I smuggled it with me into Theresienstadt and I want to thank you. That article was a great comfort to me in those dark days."[17]

Heschel had completed the German cycle of his life. Going forward, Heschel would strive to inculcate a more specifically Jewish ethos that combined reverence for the living God, regular observance, and universal ethical responsibility. Leo Baeck's concentration camp testimony had confirmed Heschel's deepest conviction: prayer was not only able to comfort the survivors; even more so, it could enable every person to encounter the reality of God.

AMERICAN JEWISH CULTURE WARS

In 1949 Heschel advanced his vision of authentic Jewish survival in a booklet entitled "To Save a Soul" ("Pikuach Neshamah"). Originally delivered as a speech to the heads of day schools and yeshivot in the New York metropolitan region, this essay echoed Heschel's YIVO speeches and his 1947 Yiddish article "Who Is a Jew?," which were intended for Jewish secularists. But "To Save a Soul," written in richly expressive Hebrew and suffused with allusions to Bible, Talmud, prayers, and religious doctrines, appealed to religiously literate Jews familiar with the traditional sources.[18]

To Heschel, spiritual survival was at stake. His title played on the well-known commandment of *pikuach nefesh*: one is obligated to suspend religious law in a life-threatening situation. The term *nefesh* referred to the vital principle, and *neshamah* to the divine soul within the human being.

After Auschwitz, Heschel wrote, Jews must do whatever is necessary to preserve the soul from extinction. The essay's subtitle, "From the Kiln of Jewish Existence," evoked both the Nazi crematoria and the furnaces of creativity. According to Heschel, "The very existence of a Jew is a spiritual act. The fact that we have survived, despite the suffering and persecution, is itself a sanctification of God's name [*kiddush ha-Shem*]." To be Jewish, he avowed, is to perceive the spiritual dimension, "to feel the soul in everything." Its essence, he explained, was the quality of "Sabbathness," spiritual refinement, which led to a universal morality. Accordingly, Jews had to surpass restrictive, ethnocentric conceptions: "Judaism teaches us that to remain a people we must be more than a people. Israel is destined to be a holy people."[19]

Heschel interpreted Sabbath observance not only as a system of rules governing Jewish behavior, but also as the most available vehicle for developing fervent concern for the sanctity of all human life. He even implied that if everyone, not just Jews, observed the Sabbath, another Holocaust might be prevented: "Perhaps people have never been as much in need of Judaism as they are in our generation. The human species is on its deathbed."

Heschel himself dealt with the crisis by enhancing the Hasidic spirit of *halakhah*. As he would later explain in *Man's Quest for God*, "'There are three ways in which a man expresses his deep sorrow: the man on the lowest level cries; the man on the second level is silent; the man on the highest level knows how to turn his sorrow into song.' True prayer is song." Heschel would sing, literally and figuratively. He loved *nigunim* and wrote essays in English that glorified East European Jewry in musical prose.

In postwar America, Heschel faced a cultural battle among American Jews as arduous as the spiritual one. He believed that mainstream Jewish organizations had remained relatively uninvolved during the Nazi atrocities because of their bias against Polish immigrants. Years later, he explained: "Everybody respected German Jewry. They produced a Heine, an Einstein, but Polish Jews, they are ne'er-do-wells. I have great respect for German Jews, but for me personally, the Baal Shem Tov is much more important than Einstein."[20]

Heschel wished to reach a national audience and oppose their prejudices; for that he would have to publish in English in respected, widely circulated magazines. The most prominent forum for Jewish readers was *Commentary*, a liberal, nonsectarian journal founded in 1945 by the American Jewish Committee. Controversial issues of cultural, political, and religious import to both Jews and Americans generally, were debated in sophisticated, often highly opinionated articles.[21]

Heschel, too, staked out his views with passion. In May 1948 (the month Israel declared its independence), *Commentary* published his essay "The Two Great Traditions: The Sephardim and the Ashkenazim." This polemical piece (introduced as a chapter from his forthcoming book on East European Jewry) represented Heschel's first critique of American Jewish values. He set up stark, oversimplified contrasts between the Sephardic culture of medieval Spain and the Ashkenazic culture of Eastern Europe. Each category delineated a distinct approach to thought and society relevant to twentieth-century Americans: Sephardic culture emphasized rationalism, scientific scholarship, and cultural elitism; Ashkenazic culture favored intuition, a sense of the holy, and a democratic community.

Heschel forcefully advanced the latter. He began by praising Sephardic culture, "distinguished not only by monumental scientific achievements but also by a universality of spirit. [The Sephardic] accomplishment was in some way a symbiosis of Jewish tradition and Moslem civilization." Heschel's appreciation was sincere and well grounded; he had written extensively on the Sephardic thinkers Saadia Gaon, Gabirol, Maimonides, and Abravanel, among others. But here he chose the other way.[22]

Praising the Yiddish language as the natural instrument for the Jewish masses of Eastern Europe, Heschel elevated it to a spiritual plane: "In this language you say 'beauty' and mean 'spirituality'; you say 'kindness' and mean 'holiness.'" Elsewhere he wrote, "Ashkenazic writers forgo clarity for the sake of depth. The contours of their thoughts are irregular, vague, and often perplexingly entangled; their content is restless, animated by inner wrestling and a kind of baroque emotion." In his essay as well, Heschel crafted a fluid, musically repetitive style that made tone as important as content.

This essay's pragmatic purpose was to denounce the tendency of American Jews to slip into bourgeois mediocrity. Acknowledging the imminent recognition of the State of Israel, Heschel warned Jews everywhere not to succumb to pride: "Magnificent synagogues are not enough if they mean a petrified Judaism. Nor will the stirrings of creative life in Palestine find any echo if brilliance is held more important than warmth."

Heschel concluded by faulting the German academic biases he had known so intimately in Berlin. He cited as an example an unnamed "prominent Jewish historian, in a work first published in 1913 and reprinted in 1931," who dismissed Hasidism for "the preposterousness of its superstitious notions and of its unruly behavior." (He was alluding to the major work on Jewish liturgy by his former teacher Ismar Elbogen, whom he otherwise respected.) Heschel thus exposed and denounced the typical contempt of German Jews (and many Americans) for the Ostjuden, East European Jews.[23]

To inspire American Jews who valued modernity, Heschel elected to deploy a neo-Hasidic counter-model. His first truly American book in English, *The Earth Is the Lord's: The Inner World of the Jew in East*

Europe (1949), would do just that—and mark his metamorphosis from Yiddish speaker and essayist to American author.

The book had developed organically from several pieces: Heschel's Yiddish review of Zeitlin's poetry, his chapter "The Mystical Element in Judaism," his essay in *Commentary*, and "To Save a Soul." By 1948 the preliminary manuscript was complete, but no publisher was interested—a normal situation for an untried foreign author.

Then the Jewish publishing world took notice. Heschel showed this work to Marc Tanenbaum, who then passed it on to his employer, Henry Schuman, the founder of Schuman Publishers. Deeply impressed, Schuman decided to craft it into a literary work of art. He commissioned Ilya Schor, a Polish Jewish silversmith and graphic artist who had studied in Paris, to embellish the book with evocative wood engravings.

In form and content, Heschel's book was designed to bridge cultures. His preface stressed the spirituality of prewar Jewish Poland: "I am justified in saying that it was the golden period in Jewish history, in the history of the Jewish soul."[24] The first page displayed a woodcut of a Hasid lovingly holding a Torah; the final page noted the book's origin in Heschel's January 1945 lecture at the Yidisher Visnshaftlekher Institut.

Inside, Heschel insisted that Judaism was not a religion of space. Judaism was not grounded in synagogues, land, or technology, but concerned with life beyond the physical: "Pagans exalt sacred things, the Prophets extol sacred deeds."[25] In the commonplace one could unveil sacred dimensions. In chapter 2, "With All Thy Heart," Heschel evoked the inwardness of East European Jewish culture: "Every part of the liturgy, every prayer, every hymn, had its own tune; . . . each object its individual stamp."[26]

Heschel also introduced his own role model: the Baal Shem Tov, who "brought heaven down to earth." The Besht, as he was also known, and his disciples, the Hasidim, had "banished melancholy from the soul and uncovered the ineffable delight of being a Jew."[27] Joy in Jewishness was desperately needed, then as now.

Consequently Heschel defined the Judaism he wanted moderns to emulate. Divine revelation was still available, and Sabbath observance could lead to a spiritual life. He even claimed that Jewish revolutionary secularism had derived its energy from religious tradition: "The fervor and yearning of the Hasidim, the ascetic obstinacy of the Kabbalists, the inexorable logic of the Talmudists, were reincarnated in the supporters of modern Jewish movements. Their belief in new ideals was infused with age-old piety."

Heschel concluded by repeating his earlier warnings: "The alternative to our Jewish existence is spiritual suicide, disappearance, not conversion into something else. Judaism has allies, partners, but no substitute. It is not a handmaiden of civilization but its touchstone."[28]

Upon publication of *The Earth Is the Lord's*, reviewers both in the popular press and Jewish newspapers sharply questioned Heschel's assumptions. Irving Kristol, book editor of *Commentary*, launched the secularist offensive. His review, entitled "Elegy for a Lost World," condemned what he perceived to be the world-denying consequences of such a spirituality and dismissed Heschel's attempt to endow the profane with a holy dimension: "This radical confusion of universes can be found in non-Jewish thinkers, too, but it is only in Judaism that the confusion is the religion itself. To be more exact, it is the Jew himself." Developing his assimilationist, hyper-rationalistic stance, Kristol explained that Heschel's dazzling literary style was dangerous because it was so seductive: "a fervor that is unrestrained and a piety that is immoderate."[29]

Maurice Samuel was the only reviewer to endorse Heschel's vision of spiritual renewal. A popular novelist, translator of Hebrew and Yiddish literature, and interpreter of relations between Jews and gentiles, he supported Heschel's mission "to build into tomorrow's American Jewry an everlasting, living and organic recollection of the

Yiddish-speaking civilization through which it received its Jewishness."[30] Samuel's brief but sophisticated essay in *Congress Weekly*, the widely read journal of the American Jewish Congress, explained that *The Earth Is the Lord's* successfully transmitted the elusive quality of *Yiddishkeit* (Jewishness). American Jews, noted Samuel, should become more, not less, identified with their ancestors.

Heschel's appeal to assimilated Jews succeeded, at least in part, with another spiritual seeker: Maurice Friedman, a young intellectual activist reared as a Reform Jew in Tulsa, Oklahoma. A socialist and pacifist, Friedman had graduated from Harvard in 1942 intent on becoming a labor organizer and educator, but he was also fascinated by mysticism, especially Asian and Christian traditions.[31]

Receiving Friedman in his JTS office, Heschel acted as a rebbe would: after listening to Friedman pour out his life story, Heschel made strong demands—learn Hebrew, study at JTS, and become observant. Heschel was not indulgent toward Friedman's personal complaints.[32] He was shocked when Friedman spoke of being angry with his mother (an insight released by group therapy): "'If I could find my mother to tie her shoestrings,' Heschel answered, 'I should be the happiest man on earth!'" As Friedman would later relate, Heschel then told him that "his family and friends and, indeed, the whole of Polish Jewry in which he had grown up, had disappeared almost without a trace. He chided me for my unhappiness over my short-lived and ill-fated first marriage. Hasidism teaches joy."

In the summer of 1950, Friedman arrived in New York to study Hasidism with Heschel. His teacher's insistence on observance was too stringent for him, however, so Friedman chose instead to earn a doctorate in the history of culture at the University of Chicago. His dissertation, "Martin Buber: Mystic, Existentialist, Social Prophet," became a foundational introduction to Buber's thought. Friedman then devoted his professional life to Buber, becoming Buber's translator and his first major interpreter in the English-speaking world.

Around the same time, Heschel formed a lifelong bond with Marshall Meyer—like Friedman, a gifted student with a deficient Jewish education, though already committed to his Jewishness. As a senior honors student at Dartmouth College, Meyer had been incited to study Judaism, ironically, by the renowned philosopher and theologian Eugen Rosenstock-Huessy, a Jewish convert to Christianity who had also inspired Franz Rosenzweig to return to Judaism rather than convert to Christianity. (Rosenzweig and Martin Buber would later establish the Frankfurt Jüdisches Lehrhaus and launch Jewish renewal in Germany.) Meyer became a disciple of Heschel and studied periodically with him (as well as with Buber, Gershom Scholem, Ernst Simon in Israel, and Paul Tillich and Reinhold Niebuhr at Union Seminary). After his ordination at JTS, he went on to revitalize Congregation B'nai Jeshurun (BJ) in Manhattan and eventually to found the Abraham Joshua Heschel Rabbinical Seminary in Buenos Aires, which continues to champion human rights and protest against government violence. And, back in New York, participants at BJ can still hear echoes of Heschel in the congregation's dynamic services and social action initiatives.[33]

Decades earlier, Will Herberg was the first prominent Jewish intellectual to recognize Heschel's significance. Herberg had gained renown for a 1947 *Commentary* essay describing his return to his Jewish roots after years as a Marxist ideologue and Communist Party activist. Two years later, *Commentary* printed his mordant critique of American Jewish life. Now vehemently against secularism, Herberg dubbed the age of Buber and Rosenzweig as "hardly more than an isolated episode in the almost unrelieved mediocrity of Jewish religious thinking in recent decades." Jews, he insisted, "needed to recognize that Judaism was a God-centered religion of crisis.[34]

Herberg enrolled at the Jewish Theological Seminary to acquire the religious education he lacked, and there he met Heschel. The repentant Marxist admired the way Heschel translated Hasidism and other forms of traditional Judaism into a bold way of thinking and living that was at once observant, open-minded, and morally courageous.

POWER SHIFT AT THE SEMINARY

While Heschel's career advanced outside his home institution, there were conflicts within it that he could not successfully navigate. The JTS faculty and administration was a tight-knit community in which professional and personal relationships were intertwined. In some ways the institution resembled a miniature shtetl: everyone knew each other, worshiped in the same synagogue, ate together in the cafeteria, invited one another over for Sabbath and holiday meals. Several faculty members were related by marriage.

Louis Finkelstein reigned over this hierarchy, and for years his primary adviser (and scholarly ideal) had been Louis Ginzberg; Mordecai Kaplan also played a secondary consultative role. Both Ginzberg and Kaplan were Heschel's original allies at JTS. Then in 1946 a major power shift occurred, and Heschel lost his two supporters. Ginzberg, seventy-three and frail, fell ill. He gradually reduced his teaching load, came less frequently to the seminary, and eventually remained at home. Kaplan retired as dean of the Teachers Institute to devote more time to his Society for the Advancement of Judaism (although he was still involved in influencing seminary policy).

Moreover, Heschel suffered from the effects of another change that had begun before he arrived. In 1940 Finkelstein had brought Saul Lieberman from Israel to take over the Talmud program from Ginzberg. Gifted with a photographic memory, Lieberman was generally acknowledged to be the greatest Talmud scholar of his generation.[35] Some claimed he was equal to the Vilna Gaon. Talmud, furthermore, was the area that defined Jewish Theological Seminary scholarship.

Lieberman incarnated the Jewish culture antithetical to Heschel. Born in Belorussia, Lieberman was educated at the *musar* (strict, ethical) yeshivot of Malch, Slobodka, and Novaredok, institutions in which Talmud was studied for its own sake, a principle known as *Torah lishmah*. (Usually Talmud study was for practical purposes, to make judicial decisions.) He attended the University of Kiev, then continued his studies in Palestine and France. In 1928 he immigrated to Jerusalem, committed to the historical-critical method of correcting scribal and other errors in sacred texts.

Lieberman applied his prodigious erudition to purely technical scholarship. He knew by heart not only the Palestinian and the Babylonian Talmuds (in itself an astounding accomplishment), but also variant readings, and he had mastered their background, along with Greek and Latin classics and early Christian literature. As an editor he restored the Talmud texts by comparing manuscripts and sources outside the Jewish canon, such as Greek and Latin legal literature. At the same time, Lieberman followed Orthodox observance and defended traditional values.

Finkelstein revered Lieberman, and as Ginzberg withdrew from JTS, Lieberman supplanted him as Finkelstein's confidant and closest adviser. From then on, what historians call "the Finkelstein-Lieberman axis" dominated the institution.[36]

Now Heschel was caught up in the traditional clash between Hasidim and their opponents, the *Mitnagdim*. At JTS, the conflict escalated as Lieberman and other textual scholars expressed their disdain for piety and religious thought. The fact that Lieberman shared with Heschel some commonalities in upbringing and temperament did not mitigate his disapproval of Heschel's mixture of erudition and fervor. He was not interested in philosophy and was hostile to theology, which he considered a Christian subject. Heschel struggled to convince Lieberman and his acolytes that traditional Judaism must be mystical—Judaism's prophetic ethos demanded no less—but Lieberman never modified his conviction that Jewish mysticism was *narrishkeit* (nonsense).

PREPARING A THEOLOGICAL REVOLUTION

All the while, Heschel was constructing his long-planned "systematology," his religious philosophy. By the summer of 1948, its manuscript was still a rough draft, consisting of his published articles on piety, holiness, faith, and prayer, with a new introduction on approaches to God. The book included only nine chapters (the completed work, *Man Is Not Alone*, would have twenty-six).

Heschel shared the manuscript with Ginzberg, who was enthusiastic. Ginzberg in turn recommended the book he described as "concerning the soul of the Jew" to Maurice Jacobs, executive vice president of the Jewish Publication Society (JPS). Jacobs told Heschel to send it on to Solomon Grayzel, the JPS president, by profession a historian and a meticulous editor.[37]

This was a great opportunity for everyone concerned. Founded in 1888, the Jewish Publication Society was America's leading Jewish publisher, with a subscriber list of thousands. Its books (including the authoritative English translation of the Hebrew Bible) were sold to reading clubs and individuals throughout North America.[38]

Heschel had matured as a writer, but his creative process remained organic, not linear. He continued to capture short intuitions on pieces of paper, place them in folders, and later compose paragraphs or chapters. Now he needed someone to help him organize a book.

Receptive to criticism, Heschel improved his manuscript considerably under Grayzel's careful direction. The editor candidly informed Heschel that several outside evaluators had trouble following his "poetico-mystical approach."[39]

By mid-November 1949 it was time to announce the book, but the manuscript was not close to being ready. Six months later, in May 1950, the book was still unfinished, albeit nearing completion.

Then Heschel made a startling announcement: his manuscript had swelled so much that he needed to publish a second volume. As inspiring as Heschel's intellectual energy might be, JPS was put in an untenable financial situation. Only co-publication with a trade house might save the project.

At this point Roger W. Straus, Jr., president of the prestigious literary firm Farrar, Straus and Company, entered the negotiations. An urbane, artistically sensitive publisher of fine books, Straus (not related to Heschel's wife, Sylvia) combined high culture with a canny business sense. Heschel and Straus enjoyed each other's company, and Heschel respected the publisher's practical advice. Most of all, perhaps, Heschel shared Straus's regard for quality literature.[40]

After much discussion, it was decided that Farrar, Straus would publish the book jointly with the Jewish Publication Society.

Heschel delivered the completed manuscript to Straus on October 5, 1950, the day after Simchat Torah, the joyous celebration of God's revelation. *Man Is Not Alone*, as the work would henceforth be known, was now slated for JPS's subscriber list as well as Farrar, Straus publication in March 1951, with the second volume planned for 1952.

A month before the official publication of *Man Is Not Alone*, Sylvia Heschel had a major launch of her own: her concert piano debut on February 15, 1951, at Manhattan's Town Hall. She had practiced every day for years for this moment, and Heschel zealously supported her.

Sylvia's performance touched many in the audience, her expressive body movements heightening the musical emotions. The next day, however, the critics diluted their praise with serious reservations. The *New York Times* stated that she had "overreached herself."[41]

Heschel's launch would prove to be considerably more successful. Finkelstein, who had read the proofs, predicted that Heschel's "lucid, easily-read, poetical prose" would inspire readers "in this day of widespread religious and philosophical confusion."[42] *Man Is Not Alone* received a sophisticated marketing campaign, organized by Farrar, Straus and Young (as the company was now called). JPS, meanwhile, secured broad distribution from its subscription lists. On the back cover was a photograph of the author by Lotte Jacobi, the German Jewish wife of Erich Reiss, Heschel's Berlin publisher. Heschel posed like a modern intellectual—young, clean-shaven, in rimless glasses, with his dark, wavy hair combed back.

For publicity purposes, the dust jacket downplayed the transcendent element. Below the portrait was a blurb from the Kirkus review service: "The author is neither a rationalist nor a mystic, but comes at his theistic position through an analysis of the human personality and through finding basic wonder there, awe and reverence, a 'sense of the ineffable.' The second part of the book deals with man's needs and his satisfaction through religious faith." Here, too, the jacket copy reduced Heschel's religion of the living God to a banal, pragmatic humanism, "man's needs," the opposite of what the author intended.

In reality, Heschel wrote *Man Is Not Alone* as a blueprint for a theological revolution. In this he vied implicitly with Franz Rosenzweig's *Star of Redemption* (1921) and Martin Buber's *I and Thou* (1923), both of which emphasized the human side of the religious quest. Heschel's spiritual itinerary was more straightforward and elegant than Rosenzweig's dense philosophical masterwork and more authentically biblical than Buber's lyrical dialogue with the sacred. Heschel would prepare readers to encounter God directly.

He sought to engage thoughtful, open-minded seekers, those whom Maimonides called the perplexed. To appeal to the modern mind, he introduced the "cognitive emotions" of awe and wonder as means to discover "radical amazement." Rigorous self-questioning, he argued, would shatter conventional categories of knowledge. Those seekers who abandoned their preconceptions would first reach a state of despair; then "radical amazement" would lead them from despair to radical insight. All thoughtful people could achieve such intuitions.

This process, Heschel explained, begins with "dark apathy," a loss of ego that allows the living God to enter human consciousness: "But, then, a moment comes like a thunderbolt, in which a flash of the undisclosed rends our dark apathy asunder." Normal, ego-centered thinking becomes reversed: "We are penetrated by His insight. We cannot think any more as if He were there and we here. He is both there and here."[43]

This paradigm shift—the re-centering of human thinking from the self to God as Subject—enabled Heschel's theological revolution. Like Immanuel Kant's "Copernican revolution" in philosophy, which had placed the focus on the human mind, Heschel described the human mind's encounter with God as a "categorical imperative" analogous to Kant's rational categories. The mind would undergo a radical "turning" (in Hebrew, *teshuvah*) to God-centered or theocentric thinking. Seekers who opened themselves up to the experience would eventually achieve "certainty" in the reality of God—and receive a form of divine revelation.

In part 2 of the volume, "The Problem of Living," Heschel applied his paradigm shift to religious observance and ethics. Rather than explain religion as a fulfillment of human needs (the jacket copy notwithstanding), he saw the essence of being human as being a need of God. God seeks the human being. The Bible was not human theology but God's anthropology.

Heschel concluded the work with the chapter "The Pious Man." By portraying an ideal awareness of God's presence as evidenced in this model of the pious person, he hoped to inspire readers to lead their own holy and righteous lives.

Man Is Not Alone revealed Heschel to be in full command of his craft. He displayed an original manner of thinking and writing and called for an imaginative reading strategy. He combined incisive philosophical analysis and lyrical passages and then vivified them with comparisons and aphorisms that condensed insights into easily grasped concepts. Spiritually audacious, Heschel sought to provoke a complete transformation of consciousness.

On a popular level, the book catapulted Heschel to national renown. Reinhold Niebuhr, America's leading Protestant theologian, set the wheels of fame in motion in a book review published in the *New York Herald Tribune*. The Protestant thinker admired the way Heschel evoked the living God and (in contrast to Irving Kristol) appreciated Heschel's elegant narrative as "the work of a poet and mystic who has mastered the philosophical and scientific disciplines and who with consummate skill reveals the dimension of reality apprehended by religious faith."[44] Niebuhr dramatically predicted that Heschel would "become a commanding and authoritative voice not only in the Jewish community but in the religious life of America."[45]

Niebuhr's gratifying words were followed by a longer, more detailed review by Jacob B. Agus in the April 1951 *Congress Weekly*. Agus, a leading thinker in the Conservative rabbinate and author of *Modern Philosophies of Judaism* (1941), the first major presentation in English of the works of Buber and Rosenzweig, associated Heschel with Buber, Rosenzweig, and Rabbi A. I. Kook in Palestine, as well as such important Christian thinkers as the nineteenth-century philosopher Friedrich Schleiermacher in Germany and Reinhold Niebuhr in America.[46]

Had Judaic studies then been an established academic discipline, Agus's review might have stimulated systematic interpretations of Heschel's works. But in 1951 there were only general forums, such as *Commentary*, in which new works of Jewish philosophy could be carefully examined. (The Association for Jewish Studies would be founded in 1969.)

Such evaluation of Heschel's works did become possible the

following year with the inception of a new scholarly review, *Judaism*, a "Quarterly Journal of Jewish Life and Thought." Sponsored by the American Jewish Congress, this nondenominational forum, which would in short order be populated with contributions from North America's leading Jewish academics and rabbis, was intended to complement—or compete with—*Commentary*, which was more favorable to secular culture and politics than to religion and philosophy. *Judaism*'s editor in chief, Robert Gordis, a leading intellectual of the Conservative movement, announced the journal's goal as nothing less than "a Renascence of Judaism." Heschel soon became a prime guide for that renewal.[47]

Judaism's inaugural issue (January 1952) placed Heschel's work at the center, while at the same time questioning his claim to be writing a "philosophy of religion." In addition to an essay by Heschel, the journal published a sophisticated review of *Man Is Not Alone* by Emil Ludwig Fackenheim, assistant professor of philosophy at the University of Toronto and already a notable religious thinker. Fackenheim defined for the first time Heschel's three modes of writing and cognition—"the aphoristic, the descriptive, the philosophico-argumentative"—although he asserted that "they will not mix."[48]

Surprisingly, Fackenheim misinterpreted what he called Heschel's "mysticism," a word Heschel had not used. With no textual proof, he deemed Heschel "frankly pantheistic," that is, experiencing God as identical to the natural world, a way of thinking that Fackenheim felt could lead to moral indifference. (In fact, the opposite was true: Heschel's 1949 essay on Jewish mysticism stressed how the kabbalists subordinated personal salvation to redemption of the world.)

Still another, even more surprising misreading flawed this important review. Fackenheim, haunted by the atrocities of the Hitler period (he would soon become known as the philosopher of the Holocaust, making the 614th commandment not to give Hitler a posthumous victory by forgetting), regretted that Heschel had not taken into account sin, the tragic, evil, and history. With an astounding blind spot, Fackenheim ignored chapter 16, "The Hiding God," which opened with these portentous words: "For us, contemporaries and survivors of history's most terrible horrors, it is impossible to meditate about the compassion of God without asking: Where is God?"[49]

The most perceptive analysis of *Man Is Not Alone* came from another philosopher, Shmuel Hugo Bergman, the first rector of the Hebrew University in Jerusalem and a close associate of Buber's. In the May 1951 *Mitteilungsblatt*, a German-language journal published at the Hebrew University, Bergman clarified Heschel's basic assumptions. Bergman related Heschel's American writings to his Berlin doctoral dissertation and his studies written in Hebrew and Yiddish. Heschel's philosophy of religion, Bergman explained, was neither a self-contradiction nor a pretentious subterfuge, "because the nature of religion lies in experience rather than in conceptual thought."[50]

Citing the revelation in chapter 9 ("The ineffable has shuddered itself into our soul"), Bergman asserted that Heschel considered "the central thought of the Jewish religion [to be] the *brit*, the *covenant*. It obligates God, and it obligates man." Pointing out how Heschel emphasized God's initiative, Bergman's insightful review (which was never translated into English) may have influenced Heschel to entitle his second volume *God in Search of Man*.

CHAPTER 8

Theological Revolution, 1952–1956

In June 1951, while absorbed in composing the second volume of his religious philosophy, Heschel also managed to complete another small book: *The Sabbath: Its Meaning for Modern Man*, an essay on the Sabbath to be promoted by the United Synagogue, the national organization of Conservative congregations.

As a part of the Farrar, Straus publicity campaign for *The Sabbath*, Heschel published one chapter in the October 1951 issue of *Commentary*. Entitled "Between Civilization and Eternity: An Ancient Debate and an Allegorical Interpretation," the essay put forth Heschel's key idea that Judaism is a religion of time as opposed to a religion of space. He urged all Jews to observe the Sabbath and, in so doing, to harmonize inward meditation and social responsibility in the world of space: "This, then, is the answer to the tragic problem of civilization: not to flee from the realm of space; to work with things of space but to be in love with eternity. Things are our tools; eternity, the Sabbath, is our mate."[1]

"Architecture of Time," a second selection from the forthcoming book, appeared in the inaugural issue of *Judaism*. Here, Heschel decried "man's unconditional surrender to space," by which he meant man's "enslavement to things."[2] He insisted that the idea of space, on its own, was limiting and individualistic. By contrast, the idea of time, which interrelated with space, included the Divine as continuous creation: "This is the task of men: to conquer space and sanctify time."[3] Consistent observance of the Sabbath would enhance "a spiritual presence" and help to sanctify the world.

The Sabbath: Its Meaning for Modern Man appeared in October 1951. It was an elegant and powerful defense of the inner life of the holy day, Shabbat, "a palace in time." (Heschel had first evoked this image in one of his early Yiddish poems.) The ten chapter titles focused on insights, such as "Only Heaven and Nothing Else?" (chapter 4) and "Eternity Utters a Day" (chapter 7). Complementing the philosophical and poetic ruminations were expressionistic wood engravings by Ilya Schor. (Schor's woodcuts for *The Earth Is the Lord's* had been more stereotypically traditional.) In addition, Heschel's copious notes accumulated a treasure of ancient Jewish sources as well as modern interpretations.

The Sabbath would come to take its place alongside *The Earth Is the Lord's* as a classic introduction to Heschel's thought. These two books would be published as one volume some ten years later, in 1962, and in the first Harper Torchbook edition in 1966. But in the short term, Heschel's polemic style was an issue in the Jewish popular press.

Heschel had become so noteworthy that he dominated the third issue of *Judaism* (July 1952). The journal included two responses to his new book, one hostile (Trude Weiss-Rosmarin), the other supportive (Nahum N. Glatzer). Heschel then answered criticisms of his spiritual approach to time in a rather technical essay, "Space, Time, and Reality: The Centrality of Time in the Biblical World-View" (which would appear as an appendix to the second edition of *The Sabbath*).[4]

The quarrel centered on whether "time" was a valid Jewish category. Refuting Heschel, Weiss-Rosmarin, the learned, combative editor of the *Jewish Spectator*, insisted that his thesis "rests on untenable premises and is supported by faulty props." She denounced his apparent "disdain of space" and claimed that there was "no proof whatsoever for his theory. . . . The evidence of the most authoritative Jewish sources proves on the contrary that Judaism identifies God with space, viz., the usage of *makom*—space—as a synonym for God in the Mishnah, Talmud, medieval literature, and colloquial Hebrew speech."[5] At the very end, revealing her bias, she objected to his "mysticism," his manner of thinking, and especially his ornate writing. Weiss-Rosmarin thus launched her lifelong campaign against Heschel.

Glatzer, a German-educated Polish Jew and professor at the recently founded Brandeis University, offered a supportive yet sober review. He had studied the classic Jewish texts as a youth in Germany and participated in Rosenzweig and Buber's movement of Jewish education before and during the Hitler period. According to Glatzer, the scientific issue of the "space-time continuum" was irrelevant to Heschel's interpretation of holiness in time.[6]

Underlying the controversy was a cultural clash. The real objection to *The Sabbath:* it was theological in content and poetic in style. At that moment in American Jewish history, the lines were firmly drawn between intuitive and analytical modes of thought. Even so, some reviewers admitted to feeling ambivalent—attracted to Heschel's spirituality despite their rationalistic objections.

ACADEMIC UPS AND DOWNS

These intellectual debates in the Jewish media were reflected in, and indeed exacerbated by, the hothouse atmosphere of the Jewish Theological Seminary. As Heschel gained stature outside the seminary, his alienation from most of his colleagues increased. His standing at JTS was undermined actively by Saul Lieberman and more covertly by Louis Finkelstein. On the surface, however, Heschel's relationship with both men remained cordial.

Finkelstein was at the height of his powers. He reorganized the

Jewish Theological Seminary administration and retained his full authority as chancellor. He was honored nationally: His portrait appeared on the cover of *Time* magazine in October 1951, during the High Holy Days, accompanied by a laudatory article entitled "A Trumpet for All Israel," praising the Seminary as being in the forefront of a national return to Judaism. Finkelstein was described as almost a holy figure.[7] Yet for all his academic and social success, Finkelstein envied Heschel's even greater celebrity in the non-Jewish world outside the seminary.

At the same time, Heschel remained acutely sensitive to, perhaps obsessed by, his colleagues' poor regard for his academic work. He even blamed himself, although he knew that the real problem was a matter of divergent values. He never lost his yearning for their approval, and he tried to compensate by seeking adulation from his favorite students. Although he rarely complained of the indignities he endured, close friends, colleagues, and even some students were aware of them. On the occasions he did confide in them, they would offer support.

Heschel's relationships with his students continued to be mixed. Many were put off by his indifferent teaching, but others found him stimulating, warm, and deeply spiritual—sometimes even droll.

Heschel was also a central figure on the Seminary Admissions Committee, through which he influenced several students even before they began their rabbinical training. He frequently supported applicants considered unsuitable by the committee's official chair, Vice Chancellor Simon Greenberg, and other committee members. A number of rabbis owe their profession to Heschel.

The high point of the committee's work was the interview with prospective students by a group of faculty. At one such session, as the distinguished professors sat around the table, Heschel, who had remained quiet during the interview, stroked his beard (as he often did), turned to the candidate, and asked, "If you were going to Alaska, what two things would you take with you?" Thinking that his answer should be Jewishly appropriate, the aspiring rabbinical student answered, "Tallis and tefillin." Heschel looked at him, and asked, "Wouldn't you take a warm coat?"[8]

Heschel was often careless with his required classes, but sometimes his neglect produced unexpected benefits.[9] One day he interrupted his lecture on Maimonides to fetch his morning mail. When he returned, he read the class a letter he had received: A synagogue in an old Jewish area of the Bronx was about to be sold. There were two potential buyers: a black Baptist church and a large bank. The synagogue board knew that according to tradition a synagogue should not be converted into a church. Nonetheless, they asked Heschel for his opinion.

"So, gentlemen, you are soon to be rabbis, what is your *pesak*, your decision?" After several seconds of uncomfortable silence, a student approvingly quoted the traditional *pesak*: "Never to a church!"

Heschel listened politely, then rose, stroked his beard, and spoke: "May I insult you? If it is sold to a bank, then it will become a temple of capitalism; if sold to a church, it will continue to be a temple of God. Should a rabbi endorse a shul being converted into a temple of capitalism?"

MARTIN BUBER'S AMERICAN LECTURE TOUR

In the fall of 1951 Louis Finkelstein arranged for Martin Buber to make a six-month lecture tour throughout the United States. It was Buber's first visit. About seventy lectures were planned at prominent locations around the country, including the Jewish Theological Seminary. Heschel would have been the appropriate person to act as the JTS faculty host, since he had been in close communication with Buber since 1935. But this was Finkelstein's project—an exceptional public relations opportunity for the seminary and for a chancellor still elated over the cover story in *Time*. Heschel was put aside.

Buber's lecture tour was successful, inaugurating his American career and helping him publish his books in English translation. On the eve of his return to Israel, the Jewish Theological Seminary hosted a farewell tribute to him at Carnegie Hall. The program that Sunday evening, April 5, 1952, did not include Heschel. On the contrary, it featured the Reconstructionist wing of Conservative Judaism: Mordecai Kaplan offered a brief tribute. So did the Protestant theologian Paul Tillich. Both Kaplan and Tillich were exponents of symbolic religion (each in his own way). Buber's farewell lecture, "Hope for This Hour," denounced "the demonic power which rules our world, the demonry of basic mistrust." Dialogue, acceptance of the other's true needs, was the solution, the hope.[10] Heschel's contact with this friend, Martin Buber, the philosopher of dialogue, was limited to a warm embrace when Seymour Siegel (a former rabbinical student who had joined the JTS faculty) brought Buber back to the seminary from the airport.

Heschel, too, was asked for the first time to lecture at an American college. Marshall Meyer invited Heschel to speak at Dartmouth College on April 28, 1952, about three weeks after Buber and his wife had returned to Jerusalem. Since Sylvia was expecting a baby at any time, Heschel did not stay long.

About two weeks later, on May 15, 1952, Sylvia Heschel gave birth to a baby girl, Hannah Susannah. The child was named Channa Shoshanah ("Anna" for Sylvia's mother; "Shoshanah," "rose" in Hebrew, for Reizel, Heschel's mother). A naming ceremony took place at the Kopitzhinitzer *shteibl* at 132 Henry Street on the Lower East Side.[11]

Heschel doted on Susie, who was precocious and lively, and loved to play with her. He also acknowledged his wife by dedicating his next book, *God in Search of Man* (1955), "To Sylvia." The only previous book he had dedicated was his 1933 collection of Yiddish poetry, in memory of his deceased father. In this way Heschel publicly honored his wife and their American family.

Judaism as a cultural force was entering the American mainstream. On January 20, 1953, for the first time, a rabbi—the tall and eloquent Abba Hillel Silver, leader of Reform Judaism and a Zionist—offered a prayer at a U.S. presidential inauguration, that of Dwight David Eisenhower. Eisenhower's landslide victory over Adlai Stevenson helped end the Korean conflict and usher in an era of relative peace.

But even as they enjoyed the postwar prosperity, Americans were becoming increasingly agitated by the Cold War and the pervasive suspicion it generated. An atmosphere of intimidation was fueled by the ongoing anti-Communist hearings held by Joseph McCarthy's Senate Committee on Governmental Operations and the House Committee on Un-American Activities. The nuclear arms race with the Soviet Union increased the general foreboding.

Heschel concentrated on spiritual authenticity as a solution to this "age of anxiety." The problem of faith, he insisted, was at the heart of the American culture wars. He deplored the prevailing American trend of interpreting religion in terms of social science, whereby God became a symbol of human values and aspirations. He positioned his lifelong polemic against symbolism in order to safeguard sacred observance; in his terms, symbolism "reduce[d] beliefs to make-believe, observance to ceremony, prophecy to literature, theology to esthetics." Above all, he rejected symbolism on ethical as well as theological grounds. There was only one "symbol" of the Divine: namely, each and every human being, body and spirit. Echoing his earliest Yiddish poetry, he proclaimed the holiness of the human: "Human life is holy, holier even than the Scrolls of the Torah. Its holiness is not man's achievement; it is a gift of God rather than something attained through merit."[12]

In June 1952 Heschel gladly accepted an invitation to present his views at the Institute for Religious and Social Studies, an interfaith conference organized by Louis Finkelstein. He spent the summer working on this paper, in addition to volume 2 of his *Philosophy of Judaism* and other essays.

At the November conference, the majority of participants—Catholic, Protestant, and Jewish—argued that symbolism could renew religious life in the same way it had energized psychology, architecture, dance, drama, and literature. For them, the Divine was replaced by an "idea" of God; ritual had salutary therapeutic and social effects.

A spiritual radical, Heschel systematically denied the value of symbolism in Jewish theology and practice.[13] Carefully defining his terms, he began with spatial symbols, such as the Holy Ark, in which God's presence could be felt. He distinguished between a "real symbol," which included something of the Divine in the image, and a "conventional symbol," which stood for something but did not partake of it, such as a flag. Even the created world was not a symbol of God: "The world speaks to God, but that speech is not God speaking to Himself." Images were not to be confused with the transcendent. In terms of practice, ritual objects possessed "no inherent sanctity."

For Heschel, religious knowledge could not be simply intellectual; it had to be direct and experiential. He countered the claim of Kant and his followers (such as Salomon Maimon) that "only *symbolic* knowledge is possible." He denounced the doctrine of a religion limited to concepts as promulgating a view that "regards religion as *a fiction*, useful to society or to man's personal well-being."[14]

Heschel's immediate target was American Reconstructionism. While he shared the Reconstructionists' goal of revitalizing observance, he held that their focus on human symbols denied its sacred essence: "Symbols are relevant to man; mitzvot are relevant to God. Symbols are folkways; mitzvot are God's ways."

Typically, Heschel overstated his position—a risky strategy. Bent on demonstrating that "nothing is more alien to the spirit of

Judaism than the veneration of images," he ignored the vast poetic and mythical resources of Kabbalah, Zohar, and mystical tradition he had studied and absorbed from his youth.[15] Why Heschel exposed himself to easy criticism remains unclear.

At the conference's end, Heschel's competitors had the last word. Mordecai Kaplan reiterated his advocacy of symbolism as the necessary vehicle of human communication and collective action. For Kaplan and his followers, Heschel's insistence upon revelation from a transcendent God was simply "supernaturalism" or "primitive religion . . . in other words, magic."[16] This interfaith conference underscored the ideological chasm.

Heschel's writings of this period concentrated on the proximity of the Divine. To consolidate the scholarly foundation of his theological revolution, he extracted material from his thesis on the prophets and the manuscript of his forthcoming *Philosophy of Judaism* and fashioned them into three articles, which he placed strategically to reach different readerships.

For religiously engaged modern Jews, he arranged to publish "The Divine Pathos: The Basic Category of Prophetic Theology" in the January 1953 issue of *Judaism*. Here, *pathos* referred to God's concern or "emotional" reactions to "what happens in the world." Heschel adapted the vocabulary of Rosenzweig ("correlation") and Buber ("dialogue") to explain the meeting of divine and human: "In sum, the divine pathos is the unity of the eternal and the temporal, of the rational and the irrational, of the metaphysical and the historical. It is . . . the correlation of Creator and creation, of the dialogue between the Holy One of Israel and His people."[17]

For politically oriented Jews, Heschel published a programmatic essay, "The Moment at Sinai," in *American Zionist*, the journal of the Zionist Organization of America. As part of his analysis of revelation, Heschel urged his activist readers not to abandon their spiritual heritage. Striking out against secularization, he distinguished between the God of the philosophers, "a concept derived from abstract ideas," and the God of the prophets, "derived from acts and events."[18]

His third essay, "A Preface to the Understanding of Revelation," directed at Liberal or Reform Jewish thinkers, appeared in a special volume published in England to honor Leo Baeck's eightieth birthday. Justifying divine revelation (by drawing from his earlier manuscript, *God in Search of Man*), he challenged the neo-Kantian view of religion as represented by Baeck's *Essence of Judaism* (1936). In each case, he wrote against what he considered to be reductionistic explanations of Judaism.

The common ground was an ethical or (as I prefer to phrase it) a sacred humanism. Connecting faith and moral sensitivity—Heschel's main task, always—he argued that insensitivity to the proximity of God, the living God of pathos, was placing humankind in mortal jeopardy, since human beings are born with "a passion and drive for cruel deeds, which only the fear of God can soothe." He graphically evoked bystander apathy during the Holocaust while suggesting that there yet remained enough religious faith to save civilization from complete destruction: "If man can remain callous to a horror as infinite as God . . . [can] make soap of human flesh, then how did it happen that nations did not exterminate each other centuries ago?"[19] The living God, he proclaimed, is the ultimate defense against human evil.

The theological debate aggravated ideological passions. Heschel's rejection of process theology (the entire cosmos as sacred) and his tendency to draw excessive contrasts provoked firm but amiable criticism from Arthur A. Cohen, one of his gifted students at the JTS Institute for Theology. In a letter, Cohen urged his teacher to demonstrate more sympathy for his opponents: "Beggars such as us cannot be choosers. To make our audience we cannot risk surrendering half." He encouraged Heschel to seek reconciliation between competing conceptions.[20] Heschel appreciated this student's bold, and brilliant, evaluation, but not enough to alter his characteristic polemic approach. He was not interested in developing a more nuanced analysis. He faithfully maintained his oppositional style.

In February 1953 Heschel again vehemently linked ethics with faith. More than three hundred teachers and school principals were debating the theme "Teaching Jewish Values" at the eleventh annual conference of the Jewish Education Committee (as the New York Bureau of Jewish Education was then known). As a featured speaker, Heschel took to task what he called "the autocracy" of psychology and sociology: "Human existence cannot derive its ultimate meaning from society, because society itself is in need of meaning." His negative example was Nazi Germany, which defined as right "what is useful to the German people."

He then spoke as a prophet, anticipating by ten years his social activism of the 1960s and demanding the highest ethical standards in public life: "How can one preserve one's integrity in a world filled with intrigue, flattery, and falsehood? . . . What is the value of being moral in spite of the defeats of the moral man in the atmosphere of cynicism in which we live?" To counter the current negativity, teachers had to help young people discover "the ultimate significance" of their lives.[21]

Education, he believed, was the key to transformation. Heschel began his talk by repudiating the debased image of the *melammed* (a Hebrew teacher of children) found in Jewish popular literature. He did not mince his words: "The fact that [the *melammed* receives little respect] seems to be nothing but blasphemy, and I am a *melammed* myself. It is treason to the spirit of Judaism, for in our teachings there is no higher distinction than that of being a teacher." He concluded by challenging the modern teacher to be "either a witness or a stranger. To guide a pupil into the promised land, he must have been there himself. . . . What we need more than anything else is not *text-books* but *text-people*. It is the personality of the teacher which is the text that the pupils read; the text that they will never forget." He counseled his audience not to be like the blacksmith's apprentice who had learned all the skills except how to kindle the spark.[22]

A SPIRITUAL DIAGNOSIS

That summer, Heschel advanced his spiritual revolution with his sharpest critique of American Jewish practice. Recognizing that the burgeoning of synagogues in suburbia had not enhanced the quality of observance and religious learning, leaders of the Reform and Conservative rabbinates separately invited Heschel to define his ideal of prayer to colleagues in the field. During the week of June 22–27, 1953, he embarked upon a sort of shuttle diplomacy, delivering his most detailed outline of what he thought rabbis of all denominations should strive for. When asked about his own institutional identity, Heschel humorously said of himself, "I am not a Jew in search of an adjective."

His critique, too, was nondenominational. To each group, Heschel asserted exactly what its partisans did not want to hear. Conservative Judaism, like Orthodoxy, emphasized *halakhah* and ritual observance over cultivation of the inner life; Reform rejected the authority of *halakhah* in favor of rational philosophy, individual choice, and social action. Heschel tailored his counter-discourse to restore the fullness of Judaism, contradictions and all.

Heschel first spoke to his Conservative colleagues, a great many of whom identified with the tenets of Reconstructionism, at their fifty-third annual convention in Atlantic City, New Jersey. Ira Eisenstein, Mordecai Kaplan's son-in-law and a leader of Kaplan's Society for the Advancement of Judaism, was then president of the Rabbinical Assembly. He was hoping to cultivate a mutually illuminating exchange of views.

Heschel's keynote speech, "The Spirit of Jewish Prayer," began diplomatically, anticipating some hurt feelings: "In advancing some critical remarks I do not mean, *God forbid* [in Hebrew], to take a superior attitude. In all honesty, my criticism will be to a considerable degree self-criticism." But his picture of the Conservative synagogue was harsh: "Our services are conducted with pomp and precision. The rendition of the liturgy is smooth. Everything is present: decorum, voice, ceremony. But one thing is missing: *Life*." Heschel's images were graphic and his tone was caustic: "Has the synagogue become the graveyard where prayer is buried? Are we, the spiritual leaders of American Jewry, members of a *hevra kadisha* [burial society]?"[23]

Asserting the need for authentic spirituality, Heschel denounced "the habit of *praying by proxy*," of letting the rabbi and the cantor do the work. He deplored the apathetic "*spiritual absenteeism*" of congregants who simply attended services without truly participating. Rigid ideologies, he claimed, were to blame.

Heschel then summarized and—provocatively—measured four "prevalent doctrines" of God and Judaism by the standards of a living God. First was "the doctrine of agnosticism," which considered "prayer [to be] a fraud." Heschel condemned those who believed that "the only way to revitalize the synagogue is to minimize the importance of prayer and to convert the synagogue into a [community] center."

Second, he denounced "the doctrine of religious behaviorism," widespread among Orthodox and some Conservative Jews, in which people "seem to believe that religious deeds can be performed in a spiritual wasteland, in the absence of the soul, with a heart hermetically sealed." Here, Heschel was alluding to the foremost exponent of modern Orthodoxy, Rabbi Joseph B. Soloveitchik, who defined the ideal Jew as "halakhic man."

Heschel then targeted Reform (and numerous Conservative) Jews imbued with the view of Judaism as a civilization. They were proponents of the "doctrine of prayer as a social act," which "is built on a theology which regards God as a symbol of social action, as an epitome of the ideals of the group, as 'the spirit of the beloved community.'" Although Heschel strategically did not name the obvious champion of this ideology, Mordecai Kaplan, his condemnation of what he called the "sociological fallacy" could not have been more explicit.[24]

Heschel's fourth and final target was a variant of "process theology" in which "the individual self of the worshiper is the whole sphere of prayer-life. The assumption is that God is an idea, a process, a source, a fountain, a spring, a power. But one cannot pray to an idea; one cannot address his prayers to a fountain of values." At its core, he asserted, such an ideology was a "doctrine of religious solipsism." Here too he did not publicly single out any proponents of process theology within his community; rather, he attacked a 1911 book by the French psychologist Joseph Segond.[25]

Heschel warned that American Jews—including their leaders—were undergoing a widespread crisis of belief: "I have been in the United States of America for thirteen years. I have not discovered America but I have discovered something in America. It is possible to be a rabbi and not to believe in the God of Abraham, Isaac and Jacob." Most American rabbis, according to a survey he cited, conceived of God as "the sum total of forces which make for greater intelligence, beauty, goodness." Heschel demanded faith in a personal God, for "if the presence of God is a myth, then we are insane in talking to Him." The risks of such intransigence were enormous.[26]

Heschel bore radical witness to the need for a living Jewish faith. But his was a lonely voice, prophetic and intense. With his demand for absolute integrity, how could he expect support from the majority? His view, compatible with Hasidic tradition and the recent cataclysm of the Holocaust, was that humans' alienation from God reflected "the soul-stirring awareness that God Himself was not at home in a universe, where His will is defied, where His kingship is denied. *The Shekhinah is in exile*, the world is corrupt, *the universe itself is not at home*" (Heschel's emphasis). Many in Heschel's audience were offended by his sarcasm, even his apparent pessimism. They felt injured and angry—perhaps, also, anxious.

The next evening, one of Heschel's theological adversaries took the floor. Reading from his paper "Prayer and the Modern Jew," Eugene Kohn, a leader in Reconstructionism, presented his movement's classic position. While agreeing with Heschel that "modern man has largely lost the art of prayer," he dismissed the traditional belief that God hears our prayers. Kohn asserted that the Jewish people had "rejected the idea that God is a transcendent person"; Jews needed an updated "idea of God" to embrace prayer once again.[27]

Blending process theology, sociology, and Buber's I-Thou dialogue, all popular trends in American Judaism, Kohn then justified the Reconstructionist movement's recent revision of the prayer book, a matter of widespread controversy. Kohn argued that the traditional liturgies retained too many ethical and scientific "errors." Prayer did not influence God, but only the worshiper; there was no room for a real God.

The battle lines were marked. Kohn's speech drew overall support from most—but not all—of his fellow leaders in the audience. For his part, Heschel was largely considered questionable from the start. Recognizing that many of his colleagues rejected Heschel a priori as "a mystic and a dreamer," Rabbi Irving Lehrman defended him by citing Abraham Lincoln's famous witticism in response to complaints that General Grant's excessive drinking made him unfit to lead the Union Army: "Ah, if I only knew the brand of liquor he uses, I would feed it to my generals."[28]

Then Heschel stood up. He was surprised, "puzzled," "amazed," and even "distressed" that his call for authentic prayer in Conservative synagogues had provoked such indignation. Yet even as he attempted to engage in a sympathetic discussion, he revealed his stubborn, insensitive side. He began defensively, insisting that he had postponed his own research to examine "the details of a problem which is specifically and uniquely yours." Then, however, he acknowledged that "your problems, too, are mine. The assurance that I was speaking in the spirit of self-criticism was not an empty phrase. All my life I have been deeply bothered by my own miserable failure to attain *kavanah* [intention] in prayer."

As the evening concluded, Ira Eisenstein took the floor and explained, somewhat apologetically, that he had planned Heschel's and Kohn's opposing presentations in the hope that they would lead to fruitful discussion. Although he could "recognize the validity" of Heschel's approach, he was disappointed that Heschel demanded that everyone "accept his theological dogma, [otherwise] you can't pray at all. I deny that."

Heschel then made an astounding admission, which drew him closer to many of his listeners: "I have been wrestling with the problem all my life as to whether I really mean God when I pray to Him, whether I have even succeeded in knowing what I am talking about and whom I am talking to. I still don't know whether I serve God or I serve something else." This was not a confession of agnosticism. Religious reality is essentially "ineffable." The task of Heschel's *philosophy* of religion, systematic reflection on the experience of piety, was to elucidate the dilemma of faith.

At the same time, it is true, Heschel continued to claim the authority of his own intuition, thereby cutting himself off from the majority that preferred intellectual constructs. He denied that he had spoken of "*a concept* or demanded the acceptance of a definition. We Jews have no concepts; all we have is faith, faith in His willingness to listen to us. We have no information, but we sense and believe in His being near to us."

He did attempt to recover some common ground by respecting his "opponents" as ethically motivated human beings: "The strange thing about many of our contemporaries is that their life is nobler than their ideology, that their faith is deep and their views shallow, that their souls are suppressed and their slogans proclaimed." Unmistakably, in this double-edged compliment, Heschel was alluding to Mordecai Kaplan: "We must not continue to cherish a theory just because we embraced it forty years ago."

Eugene Kohn had the final word, and it was both generous and uncompromising. The Reconstructionist leader refused requests from some of his partisans to "refute" Heschel. He was not offended by Heschel's critical comments; he viewed them as "motivated by love and I take them in that spirit." Kohn then reaffirmed his loyalty to God as conceived in impersonal terms: "I can talk in the same way and with the same freedom with that cosmic process which I regard as the very source and fountain of my own being."

As the conference ended, the core problem remained unresolved: Did Reconstructionism deny a transcendent Deity? Was it a disguised form of atheism or a genuine belief in the living God? Did religious naturalists—as they were also known—recognize a holy reality beyond human conceptions? All in all, Heschel felt that his challenge to the Rabbinical Assembly was a mixed success.[29]

PHILOSOPHIES OF REFORM JUDAISM

The next day Heschel took an airplane to Estes Park, Colorado to address the sixty-fourth annual Central Conference of American Rabbis convention. This Reform group was more receptive to contemporary thought—secular, Christian, and Jewish—than their Conservative and Orthodox colleagues. Adapting his approach but retaining his stringencies, Heschel challenged their historical and humanistic assumptions, emphasizing the need for a return to traditional observance.

Heschel's precarious place in the range of contemporary Jewish thought emerged clearly from the other presenters at his session: Rabbis Samuel Cohon, Heschel's former Hebrew Union College colleague, and David Polish of Evanston, Illinois. Each sought to define the most appropriate model for contemporary American Judaism.

Cohon's paper "The Existentialist Trend in Theology" traced the current "disillusionment with man, human reason and with human goals," back to Søren Kierkegaard through Jean-Paul Sartre's atheistic existentialism and Martin Heidegger's grim ontology of mystery. In Christianity, the crisis (also called dialectical) theology of Karl Barth posited God as "Wholly Other," with "an abyss separating human and divine." Cohon considered Will Herberg the most influential contemporary Jewish thinker in the existentialist vein but deemed him overly influenced by Christianity and thus not a suitable guide for American Judaism. He favored the kind of neo-Hasidism to be found in "Rosenzweig's philosophy of experience and Buber's theo-centric mysticism—despite all their ambiguities and artificialities." Apparently Cohon did not know Heschel's *Man Is Not Alone*, for he made no reference to it.[30]

David Polish's survey "Current Trends in Jewish Theology" simi-larly neglected Heschel. Polish began by considering Will Herberg's potential as a guide for Jewish doctrine, but, like Cohon, he objected to Herberg's Christian neo-orthodox influences, "a theology which is foreign and repugnant to liberal Judaism." He saw in Mordecai Kaplan's theology a remedy to Herberg, since the "idea of God" as a process immanent to the natural world favored humankind's self-liberation, and yet, Kaplan's impersonal system did not "assuage the hunger for union with God and fulfillment in Him."

In the end, Polish touted Buber's dialogical encounter as the best, since Buber emphasized human responsibility. Citing a Hasidic master—"Said the Rabbi of Kotzk: 'God dwells wherever man lets Him in.' Here the whole crucial position of man is summarized"— Polish concluded that Rosenzweig and Buber remained the prime examples of present-day spirituality.[31]

Then came Heschel's turn to inspire contemporary Jewish thought. Not referring to Rosenzweig and Buber (the true models left standing), he spoke as a traditionalist, admonishing the Reform rabbis to observe the mitzvot as expressions of God's will. His paper "Toward an Understanding of Halacha" justified the need to return to observance as the primary means of enhancing the spiritual potential of American Judaism. Heschel stressed his solidarity with the plight of Reform rabbis: "I, too, have wrestled with the difficulties inherent in our faith as Jews."

For the first time in his public life, Heschel highlighted his own path toward renewed religious commitment. He sought to reinvigorate American Judaism through an autobiographical parable: "I came with great hunger to the University of Berlin to study philosophy. I looked for a system of thought, for the depth of the spirit, for the meaning of existence. Erudite and profound scholars gave courses in logic, epistemology, esthetics, ethics, and metaphysics. They opened the gates of the history of philosophy. I was exposed to the austere disciplines of unremitting inquiry and self-criticism."[32]

But Heschel's professors in Berlin, academic philosophers and historians, did not admit religious thinking: "They spoke of God from the point of view of man. To them God was an idea, a postulate of reason. They granted Him the status of being a logical possibility. But to assume that He had existence would have been a crime against epistemology."[33]

Heschel was excavating the neo-Kantian foundations of American Reform Judaism, for whom God was at best a logical possibility. But how does one acquire faith?

Insisting upon the reality of God and the power of consistent observance, Heschel drove his point home with the memory of how, while walking in Berlin one evening, he had suddenly realized he had forgotten to recite the evening prayer.

Knowing his audience, Heschel also anticipated and addressed a number of standard objections to religious law. First, he rejected "the assumption that either you observe all or nothing." He dismissed "the assumption that every iota of the law was revealed to Moses at Sinai." He emphasized "the role of the sages in interpreting the word of the Bible and their power to issue new ordinances." In these respects, progressive Judaism could be compatible with a modern Orthodoxy. He also defined the limits of rationalist philosophy. He formulated a phrase, based on Kierkegaard's famed "leap of faith," saying: "[a] Jew is asked to take *a leap of action* rather than *a leap of thought*: to surpass his needs, to do more than he understands in order to understand more than he does."[34]

Prayer was too grave a responsibility, Heschel insisted, to depend upon impulse or even *kavanah* (focused intention): "I am not always in the mood to pray. I do not always have the vision and the strength to say a word in the presence of God. But when I am weak, it is the law that gives me the strength; when my vision is dim, it is duty that gives me insight." Heschel concluded by supporting the growing tendency toward accepting "a code of practice required by every Reform Jew." And he ended: "May it be a *return* to a *halakhic way of life*, not to customs and ceremonies."[35]

Reactions to Heschel's address were swift, as they had been at the Conservative meeting earlier that week. Several rabbis rose to their feet and berated him for rejecting the humanistic tenets of Reform so violently. Heschel was again stunned. Naively, he had expected his audience to be capable of greater self-examination.

AMERICAN ORTHODOXY AND SPIRITUALITY

While the Conservative and Reform movements remained suspicious of Heschel, he was encouraged by some recognition from American Modern Orthodoxy.

Jewish Forum, a New York monthly founded in 1917, was the first to introduce Heschel to the strictly observant public. The July 1952 issue carried a major review essay on Heschel's recent works. The anonymous author, under the pen-name "Dayyan Al-Yahud" (Judge of the Jews, a title attributed to Abraham ben Nathan, the twelfth-century Talmudic scholar and *dayyan* in Fostat, Egypt), proclaimed Heschel as the new voice for Modern Orthodox Judaism, as Reinhold Niebuhr had pronounced him for the gentile public.

Al-Yahud declared that Orthodox Judaism must be open to novelty and contradictions. In this regard he described Heschel as "unconventional," both devout and worldly. Displaying intimate knowledge of Heschel's upbringing in "the Warschawiansky milieu" as well as the contemporary American Jewish scene, he carefully examined *The Earth Is the Lord's*, *The Sabbath*, and *Man Is Not Alone*. He judged that Heschel's chief "weakness" was his tendency to exaggerate antitheses. He then corrected some of Heschel's scholarly references, citing Philo, Plato, medieval Jewish philosophy, and talmudic, midrashic, kabbalistic, and Hasidic literature.[36]

Al-Yahud also accurately highlighted two of Heschel's central ideas: the sanctity of time over space, and the partnership of God and humankind. He looked forward to Heschel's next book, which he hoped would be "a more comprehensive and adequate exposition of Judaism."

Although Heschel was not yet ready to produce the "comprehensive" account of Judaism that Al-Yahud envisioned (*God in Search of Man* would appear in 1955), by the fall of 1953 Heschel began to envisage a scholarly history of the early Hasidic movement (1720–1772). The life, teachings, and influence of the Baal Shem Tov and his disciples were at the core of his identity, and since the late 1940s, while completing his first American books, he had been laying the groundwork for this chronicle.

In fact Heschel had begun his project of preserving the Hasidic ideal even earlier, in Europe, when he started collecting Hasidic books and manuscripts. (He was forced to abandon most of them in

Warsaw.) In the United States, he found significant holdings at the Hebrew Union College library as well as at the Jewish Theological Seminary and the Yidisher Visnshaftlekher Institut Archives in New York. He conceived the idea of establishing a Hasidic archive to be housed at the YIVO Institut; the project was inaugurated in 1949.[37]

Heschel decided to publish biographical monographs in Yiddish and Hebrew for scholars with the requisite cultural knowledge. Unlike his writings in English for a general readership, he conceived these Hasidic biographies in the Wissenschaft manner: factual accounts supported by hundreds of footnotes to oral as well as written sources. These academic studies, in which matters of detail could not be disputed, may have served as Heschel's attempts to impress Gershom Scholem and other historians and thereby pave the way for scholarly acceptance of research that filled out the facts barely alluded to in *The Earth Is the Lord's*.[38]

To support his project of turning these monographs into a book-length history, Heschel applied for a Guggenheim Fellowship in the fall of 1953. His most prestigious supporters—Reinhold Niebuhr, Julian Morgenstern, Martin Buber—wrote letters of recommendation, and the subsequent April Heschel received the award. His stipend of four thousand dollars would cover the next academic year, September 1954 through August 1955.

Heschel worked on the book well into the 1960s. Over the years he placed slips of paper or paper clips in numerous Hasidic books stored in the Jewish Theological Seminary's special collections, planning to retrieve them as he wrote. But in 1966 a fire at the JTS library destroyed more than fifty thousand volumes and priceless manuscripts. As Heschel watched, with tears flowing down his cheeks, he told his student Arthur Green, "That is the end of my book on the Baal Shem Tov." Heschel never completed the book, nor did he ever complete the Hasidic Archive.[39]

By July 1954 Heschel did complete a major project, a book

on prayer and symbolism. Addressed to an interdisciplinary and interreligious audience, most chapters were adapted from previous publications: his 1945 essay on prayer from the *Review of Religion*, his paper on symbolism for Finkelstein's Jewish Theological Seminary interfaith colloquium, and his two 1953 speeches to American rabbis. Heschel added a preface, and for chapter 2, "The Person and the Word," he revised two early articles on prayer that were originally written in German and Hebrew. Scribner's officially launched *Man's Quest for God* in November 1954.

Man's Quest for God consolidated Heschel's critique of American Judaism, which he judged to be handicapped by lack of sensitivity to words. He understood that words have independent dignity and power. By projecting emotions into inherited prayers, one could bring out their richness and, reciprocally, enrich one's perception of the world and of oneself: "In prayer, as in poetry, we turn to the words, not to use them as signs for things, but to see things in the light of the words." Poetry, for Heschel, was prayer in potential. Prayer might begin as an act of empathy, identification with a printed text. But the next phase of worship could surpass human imagination. A person praying with *kavanah* could actualize an immanent force: "It is the spiritual power of the praying man that makes manifest what is dormant in the text."[40]

Heschel emphasized "the ineffable," that which lay beyond words. In prayer one realized most acutely the outer limits of language: "In no other act does man experience so often the disparity between the desire for expression and the means of expression as in prayer. . . . What the word can no longer yield, man achieves through the fullness of his powerlessness." Assuming the distance between divine and human, spiritual "fullness" could arise from a more forceful longing for the absolute.[41]

Once again, Heschel stressed the inseparability of ethics and inwardness. He updated the final chapter of *Man's Quest for God* with an allusion to the ongoing McCarthy hearings against domestic Communists: "God will return to us when we shall be willing to let Him in—into our banks and factories, into our Congress and clubs, *into our courts and investigating committees* [emphasis mine], into our homes and theaters."[42] He fused genuine prayer, which fostered ethical responsibility, with civil liberties, the heart of American democracy.

The same month that *Man's Quest for God* was published, Heschel made his début in interfaith dialogue under the auspices of the Religious Education Association, an academic and professional forum founded in 1903 that held yearly conventions and published a quarterly journal. Heschel joined roundtable discussions at Columbia University on "Judeo-Christian" values in higher education.

Reviews of *Man's Quest for God* confirmed Heschel's interfaith appeal. Analyzing the book in *Theology Today*, a Christian periodical aimed at a general, but well-informed readership, Will Herberg highlighted Heschel's spiritual radicalism: "Heschel moderates his drastic criticism of the present-day synagogue—more in the printed version than in his spoken addresses—but in the end he cannot help exclaiming: 'Better prayer without a synagogue than a synagogue without prayer.' No more shattering judgment of American religious life—and not merely Jewish—can be imagined."[43]

And, for the first time, comments on Heschel appeared in a publication whose main purpose was interfaith understanding. An admiring albeit impressionistic essay, "Heschel's Conception of Prayer," by Edward Synan SJ, appeared in the inaugural volume of *The Bridge: A Yearbook of Judeo-Christian Studies*.[44]

Within the Jewish world, the ideological battle lines had long been drawn. Ira Eisenstein's forthright review in *The Reconstructionist* asserted that Heschel had "never before come out so clearly against what we believe and for what we have ceased to believe." What galled Eisenstein the most were Heschel's attacks against psychology and rationalism. In his final judgment, Heschel was "doing religion in our time no service."[45]

Released officially in January 1956, *God in Search of Man* marked the turning point in Heschel's theological revolution. He needed the years spent writing it to sharpen his notions of depth theology, situational philosophy, awe, wonder, the ineffable, and insight that had emerged from *Man Is Not Alone*. In subsequent years he would develop essays, articles, and speeches from sections of this germinal book.

Heschel's numerous source notes validated the book's subtitle, *A Philosophy of Judaism*. An entire Judaica library of both classic and rare sources seem to be cataloged in its references.[46] By contrast, the paucity of source notes in *Man Is Not Alone* had lent credence to the charge by unsympathetic Jewish readers that Heschel's interpretation of religious consciousness was idiosyncratic or more compatible with Christianity than with Judaism.

Now Heschel had strengthened the narrative strategy needed for his broader scope. *God in Search of Man* was divided into three parts—"God" (chapters 1–16), "Revelation" (chapters 17–27), and "Response" (chapters 28–42)—each representing a station along the divine itinerary. Chapters were further divided into subtitled sections, facilitating slow, meditative reading—while frustrating readers seeking the security of a logical system.

The intellectual apologetics in part 1 culminated in a dramatic performance of divine inspiration. The central chapter (13), "God in Search of Man," reflecting the book's title, reiterated the mystical illumination of *Man Is Not Alone*, but with textual sources added as Judaic validation.[47] Heschel began with a theological assertion:

For God is not always silent, and man is not always blind. His glory fills the world; His spirit hovers above the waters. There are moments in which, to use a Talmudic phrase, heaven and earth kiss each other; in which there is a lifting of the veil at the horizon of the known, opening a vision of what is eternal in time. Some of us have at least once experienced the momentous realness of God. Some of us have at least caught a glimpse of the beauty, peace, and power that flow through the souls of those who are devoted to Him. . . . The voice of Sinai goes on for ever: "These words the Lord spoke unto all your assembly in the mount out of the midst of the fire, of the cloud, and of the thick darkness, with *a great voice that goes on for ever.*"

Integrating intuition and sacred history, Heschel bore witness that the Holy Spirit (*ruach ha-kodesh*, or prophetic inspiration) was still available. A footnote cited the Rabbinic authority: "Deuteronomy 5:19, according to the Aramaic translation of Onkelos and Jonathan ben Uzziel and to the interpretation of *Sanhedrin*, 17b; *Sotah*, 10b; and to the first interpretation of Rashi." Heschel's rendition of divine revelation now combined experience, logic, and multiple prooftext references such as these.

In part 2, "Revelation," Heschel developed his theory of biblical interpretation. As a flexible traditionalist who rejected literal readings, he understood prophetic utterances (which seem hyperbolic) as "understatements" pointing to God's overwhelming reality: "Who shall presume to be an expert in discerning what is divine and what is but 'a little lower' than divine?" He rejected the notion that the words of Scripture were "coextensive and identical with the words of God." Unambiguously, he insisted that "the surest way of misunderstanding revelation is to take it literally, to imagine that God spoke to the prophet on a long-distance telephone." Rather, he taught, God still speaks through sacred texts: "The Bible is *holiness in words.* . . . It is as if God took these Hebrew words and breathed into them of His power, and the words became a live wire charged with His spirit. To this very day they are hyphens between heaven and earth."[48]

In part 3, "Response," Heschel derided the thoughtless performance of rituals as "religious behaviorism" and backed up his view with an erudite survey of the "ancient controversy among scholars of Jewish law about the necessity of *kavanah* to validate religious acts."[49] Above all, he asserted a positive, universal principle: acceptance of inner conflicts within Torah-true Judaism. Authentic Judaism, he avowed, validates oppositions such as "the polarity of ideas and events, of mitzvah and sin, of *kavanah* and deed, of regularity and spontaneity, of uniformity and individuality, of *halakhah* and *Aggadah*, of law and inwardness, of love and fear, of understanding and obedience, of joy and discipline, of the good and the evil drive, of time and eternity, of the world and the world to come, of revelation and response, . . . of man's quest for God and God in search of man." (In later essays and speeches, Heschel would help resolve ideological clashes within the community by validating his own internal pluralism.)

Here, Heschel focused on his activist impulses. His probing analysis in "The Problem of Evil" (chapter 36) emphasized the ever-present perils of moral detachment and indifference: "Modern man may be characterized as a being who is callous to catastrophes . . . All that is left to us is our being horrified at the loss of our sense of horror." Good and evil are always mixed. The inevitable "confusion of good and evil" can be overcome only by a striving for holiness.[50]

The three short concluding chapters—"Freedom," "The Spirit of Judaism," and "The People Israel"—sketched out ideas that Heschel would elaborate on in the future, among them that the essence of human freedom is the transcendence of vanity and self-interest in service to God; that the Sabbath, as "the art of surpassing civilization," would inspire people to return to Judaism; and that Diaspora Jews have a "unique association" with the Jewish state. As he proclaimed, "Even before Israel became a people, the land was preordained for it. What we have witnessed in our own days is a reminder of the power of God's mysterious promise to Abraham."[51]

In the concluding words of *God in Search of Man*, Heschel acclaimed "the universal relevance of Judaism, the bearing of its demands upon the chance of man to remain human." To be a Jew, part of "the chosen people," was to serve God's vision of justice and compassion for the entire world.

A PUBLIC INTELLECTUAL

Widespread approval arrived via a feature article in *Time* magazine's edition of March 19, 1956, embellished with a photograph of Heschel. The author was portrayed as a modern Jewish sage who carried on the legacy of Rosenzweig and Buber: "Twinkle-eyed Dr. Heschel, a small man located beneath a bush of grey hair, labors in a blue haze of cigar smoke, and writes prose that sings and soars in the warm, intuitive tradition of the great 18th-century Hasidic leaders from whom he is descended. His just published book . . . speaks to all those men for whom the Bible is a holy book."[52] Heschel thus fulfilled Reinhold Niebuhr's prediction of 1951, becoming an authoritative source for anyone seeking to penetrate the spirit of Judaism.

In the influential Protestant journal *Christian Century*, Will Herberg cited Niebuhr to explain that Heschel's "philosophy" was really "a kind of higher phenomenology of religion linked with a critical self-examination." Herberg agreed that Heschel stood alongside Rosenzweig and Buber in "calling for a return to authentic Jewish faith in a form relevant to contemporary life."[53]

Heschel had finally found a way to reach progressive and even nonreligious Jews, in addition to gentiles. Furthermore, he impressed many open-minded traditional Jews. Two intellectual leaders of American Modern Orthodoxy, Joseph H. Lookstein and Emanuel Rackman, both congregational rabbis and Yeshiva University professors, found in what they called Heschel's "neo-Hasidism" a potential model for "Torah-true" Jews during the Cold War.

In the summer 1956 issue of *Judaism*, Lookstein, a professor of sociology and practical rabbinics, judged that Heschel, with his Hasidic experience, responded more authentically than Buber to the current religious crisis.[54] Rackman, for his part, praised *God in Search of Man* in the religious Zionist magazine *Jewish Horizon*. Humorously defining himself as a repentant *Mitnagid*, Rackman admitted, "In the past the Chasidic movement enriched Judaism; in the present it is saving Judaism. Without Chasidic thought and commitment, Torah-true Jews would simply not be able to cope with the challenge of modernism." Heschel, he argued, spelled out "in detail" how "Jewish intellectuals" might successfully live in two civilizations—their ancestral one and the secular world.[55] Heschel now had the potential to become established as a thinker who could speak to and for Modern Orthodox Jewry.

1. Heschel's father, Rabbi Moshe Mordecai Heschel, the Pelzovizna rebbe. Courtesy of Yitzchak Meyer Twersky.

2. Heschel's mother, Rivka Reizel Perlow Heschel. Courtesy of Yitzchak Meyer Twersky.

3. Abraham Joshua Heschel, age seventeen, in Warsaw. Courtesy of Yitzchak Meyer Twersky.

4. Abraham Joshua Heschel at Hebrew Union College in Cincinnati, ca. 1940.
Courtesy of Bill Liebschutz, photographer.

5. Abraham Heszel (Heschel), Declaration of Intention to become a U.S. citizen, May 29, 1940. District Court of the United States, Cincinnati, Ohio.

6. From left to right: Seymour Siegel, Abraham Joshua Heschel, and Samuel H. Dresner, ca. 1949. Courtesy of the Library of the Jewish Theological Seminary.

7. Sylvia Straus Heschel. Photograph from the program of her Town Hall début. Circa 1949. Photograph by Lotte Jacobi. © The University of New Hampshire.

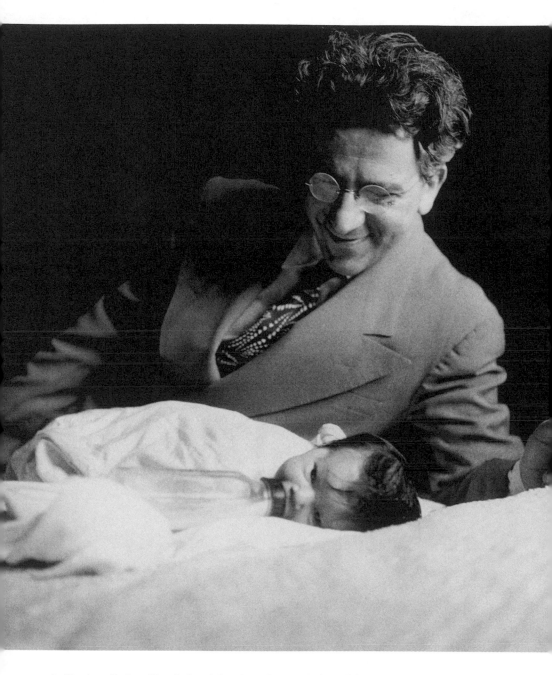

8. Abraham Joshua Heschel and daughter Susannah, born May 1952. May 1952.
Photograph by Lotte Jacobi. © The University of New Hampshire.

9. Abraham Joshua Heschel at the Jewish Theological Seminary, ca. 1960. Photograph by John H. Popper. Courtesy of the Library of The Jewish Theological Seminary.

10. From left to right: Abraham Joshua Heschel, Rabbi Marc H. Tanenbaum, and Augustin Cardinal Bea, ca. 1963. Courtesy of the American Jewish Committee. With permission of the AJC Archives. All rights reserved.

11. Abraham Joshua Heschel with Martin Luther King Jr. and other civil rights leaders at the Selma to Montgomery march, March 23, 1965. Marching in the front row, left to right: John Lewis, an unidentified nun, Rev. Ralph Abernathy, Rev. Martin Luther King Jr., Ralph Bunche, Rabbi Abraham Joshua Heschel, and Rev. Fred Shuttlesworth. Courtesy of the Library of the Jewish Theological Seminary.

12. Abraham Joshua Heschel in 1972. Photograph by Joel Orent.

13. Abraham Joshua Heschel at his desk at the Jewish Theological Seminary, December 23, 1972. This is the last known photograph taken of Heschel. Courtesy of Jacob Teshima, photographer.

PART III

Spiritual Activism

CHAPTER 9

Biblical Prophecy and Current Events, 1956–1963

Heschel now appeared on the national scene as a public intellectual. During these Cold War decades, he found his prophetic voice, speaking to and writing for Jewish and, now, interfaith or secular audiences. And as he became more prominent, his physical appearance became his enduring emblem: a bearded man with shaggy white hair, a media-friendly image of a Hebrew prophet.

The role of religion in public life became central to Heschel's reflections. After his 1956 *Time* magazine profile, Christians as well as Jews began to regard him as an authentic biblical champion of social justice. His essays and lecture tours influenced diverse constituencies; he also took part in conferences sponsored by national interfaith organizations, such as the Religious Education Association, whose annual conventions in Chicago attracted participants of all backgrounds. He keenly adapted his message to his different audiences but always insisted that authentic religion might transform every aspect of life. Shallow religion only brought collapse of values and compromised civic courage.

Audiences resonated with Heschel's biblical response to the "age of anxiety." An increasingly restless public was being challenged by the contradictory events of the 1950s. President Dwight David Eisenhower began his first term in 1953 in the midst of the congressional anti-Communist hearings. In 1954 the Supreme Court ruled against segregation in public schools as long-standing coalitions of black and white citizens (such as the National Association for the Advancement of Colored People and the American Jewish Committee) insisted on equal rights for all Americans. In 1957 the Soviet Union launched the satellite Sputnik, aggravating the Cold War and undermining confidence in the quality of American education. These political and social conflicts—and the unrelenting fear of nuclear annihilation—were inducing many Americans to seek novel means of spiritual renewal. Heschel's emerging involvement as a representative of the Hebrew prophets in interfaith meetings, in addition to Jewish audiences, spoke directly to the American people confronting these uncertainties.

As the 1960s began, the national mood became more confident. At his presidential inauguration on January 20, 1961, John Fitzgerald Kennedy promised Americans that they were on the cusp of a "new frontier." Civil rights for African Americans became a mass movement under the banner of Martin Luther King Jr. and his Southern Christian Leadership Conference; their slogan, "Redeem the Soul of America," reflected a widespread commitment to the democratic process.

Christianity, too, sought renewal. Employing his authority as a consultant for the American Jewish Committee, Heschel began working with Roman Catholic Church officials to influence what would turn out to be historic debates on Jews and Judaism at the Second Vatican Council. Between 1961 and 1965 Heschel was involved in intricate negotiations with church officials (see chapter 11 for the full story).

INTERFAITH INITIATIVES

Heschel's standing among the Protestant majority was confirmed by an invitation in 1956 to present "A Hebrew Evaluation of Reinhold Niebuhr" in a volume of the *Library of Living Theologians*, an authoritative series of scholarly studies of leading thinkers.[1]

Adapting several pages from the manuscript of *God in Search of Man* (then still in progress), Heschel formed an incisive study of moral ambiguity in Niebuhr's theology developed around the theme "the confusion of good and evil." He began by emphasizing certain commonalities in Judaism and Christianity. Niebuhr's harsh theology of original sin (sin that cannot be erased through human efforts), his "awareness of the mystery of evil," and his antagonism to optimistic or utopian conceptions of liberal religions (what Niebuhr called "sentimentality" and "unrealism") were all congruent with the teachings in certain Jewish mystical texts, as well as the biblical books of the prophets Isaiah and Habakkuk and the Psalms. Above all, Heschel agreed with Niebuhr that the world remained unredeemed. Yet, Heschel could not abide by Niebuhr's contention that human beings were incapable of acts of goodness without divine grace.

Good and evil are not entirely separable, Heschel averred. "More frustrating than the fact that evil is real, mighty, and tempting is the fact that it thrives so well in the disguise of the good, and that it can draw its nutriment from the life of the holy." Humankind's basic flaw was self-centeredness or "vanity"; the demands of righteousness were never entirely free from ego needs. Self-interest could be "redeemed," however, by action—for Jews, by fulfilling the mitzvot. This was the hope Judaism offered. Heschel concluded diplomatically: "It is, therefore, difficult from the point of view of Biblical theology to sustain Niebuhr's view, *plausible and profound as it is* [Heschel's italics]. . . . Niebuhr's life and deeds were more authoritative than his theology."[2]

Niebuhr, most significantly, rejected the Christian mission to convert the Jews as simply "wrong." He justified Judaism's spiritual autonomy by applying the "two covenant theory": God had revealed his will both at Mount Sinai and in the incarnation of Jesus, and these were separate but equally valid incursions of the Divine. In addition, Niebuhr hailed "the thrilling emergence of the State of Israel."[3]

Heschel also contributed to what turned out to be a historic moment in Jewish-Christian relations. In 1957 Louis Finkelstein had arranged the first joint meeting of the faculties of JTS and the nearby liberal Protestant Union Theological Seminary. Was it a surprise that two Union professors, the Old Testament scholar James Muilenburg and Niebuhr, delivered papers both praising Heschel's writings?

This interfaith triumph cemented the firm (and mostly undocumented) friendship of Niebuhr and Heschel, two genuine American spiritual radicals. After Niebuhr gave his historic paper to the joint faculty meeting, the two saw each other regularly, often taking long walks together. Niebuhr's wife, Ursula, a professor of religion at Barnard College, considered Heschel her husband's closest friend during the last twelve years of his life.[4]

The November 1957 Religious Education Association convention then afforded Heschel an ideal opportunity to define his sacred humanism. Academics and leaders of the nation's three major American faiths (Judaism, Protestantism, and Catholicism) gathered to reflect upon the year's topic, "Images of Man in Current Culture and Tasks of Religion and Education."

Heschel deplored the danger of defining humanity in physical terms. He drew an analogy between a materialistic definition in the *Encyclopaedia Britannica* ("Man is a seeker after the greatest degree of comfort for the least necessary expenditure of energy") and a view held in pre-Nazi Germany: "The human body contains a sufficient amount of fat to make seven cakes of soap, enough iron to make a medium-sized nail."[5]

For Heschel, the chief mission of religious education was to "become aware of the sacred image of man." Borrowing from *Man's Quest for God*, he stated that a human being is the only "real symbol" of the Divine—a combination of dust and the divine spark. All human life, each and every individual person, is holy. For Heschel, this noble definition of the human was not just a theological construct, but a visceral, even passionate intuitive certainty.

Heschel argued for a universal ideal of world peace already present in the Hebrew Bible. He cited a daring assertion in Isaiah (19:23–25) predicting a future reconciliation of Egypt, Assyria, and Israel: "Our God is also the God of our enemies, without their knowing Him and despite their defying Him. The enmity between the nations will turn to friendship. They will live together when they will worship together. All three will be equally God's chosen people."[6] Heschel was advancing a biblical philosophy of the human being.

He sought to find common ground for Judaism and Christianity, and even Islam and Asian religions, on the foundation of the Hebrew Bible. He went on to expand the "Sacred Images of Man" speech into an article, which first appeared in the *Christian Century*. He then carefully revised the piece for the convention issue of *Religious Education*. Next he enriched the essay to represent the Jewish viewpoint alongside Greek, Chinese, Christian, and Hindu views in his contribution to the impressive collection called *The Concept of Man: A Study in Comparative Philosophy*, edited by two Indian philosophers, Sarvepalli Radhakrishnan (also a statesman) and P. T. Raju.

By 1958 the role of religion in a free society was widely recognized as a national concern. That May, Heschel joined more than a hundred distinguished lawyers, professors, clergy, educators, and publicists at the World Affairs Center in New York in a multiday interfaith conference organized by the noninstitutional think tank Fund for the Republic. Among the conference participants were Paul Tillich, professor of systematic theology at Harvard Divinity School; Will Herberg, who was now teaching Judaic studies at Drew University; and Reinhold Niebuhr, a member of the Fund's Committee of Consultants. Forums were held on religious pluralism and civic unity, church and state, the question of religion in the public schools, the secular challenge, and other national policy issues.

Adhering to the American constitutional separation of "church and state," Heschel had clarified his religious critique of contemporary politics. Briefly put, he identified "politics" with expediency. Religion, he observed, must rise above pragmatism to represent absolute values, the first of which was the holiness of humankind. Social ills were due in large part to the trivialization of the human image and the degradation of language—a debasing of words, which had to remain truthful repositories of the spirit. Alluding to the ongoing civil rights struggle, Heschel asserted his support for ideological pluralism and faulted the narrowness of institutional religion: "It is an inherent weakness of religion not to take offense at the segregation of God, to forget that the sanctuary has no walls."[7]

Most audacious was Heschel's challenge to America's consumer culture. With questionable logic, he associated the economic depression of pre-Nazi Germany with the worship of comfort and success prevalent in the United States. Referring to sociologist Vance Packard's best-selling exposé of advertising strategies, *The Hidden Persuaders* (1957), Heschel implied that both fascism and capitalism could lead to the abandonment of basic human values: "In times of unemployment, vociferous demagogues are capable of leading people into a state of mind in which they are ready to barter their freedom for any bargain. In times of prosperity, hidden persuaders are capable of leading the people into selling their conscience for success."[8]

Finally, Heschel attacked U.S. government policies that were justified by self-interest rather than democratic generosity: "Foreign aid, when offered to underdeveloped countries, for the purpose of winning friends and influencing people, turns out to be a boomerang. Should we not learn how to detach expediency from charity?"[9]

THE PROPHETS

Heschel was laboring on at least two fronts, one public and the other scholarly, for the ancient Hebrew prophets had become his models of spiritual and ethical renewal. While completing his translation and major revision of his 1933 doctoral thesis from the University of Berlin, he continued to promote religious education and his masterwork on the prophets. In February 1958 he explained his bold pedagogy of biblical Judaism to religious school teachers attending a Cleveland Bureau of Jewish Education conference. With this sympathetic and knowledgeable audience, Heschel was relaxed, a master teacher.

He came right to the point. Judaism had been "trivialized." The chief problem facing religious teachers was to confront "spiritual illiteracy" by elevating the level of thinking among their students. "Intellectual vulgarity" was detaching Judaism from "the living issues of the human soul." Americans tended to be hedonists, viewing religion in pragmatic terms: "The body is the supreme object of worship. Of course, God is also served, because He is useful. Why not let there be a God? It's nice," he declared sarcastically. Heschel provoked his fellow educators, hurting some feelings when he added: "Sometimes I wonder whether bad Jewish education isn't worse than no education at all."[10]

In his battle against mediocrity, Heschel urged teachers to concentrate on spiritual insight. Above all, he explained, teachers should cultivate awe: "The real theme of most of my books is the problem, why have faith at all? . . . The first step is the sense of wonder in the face of all existence, the entrance to faith."

In the question-and-answer session that followed, Heschel skillfully elucidated some pragmatic but fundamental issues facing teachers of the biblical prophets:

Question: "How can one make this subject concrete and real to the eighth grade children?"

Heschel: "I think one can. But first of all let us ask: 'Is this subject concrete and real to us?' . . . I have said this to teachers many times: Important as technique is, the *neshamah* [the soul] is more important than technique."[11]

Once again, Heschel was transforming a nagging pedagogical problem into a spiritual opportunity.

He was pressed about divine revelation, the main dividing line between traditional and progressive religionists. When asked whether prophecy was possible today, he affirmed it, now expanding on a crucial source he had first cited in his 1950 Hebrew essay on the Holy Spirit:

> In the Book of Deuteronomy [5:19], after describing the voice the people heard at Sinai, there occurs the following phrase: *kol Gadol v'lo yasaf*, a great voice, and *v'lo yasaf*. What does *v'lo yasaf* mean? Two interpretations are found in rabbinic literature. One, a great voice was at Sinai, but nevermore. The second interpretation is, a great voice that never ceased. The voice of Sinai goes on forever. I am very excited about the fact that we have both interpretations. If we only had one interpretation; namely, a great voice but nevermore, we would have petrified Jews. If we had only the second interpretation, a great voice that never ceases, we would have slippery Jews, relativists. How marvelous that we have both interpretations. They supplement each other.[12]

Traditionalists, Heschel was saying, could also be pluralists, tolerant of and even recognizing contradictory views. Pluralists, on the other hand, by affirming the factuality of divine revelation, could also become traditionalists. Through this application of depth theology, he hoped to bridge the abyss dividing secular, liberal, and "Torah-true" Jews.

ISRAEL AND THE DIASPORA

In addition to exploring issues of religion for both interfaith and Jewish audiences, Heschel was now challenging his Jewish audiences politically, through a series of lectures on the Israel-Diaspora relationship.

Growing up in prewar Europe, Heschel had encountered virtually all approaches to Zionism. His elders in Warsaw were leaders in the Agudah, the ultra-Orthodox organization that resisted modernity and opposed settlement in Palestine before the coming of the Messiah. Yet his daily prayers, like those of all observant Jews, called for the eventual ingathering of the dispersed people in the Holy Land. In Poland, Heschel had become close to dedicated Zionists such as Fishl Schneersohn and Schneur Zalman Rubashov (as Zalman Shazar, the third president of Israel, was then known); in Germany, his closest friends had included the Zionists David Koigen and Martin Buber.

In America, Heschel's zeal for the Jewish state was eclectic, tempered by his universal standards, his prophetic integrity. His social and political commitment to the Jewish state, however, was essentially spiritual, as he had asserted in *God in Search of Man*—justified by the Bible's ancient claims. Meanwhile, Heschel was also adept at Modern Hebrew literature and its cultural nationalism. And while he was not a Zionist in the classical sense, intent upon settling in Palestine or the new State of Israel, he nonetheless considered Israel inseparable from Jewish communities in the Diaspora, where he chose to remain.

His publications challenged Jewish secularism. In 1951 he published his programmatic essay "To Be a Jew" in the inaugural issue of *Zionist Quarterly*, founded by the Zionist Organization of America. In it he unequivocally proclaimed the priority of God: "Israel is a spiritual order in which the human and the ultimate, the natural and the holy, enter a lasting covenant, in which kinship with God is not an aspiration but a reality of destiny."[13]

Heschel longed to visit the Holy Land, and in August 1957 he was finally able to do so. Zalman Shazar, as acting chairman of the Department of Education and Culture in the Diaspora, an Israeli government agency, invited Heschel to speak at the "Ideological Conference," an international gathering of Zionist representatives in Jerusalem. (This was a tremendous gift because Heschel could not afford the trip without institutional support; his salary at the Jewish Theological Seminary remained low despite his growing prominence.) Given the approaching tenth anniversary of Israel's Declaration of Independence and the controversial Sinai invasion of October–November 1956, Israelis felt the need to reflect on their past—and their future. Heschel and other leaders would help evaluate the spiritual health of the developing Jewish state.

Shazar's invitation inspired Heschel to grow a beard. "How could I visit the Land of Israel without a beard?" he told Wolfe Kelman. Heschel formed his appearance prudently, beginning with a neat goatee.[14]

Heschel, Sylvia, and now five-year-old Susannah first flew to London, where they spent a week visiting Heschel's brother Jacob. The Heschels went on to Paris for another week, where they probably saw Heschel's first cousin Tova Perlow Monthéard. Heschel wrote enthusiastically to his friend Wolfe Kelman: "Such experiences add perspective and scope even to a parochial mind." Then the Heschels flew to Jerusalem, settling in a pension on Abravanel Street.[15]

The Israeli press expected substantial insights to emerge from this international Zionist gathering, especially from Heschel, whose reputation as a unique Jewish theologian had preceded him. After ten days in the country, Heschel was featured in an article in the English-language *Jerusalem Post* as a "fusion" of "Jewish mystic" and "modern scholar." The reporter commented that Heschel's provocative stances might help "emancipate people's minds from the clichés and banalities in which so many of us are involved."[16]

On August 15, 1957, Heschel brought his challenge to the conference participants at the Hebrew University. Speaking in Hebrew, he sought to persuade intransigent nationalists that Jews in the Diaspora were one with the Israeli people and to persuade belligerent secularists that authentic Judaism demanded more than just acquiescence to ritual law. True to his oppositional stance, as an American Jew he insisted upon the necessity of Jewish life outside the Holy Land: "The people of Israel is a tree whose roots are in Israel and the branches in the Diaspora. A tree cannot flourish without roots. But how can it bear fruit without branches? Be careful with the branches!"[17]

He also examined the relationship of Jewish religion to the nation and to God: "Only in Israel are the people and Torah one. . . . The depravity of civilization is proof that a godless people [the Nazis] is bound to become a satanic people." Going deeper, he evoked Zechariah's image of the brand plucked from the fire (Zech. 2:3) to proclaim: "Every one of us alive is a spark of an eternal candle and a smoldering ember snatched from the fire. Without his knowing it, every one of us is crowned with the Holy. Let us learn to be aware of the majesty which hovers over our existence."[18]

Opposing Israel's pervasive secularism, Heschel asserted the primacy of religion for all Jews. In fact, he subordinated the "national problem" of establishing a Jewish homeland to "the spiritual plight of the individual . . . especially in the Diaspora." In order for Judaism to survive, rabbinical authorities must become more flexible, he warned: "A Judaism confined to the limits of *halakhah*, with all due respect be it said, is not exactly one of the happiest products of the Diaspora. Such condescension and parochialism has little of the sweep and power of the prophets."

Even as he recognized that few individuals enjoyed "perfect faith," Heschel quixotically demanded an uncompromising religious commitment. He urged his audience, many of whom were fierce atheists, to cultivate humility and a yearning for God. Religion and nation were interdependent, and there was a definite scale of importance: "Judaism stands on four pillars: on God, the Torah, the people of Israel, and the land of Israel. The loss of any one of these entails the loss of the others; one depends on the other."

A post-conference meeting with several leaders at the home of

Prime Minister David Ben-Gurion confirmed for Heschel the necessity of continuing to advance spiritual values. In his report to the Conservative movement's Rabbinical Assembly (RA) conference the following April, Heschel explained that Ben-Gurion had not asked his visitors about "forming new organizations or arranging national demonstrations," but rather: "Why do you believe in God?"[19]

Heschel also refocused and presented his Israel speech to the RA. He joined Mordecai Kaplan in the session on interpreting the relations between "the people" (*am*), "the land" (*eretz*), and "the community or state" (*medinah*). For Heschel, Israel's mere existence was not enough; what mattered was its quality of Jewish life: "The question is not how to make the State meaningful to the Jews of America, but how to make the State worthy of 2,000 years of waiting."

Heschel applied the notion of *galut* (exile), which usually pertained to Jews living outside the Holy Land, to "the spiritual condition" of all Jews, especially Americans: "Some bar mitzvah affairs are *galut*. Our timidity and hesitance to take a stand on behalf of the Negroes are *galut*." Furthermore, Americans were not the only "exiles": "There is *galut* whenever Judaism is judged by the standards of the market-place and whenever the sense of the holy is replaced by spiritual obtuseness." Even in the Jewish state, "the vital, unquestionable, and indisputable need of maintaining an Israeli army is *galut* too. The fact that the State of Israel must celebrate its birthday by demonstrating its guns and tanks in the streets of Jerusalem, cries out tragically that redemption has not come. In a world which is dark and enmeshed in evil, Israel is not redeemed." Heschel's love for Israel was inseparable from his agonized, prophetic vision of peace.[20]

Yet he had been impressed by the spiritual thirst throughout Israel, the desire for God: "Soldiers complain that the chaplains are concerned with the kashrut of the kitchen rather than with the questions of the mind and the longings of the heart." He suggested that American Jews might show Israelis the right path. Rabbis and laity could cooperate in bringing "the spirit of the Sabbath into the Jewish home, or in trying to build day-schools, or in establishing the habit of studying Torah." A ladder of observance, flexibility, was the way.[21]

Heschel's views were faced with a practical test five months later. On October 27, 1958, Prime Minister Ben-Gurion called on authorities worldwide—writers, academics, and rabbis—to evaluate the status of children of mixed marriages. Along with forty-six other *chachmei Yisrael* (Jewish sages or scholars) from Israel, Europe, and North America, Heschel was invited to answer Ben-Gurion's questionnaire on Jewish identity, designed to determine that status. Here, the ancient conundrum "Who is a Jew?" was being applied to practical matters in the Jewish state—to civil as well as spiritual identity.

Attempting to reconcile the usually antagonistic standards of pluralism and Orthodoxy, Heschel derived his interpretation from "both the *Halakhah* and reality." He affirmed traditional law but welcomed with compassion those who wished to be recognized as Jews yet did not qualify under strict rabbinic standards. At the same time, he rejected those who "tried to base Jewish existence on nationality alone, and to make a distinction between people and religion." A "schism" would spell disaster.[22]

Heschel regretted the Israeli government's loose secular definition: "A theory which proposes that there is a Jewish people without a religion necessarily implies that there is a Jewish religion without a people." He sympathized with the anguish of those for whom the confines of the law were too restrictive: "We cannot force people to believe. Faith brought about by coercion is worse than heresy. But we can plant respect in the hearts of our generation." This was Heschel's lifelong task.

To resolve the civil issue of Jewish identity, he formulated an administrative definition that did not undermine the authority of *halakhah*. First, he distinguished between spirit and politics: "The term 'Jew' is a concept both religious and national. As a religious concept it has a fixed definition; as a national concept its meaning is obscure." Therefore, for immigrants whose mothers were not Jewish, it would be better not to define the term "Jew." "If for security reasons a legal resident of Israel needs a document to identify himself, it might be possible for those unable to identify themselves as 'Jews' to be registered as 'Hebrews.' As for the 'Law of Return,' we need not impose rigorous tests."

A year later, in November 1959, Heschel took center stage in an American controversy about politics, Zionism, and religion. "The Great Debate," as it was called in the media, occurred at the biennial convention of the United Synagogue of America, the congregational arm of the Conservative movement. Heschel unexpectedly provoked discord among the thirteen hundred delegates when, speaking at a session on "the future of Zionism and its role in Judaism," he opposed the United Synagogue's joining the World Zionist Organization (WZO), a political action group founded in 1898 to help establish a Jewish state. Since the creation of Israel, the WZO had concentrated on education and problems affecting new immigrants.

Heschel opposed the involvement of religious institutions in politics as firmly as he judged politics according to prophetic standards: "The primary function of the synagogue is to inspire the soul and to instruct the mind; its task is to cultivate faith in God, love of man and understanding of Torah; its goal is holiness; its methods are personal, intellectual, spiritual. The primary function of a political organization is to serve the self-interest of the group it represents; its goal may be holy, yet its methods are adroitness, opportunism and expediency." Even sacred ends could not justify some means.[23]

After Heschel finished his speech, Mordecai Kaplan immediately demanded the floor to give a strong rebuttal. The *New York Times* reported, in "Jewish Split over Zionist Ties," that Kaplan "denied that the World Zionist Organization was a political party in any sense, and expressed 'amazement' at Dr. Heschel's views." WZO president Nahum Goldmann similarly rejected Heschel's reasoning as "an empty excuse." But Simon Greenberg, a JTS professor and Conservative pulpit rabbi, agreed with Heschel that support for Israel did not require a religious entity to join the World Zionist Organization, and ultimately the delegates decided against affiliation.[24]

THEOLOGY AND ACTIVISM

Due to his unique writing style and often sublime perspective, Heschel's works lacked careful interpreters. That changed in 1959, when Heschel's Jewish Theological Seminary colleague and ally Fritz Rothschild undertook to clarify the fuller context of Heschel's method and system. Heschel had told Rothschild, with some regret, that he himself was not a systematizer and therefore was happy to cooperate in Rothschild's project, *Between God and Man*.

The 1959 anthology included forty-one selections taken from most of Heschel's published works and the manuscript of *The Prophets*, not yet published. Rothschild's meticulous introduction to Heschel's life and works explained his terminology and theological system. Heschel assumed "the fact" of God's concern for humankind and the world; Rothschild called this "the *root metaphor* of his ontology." This divine involvement in human history became Heschel's "conceptual tool to render intelligible such different fields of inquiry as theology, ontology, and ethics." Rothschild also coined a phrase that Heschel happily adopted (with Rothschild's permission): "The pathetic God [that is, the God of pathos] as distinguished from the God of Aristotle is not the Unmoved Mover but the *Most Moved Mover*."[25]

For the first time, Rothschild's anthology provided readers with Heschel's vast Judaic context: Heschel's "exposition is a masterly synthesis in which elements from the whole of Jewish religious tradition from the Bible, Talmud, Midrash, medieval philosophy, Kabbalah, and Hasidism are welded into an organic whole that is held together by the central framework of his philosophy of religion." As John Herman Randall, Rothschild's philosophy professor at Columbia University, exclaimed to Rothschild's delight, "You have succeeded where God himself has failed: making a consistent, systematic philosopher out of Heschel."[26] Indeed, critics could now evaluate Heschel for what he was actually trying to accomplish.

Between God and Man became a prime textbook for courses in modern Jewish philosophy. And its bibliography of Heschel's writings in Europe, Israel, Argentina, and the United States made it a valuable research tool as well.

With that said, Heschel became most intelligible through his public actions. He was now entering a dramatic new phase as a speaker on the national scene. Still more comfortable in his office or in the library, he was being urged to speak at prestigious events by former students who now held influential positions. Wolfe Kelman was executive vice president of the Rabbinical Assembly, and Marc Tanenbaum was executive director of interfaith relations at the Synagogue Council of America, an umbrella group representing all Jewish denominations. Separately and together, the two acted as Heschel's impresarios.[27] Also supporting Heschel was Samuel Dresner, now a pulpit rabbi and editor of *Conservative Judaism.* Although Heschel still lacked support from the Jewish Theological Seminary, he now had a dedicated network.

The first prestigious national forum Heschel was asked to address was the White House "Conference on Children and Youth," initiated in 1909 by President Theodore Roosevelt and held every ten years. Marc Tanenbaum and American Jewish Committee executive vice-president John Slawson, both members of the national group that was organizing the fiftieth-anniversary gathering, chose Heschel to develop the Jewish perspective. More than seven thousand delegates representing a variety of professional fields and religious origins attended from March 27 through April 2, 1960.[28]

President Eisenhower opened the convocation at the University of Maryland in College Park. In keeping with the tenor of the time, he supported any religious faith that would convey "such truths as the transcendent value of the individual and the dignity of all people, the futility and stupidity of war, its destructiveness of life and its degradation of human values."[29]

Heschel's message, which applied "moral and spiritual values" to social issues, was received with enthusiasm. Echoing resolutions against discrimination based on race, color, or creed, he stood behind the civil rights movement: "How can we speak of reverence for man and of the belief that all men are created equal without repenting the way we behave toward our brothers, the colored people of America?" In the idiom of a spiritual revolutionary, he thrilled the audience with a call for "*a radical reorientation of our thinking.*"

The American Jewish Committee's interfaith relations department distributed hundreds of mimeographed copies of Heschel's speech around the country.[30] The next day many of his striking formulations were featured in the *Washington Post*: "the greatest threat" was not the atomic bomb but our "callousness to the suffering of man."[31]

Soon after his electrifying speech, the University of Minnesota offered him a nine-week appointment (April–May 1960) at the prestigious religion program sponsored by the Danforth Foundation. As Heschel, Sylvia, and now eight-year-old Susannah settled in Saint Paul, Heschel taught an undergraduate course on Maimonides and a graduate seminar on the prophets. He also gave nine public lectures under the general topic "The Intellectual Relevance of Judaism."[32]

During his two months in Minnesota, Heschel took a step that would enhance his public image in the years to come: he had let his goatee and graying hair grow longer. With his salt-and-pepper waves and full whiskers, Heschel looked more the way the public expected a major Jewish thinker to look. Especially during his civil rights and antiwar activities, he would appear as an "Old Testament prophet" to the Christian majority.

In the fall of 1960, John F. Kennedy was attempting to become the first Catholic president of the United States. Upset by the media obsession with Kennedy's minority religion, *CrossCurrents* editor Joseph E. Cunneen dedicated a full issue of the interfaith journal to the national problem of religious bigotry. Cunneen positioned an essay offering a Jewish perspective by "Rabbi Heschel" (as Heschel was described) directly after his own editorial, which offered possible solutions to the political prejudices of the American majority. Here Heschel turned his first University of Minnesota lecture, "Depth Theology," into a well-constructed rationale for religious pluralism.[33]

Heschel's pedagogically astute notion of depth theology assumed a firm distinction between dogma and experiential, intuitive awareness of the living God. Referring to the dangers of fundamentalism, he described dogma as "a poor man's share in the divine. A creed is almost all a poor man has. Skin for skin, he will give his life for all that he has. Yea, he may be ready to take other people's lives, if they refuse to share his tenets." On the contrary, depth theology, he taught, was committed to finding common ground between seekers of faith.

Owing to the continued efforts of his former students, Heschel was being asked to supply the "Jewish perspective" on a number of national issues. On January 9, 1961, two days before his fifty-fourth birthday, he returned to Washington to deliver a paper to the White House Conference on Aging. Attending the four-day meeting were more than seven hundred activists and practitioners in the fields of gerontology, religion, family life, education, medicine, and social welfare. Organized by the outgoing Eisenhower administration, the conference was strongly influenced by the agenda of president-elect John F. Kennedy, especially his far-reaching plan to broaden health care for the elderly by tying it directly to the Social Security system.

Heschel broadcast one of his most vivid analyses of the human condition. "The Older Person and the Family in the Perspective of Jewish Tradition" began by elevating the ethical commandment to honor your father and mother to its spiritual essence: "There is no reverence for God without reverence for father and mother." With sarcasm, he then deplored widespread attempts to disguise age: "You find more patients in the beauty parlors than in the hospitals. We would rather be bald than gray. A white hair is an abomination."[34]

Most grievous, Heschel asserted, was the spiritual crisis of old age, the "sense of emptiness and boredom, the sense of being useless to, and rejected by, family and society, loneliness and the fear of time." For this Heschel offered some practical solutions. By attending to their own inner growth, older citizens could transform society: "What the nation needs is *senior universities*, education toward wisdom in the value of time. . . . *Just to be is a blessing, just to live is holy. The moment is a marvel*; it is in evading the marvel of the moment that boredom begins which ends in despair." In an era where religion and ritual no longer enriched family communication, parents needed to find ways to share with their children "moments of exaltation," so when the children grew up and their parents aged, they would willingly remain connected to their elders as they entered their final years.[35]

Heschel was the star of the conference. His audience was transfixed by his assessment, his astute solutions, and his eloquence. Subsequently, the Synagogue Council of America distributed the speech as an attractive pamphlet, "To Grow in Wisdom." It also appeared in two issues of the *Congressional Record* and became one of Heschel's most widely reprinted occasional writings.[36]

SPIRITUALLY RADICAL PEDAGOGY

In the spring and fall of 1962, Heschel took up the fight for religious education at three conferences: the Rabbinical Assembly, the World Council of Synagogues, and the interfaith Religious Education Association. He used the phrase "spiritual audacity" throughout them all.

That year the Rabbinical Assembly devoted its convention to institutional self-examination. According to Wolfe Kelman's yearly report, the main problem for American Jews was not assimilation or intermarriage but rather the quality of Jewish education.[37] Heschel, featured at a session on "The Values of Jewish Education," immediately challenged his colleagues: "The disease from which we suffer is *intellectual* as well as *spiritual illiteracy*; *ignorance* as well as *idolatry of false values*. We are a generation devoid of learning as well as sensitivity. . . . I insist that the *vapidity of religious instruction* is a major cause of this failure."[38] Heschel deplored the "trivialization" of Judaism though secularization, in which sacred "mysteries" were replaced with "customs and ceremonies," thereby demoting God's commandments to folkways. Teachers had to learn to inspire the inner person, to unlock the reverence and awe contained in Judaism's most common prayers. Education had to become "an event."

At the same time, Heschel acknowledged his own feelings of inadequacy as a teacher: "I have been a *melammed* [teacher] all my life. I know how hard it is to teach. The first moment of each class is like the hour in which the Jews stood at the Red Sea."[39]

Meanwhile, Heschel continued to promote a sacred humanism, reverence for all individuals throughout the world. Challenging the current death-of-God ideologies, he demanded a renewal of faith in the holy potential of human striving: "The central issue is not man's decision to extend formal recognition to God, to furnish God with a certificate that He exists, but the realization of our importance to God's design; not to prove that God is alive, but to prove that man is not dead." (At the World Council of Synagogues convention, Heschel would deliver essentially the same speech.)

The following November he adapted his Jewish educational manifesto for the more than eight hundred predominantly Christian delegates attending the Religious Education Association convention.

Now excised of Hebrew quotations as well as almost all references to specifically Jewish problems, his retitled "Idols in the Temples" speech retained the same message: the Hebrew Bible was for everyone a source of divine presence and a call to action.[40]

TALMUDIC PLURALISM AND THE PROPHETS

Heschel did not let his enterprising public life hold back his specialized scholarship. Drawing from his lifelong memory of the Bible, medieval and modern commentaries, Kabbalah, and Talmud, his new book in Hebrew, *Heavenly Torah as Refracted through the Generations* (*Torah Min Ha-shamayim Be-aspaklaryah Shel Ha-dorot*), traced the classical sources of his pluralistic theology. In his own modern voice, Heschel asserted: "There is a grain of the prophet in the recesses of every human existence."[41]

In 1962 Soncino Press in London and New York published the first volume of this encyclopedic study of the Talmud, written in richly evocative Hebrew. Heschel's scholarly agenda was again oppositional: first, to demonstrate how the Talmud conveyed dynamic theological reflections, not just legalistic dialectics; and, more importantly, to display the congruence of Rabbinic theology and prophetic inspiration.

True to his system of polarities, Heschel organized the vast corpus around two opposing "schools" and personalities, those of the first- and second-century talmudic sages Rabbi Akiva (Akiba ben Joseph) and Rabbi Ishmael (Ismael ben Elisha). Both rabbis, of course, believed that Moses received the Torah at Mount Sinai, but they diverged on how to interpret the meaning of this divine revelation. According to Heschel's contrast, Akiva was a mystic for whom every word, jot, and tittle of the Torah scrolls, even the crowns on the Hebrew letters, held hidden meaning. For Akiva, "the true Torah is in Heaven." Rabbi Ishmael, on the other hand, was a rationalist who emphasized the text's plain meaning. For him, "the Torah speaks the language of human beings." Together, these two personalities reflected Heschel's complex temperament and theological inclusiveness, which welcomed contradictions.[42]

However, Heschel's sympathy lay with Rabbi Akiva, a "poet at heart, and at the same time a razor-sharp genius." Akiva sought to "arouse the public, to demand action from them, to be their guide. . . . He was a man of action, a spokesman for his people, a public servant, and a traveler to lands beyond the sea." Above all, Heschel located his own synthesis of intellect and intuition in Akiva, and his activism as well.

There was also a professional reason to write this major book on the Talmud. Heschel was seeking a *heksher* (certificate of kashrut) for his open-minded theology of revelation. This study, provisionally called the "Battle of the Books," defined Rabbinic Judaism as both supernatural in its origin and open to diverse interpretations.

Furthermore, Heschel was impelled to write *Heavenly Torah* for even more intimate reasons. At the heart of his approach to Talmud was a desire for attachment to God, as he would state in the introduction to volume 2, published in 1965.

The book's dedication implies yet another poignant motivation, as it recalls his most acute personal losses: "To the memory of my mother, the saintly Rivka Reizel, and to the memory of my sisters, Devorah Miriam, Esther Sima, and Gittel, who perished in the Shoah. May their souls be kept among the immortals." Heschel then cited a midrashic reflection on Deut. 32:4: "The Rock! His deeds are perfect, / Yea, all His ways are just." In this both explicit and discreet manner, cloaked in bitter irony, Heschel advocated Akiva's affirmation of God's justice despite the horrible state of the world.[43]

While writing *Heavenly Torah*, Heschel also finished transforming his German doctoral dissertation on the prophets into an inspiring book for Americans. In the meantime, he published excerpts from the manuscript. He placed one selection in *Judaism*; another in a volume honoring Rabbi Leo Jung, an intellectual leader of Modern

Orthodoxy; and translations in *Évidence* (published in France by Congrès juif mondial), among others.

Finally, in May 1962 Heschel delivered the almost completed manuscript to Harper and Row. *The Prophets*, published in February 1963, was an impressive volume of nearly five hundred pages.

Heschel had now completed the bridge between his European and American lives, both of which were defined by the prophets of ancient Israel. In his introduction, dated August 1962, Heschel asserted his preference for phenomenology over the historical-critical methods favored by most scholars. Contrasting the scientific approach he had practiced as a doctoral candidate in Berlin—"pure reflection" on prophetic consciousness—and his present stance of personal involvement, he now insisted that a detached, academic approach is impossible, even irresponsible.[44] For Heschel, the prophets spoke compellingly to the present world.

Heschel employed some of his most captivating prose, replete with poetic devices such as alliteration and assonance, to evoke his empathy with those ancient radicals, the prophets: "The situation of a person immersed in the prophets' words is one of being exposed to a ceaseless shattering of indifference, and one needs a skull of stone to remain callous to such blows." He hoped readers of all faiths would experience "communion with the prophets," who were models of *"exegesis of existence from a divine perspective."* Thus Heschel laid the biblical groundwork of his activism.

Heschel began with a dedication "to the martyrs of 1940–45" and ended the dedication with the bitterest question to God: "Why dost Thou hide Thy face?" He was continuing to ask, as he had a decade earlier in *Man Is Not Alone*: What is the meaning, if any, of the Nazi genocide?[45]

Each prophet provided a specific approach to truth. The preface and early chapters sketched their personalities, historical background, and messages. The middle chapters defined biblical notions of history, justice, chastisement, the theology of pathos, and the religion of sympathy. The latter chapters examined various methods in order to shield the mystery of divine revelation from being minimized by psychological or anthropological explanations of ecstasy, poetic inspiration, or psychosis. Heschel concluded with the notion of God as divine Subject, the keynote of his theology.

This apparently objective treatise took on vehement tones as he showed how the prophets criticized opportunistic religion and power politics: "Few are guilty, but all are responsible. If we admit that the individual is in some way conditioned or affected by the spirit of society, an individual's crime discloses society's corruption." Prophetic Judaism was a forceful and subversive antidote: "The purpose of prophecy is to conquer callousness, to change the inner man as well as to revolutionize history." The prophet was not a diplomat; he stood outside social norms: "The prophet hates the approximate, he shuns the middle of the road. . . . The prophet is strange, one-sided, an unbearable extremist."[46]

Perhaps the book's most powerful contribution was its autobiographical dimension. Close to Heschel's own sensibility were the prophets Hosea, Isaiah, and Jeremiah, in part because they voiced something of his own piercing marginality: "[The prophet] alienates the wicked as well as the pious, the cynics as well as the believers, the priests and the princes, the judges and the false prophets."

Hosea, especially, suffered because of his sympathy with God's anger at unfaithful Israel. According to Heschel, God made Hosea suffer the sorrow and anguish of his wife's infidelity for one purpose: so that the prophet would feel in his gut God's own suffering because of Israel's betrayals of the covenant. Hosea was Heschel's model of the divine pathos.

Later, during the Vietnam War, Heschel would emulate Isaiah in denouncing the U.S. government's arrogance and most Americans' moral apathy: "Callousness is sovereign and smug; it clings to the soul and will not give in." Isaiah rejected tactical politics and military power; instead, he devoted himself to "the day when nations 'shall beat their swords into plowshares and their spears into pruning hooks.'"[47]

The prophet known as Second Isaiah became Heschel's model of faith after the Holocaust: "It is a prophecy tempered with human tears, mixed with a joy that heals all scars. . . . No words have gone further in offering comfort when the sick world cries." The people Israel, who were God's "suffering servant," were thus prepared to accept the mystery of unjust suffering. In the end, God's love would prevail. Human agony could be given meaning.[48]

Most intimately, the prophet Jeremiah reflected Heschel's inner, emotional combat. Both men could be raw, hypersensitive, extremely vulnerable. Jeremiah endured a "hypertrophy of sympathy" in which emotions carried him way beyond the limits of his better judgment: "Such excess of sympathy with the divine wrath shows the danger of sympathy grown absolute," Heschel declared. Sometimes Heschel, too, seemed to lose control of his indignation, as when he would demonstrate acute highest sensitivity in the presence of ranking government officials. Once, for example, as part of a committee of clergy opposed to the Vietnam war, meeting in 1967 with Robert McNamara, secretary of defense, Heschel suddenly burst forth with dismay at the needless killing.

Of all Heschel's books to date, *The Prophets* received the widest critical attention in both academic and general, Christian and Jewish, publications. Christians admired his dramatic account of their Old Testament precursors. Samuel Terrien of Union Theological Seminary concluded, "It would be difficult, if not impossible, to find elsewhere a more lucid and compelling appreciation for the reality of the divine pathos."[49]

Jewish critics involved in ideological debates were more divided. In *Commentary*, David Daiches, professor of literature at the University of Sussex, England, objected that Heschel avoided the enigma of why the righteous suffer, and he dismissed the author's contention that "history is a nightmare" as another of his "vague generalizations." On the positive side, Daiches appreciated Heschel's poetic instinct for the prophet's compassion for God.[50]

Confusion about Heschel's views on (and use of) metaphorical language aroused the ire not only of Daiches, a secularist, but also of Eliezer Berkovits, an Orthodox Jew. Writing in a new journal, *Tradition: A Journal of Orthodox Thought*, Berkovits rejected Heschel's notion of divine pathos as non-Jewish: "The boldness of Dr. Heschel's thought consists, first, in taking literally all biblical expressions that ascribe to God emotions of love and hatred."[51]

On the other side of the argument, the Bible scholar and Orthodox rabbi David Shlomo Shapiro, writing in Hebrew in *Hadoar* (the American Hebrew-language newspaper), praised Heschel's synthesis of theology and ethics: "There is no dichotomy of pathos and ethos, of motive and norm. . . . It is because God is the source of justice that His pathos is ethical; and it is because God is absolutely personal, devoid of anything impersonal, that His ethos is full of pathos."[52]

Especially among Christians, *The Prophets* was widely perceived as a reanimation of the Hebrew spirit, with focus on prayer as well as action. The book soon provided Heschel himself with inspiration—and quotations—as a defender of civil rights and, especially, as an opponent to America's intervention in Vietnam.

CHAPTER 10

A Sacred Humanism, 1963–1966

The year 1963 was a historical watershed for the United States, when highest hopes clashed with bitter disillusionment. The presidency of John F. Kennedy and the civil rights movement seemed to become the nation's spiritual barometers. That January, Americans celebrated the centenary of the Emancipation Proclamation, the abolition of slavery signed in 1863 by President Abraham Lincoln. On June 3 Pope John XXIII passed away, but hopes for the Roman Catholic Church's renewal through the ongoing Second Vatican Council remained strong. Later that summer, on August 28, more than two hundred thousand citizens gathered in Washington DC to demand equal opportunity for blacks and were uplifted by Martin Luther King Jr.'s "I Have a Dream" speech. Then, on November 22, President Kennedy was assassinated, a catastrophe that threatened to destroy the nation's self-confidence.

Heschel took sober measure of the historical moment: "Our world, which is full of cynicism, frustration, and despair, received in 1963 a flash of inspiration; 1963 was a noble year, a triumph of conscience, a triumph of faith. It will depend upon us whether 1963 will remain a chapter in sacred history."[1]

Having experienced the ravages of European antisemitism, Heschel abhorred American racism of any kind—a sentiment that took hold soon after he stepped off the boat in 1940. Among the affronts he witnessed were the prejudices African Americans endured. The year after the 1954 Supreme Court decision outlawing segregation in public schools, Heschel began to denounce racial discrimination, making a sharp pronouncement to the Rabbinical Assembly evoking the decision that deplored "our timidity and hesitance to take a stand on behalf of the Negroes." By 1963 the imperative to act had arrived.[2]

For the first time in American history, leaders of the country's three major faiths—Catholicism, Judaism, and Protestantism—organized a nationwide meeting for a candid discussion of race relations. Again, it was Marc Tanenbaum, seconded by Wolfe Kelman, both forceful supporters of civil rights, who featured Heschel. Tanenbaum presided over a planning session for the first National Conference on Religion and Race, to be held in Chicago in January 1963. Heschel was chosen to be the keynote speaker at the opening plenary session, where he would provide "the prophetic inspirational statement," according to an internal memorandum.[3]

Heschel, now author of the newly published magisterial book *The Prophets*, would be transformed. More than 650 voting delegates and 200 local observers were present at the opening plenary on January 14, at which the conference chairman, Morehouse College president Dr. Benjamin E. Mays, read greetings from President Kennedy and then introduced Abraham Joshua Heschel.[4]

Heschel's address, "The Religious Basis of Equality and Opportunity," drawing on striking formulations from *The Prophets* and delivered in dramatic biblical cadences, stirred the predominantly Christian audience. Alluding to international summit meetings of the Cold War era, Heschel associated the current racial situation with the Israelite epic of liberation from slavery:

At the first conference on religion and race, the main participants were Pharaoh and Moses. Moses' words were: "Thus says the Lord, the God of Israel, let my people go that they may celebrate a feast to me." While Pharaoh retorted: "Who is the Lord, that I should heed this voice and let Israel go? I do not know the Lord, and moreover I will not let Israel go." The outcome of that summit meeting has not come to an end. Pharaoh is not ready to capitulate. The exodus began, but is far from having been completed. In fact, it was easier for the children of Israel to cross the Red Sea than for a Negro to cross certain university campuses.[5]

Heschel then restated one of his most forceful injunctions from the Talmud: "It is better . . . to throw oneself alive into a burning furnace than to humiliate a human being publicly."

He further proclaimed that indifference was the attitude preventing the white majority from embracing the imperative of universal human dignity. Urgently needed was nothing less than a transformation of the nation's soul: "*The Negro problem is God's gift to America*, the test of our integrity, a magnificent spiritual opportunity." Hopeful, even optimistic, he cited Pope John XXIII, who had opened the Twenty-First Ecumenical Council with the following words: "Divine Providence is leading us to a new order of human relations." Heschel concluded, "History has made us all neighbors. The age of moral mediocrity and complacency has run out. This is a time for radical commitment, for radical action."

Martin Luther King Jr. closed the Chicago conference with a bold, authoritative speech entitled "Challenge to the Churches and the Synagogues." Like Heschel, who deplored the mediocrity of institutional religion, King chastised organized Christianity as untrue to its root values. He shared Heschel's central focus on the sanctity of the human being in the eyes of God: "Segregation denies the sacredness of the human personality. . . . Human worth lies in relatedness to God. An individual has value because he has value to God."[6]

Time magazine published a brief, though pessimistic, account of the event: "The dominant mood of the four-day meeting . . . was what one participant called 'that awful fatalism.'" However, the issue also devoted two columns to Heschel's recent book *The Prophets*, accompanied by a photograph. Touting him as "one of the world's most illustrious Jewish theologians," *Time* praised Heschel for his "prophetlike" intervention at the conference: "He was a mordant critic of religious ineffectiveness in U.S. race question [*sic*]."[7]

Heschel and Martin Luther King Jr. had met for the first time at this conference and quickly became allies. They realized they shared basic ways of perceiving the world, not least a commitment to nonviolence and a biblical theology grounded in the Israelites' liberation from slavery in Egypt. Both men were charismatic orators at the fullness of their powers—Heschel as a writer and speaker, the younger King as a preacher and movement leader. Each had also been influenced by Reinhold Niebuhr's activist theology and was using it to help communicate a minority perspective to the American mainstream.

For Heschel, another consequence of the conference was being invited to join four hundred Christian and Jewish clergy for a meeting with President Kennedy and his brother Robert, the attorney general, in the East Room of the White House. On June 16, 1963, the day before the event, Heschel sent the president a telegram, proclaiming, "Let religious leaders donate one month's salary toward fund for Negro housing and education. I propose that you Mr. President declare a state of moral emergency. A Marshall Plan for aid to Negroes is becoming a necessity. The hour calls for high moral grandeur and spiritual audacity."[8]

The national event served as a model for action. Similar conferences to the Chicago assembly continued to be instituted across the country after President Kennedy's assassination on November 22, 1963. These local meetings became the most practical manner of forming coalitions among people of different races, religions, and classes. In February 1964 Heschel addressed one such interfaith meeting in Manhattan, under the auspices of the Metropolitan New York Conference on Religion and Race. More than two thousand clergy and laity participated in the daylong series of meetings.[9]

Heschel spoke at the dinner session along with New York mayor Robert Wagner and archbishop of New York Francis Cardinal Spellman. Updating his Chicago speech, Heschel delivered an even more forceful presentation, "The White Man on Trial." With the memories of the civil rights and anti-poverty March on Washington the preceding August still vivid, Heschel again cited the Exodus from Egypt. This time he compared the grumbling of the Israelites wandering in the desert to the legitimate complaints of African Americans, speaking ironically: "The Negroes of America behave just like the children of Israel. . . . Now three months later they have the audacity to murmur: 'What shall we drink? We want adequate education, decent housing, proper employment.' How ordinary, how unpoetic, how annoying!"

Sharpening his criticism of white complacency, Heschel mockingly condemned the optimistic national mood: "Life could be so pleasant. The Beatles have just paid us a visit. The AT&T is about to split its stocks. Dividends are higher than ever. Vietnam has a sensible government. Castro is quiet and well-mannered. Khrushchev is purchasing grain from us. Only the Negroes continue to disturb us: What shall we drink?"[10]

Heschel's rhetoric was provocative, and his goals ambitious: he envisioned nothing less than a worldwide "spiritual revolution." Religion, which demanded inner integrity of its adherents, was the most authentic vehicle for social transformation. Legislation was indispensable, of course, but "true fellowship" and "democratization" of education had to be founded not only on "riding on the same bus," but on the ability to share "moments of joy, cultural values, insights, commitments."

Meanwhile, world history was at a turning point, and Heschel believed he was speaking for all persecuted peoples, not only American blacks, but also "the people in Tibet, the hungry masses in India and Brazil, the sick and the poor, the wetbacks, the Braceros in our own country."

Locally, Heschel became involved in the power struggle between neighborhood black leaders and the predominantly Jewish Teachers Union in New York City. For example, who should control the curriculum? (He was not able to help the antagonists find a satisfactory compromise.) He opposed school boycotts threatened by community activists, but he also supported a busing system for the higher grades so that black students could attend the more successful schools. Heschel signed a letter to the *New York Times* urging that the city provide superior integrated education to all its children. He also joined the Coalition for Integrated Education and forcefully expressed his views at meetings.[11]

By 1965 Heschel moved beyond giving speeches, publishing essays, and attending meetings condemning racial discrimination to join protests in the streets. His fuller involvement was instigated by a brutal police assault on nonviolent black protesters in Selma, Alabama. John Lewis, chairman of the Student Non-Violent Coordinating Committee, and Hosea Williams, aide to Dr. King in the Southern Christian Leadership Conference, had initiated a small, relatively spontaneous march from Selma to the state capital at Montgomery. On Sunday, March 7, as the hundred or so demonstrators started to cross the Edmund Pettus Bridge to the highway, mounted state troopers unleashed attack dogs and tear gas and severely beat them with clubs. The attack immediately acquired the name "Bloody Sunday."

That evening, an ABC documentary, "Trial at Nuremberg," was interrupted by graphic footage of the current American violence. Heschel was not alone in recognizing the parallels with Nazi Germany proclaimed in nationwide headlines the next day. (The Kristallnacht pogrom of the night of November 9–10, 1938, was originally known as "Bloody Thursday.") Horrified, President Lyndon Johnson pressed his attorney general for solutions, while members of Congress championed legislation to secure voting rights for Americans of African descent.[12]

Americans could no longer deny the racial crisis. Tremendous moral outrage was sparking hundreds of demonstrations throughout the country. Mayors, governors, and religious leaders condemned the segregationists and championed the nonviolent activists. The battle lines could no longer be ignored.

In this atmosphere of upheaval, on March 9, Heschel became a co-leader of a New York City demonstration to protest the attack. Along with young activists from the Student Non-Violent Coordinating Committee (SNCC) and the Congress for Racial Equality (CORE), two groups considered "militant" (code word for extremist) by more established groups, Heschel took part in a "freedom march" to the New York FBI headquarters to deliver a petition demanding protection for voting rights workers and the arrest of violators of federal law. The approximately eight hundred marchers—including students, clergy, and doctors—staged a two-hour protest in front of the FBI offices at Sixty-Ninth Street and Third Avenue. Agents had erected barricades around the entrance to control the demonstrators, who held up traffic as they marched and sang protest songs. Several leaders demanded to see John F. Malone, assistant director of the New York FBI office, but fearing a sit-in, government agents initially refused to let the protestors enter the building.

Director Malone's report stated that he agreed to meet the group's leaders in the lobby, but once he arrived, the SNCC representatives demanded that two additional protestors be included in the meeting. Heschel calmly mediated this dispute. After Malone "explained to the Rabbi that certain representatives of the group had obviously deceived him," Heschel persuaded the delegation of protestors to respect the original agreement. Although Malone's subsequent report had highlighted his composure and restraint during the confrontation and forty-five-minute meeting, this action led to Heschel's inclusion on the FBI list of potential subversives.[13]

The next day Heschel's name was recorded as one of three hundred signers of a *Washington Post* advertisement calling for the repeal of the 1950 McCarran Act, which required that Communists and other suspected "subversives" register with the attorney general. (Senator Joseph McCarthy used it as the basis for his anti-Communist hearings.) "Born in panic and productive of fear," the ad read, "[the McCarran Act] adds nothing to our security and diminishes the honor of a democracy."

From that time on, Heschel appeared on the wide-ranging FBI list of citizens to track. Once the FBI identified someone as a troublemaker, the agency was swift to investigate. Heschel's public stands were documented through direct observation by special agents, reports from informants, and newspaper accounts. Reports marked "secret" were then distributed to several security agencies, as well as to J. Edgar Hoover, who was widely known to be hostile to civil rights.[14]

Heschel was not long in giving them more reports to file away. In the two weeks after Bloody Sunday, a call went out nationwide for a now massive march from Selma to Montgomery, Alabama. This time the five-day march was carefully planned with the major civil rights organizations, including the Southern Christian Leadership Conference (which raised most of the money and prepared the local people), the Student Non-Violent Coordinating Committee, the National Association for the Advancement of Colored People, and the Urban League. This larger protest event also had the protection of the Johnson administration. Under orders from the president, more than eighteen hundred armed Alabama National Guardsmen patrolled the route, with the help of the U.S. Army and about a hundred FBI agents. Helicopters hovered overhead. All around the country, thousands of people chartered airplanes and buses to join the march.

For his part, Heschel felt commanded to protest conspicuously as a voice of biblical justice by exercising his constitutional rights as an American citizen. Despite fears for his safety from his wife and twelve-year-old Susannah, he was ultimately swayed by the urging of his former JTS student Rabbi Everett Gendler, a pacifist, and agreed to join the march. Heschel had accepted his public role as Hebrew prophet.

On March 20, the Saturday night after the Sabbath, just one week after his confrontation with the New York FBI, Heschel and Wolfe Kelman took an airplane to Atlanta, where they stayed overnight. Andrew Young, King's executive assistant at the Southern Christian Leadership Conference, met them, and they drove to Selma in time to begin the march.

Heschel joined Martin Luther King Jr. on Sunday morning at a religious service at Brown's Chapel, where about two hundred people had spent the night, while more than three thousand waited outside. King welcomed the out-of-state participants; then Heschel read from Psalm 27: "The Lord is my might and my salvation; whom shall I fear? / . . . When evil-doers came upon me to eat up my flesh, / Even mine adversaries and my foes, they stumbled and fell." King ended the service with a sermon on the Israelites' long wandering in the wilderness after the Exodus from Egypt.[15] The idiom of the Hebrew Exodus defined what was later known as "the alliance between blacks and Jews."

When it came time to march, Heschel was in the first row of the marchers. With Ralph Bunche, former undersecretary of the United Nations, on his right, and the Reverend Fred Shuttlesworth of the Southern Christian Leadership Conference on his left, Heschel joined Dr. King and the Reverend Ralph Abernathy, King's key aide. Also in front were Archbishop Iakovos of the Greek Orthodox Church, Walter Reuther of the American Federation of Labor and Congress of Industrial Organizations labor union, and John Lewis, the Student

Non-Violent Coordinating Committee chairman, one of the leaders beaten in the previous demonstration. Kelman marched in the second row with Young, who remained attentive to Heschel's well-being.

Afterward the essence of his brief, but deeply felt, participation in the Selma to Montgomery march was captured by a United Press International photograph of him standing with King, Bunche, Shuttlesworth, and Lewis. With his yarmulke, white hair, and beard, he looked like what the popular imagination thought of as a "rabbi." Even more so, Heschel typified and symbolized the media's imagined Hebrew prophet.

Fears for Heschel's safety on the march had been realistic. The onlookers expressed bitter antisemitism in addition to anti-black bigotry. As the demonstrators of all races and faiths, though mostly black, filed slowly through the white section of Selma, hostile spectators cursed and jeered, while old women with sour looks sat in rocking chairs on their porches as above them displayed banners bore such messages as "Koons, Kikes and Niggers Go Home!" Adding to the intimidation, the police drove by, filming the marchers, many of whom found the National Guard presence as intimidating as it was protective.

After four or five hours the procession stopped to rest. Many prominent individuals had planned to return home before reaching the end, after making their gesture of solidarity, among them and Kelman. Other witnesses joined the march along the way or went straight to Montgomery for the culmination.

The Selma to Montgomery march ended four days later on March 25. Nearly fifty thousand people had poured into the capital to hear the final speeches. Back in New York, in a private memorandum, Heschel formulated the spiritual meaning of the protest as he had experienced it. He wrote of previously "having walked with Hasidic rabbis on various occasions." Comparing those times with the present, "I felt a sense of the Holy in what I was doing. . . . Even without words our march was worship. I felt my legs were praying."[16]

Four months later, on August 6, 1965, President Johnson signed the Voting Rights Act, which secured the right to vote for racial minorities throughout the nation.

SAVING SOVIET JEWRY

While expressing his solidarity with African Americans, Heschel was foremost among Jewish leaders in speaking out against the catastrophic situation of Jews in the Soviet Union. Again through the lens of the Holocaust, he judged that Russian Jews were now undergoing a cultural genocide. The Soviet constitution guaranteed freedom of religion to all peoples, but in reality, this applied only to the Russian Orthodox Church and a few Protestant denominations. Roman Catholics had been marginalized, while the Jewish population of more than three million was beset by severe restrictions. Jews were forbidden to operate religious schools; only one theological seminary was still operating, and it was foundering. In addition, approximately four hundred synagogues had been forcibly shut down, leaving only ninety-five. Jewish cemeteries were closed in Moscow, Kiev, and Minsk. There were no prayer books. Sanctioned by the government, antisemitic propaganda proliferated in newspapers.

In America, the Jewish establishment was slow to respond to the situation, held back by political caution, simple ignorance, or moral lethargy. (Similarly, Hayim Greenberg had diagnosed American Jewry's "moral bankruptcy" during the exterminations.) Wolfe Kelman initially reported that the plight of Soviet Jewry was high on the RA list of priorities; the previous year, the RA and the Synagogue Council of America (the Jewish community's interdenominational umbrella organization) had made widely publicized efforts to promote visits between the Russian Jewish and the American Jewish communities. "I feel we can be justifiably proud of our role in that situation," Kelman reported, without acknowledging the poor results.[17]

In fact, bolder—and especially interfaith—diplomacy was

imperative. In 1961 the Synagogue Council of America launched a new initiative intended to pressure Soviet authorities: a delegation to the then "political counselor" of the Soviet Embassy, Georgy Kornienko, to review a list of "concerns," including the recent death sentences for Jews accused of "economic crimes," the Soviets' refusal to allow contacts between American and Soviet Jewish leaders, and prohibitions against baking matzah and other elements of religious observance. When Soviet authorities did not respond, the Synagogue Council enlisted help from the National Council of Churches.

The coalition of Christians and Jews met with greater success. A delegation of American Christians visited the Soviet Union and reported that the Jewish community was suffering from "poor, run-down" synagogues and "a lack of rabbis." A group of Soviet Christians then came to New York to meet with Jewish groups; later they visited Jewish leaders throughout the country. On July 3, 1963, Jewish and Christian activists met with Anatoly Myshkov, an official at the Soviet Embassy in Washington. Formal negotiations on the Jewish question had begun.

On September 4, shortly after the August 1963 March on Washington (which he did not attend), Heschel addressed Conservative rabbis at the Rabbinical Assembly conference on the topic of moral responsibility. Heschel was uncompromising, unusually severe. At this season of the High Holy Days, he judged that the soul of American Jewry was once again threatened by apathy, as it had been in 1940–1943.[18] He bitterly named several ways in which modern American Jews were trying to assuage their consciences, commenting, "We are busy in 1963 just as we were busy in 1943."

Furthermore, Heschel deplored other historical instances of indifference to the mass persecution of Jews. As a boy, he recalled, he had been amazed that there was "no moral indignation in Europe, when a whole people was driven out of Spain in 1492. Was there no outcry, no outburst of anger when human beings were burned alive in the auto-da-fé?" He then denounced another, more ancient failure, "the indifference of our people to the Ten Tribes" of ancient Israel, who disappeared from history.

The present situation was also catastrophic. Soviet Jewry, he insisted, was "the last remnant of a spiritual glory that is no more," and it was in danger of annihilation.[19]

Heschel recognized the political hazards of his position. Détente was the diplomatic order of the day. Relations between the United States and the Soviet Union remained unstable, even though the Nuclear Test Ban Treaty had recently been signed. Everyone recognized the danger in provoking the Soviets. But Heschel considered politics secondary to ethical demands. He concluded with this outcry: "Let the twentieth century not enter the annals of Jewish history as the century of physical and spiritual destruction!"

The next fall, again during the High Holy Days, Heschel challenged the conscience of American Jews even more aggressively. At the October 28, 1964, meeting of the New York Conference on Soviet Jewry at Hunter College, facing an audience of more than two thousand, he relentlessly condemned the Soviets. Although there was some hope that Leonid Brezhnev would bring in new leaders who would be more favorable to Jews, Heschel insisted that Stalinism was not dead. To stir his audience, he reached as yet unprecedented heights of invective. He excoriated the all-too-familiar disease of official racism as if he himself was an ancient prophet: "Malice, madness and blind hatred had combined in Stalin's mind to produce a foul monster whose work goes on to this very day. It is a sinister fiend whose work is a kind of blood-sucking cruelty in depriving Jewish citizens of their pride, of their human dignity, of their spiritual authenticity."[20]

Two years later Heschel was not satisfied with the progress made by two national conferences on Soviet Jewry. At the Rabbinical Assembly's 1966 annual convention, held for the first time in Toronto, he ignited a controversy that spread beyond the conference when he condemned the American establishment for "spending their energy on dealing with marginal non-vital issues rather than on the most important emergency of our day."[21]

In fact, Heschel spoke twice, first on his announced topic of interfaith dialogue, and then at the session on Soviet Jewry—at which Elie Wiesel, who had recently returned from the Soviet Union, gave Heschel credit for impelling him to action: "I went for a very simple reason. I was moved by what Rabbi Heschel, the first to raise his voice, had said and written about the Jewish tragedy in Russia." Like Heschel, Wiesel spared no words as he drew a parallel with the Holocaust and indicted Jews around the world for abandoning their three million Soviet brethren. As the *New York Times* reported the next day, Wiesel "charged that the Soviet Jewry issue 'was being utilized by some Jewish leaders for self-aggrandizement and fundraising and not in an effort to evoke the conscience of the world to the plight of Soviet Jews.'" The same article quoted Heschel's rebuke of the leaders and was widely disseminated.[22]

This public intra-Jewish criticism provoked explosive anger. The establishment immediately struck back. Rabbi Joachim Prinz, chairman of the Conference of Presidents of Major American Jewish Organizations (and the Jewish speaker at the 1963 March on Washington), now deliberately targeted by Heschel's criticism, dismissed his accusation as without merit. An even more personal attack came from Rabbi Israel Miller, chairman of the American Jewish Conference on Soviet Jewry, who denounced Heschel for "vocal demagoguery."

Jewish newspapers all around the country picked up Miller's words.[23] Heschel's prophetic idiom was too extreme for the Jewish mainstream.

However, some leading Jewish institutions felt that Heschel had been justified in his criticism. The Rabbinical Assembly officially expressed "dismay" at the establishment's repudiation of Heschel, "who has been a prime mover in awakening the conscience of American

Jewry about the conditions of our brothers in the Soviet Union."[24] An editorial in the Washington DC *Jewish Week* developed a realistic analysis of the dispute: "When the Conference on Soviet Jewry accused its critic, Rabbi Abraham Joshua Heschel, of 'demagoguery' it sounded very much like the indignation of a disturbed conscience."[25]

Heschel's persistent support for Soviet Jews also attracted FBI scrutiny. On December 7, 1966, the first night of Hanukkah, he participated in a vigil at Columbia University. The Newark FBI office took the account from the *New York Times* and, classifying it as relevant to the "CP [Communist Party], Counterintelligence Program," forwarded it to the national director with this note: "Bureau authority is requested to mail this clipping on four CP subjects of Jewish background."[26] This biased judgment, as far as we know, remained neatly classed in the FBI files.

A SACRED HUMANISM

While energetically pursuing a politics of witness, Heschel remained a thinker. An opportunity arose for Heschel to refine his ethical and religious philosophy. From his biblical perspective, theology and ethics were inseparable, but he had not yet clarified the nuances of their interdependence. An endowed speaking program was bringing leading intellectuals to the Stanford University campus to reflect upon "Immortality, Human Conduct, and Human Destiny." Heschel's appointment represented significant academic recognition; his predecessors included Reinhold Niebuhr, the social philosopher Joseph Wood Krutch, and the biologist Julian Huxley.[27]

Heschel's three lectures, delivered on May 5, 6, and 7, 1963, aroused considerable interest among Stanford's activist students and faculty. The opening lecture, "In the Likeness and Unlikeness of God," focused on the inner nature of human beings. Drawing an ironic contrast between people and unreflective animals, Heschel observed, "Man is a beast who knows he will die; he is cultivating the doubt that man is worthy of being saved. Thus he has a 'superior sense of inferiority.'" The second lecture, "In Search for Meaning," stressed the dangers of a negative humanism precipitated by "the liquidation of the inner man." Heschel insisted that a life without commitment was not worth living. In his final lecture, "Existence and Exaltation," he directed contemporary thinkers to "save the inner man from extinction." Social responsibility should be strengthened: "Millions are starving while new hotels are being built in Las Vegas."[28]

Heschel went on to revise his Stanford lectures into a small, intense book, *Who Is Man?*, which Stanford University Press published in 1965. Reversing his usual creative process—expanding paragraphs into essays and essays into books—Heschel distilled the arguments of *Man Is Not Alone*, *God in Search of Man*, and *The Prophets*.[29]

Here, for the first time, Heschel systematically addressed the philosophical meaning of the Nazi genocide. This intellectual process had consequences, for Heschel believed that a negative definition of the human had made the century's atrocities possible: "Massive defamation of man may spell the doom of all of us. Moral annihilation leads to physical extermination."[30] And, for the first time, he explicitly challenged Martin Heidegger, the prestigious philosopher who had supported Nazi ideology.

Defining "the logic of being human," Heschel refuted the materialistic and hedonistic "definitions of man" that would lead to "the eclipse of humanity" and replaced them with the value of "preciousness." He asserted, "Human life is the only type of being we consider intrinsically sacred, the only type of being we regard as supremely valuable." Each person was an example of "ultimate preciousness." Furthermore, Heschel declared his own faith in God the creator: "I have not brought my being into being. Nor was I thrown into being. My being is obeying the saying, 'Let there be!'"[31]

Heschel thus laid the foundations for an alternative to

existentialism. He elevated Descartes's rationalist dictum "I think, therefore I am" with "I am commanded—therefore I am."

Ultimate human responsibility became his last word: "By whatever we do, by every act we carry out, we either advance or obstruct the drama of redemption; we either reduce or enhance the power of evil."[32]

In Heschel's eyes, every person, regardless of age, was meant to embrace this responsibility. Heschel's dedication of the book to his daughter Hannah Susannah (around the time of her bat mitzvah), followed by the biblical citation 1 Chron. 28:9–20, signaled his legacy to the next generation. Referring to King David's final words to his son Solomon, the Bible passage concludes, "David said to his son Solomon, 'Be strong and of good courage and do it; do not be afraid or dismayed, for the Lord God, even my God is with you; He will not fail you or forsake you till all the work on the House of the Lord is done.'" This work was the closest Heschel ever came to writing a systematic theology.

Heschel's other book of sacred humanism, *The Insecurity of Freedom* (1966), documented his years of political, social, and religious activism. These "essays on human existence," as the subtitle read, encompassed his writings and speeches published or delivered publicly from the 1950s to 1966. He dedicated the book simply "To Wolfe," the former student and friend who, with Marc Tanenbaum, had helped promote him as a public intellectual.

Heschel divided the book into three (untitled) sections. Part 1 focused on national issues: religion in a free society, youth, aging, the patient as a person, racism, and civil rights. Part 2 contained theological essays on depth theology, Reinhold Niebuhr's theology of evil, Protestant renewal, Jews and Catholics, and the "sacred image of man." Part 3 addressed Israel and the Diaspora, religious education, Soviet Jewry, and, in the final essay, "the last Years of Maimonides."

By concluding the book with a chapter on the medieval Jewish sage, Heschel unified the two distinct periods of his life: before and after the Holocaust. Both his European and American lives embraced contemplation and action. The author of *The Insecurity of Freedom* had become a professor of Jewish ethics and mysticism who, like Maimonides, one of his earliest role models, had reconciled the inward, meditative life with worldly responsibility: "Contemplation of God and service to man are combined and become one." And, like Maimonides, Heschel spent his final years consumed by his service to God, to the Jewish people, and to humankind.[33]

CHAPTER 11

Apostle to the Gentiles, 1961–1966

During these same years of intensely publicized activism, scholarly research and writing projects, and teaching, Heschel carried on a largely confidential role in a great historical drama: the modernization (aggiornamento, or updating) of the Roman Catholic Church.

Within the church, the prospect for developing positive relationships with other religions—especially Judaism—looked brighter in 1958 after the election of Angelo Giuseppe Roncalli as Pope John XXIII. A warm and compassionate man of peasant origins, Roncalli, as apostolic delegate to Turkey and Greece during World War II, had saved thousands of Jews from deportation and certain death by providing them with forged baptismal papers. Now the Vatican diplomat recognized that church-sanctioned accounts of the crucifixion of Jesus were often used to justify, and even inspire, Christian antisemitism and the persecution of Jews. It was time for Jews and Christians to achieve mutual understanding on an international basis.

This initiative had begun years earlier with research by the Frenchman Jules Isaac, a historian and an inspector of schools. In his 1947 *Jésus et Israël* (*Jesus and Israel*), Isaac documented the Christian roots of antisemitism. He had some influence on Pope Pius XII, who had already made important changes favorable to the Jews in the Good Friday liturgy. The traditional Easter service had characterized Jews as a "treacherous" (*perfidus*) people. Now *perfidus* was understood more objectively as "unbelieving," not accepting Christ.[1]

Even as the Roman Catholic Church had begun to acknowledge, and address, at least a small part of its role in spreading antisemitism, much more needed to be done. In 1960 the elderly Isaac provided Pope John XXIII and three members of the Curia (the church's doctrinal authority) with examples of the church's pernicious "teaching of contempt," such as the notion that the Jews were a "deicide" race, responsible for killing Christ, and had been scattered around the world as punishment for their crime.

Pope John XXIII then personally charged Augustin Cardinal Bea, president of the Secretariat for Christian Unity and an Old Testament scholar, to prepare a draft on "the inner relations between the Church and the people Israel [the Jews]." This draft was conceived as a key document, to be considered by the upcoming Ecumenical Council (as the Second Vatican Council was originally called). Thus began years of intense and often troubled cooperation between Jewish and Christian promoters of progress.

Bea sought the advice of the American Jewish Committee (AJC), a Jewish self-defense and civil rights agency, and other organizations.[2] Marc Tanenbaum, the incoming director of interreligious affairs at the AJC, believed that his teacher, Abraham Joshua Heschel, was supremely qualified for scholarly discussions with Cardinal Bea and other Vatican officials.

Heschel eagerly accepted his new role as primary theological consultant to the American Jewish Committee. He believed this mission to the Vatican would be his greatest opportunity to eradicate Christian sources of antisemitism and save future Jewish lives.

Notwithstanding the inevitable complications, Heschel would go on to influence—significantly—the drafting of *Nostra Aetate* (*In Our Times*), the "Declaration on the Relation of the Church with Non-Christian Religions" (1965), which, for more than fifty years now, has sustained a positive relationship between Catholics and Jews. Despite the revulsion of some Orthodox Jewish leaders at the idea of debating with Christians, which would be required, Heschel was inspired to launch a powerful defense of Judaism. More broadly, in this interreligious work, Heschel would give voice to his most fervent hopes and expose his most intimate vulnerabilities as a Jew who had never healed from the ravages of the Holocaust. Nowhere else do we get a closer glimpse into his inner battles.

CONFRONTING THE CHURCH

Heschel entered the process of Vatican II in 1961. The American Jewish Committee provided him with information, secretarial and logistic support, and constructive criticism. Marc Tanenbaum would supervise and fortify his former teacher, whom he revered.

In addition to Tanenbaum, Heschel collaborated most closely with Zachariah Shuster, the American Jewish Committee's European director, stationed in Paris, who kept the New York headquarters informed of events—public and secret—occurring at the Vatican. A canny diplomat, Shuster regularly sent exquisitely detailed reports of the inner workings of this process, many of them leaked and confidential.

Heschel quickly became very close to Shuster, an East European Jew who had immigrated to New York in the 1920s and worked as a Yiddish journalist for *Der Tog* (The morning) before the American Jewish Committee sent him to Paris in the early 1940s, to work in Jewish international relations. Shuster developed close ties with Christians favorable to the Second Vatican Council.

In 1960 Shuster visited Jules Isaac at his home in Aix-en-Provence and learned about Isaac's audience with Pope John and the upcoming council, which had just been formally announced.[3] Cardinal Bea had written to Isaac of his charge to develop a declaration on the Jews, and Isaac repeated to Shuster the cardinal's encouraging words: "You are assured of more than hope"—echoing a phrase the pope himself had used when meeting with Isaac. Now the AJC depended on Heschel's theological expertise and humane sympathy to communicate across the abyss of sacred history.

First and foremost, Heschel proposed to establish a close working relationship with Cardinal Bea. Judaism and the Jews already had their most dedicated sponsor in the eighty-one-year-old Bea, a learned scholar of the Old Testament and Vatican veteran.[4] Born and reared in Germany (his father changed their family name from Behan to Bea), he had studied philosophy and theology at Freiberg University, entered the Jesuit order in 1912, and continued his biblical studies in Berlin and Holland until he settled permanently in Rome in 1929. A professor of biblical exegesis and the history of the Jewish people, he was appointed rector of the Pontifical Biblical Institute and editor of the academic journal *Biblica*, positions he held until Pope Pius XII chose him as his confessor. Bea was fluent in Hebrew, Aramaic, ancient Greek, Latin, Italian, French, and, of course, his native German; he had recently learned English. Bea not only possessed specialized knowledge of the Hebrew Bible; he also cherished Judaism as a living religion.

Although the AJC already enjoyed access to Vatican officials through the International University for Social Studies "Pro Deo" in Rome (founded in 1950 to foster joint research programs among different faiths and to promote democracy and religion in Europe and the developing world), Cardinal Bea was offering more direct influence. Bea informed American Jewish Committee officials that his subcommittee was working on the declaration on the Jews and that he wished to work closely with the AJC on this. Heschel, in turn, and through him the AJC, might influence the subcommittee's progressive proposals to develop a declaration on Judaism that would transform the Roman Catholic dogma that had been so harmful to Jews over the centuries. A preliminary draft cited Paul's Epistle to the Romans (chapters 9–11), which addressed the "mystery of Israel" and its relation to Christ, to be interpreted positively toward the Jews. More precisely, Bea asked the AJC and other organizations to prepare memoranda on "teachings of contempt" they wished the Secretariat to critically examine.

The American Jewish Committee then launched an international diplomatic initiative (a lobby, to speak crudely) to promote Jewish interests. They contacted prominent Jews: Elio Toaff, chief rabbi of Rome; Jacob Kaplan, chief rabbi of France; Joseph B. Soloveitchik, professor of Talmud at Yeshiva University; Louis Finkelstein, chancellor of the Jewish Theological Seminary; Salo W. Baron, professor of Jewish History at Columbia University; and Harry A. Wolfson, professor of philosophy at Harvard University. Heschel, however, would remain the most active of the AJC's advisers.[5]

In May 1961 Tanenbaum asked his American team to evaluate a draft of the AJC's report on Catholic teachings regarding Judaism. Then in July a confidential meeting arranged by Pro Deo University took place in Rome, where Cardinal Bea, Shuster, and Ralph Friedman, head of the American Jewish Committee's Foreign Affairs Department, discussed the report. Within a year, the American Jewish Committee had completed two researched documents: "The Image of the Jew in Catholic Teaching," co-sponsored by the Catholic institution St. Louis University and the AJC, and "Anti-Jewish Elements in Catholic Liturgy," a critique of the "deicide" accusation and other elements in the liturgy that degraded Judaism.

Heschel's personal relationships with sympathetic Vatican officials were crucial. He made his first significant contacts that November. Flying to Rome, he met Zachariah Shuster and arranged "fortuitous" encounters with several Vatican officials, including Father Felix Morlion, president of Pro Deo University as well as a personal friend of the pope, and Cardinal Bea, the American Jewish Committee's most highly placed ally. In a four-hour meeting, Morlion gave Heschel pointers on Vatican etiquette (including the suggestion that he send his writings on biblical theology to the pope and other named officials, which Heschel subsequently did).

Heschel, accompanied by Shuster and Professor Max Horkheimer (the AJC's German consultant), was introduced to Cardinal Bea on Sunday, November 26, 1961. (The original appointment, on Saturday morning, had been changed so as not to violate Heschel's Sabbath observance.) Also present were the cardinal's closest associates: Monsignor Johannes Willebrands, secretary of Bea's committee; Father Stefan Schmidt, Bea's personal secretary; and Father Morlion. Both Heschel and Bea had prepared carefully for this formal encounter. Heschel had studied Bea's introduction to a critical Hebrew edition of the Song of Songs. Bea, who admired Heschel's Berlin dissertation on the prophets, had reviewed references to Heschel's writings in Catholic academic sources.

Shuster's subsequent memorandum to the American Jewish Committee's Foreign Affairs Department meticulously recounted the orchestrated event. Heschel, the presenter, spoke in German. There was an immediate rapport between these two devout biblical scholars. Heschel gave the cardinal "two large Hebrew volumes of *Midrash Rabba* [the basic Rabbinic commentary on the Torah] with place markings indicating commentaries on The Song of Songs." He expressed admiration for the cardinal's scholarly edition of the Song of Songs, "even including subtle points of punctuation. Cardinal Bea was obviously very pleased."

After creating this "warm and friendly" atmosphere, Heschel referred to the two American Jewish Committee memoranda, which offered "specific suggestions regarding changes in Catholic liturgy and catechism." He asked the cardinal for permission to send another, more affirmative memorandum, urging the church to "bring about a greater knowledge of Jewish religion and Jewish teaching." Above all, he explained, "Jews want to be known, and understood, and respected as Jews [als Juden]."

Shuster was elated by Heschel's visit. He reported to Tanenbaum, "I personally found Dr. Heschel a most charming, inspiring and delightful personality. He is a man of spirit and understanding." Then, upon his return to Paris, Shuster wrote to Heschel to ratify their partnership in helping inaugurate an era: "The beginnings of a new spirit are clearly visible."

Soon after returning to New York, Heschel hurried to draw up what became known as "The Third Memorandum," which he had promised to Cardinal Bea. Sympathetic informants inside the Vatican were urging the American Jewish Committee to submit the text soon, since Bea's statement on the Jews was nearing completion.

Drafts circulated among the home team: Shuster, Tanenbaum, Judith Hershcopf of the AJC, Finkelstein, Soloveitchik, and officials of Pro Deo. They offered further refinements. On May 22, 1962, with a covering letter in German, Heschel sent the final report to Cardinal Bea.[6]

Heschel's memorandum, titled "On Improving Catholic-Jewish Relations," became the foundational AJC contribution to the Vatican declaration on the Jews. Tanenbaum summarized its contents for his AJC colleagues: "1) A declaration rejecting the deicide charge; 2) recognition of the Jews as Jews; 3) A statement calling for more knowledge and understanding, to be prompted through: a) A forum to make knowledge of Judaism available to Catholic priests and theologians; b) Joint Cath[olic]-Jewish research projects and publications; c) Encouragement of interreligious cooperation in civic and charitable endeavors; 4) Explicit rejection of anti-Semitism by the Church; a) A permanent high-level commission at the Vatican, for eliminating prejudice and watching over Christian-Jewish relations; b) Similar commissions in all dioceses." Shuster and Tanenbaum had directed

Heschel to emphasize point 1 (the deicide issue) in his memorandum "because it was learned that the draft being prepared by Bea's working group did not cover it."[7]

The American Jewish Committee was pleased with Heschel's unique contribution to this memorandum—a spiritual perspective. Heschel's "Third Memorandum" had elevated a functional document into a prophetic proclamation, conveying to Vatican officials its significance not only for Jews, but for all people. The document opened by declaring the universal necessity to serve the Divine: "With humility and in the spirit of commitment to the living message of the prophets of Israel, let us consider the grave problems that confront us all as the children of God." The Hebrew prophets were a vital common source for the two religions: "Both Judaism and Christianity live in the certainty that mankind is in need of ultimate redemption, that God is involved in human history, that in relations between man and man God is at stake."[8]

Heschel asserted that the strained relationships between Jews and Christians constituted "a divine emergency." Among the multiple causes of antisemitism, he judged the foremost to be "the slanderous claims that 'the Jews' are collectively responsible for the Crucifixion of Jesus, that because of this the Jews were accursed and condemned to suffer dispersion and deprivation throughout the ages. For centuries, anti-Semites had invoked this charge to justify the most cruel and inhuman treatment of Jews; it was even advanced to rationalize the fate of six million Jews during the Nazi Holocaust." (The term "Holocaust" had become symbolic of the genocide.) The upcoming Ecumenical Council, Heschel averred, should "issue a strong declaration stressing the grave nature of the sin of anti-Semitism as incompatible with Catholicism and, in general, with all morality."

Overall, Heschel was concerned less with doctrinal formulations than with creating a new spirit. For him, says his daughter Susannah Heschel, now the Eli Black Professor of Jewish Studies and chair of the Jewish Studies Program at Dartmouth College, "the central question was whether the Catholic Church could come to recognize the holiness in Judaism as a source of blessing for Christians. And that holiness could only be recognized if the Church abandoned proselytism and instead understood Jews as standing in unbroken covenant with God."[9]

After reviewing the "Third Memorandum," Cardinal Bea's sub-committee completed a forty-two-line Latin document, *Decretum de Iudaeis* (Statement on the Jews), to be submitted to the Central Preparatory Commission. If approved, it would then go to the council prelates for open discussion. There was great hope on both sides.

Negative forces now threatened the negotiations. Vatican II was a spiritual milestone, but it was also a political minefield. Bishops from Arab countries were fearful of appearing sympathetic to Jewish and Israeli interests. In fact, Arab political interests became such a strong issue in the council's deliberations that Israel's government decided to dispatch its own representative to Rome.

In May 1962, several months before the council was due to open, World Jewish Congress president Nahum Goldmann announced, to everyone's astonishment, that he was sending, uninvited, a former member of the Israeli Ministry of Religious Affairs, Dr. Chaim Wardi, to Rome as "an unofficial observer and representative." Other Jewish organizational leaders and church officials were outraged. Most problematic, the "Wardi incident" provoked further partisan resistance among Arab and conservative Catholic prelates, which in turn forced the Preparatory Commission to remove the draft statement on the Jews from the agenda of the opening session.

AJC officials were dismayed. In September, Shuster and Friedman secured a meeting in Rome with Bea and Eugene Cardinal Tisserant, dean of the Sacred College of Cardinals and a member of the Preparatory Commission. Bea reassured the Jewish officials. He reported on his discussion of the matter with Pope John, who had declared, "The Jews also have immortal souls, and we have to do something for them too." Bea admitted, however, that other church officials would need more persuasion.

THE FIRST AND SECOND SESSIONS

Spiritual generosity was in the air as Pope John XXIII opened the Ecumenical Council on October 11, 1962. Yet the council's first session ended two months later, on December 8, without having considered two progressive statements, one on religious liberty and the second the declaration on the Jews. To make matters worse, a few days before the session ended, a scurrilous, nine-hundred-page antisemitic attack entitled *Il complotto contro la Chiesa* (The plot against the church) was distributed to every prelate. The anonymous volume claimed to have unmasked a worldwide Jewish conspiracy, including Jewish infiltration of the Vatican.

After the council failed to consider the declaration on the Jews, Cardinal Bea tried to rally support via a promotional visit to the United States. The American bishops were strong advocates of religious freedom, with favorable views of Judaism. The centerpiece of the March 1963 trip would be an unpublicized meeting at AJC's New York headquarters between the cardinal and about ten "national Jewish religious and cultural personalities." Heschel would chair the "unprecedented" meeting (as the AJC proudly termed it).

On March 26, Bea kicked off his tour by presiding over a joint meeting of Catholics and Protestants at Harvard University in Boston. The next morning, Heschel and Tanenbaum, who had been invited to meet privately with Bea, arrived at the chancery of Archbishop (soon to become Cardinal) Richard Cushing. Several weighty conversations took place. Heschel and Bea first spoke alone, like old friends, for about thirty minutes. Then Tanenbaum, Father Schmidt (Cardinal Bea's personal secretary), and Monsignor Willebrands (secretary of Bea's committee, who was soon to become cardinal) joined them.

Heschel spoke a few formal words of appreciation regarding their common goals. Bea, for his part, warned the group not to publicize "these contacts," since "bitter enemies of the Jews in Rome" and outside the church might turn this information to their advantage.

Heschel introduced specific requests, some of them quite exacting, all recorded in a confidential American Jewish Committee report. Informally, Heschel suggested that Pope John might "condemn the charge against the Jews of deicide as a heresy or as a blasphemy. . . . Cardinal Bea said that he thought something like this might be possible." Heschel pressed for Bea's plan to establish a permanent organization, after the Vatican Council, for interfaith study projects. Bea next astonished his Jewish guests by asking them what they would think if the Vatican were to officially recognize the State of Israel. The stunned rabbis took a moment to catch their breath, then answered that Jews all around the world would welcome such news. (Three months later, this great-hearted idea died with Pope John XXIII. The State of Israel would not be accorded Vatican recognition until 1993.)

Returning to New York, Tanenbaum and Heschel completed arrangements for the confidential meeting of Cardinal Bea and prominent rabbis at AJC headquarters. On March 31, the "unprecedented" meeting of the cardinal and representatives of all branches of American Judaism—Reform, Conservative, and Modern Orthodox—ensued. (Rabbi Soloveitchik could not attend, since his wife was undergoing surgery the following day.) As chair of the meeting, Heschel opened the formal program in German by introducing the cardinal and his associates and then the Jewish leaders. He reminded his colleagues that the meeting was "informal and unpublicized." Heschel then read, in English, questions that had been submitted in advance to Bea.[10]

Responding first in German, Bea said that he was very pleased to meet with Jewish scholars and theologians, since he was an Old

Testament scholar himself; more to the point, his "activities on behalf of a Jewish-Christian understanding [were] not the result of some temporary situation or political opportunism, but based on a very deep conviction held for many years." He explained to the group that the notion of an accursed people and other negative teachings about Jews were not justified by the Gospel texts. The cardinal then proceeded to answer every question, in English. He reminded his Jewish colleagues not to expect too many specifics, as the council was dealing with some seventy documents totaling more than two thousand pages. He acknowledged "the great political difficulties which have arisen and some protests" that the Vatican had received, and he concluded by reiterating that the pope "fully endorse[d]" his views.

The next morning, Bea publicly addressed Jewish concerns at a press conference in the New York apartment of J. Peter Grace, president of the American affiliate of Pro Deo University, the American Council for the International Promotion of Democracy Under God. Significantly, the cardinal borrowed phrases from Heschel's 1962 Third Memorandum: "Through the centuries the Jewish people have paid a high price in suffering and martyrdom for preserving the Covenant and the legacy of holiness in faith and devotion." The cardinal made clear his "sincere desire that the Catholic Church and its faithful will acknowledge the integrity and permanent preciousness of Judaism and the Jewish people." Bea emphasized his hope for "the continued cooperation of Rabbi Heschel and members of the American Jewish Committee who have contributed so significantly thus far to removing the bases of misunderstanding between Catholics and Jews."[11]

That evening, at the Plaza Hotel in Manhattan, local, national, and international leaders gathered for a ceremonial feast of agape (fraternal love)—an interfaith banquet to honor Cardinal Bea sponsored by Pro Deo University and its American affiliate. Prominent politicians—such as Mayor Robert Wagner, Governor Nelson

Rockefeller, secretary general of the UN U Thant, president of the UN General Assembly Sir Muhammad Zafrulla Khan, and more—lent their authority to representatives of the three Abrahamic faiths: Christianity, Judaism, and Islam.

By now Heschel had become the model Jewish spokesman. His speech was warm and generous, but also politically audacious. Inter-religious dialogue was imperative, he insisted, because of the Cold War and the possibility of nuclear annihilation: "Is it not true that God and nuclear stockpiles cannot dwell together in one world?" he asked rhetorically. Heschel called for radical humility and a revival of reverence for all human beings. He also paid tribute to Bea and expressed enthusiasm for both the Ecumenical Council and Pope John's 1963 (posthumously published) encyclical *Pacem in Terris* (Peace on earth), which promoted nuclear non-proliferation. Heschel then affirmed his commitment to religious pluralism by citing the prophet Malachi (1:11) and Rabbinic sources: "God's voice speaks in many languages, communicating itself in a diversity of intuitions. The word of God never comes to an end. No word is God's last word."[12]

The immediate outcome of Cardinal Bea's American tour was modest: the decision to create an Institute for Judaic Studies to be part of or associated with the Institute for Social Studies Pro Deo in Rome. The larger goal—a declaration on the Jews—would take three more years to accomplish, owing in part to human mortality. Pope John XXIII passed away on June 3, 1963, at age eighty-one. He had held the Throne of Saint Peter for only four years and seven months. Yet Pope John had redirected the tide of church history forever.

Two weeks later, on June 21, the liberal-minded Giovanni Battista Cardinal Montini, archbishop of Milan, was elected pope. The sixty-five-year-old Montini was an experienced diplomat who had been close to the previous pontiff. He took the name of Paul VI, "after the apostle who transformed Christianity into a world religion." Progressives worldwide were encouraged by the selection.

The new pope was installed at a majestic outdoor ceremony on Saturday, June 30. After a blessing in Latin, the pope stated his intention to reconvene the Ecumenical Council. The American Jewish Committee team could continue its mission.

Supporters of the declaration on the Jews had great hopes for the second session of the Ecumenical Council, which Pope Paul VI had called for September 29, 1963. In the meantime, Zachariah Shuster had learned "from reliable sources" that Bea's Secretariat had drafted an excellent text that addressed most of the Jewish concerns. He secured a copy of this top-secret document, summarizing its essential elements in a letter to Heschel: "A solemn affirmation that Christianity has emerged from Judaism and originated from the Jewish religion and history. . . . It then says in clearest terms that the Church rejects the accusation of deicide made against the Jews; that it deplores anti-Semitism in past and present times; and concludes with a statement deploring the persecutions of Jews and declaring anathema any person who has contempt of or persecutes the Jews." Shuster went on to explain that "friends in Rome" advised against making any aspect of the document public, especially before the council opened.

Impressed by these details, Heschel replied to Shuster's glad tidings in very large script: "Just received your letter of 9.12, and I am overjoyed! Let us pray that the draft may receive the necessary votes."[13]

THEOLOGY AND POLITICS

A public relations calamity, due to a leak, soon stifled these ecstatic expectations. Milton Bracker, the Rome bureau chief of the *New York Times*, published an article on October 4 revealing the existence of the revised declaration, just as Shuster had feared. Two weeks later, Bracker outlined the proposed text in a front-page article with the headline "Vatican Council Paper Decries Blaming of Jews in Jesus's

Death." Bracker also divulged Cardinal Bea's contacts with Heschel and other Jewish representatives. These unauthorized disclosures provoked storms of antagonism and support that took months to subside.

The draft statement, "On the Catholic Attitude toward Non-Christians, and Especially toward Jews," was finally distributed to the council members at their November 8, 1963 meeting. When it was announced that Cardinal Bea would present chapter 4 (the declaration on ecumenism and the Jews) and Bishop Emile de Smedt of Bruges chapter 5 (the declaration on religious liberty), the prelates applauded loudly.

Heschel, Shuster, and their team were confident, and the American Jewish Committee's tendency to micromanage its program went into action. Since the text had been widely discussed in the press, Shuster believed that Heschel should meet with Cardinal Bea to persuade him to fine-tune details. Heschel flew immediately to Rome. But Bea, cautiously avoiding internal opposition, judged it impolitic to receive a Jewish representative at that sensitive moment. Heschel and Shuster met with Willebrands instead, and Heschel, according to Shuster's letter, "made a very forceful and effective plea for the alteration of . . . two passages" that might be misinterpreted as blaming the entire Jewish people for the death of Jesus.

Then, another anonymous antisemitic tract, *Gli Ebrei e il Concilio alla luce della Sacra Scriturra e della tradizione* (The Jews and the council in the light of Scripture and tradition), was stealthily distributed to the council members. These pressures enabled Vatican conservatives to maneuver behind the scenes to delay the vote on chapters 4 and 5. Sure enough, the second session of the Ecumenical Council ended on December 4, 1963, again without consideration of these broad-minded policies. In public, Cardinal Bea blamed the delay on lack of time in the council meeting. Heschel and the American Jewish Committee knew better. Shuster reported to Tanenbaum, "I know that [Heschel] left [Rome] in a state of depression. . . . I trust, however, that he has succeeded in overcoming his pessimism and [is] seeing matters now in a more balanced perspective."[14] Heschel never achieved that equanimity.

From then on Heschel was swept onto an emotional roller coaster. Now the risk was that given the approximately ten months before the Ecumenical Council would hold its third session, the draft of "On the Catholic Attitude toward Non-Christians, and Especially toward Jews" might be revised by a less sympathetic committee. The AJC and its allies launched an international campaign to save the declaration on the Jews.

Meanwhile, conflicts were breaking out within the Jewish camp as well. In February 1964 the *Jewish Chronicle* of London reported that Rabbi Joseph Soloveitchik, forcefully opposing "theological discussion" with Christians at the Rabbinical Council of America's midwinter conference, had repudiated the Vatican document as "nothing more or less than evangelical propaganda." Tanenbaum attempted to mediate. Soloveitchik agreed not to act, but other Orthodox colleagues disparaged some unnamed "Jewish laymen" (certainly the American Jewish Committee), as reported in the *New York Times* on June 23.

The American Jewish Committee did everything possible to support Cardinal Bea and other forward-looking clerics. Over the succeeding months, AJC contacted American cardinals and bishops favorable to the declaration and distributed their speeches to the press.

In May, however, rumors circulated that the draft had been seriously "watered down" and the repudiation of the deicide charge had been removed—a critical failing. In desperation the AJC called three exceptional meetings. On May 11, about twenty-five Jewish, Protestant, and Catholic representatives gathered to discuss the decree. As before, Heschel chaired that exchange of views.

The American Jewish Committee then arranged an audience of its highest officers—including president Morris Abram, director

John Slawson, and Zachariah Shuster—with Pope Paul in Rome. (Before flying to Italy, they met with U.S. Secretary of State Dean Rusk, who endorsed their endeavor.) Despite Jewish law and custom, the papal audience took place on May 30, a Saturday.[15]

Unfortunately, this emergency audience provoked disapproval in several quarters. The Rabbinical Council was incensed that AJC leaders had met with the pope on the Sabbath. Moreover, Bea and the recently elevated Cardinal Willebrands were also offended at the American Jewish Committee's public violation of religious law; to their knowledge it was the first time a Jewish group ever had an audience with the pope on their own holy day. Privately, Bea also regretted that the meeting with the pope had not been cleared with him, since this area was his major responsibility. Bea assured his Jewish consultants, however, that the new text of the declaration was an improvement on the old and admonished them not to seek "more complete statements" of its contents.

It was soon learned that the text had indeed been revised, but in a manner detrimental to progressive interests. Again, the media were responsible for the exposure. On June 12, 1964, the *New York Times*'s headline described the secret document: "Text on the Jews Reported Muted." Meanwhile various "informants" from Rome were giving Heschel and the American Jewish Committee conflicting views about whether the declaration would even be considered at the third session. The Jews feared the worst.

Adding to Heschel's stress was the death, on June 30, 1964, in New York, of his only surviving sister, Sarah Bracha Heschel, the wife of his first cousin the Kopitzhinitzer rebbe. Heschel would continue his myriad activities after the week of shivah, during the monthlong mourning period (*sheloshim*).

The following month, as he was traveling to a speaking engagement, Heschel arranged to spend the night of July 13 at the Trappist Abbey of Gethsemani in the Kentucky hills as the guest of the monk and poet Thomas Merton. A spiritual radical like himself, Merton was both devout and forward-looking. The two men had been corresponding since 1960. Heschel's writings were familiar readings among monastics, and as a master of novices, Merton had used *God in Search of Man* and *The Prophets* as teaching texts. Now he wanted to meet the man behind the author.

The exuberant Merton and the rabbi connected immediately. Central to their conversation was the declaration on the Jews at the Ecumenical Council, soon to convene its third session. Affected by Heschel's pessimism, Merton noted in his diary that Heschel was "convinced that . . . the Jewish Chapter will never be accepted in the Council." Merton felt that it was time for the church to repent, but Heschel "thinks [Cardinal] Bea is really finished, that he suffered a crushing defeat in the Second Session (obvious). The envy aroused by his American trip brought him many enemies, and he had plenty before that."[16]

Their encounter, under the pall of Vatican politics, confirmed Merton's deep sympathy for, and even identification with, Judaism and the Jewish people.[17] The immediate upshot of this brief but poignant visit (which is still remembered at the monastery) was Merton's vigorous letter the next day to Cardinal Bea. In supporting the declaration on the Jews, Merton declared, "I am personally convinced that the grace to truly see the Church as she is in her humility and in her splendor may perhaps not be granted to the Council Fathers if they fail to take account of her relation to the anguished Synagogue."[18]

Faced with the horrifying possibility of failing in his mission to end the Catholic Church's anti-Jewish teachings, Heschel was filled with tension, as were most Jewish advocates and their allies. Media "leaks" were a hazardous resource, and supporters of the Jewish cause were disconcerted by yet another unauthorized publication of the latest revised draft of the Vatican text on the Jews in the *New*

York Herald Tribune on September 3, 1964. An anonymous "special correspondent" published a translation of the Latin original, "Schema of the Doctrine on Ecumenism, Second Declaration: On the Jews and Non-Christians." The following day, another version of the draft appeared in the *New York Times*.[19]

Internal American Jewish Committee reaction to this revised document was temperate, but urgent. A memorandum dated the same day, September 3, detailed the draft's shortcomings and urged the Ecumenical Council to restore the previous document, "eliminating any spirit of conversion, condemning in unequivocal terms the charges of deicide against the Jews of Christ's time or of later times, and repudiating anti-Semitism." Heschel, however, abandoned diplomacy, sending mimeographed copies of his critique to several Catholic friends, which was picked up by the *New York Times* and, the following week, *Time* magazine. His indignation led him to use unusually strong language, even sarcasm: "Since this present draft calls for 'reciprocal understanding and appreciation, to be attained by theological study and fraternal discussion,' between Jews and Catholics, it must be stated that *spiritual fratricide* is hardly a means for the attainment of 'fraternal discussion' or 'reciprocal understanding.'"

In particular, Heschel assailed the notion that Jews were "a candidate for conversion." That Christian "hope," he asserted, was tantamount to annihilation. The bitterness with which he spurned church triumphalism would shock even some of his closest Christian allies: "As I have repeatedly stated to leading personalities of the Vatican, I am ready to go to Auschwitz any time, if faced with the alternative of conversion or death."[20]

No compromise was possible. Christianity must answer to history, Heschel continued: "Jews throughout the world will be dismayed by a call from the Vatican to abandon their faith in a generation that witnessed the massacre of six million Jews and the destruction of thousands of synagogues on a continent where the dominant religion was not Islam, Buddhism or Shintoism."

Among the friends to whom Heschel mailed copies of this prophet-like rebuke was Thomas Merton. In the solitude of his hermitage, the monk confronted his own conscience. Answering Heschel on September 9, Merton declared his solidarity: "My latent ambitions to be a true Jew under my Catholic skin will surely be realized if I continue to go through experiences like this, being spiritually slapped in the face by these blind and complacent people of whom I am nevertheless a 'collaborator.'"[21]

At home, however, Heschel's rebuke itself faced rejection. On August 16, the *New York Times* reported that the Modern Orthodox Rabbinical Council of America had reinforced its interdiction of interfaith theological discussions.

SECRET SUMMIT MEETING

Heschel now faced the most enormous emotional test of his life since the Holocaust. The third session of the Ecumenical Council was due to convene on September 14, 1964. As the day approached, tensions were almost unbearable. The timing was particularly bad for Jews, who were entering the Days of Awe, the hallowed ten-day period between Rosh Hashanah and Yom Kippur. The council's opening date, the day before Yom Kippur, seemed to symbolize the theological abyss separating Jews and Christians.

Still desperate to save the declaration on the Jews, the American Jewish Committee took an emergency measure: pressing its highest Vatican contacts to obtain a private audience for Heschel with Pope Paul himself. The political risks involved were high. If advertised, Heschel's meeting with the pontiff could compromise the AJC's long and deliberate lobbying efforts and discredit Cardinal Bea's initiatives. Heschel's prestige within the Jewish community was also at stake. By meeting with the head of the Catholic Church during the High Holy Days, he might appear to be demeaning Jews everywhere.

Richard Cushing of Boston (now elevated to cardinal) expedited the arrangements, but difficulties in scheduling increased the stress on Heschel. Vatican officials first set the meeting on the Jewish Sabbath, but Heschel refused to violate the holy day. The audience was then moved to Monday, September 14, the council's opening day itself.

Before the Sabbath, Heschel flew from New York to Rome, where his presence remained covert. He did not even attend synagogue on Shabbat Shuvah, the solemn Sabbath of repentance preceding Yom Kippur.

Around noon on Monday, Heschel and Zachariah Shuster entered the pope's private study in the Vatican. Heschel brought a new memorandum for consideration. Although the pope spoke English well, a translator was present: a young American monsignor, Paul Marcinkus, a tall and imposing presence—years later to be enveloped in the scandal of the Vatican Bank.[22]

There are two versions of this papal audience in the American Jewish Committee's archives: an official report written by Shuster in collaboration with Heschel, and a (then) top-secret memorandum written by Shuster alone and intended only for Marc Tanenbaum and his supervisor, AJC director John Slawson.[23] From an analysis of these documents, readers can follow the creation of the historical record.

The official report distilling the substance of Heschel's thirty-five-minute conversation with the pontiff was sanitized but essentially accurate.[24] Here is the gist of the "facts."

After the initial ceremonial formalities, Heschel introduced his topic: "The paragraph [of the new draft declaration] stating that the Church has 'unchanging hope' and 'ardent desire' that the Jews will enter the Church" would "defeat the purpose" of the declaration. The pope "expressed his bewilderment" at Heschel's remark; he explained that the statement "was conceived in a spirit of benevolence and abundant friendship to the Jew and does not contain anything offensive. . . . As a matter of fact, there are some people who consider the proposed declaration as being too favorable to the Jews." Obviously, Heschel and the pope viewed the declaration from opposing, perhaps irreconcilable, theological assumptions.

A brief debate on conversion (Heschel's most contentious topic) ensued. Diplomatically, Heschel asked the pope to respect "the sensitivity of the Jewish people and [recognize] that any reference to the eventuality of the acceptance by Jews of the Christian faith might create misunderstanding." The pope's "firm" answer was unmistakable: "The declaration is a religious document, addressed to all the Catholic world and cannot be guided by political or journalistic motivations. . . . Unsolicited counsel and advice from elements outside the Church cannot influence the position of the Church." Heschel reiterated his point and agreed that "it was not our intention to question the right of the Council to proclaim its beliefs." Responding to Heschel's request that he intervene personally on the wording of the declaration, the pope refused: "The Council is a democratic body and follows democratic procedure. The appropriate commission of the Council will have to consider this text and whether any modifications should be made in it."

Heschel then appealed to the pontiff's compassion. He attempted to convey the extent of Jewish suffering at the hands of Christianity. He urged the pope to condemn antisemitism ("a unique evil and unlike any other kind of discrimination") and to remove it once and for all from church teachings. At that point, Shuster spoke for the first time and "called the Pope's attention to the passage on deicide and said that . . . the implication is that the Jews of ancient times and of subsequent generations *were* responsible for [Christ's death]."

As the discussion ended, the pope accepted Heschel's memorandum, saying that he would submit it to the appropriate commission of the council. Heschel presented the pope with a copy of *The Prophets* that contained an inscription.

For the historical record, Heschel and Shuster had indeed placed the essential issues before the pope; not surprisingly, they were unsuccessful in enlisting him to their side. Shuster added to the official account: "The entire conversation was conducted in a spirit of give-and-take without any restrictions. While the Pope was firm and definite in his remarks, he was most cordial and friendly to us." With this official report in hand, the American Jewish Committee, which had arranged this extraordinary secret audience, might subsequently choose to highlight the positives in the theological impasse.

Shuster's private, super-confidential report (consisting of twenty-one numbered points) was brutally direct. The seasoned interreligious diplomat, who admired Heschel, nevertheless deemed the rabbi's performance a failure. The American Jewish Committee had counted on this secret meeting to tip the balance toward the Jews; now, Shuster believed, they had to face reality. Reporting only to his immediate superiors—Slawson and Tanenbaum—Zachariah Shuster blamed Heschel by cataloging his shortcomings.[25]

Shuster's disgruntled version set the scene with body language: "The Pope was at ease, while Dr. Heschel sat on the edge of his chair, fidgeting, extremely tense, betraying great nervousness." Heschel's introductory remarks were "too long, obsequious in manner, repetitious in addressing the Pope innumerable times as 'Your Holiness,' and lacked point and clarity." The pope reminded his visitors that "he was ready to listen but that we should remember that the Council was a deliberative body, one that made its own decisions, and that he cannot impose on it in any way."

Despite that reminder, Heschel attempted to persuade the pope to support the previous statement on the Jews, because, according to Shuster's report, the revised text "would create a bad impression on public opinion." The pope answered by reminding Heschel that the document was addressed to believing Catholics, not outsiders. Refusing to drop this line of argument, Heschel repeated his view, probably thinking of the talmudic principle by which some religious laws can be subordinated to the higher good of maintaining peace.

Shuster found this part of Heschel's performance particularly shameful: "My eyes sank to the ground because I heard a Jew speaking to the head of the Catholic Church and bring in such irrelevant, unsuitable and alien considerations as *public relations* in a matter of the highest religious import and significance." Heschel, he wrote, was in a state of panic; unable to introduce further arguments, he "return[ed] again and again to obsequious remarks, pointing out the great public role the Council had assumed in the world, and that the passage, as it stood, would be misunderstood."

Frustration overcame both emissaries. Shuster believed the pope was "ready apparently to listen to further arguments and discussion, but none were forthcoming. Finally, in a state of near exhaustion, Dr. Heschel presented a copy of his own book on the Prophets."

The two men left the pope's study extremely agitated. Soon after, they were seen arguing—Shuster, his face ashen, exploding at Heschel. As Shuster admitted in his top-secret report: "I recall definitely that on leaving the Vatican, the words that came spontaneously to my mind and lips were *hillul ha-Shem v'Yisrael* [the desecration of God's name and of the Jewish people]."[26] Shuster's warm and impassioned alliance with Heschel had collapsed in bitterness.

While completing this candid report the next day, Shuster noted with horror that the pope's intimates had already learned of Heschel's poor performance. From then on, the American Jewish Committee relegated Heschel to the background while Shuster, Tanenbaum, Slawson, and especially their numerous Catholic allies at the council carried the battle forward.

Ironically, on the very day of Heschel's secret audience with the pope, Rabbi Joseph Soloveitchik publicly reasserted his opposition to interfaith theological discussions. As reported by the *Jewish Press Agency*, the Modern Orthodox leader alluded negatively to Heschel's earlier "Auschwitz" memorandum without naming him: "The situation does not call for hysteria and readiness to incur martyrdom. All it requires is common sense, responsibility, dignity and particularly a moratorium on theological 'Dialogue' and pilgrimages to Rome."[27]

Now Heschel, perhaps unknowingly at first, was alone. Without the American Jewish Committee's support, he continued his role as an uncompromising prophetic voice. Heedless of the diplomatic dangers, and despite his pledge of secrecy, he began to speak privately about his meeting with the head of the Roman Catholic Church.

Heschel's clandestine audience soon became news. It was impossible to staunch the flow. Rumors of his papal audience were first aired by the *Religious News Service*, a worldwide press outlet reporting on issues concerning all religions. Two weeks later, a few distorted pieces of information reached print. One was an article, in Yiddish, in the *Day-Morning Journal* on October 2, 1964, by Gershon Jacobson, the Yiddish-speaking Russian Jewish journalist who had interviewed Heschel in the 1940s and who now traced the outlines of the still-confidential meeting.[28]

The threshold between rumor and story was crossed the following week, as more details reached the London *Jewish Chronicle* "from our correspondent, New York," probably the same Jacobson, who announced, "Rabbi Dr. Abraham Joshua Heschel, who has been in close touch with Cardinal Bea . . . was invited by Pope Paul VI to an audience on the Monday before Yom Kippur, it is now disclosed." The reporter emphasized Heschel's refusal to discuss what was said but added that he "has reason to believe that Pope Paul was greatly impressed by Rabbi Heschel's statement."[29] Heschel was boosting his authority, according to the anonymous reporter.

Alarmed and outraged at these infringements, Shuster feared that the entire American Jewish Committee project might collapse. Immediately he dispatched a "personal and confidential" memorandum to Slawson, carefully explaining his reactions. Only

Heschel could be the source of this "flagrant breach of faith," Shuster asserted. The rabbi's reported claim that the pope was "greatly impressed" was especially shocking. Alarmed that opponents would accuse the pope of allowing himself to be unduly influenced, Shuster urged that Heschel be silenced and the papal audience "be kept in total secrecy."[30]

It was too late. The brief *Jewish Chronicle* article quickly led to a cover story in the October issue of the *Jewish World*, an independent illustrated monthly published in New York. The cover featured photographs of Heschel and Pope Paul along with the misleading headline, repeated inside, "What Happened on Yom-Kippur Eve at the Vatican?" (The article did explain that Heschel, refusing to meet with the pope on the Sabbath, had rescheduled the audience for the following Monday, the day *before* Yom Kippur eve.)[31]

Again, the reporter was anonymous, but he was well informed. Furthermore, this longer account was provocative, calculated to nettle its partisan readership. It cited some antisemitic innuendoes expressed at the council itself while praising the supportive American bishops, especially Cardinal Cushing: "A new tone was introduced by a plea from several Church Fathers asking for *an act of contrition* by the Church on behalf of the Jews." Its conclusion, however, alluded sarcastically to Hitler: "[This Vatican source] added that the Most Holy Father still has not made up his mind on the Jewish issue at this time, the *final solution* is still to come." Such rhetoric could only offend Jews and Christians motivated by trust or magnanimity.

VATICAN II: THE THIRD AND FOURTH SESSIONS

Realistically speaking, even Pope Paul himself could not have revised the draft declaration on the Jews. Its fate was sealed well before his confidential meeting with Heschel and Shuster. The council prelates discussed the text on September 18–19, 1964, and, predictably it was opposed by prelates from Arab countries and church conservatives.

The Curia even attempted to remove the document from Cardinal Bea's Secretariat, though without success.

A vote on the declaration on the Jews was scheduled for November 19 and the vote on religious liberty for the following day. Using a dubious parliamentary tactic, council president Cardinal Tisserant announced that both votes would be postponed, eliciting a tremendous outcry among supporters. More than a thousand bishops signed a petition urging Pope Paul to reconsider the decision. The pope refused to do so, but he promised that the issues would be treated in the fourth and final session.

Hopes rose on November 20, the last Friday of the third session, when Cardinal Bea was allowed to introduce the draft statement on the Jews for preliminary approval. It passed enthusiastically with 1,770 in favor, 185 opposed. (The text on non-Christian religions was adopted by a similar majority.) Pope Paul promised that the definitive text would be presented at the final session the following year. Grateful American Jewish Committee officials thanked their allies at the Vatican for their efforts on behalf of the vote. It was a triumph for church progressives—at that moment. Nonetheless, the text, although approved for discussion yet arousing vehement dissent, was still subject to revision.[32]

Did Heschel realize that he had been marginalized? By early December, Shuster judged that Heschel had become a major liability. He telephoned Tanenbaum, then followed up with a firm but tactful letter revealing that "Dr. Heschel is now a *persona non grata* to the highest Vatican authorities." Shuster urged Tanenbaum to keep the matter secret.[33]

Heschel indeed gave them additional reason to worry: he had made a gigantic blunder. On the evening of November 21, the very day after the preliminary vote on the Jewish declaration, he had accorded an in-depth interview in Hebrew to Geula Cohen, a visiting Israeli journalist from the widely circulated Tel Aviv newspaper *Ma'ariv*. A formidable personality and right–wing Zionist, notorious as a "girl terrorist" and "unyielding Israeli warrior," Cohen had worked as a radio broadcaster in the early 1940s for the Stern Gang, a paramilitary organization outlawed by both the British and the Zionists. Captured by the British and sentenced to nine years in prison, she escaped two years later. After independence in 1948 she became a school teacher and a journalist.[34]

Her interview with Heschel, speaking in Modern Hebrew, probed the rabbi's complex identity. Meanwhile, Heschel did not realize that he was a perfect foil for Cohen's contempt for Christianity. As this adroit interviewer directed Heschel to his memories of helplessness during the Holocaust, forceful emotions were discharged. His mission to Rome was to save future Jewish lives, he explained: "I live in Auschwitz. Since Auschwitz I have only one rule of thumb for what I say: would it be acceptable to those people who were burned there?"[35]

Cohen then applauded Heschel's proclamation about being "ready to go to Auschwitz" if faced with conversion or death: "This statement of yours made me proud." Then, she added, "Yet, I would have written it differently, saying: 'if this were the only way in which I would be permitted to live, I would have endeavored to send *them* [Christians] to Auschwitz.'" According to Cohen, Heschel did not seem "shocked by [her] words" as he naïvely displayed his vanity: "Permit me to avoid modesty at this moment. Frankly, I assert that the statement on Auschwitz, of which you are proud, is the strongest statement possible, and it has shaken many people throughout the world."[36]

Heschel, to the contrary, had greater respect for the Christian conscience. The reporter's startling anti-Christian statement highlighted their radical opposition. Without compunction, she pushed beyond the brink of common sense by condemning Christianity: "But they are the murderers. For they are guilty not only of killing Jews but of killing God." Heschel was enough of a pragmatic negotiator not to rise to this particular bait. He pointedly rejected Soloveitchik's position (without naming him) or that of other Jewish leaders who refused to engage with the Vatican. Rather, he affirmed, "The moment I became convinced that I could contribute toward the death of the Christian myth about the Jewish killing of God (which was the cause of so much sacrifice and suffering), I rose and went to the Pope."

Cohen then invited Heschel to elaborate his personal narrative of his audience with the pope. Instead of crediting the AJC initiatives (which would have violated the bond of secrecy), he switched topics, recalling his first meeting with Cardinal Bea in November 1961. Heschel focused on the memorandum he had prepared at Cardinal Bea's request, which, he said, had led to his meeting with the pope: "At the initiative of very important theologians, I was invited to an audience by the Pope."

Cohen then prompted Heschel to restate his version of the papal audience. According to Cohen, he offered a solution to the conversion issue: "Inasmuch as this Christian hope is a hope for the end of time, and since what will happen at the end of time is God's mystery . . . one can therefore formulate this hope in an eschatological form which would be acceptable also to Jews, expressing the hope that at the end of time all men will worship our Father in Heaven." Heschel reported the pontiff as answering, "'I shall do what I can, but you know that the Council is a democratic body.'"

When Cohen's blockbuster interview in Hebrew with Heschel appeared in *Ma'ariv* on Christmas Day 1964, Vatican officials were stunned. (It had been immediately translated for all concerned.) The scandal might still contaminate the council's deliberations.

The first intimation came from Vatican Radio, which picked up a short notice from Radio Cairo about the interview, stressing Heschel's supposed inference (by his silence) that church officials were comparable to Nazis. Some opponents of the declaration on Judaism prepared a strong rebuttal for *L'osservatore romano* (The Roman observer; a quasi-official Vatican newspaper), and Cardinal

Bea was able to stop its publication. Less than a week later, Shuster learned from his Vatican informants that Heschel's indiscretion had reached the highest authorities: not only Cardinal Bea but also Amleto Giovanni Cardinal Cicognani, the Vatican secretary of state and a powerful conservative, and furthermore, the pope himself. Cooperative ties between Jews and Catholics, so cautiously cultivated for years, were now severely menaced. Shuster was horrified that the American Jewish Committee's project might be aborted.[37]

Cardinal Bea, whose personal bond with Heschel was particularly deep, suffered excruciatingly. Called before Cardinal Cicognani, Bea took in Cicognani's eyewitness account of the pope's reactions and later conveyed it to Shuster: "The Pope was angered and chagrined by the presumption of the tone used in the article; by the distortion of actual historical facts as he, the Pope, knows them; the implied insults to Christianity." Bea also reported that the Vatican secretary of state "is convinced that Heschel and his visit was the American Jewish Committee in person. *The entire faithlessness of this man is ascribed totally to the American Jewish Committee*" (Shuster's emphasis). Bea concluded that the American Jewish Committee must dissociate itself completely from Heschel, privately and publicly.

How will history judge Heschel's actions? While we cannot justify the humiliation Heschel inadvertently inflicted on the American Jewish Committee and its Vatican partners through his interview with Geula Cohen, we can try to understand why he appears to have panicked and been rendered speechless, unable to protest Cohen's outrageous comparison of church officials to Nazis.

Heschel was vulnerable on two major levels. The first was identity: he held in memory almost two thousand years of persecution by the Catholic Church—periodic killings, expulsions, demeaning public disputations, papal burnings of the Talmud. The second was political: The American Jewish Committee had been unrealistic in expecting one single papal audience to resolve policy in a document hotly debated for over two years. This gamble, furthermore, was based on the faulty assumption that Pope Paul could (and would) interfere with the "democratic" (or collegial) process in which more than a thousand bishops from around the world discussed, amended, and voted on legislation.

Another possible factor may have been Heschel's own diplomatically unexpressed resentment. The Vatican had repeatedly put Heschel in the situation of having to refuse to meet with the pope on the Jewish Sabbath. Furthermore, Heschel had also endured attacks for agreeing to engage the Vatican between Rosh Hashanah and Yom Kippur.

Moreover, Heschel was still in mourning for his sister. His observance of the Days of Awe was disrupted. All this undermined Heschel's unreasonably expected performance.

VATICAN II: THE GRAND FINALE

With the cooperation of the Vatican, however, and leaders of the American Jewish Committee, the historical record eventually placed Heschel's papal audience as one ambiguous bump on the royal road to victory. Proof of the more complex reality languished in the American Jewish Committee files until the publication of the first Heschel biography in 2007.[38]

When the fourth session of the Ecumenical Council opened on September 14, 1965, the revised texts of the Jewish declaration and the statement on religious liberty were examined quickly. On September 21, the latter was adopted by a large majority. On September 30, Cardinal Bea's Secretariat distributed a version of the Jewish declaration that was somewhat less favorable than the previous one. Notably, the *deicide* charge was not explicitly condemned.

As a last attempt to strengthen the declaration, Heschel, now interacting as a freelancer, rallied his polemic skill to denounce this lack of specificity. He wrote his own press review: "The deicide charge is the most dreadful calumny ever uttered. It resulted in rivers of blood and mountains of human ashes. . . . It is absurd, monstrous, and unhistorical, and the supreme repudiation of the Gospel of love." Persisting in his prophetic role, he amplified his hyperbole even further: "Not to condemn the demonic canard of deicide . . . is a defiance of the God of Abraham and an act of paying homage to Satan."[39]

On October 14, Cardinal Bea presented the revised text on Judaism and the Jews. That afternoon, the prelates approved a number of clauses: asserting that the death of Jesus was not to be blamed on all Jews collectively; eliminating the word "deicide"; and including a passage that "deplored" antisemitism. On October 28, 1965, the anniversary of John XXIII's election to the papacy, the final document was adopted by a vote of 2,312 to 88. Pope Paul VI promulgated the text immediately as official church doctrine.[40]

The document that had begun with a declaration on Judaism and the Jews had expanded into "Declaration on the Relation of the Church with Non-Christian Religions," and this final, short, five-paragraph statement became known as *Nostra Aetate* (In our times). The fourth paragraph in this statement, dealing with Judaism, comprised only seventeen sentences—but it would dramatically change how the Roman Catholic Church viewed Judaism and treated Jews.

Finally, after some two thousand years, Catholics were now directed to renounce antisemitism, to recognize Judaism as possessing an ongoing covenant with God, and to stop missionizing Jews. A solid foundation had been established for future decades of Jewish-Christian dialogue and cooperation.

As for Heschel, his "Third Memorandum"—"On Improving Catholic-Jewish Relations"—had served as *the* foundational AJC contribution to the Vatican declaration on the Jews. Rabbi Abraham Joshua Heschel thus emerged as an honored critic of the church and a unique spiritual resource for progressive Christians

(Protestants and Catholics) seeking to animate the momentum of religious renewal.

NEW INTERFAITH TRIUMPHS

While pursuing his (mostly confidential) activities at Vatican II, Heschel had been gaining prominence in the American Protestant community. Protestants at this time were especially attentive to the Second Vatican Council, and discussions among the Roman Catholic clergy had roused them to intensive self-questioning. Yet even earlier, starting with Reinhold Niebuhr's laudatory review of *Man Is Not Alone* in 1951, Heschel's authority as a spiritual voice had gained wide public esteem. Over the next decade or so, this was reinforced by articles in *Time* magazine, reviews of *God in Search of Man*, Heschel's participation at interfaith conferences, and his invited articles. With the publication of *The Prophets* in 1963, Heschel's biblical theology became required reading in many Protestant seminaries.

By 1962 Heschel had also found a major Christian ally and friend in John Coleman Bennett, dean of faculty and the Reinhold Niebuhr Professor of Social Ethics at Union Theological Seminary. Bennett had replaced the elderly Niebuhr as the theologian of progressive, politically engaged Protestantism.

In December 1963, anticipating the triennial General Assembly of the National Council of Churches, editors of the preeminent Protestant journal the *Christian Century* devoted an issue to religious renewal and invited Heschel to present a Jewish view. Heschel's theological answer to the call for religious renewal was bold. Still keenly involved in the drama of Vatican II, he detailed, for the first time in print, what he considered deficiencies in Christian observance and thought. He deplored two trends, both connected with Judaism: "the age-old process of dejudaization of Christianity, and the modern process of desanctification of the Hebrew Bible." He went so far as to scold those he was trying to reach: "How dare a Christian substitute his own conception of God for Jesus' understanding of God and still call himself a Christian? . . . Only a conscious commitment to the roots of Christianity in Judaism could have saved it from such distortions."[41]

Heschel's criticism of Christian theology did not bother Bennett. After his inauguration as Union Theological Seminary president in April 1964, Bennett invited Heschel to join the faculty as the Harry Emerson Fosdick Visiting Professor. John D. Rockefeller III had established the professorship in 1953 to honor Fosdick, one of America's great religious progressives and a former member of the Union faculty. Located on Broadway across from the Jewish Theological Seminary, Union (as the seminary was known in shorthand) was proudly liberal.

Bennett offered Heschel two courses for the first semester; for the second semester, Heschel would tour the country as a "roving professor under the auspices of Union Seminary." Bennett expected Heschel to embody Jewish tradition as well as to teach it. It was time for Protestants to have a share of him along with the Catholics, he added.[42]

Heschel was pleased to accept. This was a tremendous opportunity for him to influence Protestants, who dominated American social and political life.

He was also the first Jew to be honored with the Fosdick Visiting Professorship, and an institutional change made the appointment even more noteworthy.[43] Union's constitution required all faculty members to identify with a specific Christian denomination. It was necessary to formally change that rule in order to appoint Heschel. Union's Board of Directors accordingly voted to amend the section of the constitution and bylaws to define *permanent* members of the faculty.[44]

The next day, a press release went out that quoted Niebuhr on Heschel's "commanding and authoritative voice," along with a page-long biography, including his European background, his abundant American publications, and a list of fifteen lecture topics. Invitations to speak soon arrived. Heschel's national teaching tour would include twenty-five institutions.[45]

In the meantime, Heschel's family was preparing to celebrate Susannah's bat mitzvah on May 15, 1965, her thirteenth birthday. Susannah herself, independent and strong-willed, had requested the ritual, contrary to the custom prevailing among Jewish Theological Seminary faculty, who did not mark their daughters' b'not mitzvah, and Susannah's parents were quick to support her. (At the time, only about half of the Conservative congregations followed Reform and Reconstructionist Jews in dedicating girls to Judaism in this way.) The Heschels decided not to involve their Hasidic relatives, who would neither accept the idea of a bat mitzvah nor enter a Conservative synagogue.[46]

Susannah chanted the haftarah (a reading from the prophets) and gave two speeches, one in Hebrew, the other in English. Several obligations at the seminary prevented Finkelstein, Saul Lieberman, and many others from attending, so they claimed. Their absence reinforced Heschel's sense of isolation from the tight-knit JTS community.

An entirely different feeling reigned at Union. Officials recorded Heschel's inaugural lecture "No Religion Is an Island" (November 10, 1965) and published it in the *Union Seminary Quarterly Review*. It was a magnificent oration, a wide-ranging and eloquent analysis of the foundations of Jewish-Christian cooperation. Heschel's dramatic opening defined his place in the historical moment:

I speak as a member of a congregation whose founder was Abraham, and the name of my rabbi is Moses.

I speak as a person who was able to leave Warsaw, the city in which I was born, just six weeks before the disaster began. My destination was New York, it would have been Auschwitz or Treblinka. I am a brand plucked from the fire, in which my people was burned to death. I am a brand plucked from the fire of an altar of Satan on which millions of human lives were exterminated to evil's greater glory, and on which so much else was consumed: the divine image of so many human beings, many people's faith in the God of justice and compassion, and much of the secret and power of attachment to the Bible bred and cherished in the hearts of men for nearly two thousand years.

Expanding upon his powerful image based on the prophet Zechariah, as "a brand plucked from the fire of an altar of Satan," Heschel asserted that the Holocaust was a catastrophe for all civilization. He proclaimed too that Judaism and Christianity shared a common fate and a common legacy: the living God, the Hebrew Bible, and the sacred image of humankind.[47]

Heschel also reiterated his earlier contention that "the fate of the Jewish people and the fate of the Hebrew Bible are intertwined." Jews and Christians were united against the common enemy: nihilism. Religious people were threatened not by competing theologies but by alienation from the living God.

Heschel saw depth theology as the common ground of interfaith dialogue. After summarizing "four dimensions of religious existence" (creed, faith or inwardness, the law, the community), he evoked in one long peroration the existential situation preceding religious commitment and statements of belief:

I suggest that the most significant basis for meeting of men of different religious traditions is the level of fear and trembling, of humility and contrition, where our individual moments of faith are mere waves in the endless ocean of mankind's reaching out for God, where all formulations and articulations appear as understatements, where our souls are swept away by the awareness of the urgency of answering God's commandment, while stripped of pretension and conceit we sense the tragic insufficiency of human faith.

According to Heschel, this "tragic insufficiency of human faith" set the stage for "depth theology." Coupled with an acute yearning for God's presence, "humility and contrition," open-mindedness, were necessary preconditions of true interfaith dialogue. Such courage could foster real spiritual companionship.

Taking up the issue of the Christian mission to the Jews that had so vexed his audience with Pope Paul, Heschel proclaimed, "No religion is an island." In other words, no tradition holds primacy in interfaith exchange: "Thus any conversation between Christian and Jew in which abandonment of the partner's faith is a silent hope must be regarded as offensive to one's religious and human dignity. . . . Is it not blasphemous to say: I alone have all the truth and the grace, and all those who differ live in darkness, and are abandoned by the grace of God?" Heschel justified his own pluralism "in this aeon diversity of religions is the will of God," quoting a talmudic source: "The ancient Rabbis proclaim: 'Pious men of all nations have a share in the life to come.'" He cited other Jewish sages, including Yehuda Halevi and Maimonides, who affirmed the legitimacy of Christianity and Islam, along with Judaism. He concluded with a call to cooperative action.

After thunderous applause, there was a reception, at which Mordecai Kaplan came up and threw his arms around him, calling the event a *kiddush ha-Shem* (an action that brings honor to God). Ironically, it was Kaplan, the devout old Reconstructionist, and not Finkelstein, the traditionalist, who most earnestly applauded Heschel's defense of Jewish spirituality. For Kaplan, seeking the value of all religions triumphed over ideology.[48]

Heschel revised his speech for publication in the *Union Seminary Quarterly Review*; it became his classic defense of religious pluralism, as well as his forthright rejection of mission to the Jews. Over time it would strengthen his spiritual authority among Catholics, Protestants, and eventually Muslims.

Heschel was happy and at ease at Union Theological Seminary. From October 1965 through January 1966, he taught two courses and made himself available for private conversations. His classroom performance was quite successful, for several reasons. For the first time in his life, a religious academy had asked him to offer courses based on his own books. Furthermore, most of his Christian divinity students were disposed to be impressed by him, as were their professors. More students signed up for his classes than for those of any previous Fosdick visiting professor. They also appreciated his charisma. For them he was an embodiment of Judaism. Moreover, Heschel was frequently available to them; he kept the door of his office open, welcoming students and faculty who wished to speak with him.

In the classroom he transmitted a religious sensibility, a dynamic, personal presence that endured in memories. Students remembered many ideas that were new to them: for example, Heschel explained that Jews never write the word "God" on the blackboard "because you could erase it."[49] He told the story of a rabbi who continually studied the first words of Genesis. When his disciple returned six months later to find him reading the same text, he asked, "You haven't moved from that one verse yet?" The rabbi answered, "Well, I still haven't grasped everything in it."

Most gratifying for Heschel during his year at Union were the warm relationships he and his wife developed with several colleagues. Heschel became closest to W. D. Davies, Edward Robinson Professor of Biblical Theology, and James A. Sanders, the recently appointed professor of Old Testament. Both scholars were ordained Christian ministers with profound knowledge of biblical and Rabbinic texts, and both revered Judaism.

Davies appreciated Heschel's ability to convey Jewish spirituality and liturgical sensibility to Christians. He considered Heschel essentially a Hasidic rebbe, a personification of Torah and Jewish tradition with a modern European way of thinking. At the same time, Davies judged that Heschel's scholarship "lacked critical austerity."[50] Like Davies, James Sanders admired Heschel as a biblical witness: "For Heschel, God was overwhelmingly real and shatteringly present." Sanders considered Heschel "a *shalliah la-goyim*, an apostle to the gentiles."[51]

In spite of generous conversations, Heschel's Christian colleagues found shortcomings in his personal approach to interfaith dialogue. In gatherings of Jewish Theological Seminary and Union faculty, there were matters Heschel refused to discuss, even on a theoretical level, such as the Christian mission to the Jews. In this regard Heschel was both inflexibly conservative and respectful of other religions. He also refused to discourse on the current fascination with "death of God" theology, even as an academic hypothesis. To him, pronouncing those very words was blasphemous.

That said, recognition by the liberal Protestant establishment validated, as it were, a mandate to represent biblical Judaism in interfaith dialogues. Heschel launched his lecture tour for Union on January 10, 1966 (the day before his fifty-ninth birthday). An article in the January 31 issue of *Newsweek* by the religion editor, Kenneth Woodward, a progressive Catholic, featured Heschel's "radical Judaism": "With his appointment to Union, Heschel has become the center, and in a sense the source, of a new understanding between Christians and Jews which transcends the superficialities of conventional brotherhood."[52]

While lecturing under Union auspices, Heschel was also gaining prominence in the Catholic academic world. In March, Saint Michael's College in Winooski, Vermont, awarded Heschel his first honorary doctorate. (He was the first Jew to receive this honor from the Catholic institution.) Two weeks later, the University of Notre Dame also bestowed an honorary degree on Heschel. He had come to Indiana to participate in a weeklong international conference on Vatican II that also marked the opening of Notre Dame's Graduate School of Theology and Institute for Advanced Religious Studies, the very type of program for which Heschel had pressed strongly in Rome.[53]

Heschel's vigorous interfaith efforts continued unabated after he completed his visiting professorship at Union in May 1966. In August 1967, for example, he addressed an international gathering of Catholic leaders in Toronto—a veritable summit of Catholic theologians, who had come from France, Germany, Holland, the United States, and Canada. Forty-three papers were given to some two thousand participants and outside spectators via closed-circuit television, broadcast television, and radio.[54]

Attentive to his listeners' theological sophistication, Heschel asserted that Christians had to accept the continuity of their tradition with the Hebrew Bible: "The saying 'God of Israel' has no possessive or exclusive connotation: God belonging to Israel alone. Its true meaning is that the God of all men has entered into a Covenant with one people for the sake of all people."[55] Even more audaciously, Heschel criticized Christianity for reducing theology to Christology, placing Jesus the Son (rather than God) at the center of the faith. This emphasis not only excluded Jews, he insisted; it created hazards for believing Christians, who might do without God by hanging onto Jesus of Nazareth.

Heschel had consolidated his authority as a Jewish theologian among Roman Catholics committed to the spiritual revolution of Vatican II, as he had with the liberal Protestant establishment. These spiritual alliances would soon be sorely tested politically.

CHAPTER 12

Civil Rights, Vietnam, and Israel, 1965–1969

Heschel's dissent became more overtly political. On January 20, 1965, Lyndon Baines Johnson was inaugurated president of the United States, elected in a landslide over Barry Goldwater, a conservative Republican feared as too militaristic. That February, Johnson intensified the war in Vietnam, unleashing massive bombings on the north while the U.S. Marines arrived in the south on March 8. The U.S. escalation became Johnson's war, an affair of relentless military destruction. Yet he remained optimistic about achieving his "Great Society" of economic and racial equity. "Guns and Butter" became his slogan.

Heschel kept close watch on national events—reading the *New York Times* every day, following other news sources, studying books on the international situation—all the while continuing to teach, write, give speeches, travel to conferences—and endeavor to influence the Second Vatican Council. On top of it all, his opposition to the Vietnam War was consuming him. An inner crisis had led Heschel to conclude that the United States' assault on North Vietnam was "an evil act."[1] He deemed the Johnson administration misguided, wedded to the Cold War notion that "Communism [is] the devil and the only source of evil in the world." He vociferously opposed military support for the corrupt Saigon regime and rebuked the silent American majority for their apathy toward the military intervention in Southeast Asia: "If . . . deep sensitivity to evil is to be called hysterical, what name should be given to the abysmal indifference to evil which the prophet bewails?"[2]

Yet his activism had no institutional backing. He was not connected to Reform Judaism, whose leaders were in the vanguard of the antiwar movement, as well as the civil rights movement and other social justice issues of the day. Orthodox rabbis, closer to his observance, either rejected political protest or upheld the U.S. government's commitment to military victory. The Conservative movement had less unanimity, while leaning in temperament toward moderate, nuanced support. A majority of the Jewish Theological Seminary faculty deliberately dissociated themselves from Heschel's involvement, among them Heschel's closest colleagues and friends—Wolfe Kelman, Fritz Rothschild, and Seymour Siegel (a former student). Mordecai Kaplan's small Reconstructionist movement did not yet embrace the political militancy shared with other progressive Jews in later years.

Heschel soon became the most visible traditional Jew in the anti–Vietnam War movement, judging events according to sacred Jewish values.

COMMUNITY OF FAITH AND DISSENT

Heschel had—of necessity—been aware of political currents since his youth in Warsaw, and especially in Vilna and Berlin during the rise of Hitler. Yet at heart, Heschel was a contemplative personality who craved solitude for prayer, study, and reflection. "Loneliness was both a burden and a blessing," he later wrote, "and above all indispensable for achieving a kind of stillness in which perplexities could be faced without fear."

When asked, he traced his newly found activism of the early 1960s to his expansion (both revision and translation) of his 1933 doctoral dissertation into *The Prophets*. Although he had attempted, unsuccessfully, to publish a translation of his thesis around 1954—it was deemed too technical, dry—his plumbing the depths of lives and feelings of these ancient radicals inspired a more personal approach. As he wrote in the introduction to *The Prophets* dated August 1962, "The situation of a person immersed in the prophets' words is one of being exposed to a ceaseless shattering of indifference, and one needs a skull of stone to remain callous to such blows."[3]

His phenomenology of prophetic consciousness, the detached analysis of the biblical narratives, led him to identify with their sacred demands: "Reflection about the prophets gives way to communion with the prophets." This new book became a sacred blueprint for his present commitments. He believed the United States could not defeat North Vietnam without destroying the country's human as well as natural resources. Citing Leviticus 19:16, "Thou shalt not stand idly by the blood of thy neighbor," he declared that the American government needed to withdraw immediately from Vietnam and that American citizens were duty-bound to publicly oppose the war. For people of faith, protesting against this injustice was a religious obligation, "a supreme commandment."

Perhaps above all, as a patriotic naturalized citizen, Heschel feared for the American soul. "In regard to the cruelties committed in the name of a free society," he wrote, "some are guilty, all are responsible."[4] In his judgment, most citizens were indifferent to what he deemed the criminal behavior of their elected government. And even though religious law required Jews to obey the rules of the country in which they lived, it also recognized that "whenever a decree is unambiguously immoral, one nevertheless has a duty to disobey it." Militaristic thinking as such was an immediate peril: "I . . . previously thought that we were waging war reluctantly, with sadness at killing so many people. I realize that we are doing it now with pride in our military efficiency."

In the fall of 1965, while still teaching at Union Theological Seminary, Heschel joined a protest rally organized by a local committee of both Christians and Jewish clergy. At issue were the Johnson administration's maneuvers to stifle dissent. On October 25 (about two weeks before his Fosdick inaugural lecture), he joined a Lutheran minister and a Jesuit priest in speaking out at the United Nations Church Center, 777 UN Plaza in New York. The Lutheran, Richard John Neuhaus, pastor of St. John the Evangelist in the poor and predominantly African American Bedford-Stuyvesant neighborhood of Brooklyn, expressed shock that "the President should be amazed by dissent." The Jesuit, Daniel Berrigan, a poet and ardent pacifist, insisted that it was the duty of all religious persons to involve themselves in politics. Heschel proposed a national religious movement to end the war. He told a *New York Times* reporter that this group would establish an official body to continue its opposition. Neuhaus and Berrigan were taken by surprise, but they approved the idea.[5]

In November, Heschel participated in a "teach-in" on Vietnam with more than five hundred clergy. Absent was the charismatic Berrigan, who, the FBI noted in their files, "had been sent to South America by his superiors in an effort to prevent his further participation in protests against the Vietnam War." (Francis Cardinal Spellman had begun wielding his authority against Catholic dissenters.) It was probably Heschel's idea to represent the exiled Jesuit with an empty chair on stage. The Hasidim of Bratslav continued to honor their revered leader Rabbi Nahman after his death by placing his empty chair in their Jerusalem synagogue.[6]

The National Emergency Committee of Clergy Concerned about Vietnam was founded on January 11, 1966 (Heschel's fifty-ninth birthday), at the apartment of Union Theological Seminary president John Coleman Bennett. Elected co-chairs were Neuhaus, Berrigan, and Heschel—a Protestant, a Catholic, and a Jew.

Liberal Protestants dominated the movement. Catholic priests and nuns were slower in coming to the fore due to their vows of obedience to American bishops and Roman authorities who objected to their participation. But soon, incited by students in Catholic universities, thousands of Catholic clergy—even a few bishops—joined the protests as individuals of conscience. By April, the committee obtained office space from the National Council of Churches (Protestant) at its center at 475 Riverside Drive. Volunteers helped establish nearly 165 local committees in more than twenty states. With the energetic Yale University chaplain William Sloane Coffin Jr. serving as acting executive secretary, this network of notables soon achieved national outreach.[7]

The committee's first act was to send a telegram to the recently inaugurated President Johnson urging him to extend the bombing halt that had begun the previous Christmas and to pursue negotiations with the National Liberation Front and the North Vietnamese. Among the twenty-eight signatories were Philip Berrigan (a Josephite priest and brother of Daniel), Reinhold Niebuhr, Martin Luther King Jr., editors and theologians, presidents of the Reform and Conservative rabbinical associations, and other national and international religious leaders. For the next few months, the group added members and organized or sponsored acts of spiritual resistance to the war— rallies, fasts, vigils, and other forms of nonconfrontational protest. Their approach was moderate, cautious, and patriotic. Even peaceful violations of laws, the staple of nonviolent civil rights actions, were rejected. The means had to be compatible with the ends.

Many supporters of the new interfaith anti-Vietnam movement considered Heschel to be "the most influential Jewish leader on the National Emergency Committee" and "its prophetic voice." As had been the case during the Vatican II negotiations, his philosophical training and immense knowledge of Christian and Jewish sources boosted his ability to interpret the religious significance of current issues. Far more than a photogenic figurehead, Heschel was also involved in the day-to-day details, participating regularly in meetings, helping to draft position papers, even raising money. He sent letters to rabbis and influential Jewish laity, asking them to join as sponsors.

Heschel had finally found his true religious-political community. He relished these principled activists, who in turn admired him as an embodiment of their shared biblical vision of peace and prophetic outrage. His closest bond was with William Sloane Coffin Jr., a charming, immensely talented, devout Presbyterian minister who was zealously committed to social justice and fascinated by Judaism. He had married a Jewish woman, Eva Rubinstein, the daughter of the pianist Arthur Rubinstein.

Coffin and Heschel met during their first week of organizing the Emergency Committee and connected almost immediately. The activist pastor felt himself to be in the presence of a venerable prophet, "the most rabbinic figure I had ever seen or heard."[8] Heschel invited him to share the family Sabbath dinner the very next evening.

Coffin was impressed by Sylvia Heschel, with whom he shared musical affinities, and their "precocious fourteen-year-old daughter," Susannah. Already he felt enough at ease with Heschel to press the volatile issue of conversion. Wouldn't it be "to the greater glory of God" (*ad majorem Dei gloriam*, the Jesuit motto) if the Jewish people accepted the divinity of Christ? he asked. Heschel countered with a personal, rather than a theological question: "Tell me, my friend, were the Sabbath never again welcomed in this fashion, were the Torah and Talmud no longer studied, were the ark of the covenant of the Lord no longer opened in synagogues the world around, tell me, would that be *ad majorem Dei gloriam?*" Taking this stirring testimony as a test of wits, Coffin answered indirectly: "Father Abraham, you are not only a great philosopher and theologian, you're a shrewd old Jew."

Heschel, taken aback at this unaccustomed familiarity, asked for an explanation. Coffin replied from a less dogmatic viewpoint: "Well, I have a question for you. Do you think it is *ad majorem Dei gloriam* that God's chosen people should not have recognized God's love, in person, on earth?" Heschel was silent for some time. "Then," Coffin would later relate, "raising his shoulders and turning up the palms of his hands, [Heschel] said: 'Put it that way and we have a dilemma.' Then he proceeded to prove how possible and interesting it is to live with that dilemma. . . . Heschel wasn't out to convert me, and I couldn't see why any Christian would want Heschel to accept Jesus Christ as his Lord and Savior. Wasn't it enough that he was close to [being] a saint?"

PROTEST AND POLITICAL ACTION

The National Emergency Committee of Clergy Concerned about Vietnam (which in May 1966 changed its name to Clergy and Laymen Concerned about Vietnam) continued its "middle ground" strategy of attempting to persuade the U.S. government to decrease bombings and press for a negotiated settlement. Deciding that the organization should remain in existence until the end of the war, they hired a full-time executive director: Richard Fernandez, a young, brash, witty minister who had served in the army and later, as part of his campus work, participated in the civil rights movement.

Fasting and prayer were Heschel's favored tactics of opposition. Through such acts of repentance, he hoped to bring others to a recognition of error or sin, and thus to positive acts of restoration. The clergy were innocent of the crimes for which they "repented," but as Heschel repeatedly insisted, "in a free society, some are guilty, all are responsible."

In September 1966 he published a fierce sermon, "The Moral Outrage of Vietnam," in *Fellowship*, the magazine of the interfaith pacifist organization Fellowship of Reconciliation. To dramatize the national dilemma, he opened with a surrealistic scene: "It is weird to wake up one morning and find that we have been placed in an insane asylum while asleep at night. It is even more weird to wake up and find that we have been involved in slaughter and destruction without knowing it."[9]

Even the idea of an enemy is "obsolete," he asserted, since

"yesterday's enemy is becoming today's ally." He praised the rise of "engaged Buddhism, as evidenced in the growing involvement of the Vietnamese monks in the daily life of the people," and expressed empathy with the Vietnamese victims through the lens of the God of pathos: "God is present whenever man is afflicted, and humanity is embroiled in every agony wherever it may be."

Clergy and Laymen Concerned about Vietnam staged its first national mobilization, in Washington DC, January 31–February 1, 1967. Using the 1963 civil rights March on Washington as its model, the event encompassed action workshops, visits to high government officials, and picketing in front of the White House. More than two thousand clergy and laity from forty-five states participated, most of them bringing sleeping gear in order to spend the night on the floors of local churches.[10]

The assembly marched to the White House, where a silent vigil was held. Refused a parade permit, the marchers had to keep moving in circles. Nearby, an anti-Communist zealot displayed signs and sang "God Bless America." When he pulled out a poster that read "Communism Is Jewish from Beginning to End," the police carried him away—but he had managed to monopolize the newspaper photographers. Also opposing the protesters were about 250 people from a well-organized Christian fundamentalist group carrying "Communist Stooges," "Victory," and other signs. After the picketing, the Clergy and Laymen Concerned about Vietnam group walked silently to the Capitol.

The significance of their Washington mobilization far surpassed the mammoth media event. At the center was a solemn interfaith worship "Service of Witness in Time of War" at the New York Avenue Presbyterian Church that combined ethics, politics, and spiritual transformation—crowning the first day of lobbying with heartfelt sanctity. Worshiping together for peace cultivated an ambiance of harmony, despite striking theological differences and the overwhelmingly Protestant content.

Heschel's speech, crafted from his "Moral Outrage of Vietnam" article, electrified the audience. He began by quoting Ezekiel 34:25–30: "I will make with them a covenant of peace, and will cause evil beasts to cease out of the land. . . . And they shall know that I, the Lord their God, am with them"—the poignancy heightened by his sing-song and plaintive, high-pitched voice inflected with his Yiddish accent. He contrasted Ezekiel's pastoral utopia protected by God's loving care with the ravaging "wild beasts" of Vietnam: "We implore Thee, our Father in heaven, help us to banish the beast from our hearts, the beast of cruelty, the beast of callousness. . . . In the sight of so many thousands of civilians and soldiers slain, injured, crippled, of bodies emaciated, of forests destroyed by fire, God confronts us with this question: Where art thou?"[11]

The next day, a notable delegation from the group—Heschel, Bennett, Coffin, Neuhaus, Protestant theologian Robert McAfee Brown, Central Conference of American Rabbis president Jacob Weinstein, and Stanford University's Catholic chaplain Michael Novak—met with Secretary of Defense Robert McNamara. The *New York Times* reported that they spent forty minutes with him in his Pentagon office, attempting to persuade McNamara to suspend the bombing of North Vietnam and begin peace negotiations. "Mr. McNamara's reply to the clerics' requests was not disclosed," the *Times* vaguely concluded.[12]

The inside story of the meeting reveals an emotional drama beneath the diplomatic give-and-take. A fifteen-minute appointment had been made. Television cameras and reporters swarmed about while the delegation was led to McNamara's office. In his later account Coffin savored every detail: "Over the far door the clock registered 4:13. There was no question in my mind that at exactly 4:15 the door would open. At 4:15 it did, revealing a handsome woman in an Air Force uniform who announced, 'The Secretary of Defense.' We turned to see the immaculately dressed man we had seen so often on television and in the newspapers. But news photos could never do justice to the energy that literally bounded into the room. Nor could they do more than hint at what I sensed immediately—his decency. It was disconcerting."[13]

The conversation started awkwardly. McNamara shook everyone's hand and began by thanking the clergy for their concern. Coffin summarized the Clergy and Laymen Concerned about Vietnam position paper and handed McNamara a copy. At that moment, without visible cause, Heschel erupted with indignation. He was out of control, Coffin believed, as "he poured forth his anguish, his hands gesticulating pathetically." The secretary of defense showed no emotion and listened carefully, "more with astonishment than understanding." But, sympathizing with the rabbi's anguish and righteous anger, McNamara was moved to extend the meeting another fifteen minutes.

Coffin and his colleagues were not impressed by McNamara's arguments. He claimed to favor restraint in the bombing while hoping that the North Vietnamese would be more willing to negotiate, but he maintained the right of U.S. forces to bomb North Vietnam without an official declaration of war. The clergy considered McNamara a war criminal because of his actions, yet on the human level, they found him to be "a nice guy," a man of decency and integrity, "a true innocent." For the Clergy and Laymen Concerned about Vietnam group, the meeting ended unsatisfactorily. But Heschel's outburst might have reinforced McNamara's own nascent opposition to American military policy.

As the next year's events were being planned, the group leaders enlisted Martin Luther King Jr., a sponsor of Clergy and Laymen Concerned about Vietnam from its inception, to mark a turning point in opposition to the war. Along with Heschel and other highly regarded figures, King delivered a major address against the war on April 4 at New York's imposing Riverside Church. The spiritual alliance of King and Heschel was reinforced before an audience of more than three thousand.[14]

King had criticized the government's Vietnam policy as early as 1965, but up to this time he had been reluctant to jeopardize public and government support for civil rights and President Johnson's War on Poverty by taking too vocal a stand. Now he decided to end what he called his "shameful silence."[15]

Greeted by a standing ovation, King began, "I come to this magnificent house of worship tonight because my conscience leaves me no other choice. . . . I am in deepest agreement with the aims and work of the organization which has brought us together: Clergy and Laymen Concerned about Vietnam." Answering his critics from the civil rights camp who opposed his foreign policy pronouncements, he declared that the Vietnam War had become "the enemy of the poor," for President Johnson's poverty program was "broken and eviscerated as if it were some idle political plaything of a society gone mad on war." African American soldiers were being killed in disproportionate numbers. Violence in the urban ghettos, primarily black crime, was a symptom of a larger American illness. His government, King asserted, had become "the greatest purveyor of violence in the world today."[16]

Speaking after King, Heschel condemned the Vietnam War as threatening our very humanity and offered compassion as the guide to positive action: "Has our conscience become a fossil? Is all mercy gone? If mercy, the mother of humility, is still alive as a demand, how can we say 'yes' to our bringing agony to that tormented country?"[17]

Clergy and Laymen Concerned about Vietnam printed a slim volume, *Vietnam: Crisis of Conscience*, in May 1967. Heschel again offered "The Moral Outrage of Vietnam," framing the short essay as "an appeal to the individual conscience." Among his striking formulations was a denunciation of militarism as "whoredom, voluptuous and vicious, first disliked and then relished." The religious anti-war movement now had its official sourcebook. Within the year *Vietnam: Crisis of Conscience* sold more than fifty thousand copies.

THE SIX-DAY WAR

Much the same as King and his civil rights allies, Heschel continued to be pressured by many Jewish allies to halt or modify his public opposition to the Vietnam War. Tensions were mounting in the Jewish community. Many supporters of Israel feared that if American Jews opposed the Vietnam War too blatantly, the Johnson administration would withdraw its economic and military aid to the Jewish state.

Meanwhile Heschel received direct demands from Israel to end his anti-war activities. A member of the Israeli embassy came to his office to insist that he abandon public protest. Another influential Israeli asked Elie Wiesel to talk to Heschel. Wiesel and Heschel spent an entire afternoon together, walking back and forth, discussing what a Jew should do in this situation. At one point, Heschel stopped in the middle of the street: "Listen, there are people in Vietnam who have been bombarded for years and years and years and they haven't slept a single night. How can we simply go on and not try to help them sleep at night?" This vivid image stayed with Wiesel. He took Heschel's side, though with discretion.[18]

Intensifying these debates, the leaders of Egypt, Syria, and Jordan were increasingly menacing Israel. The pan-Arabist luminary Gamal Abdel Nasser was repeatedly broadcasting his pledge to drive the Jews into the sea. Despite the Arabs' penchant for rhetorical excess, the Israelis were forced to take these declarations seriously. Heschel, and most Israelis and Jews around the world, relived nightmares of the Nazi genocide.

The situation reached its crisis point on May 23, 1967, when

Nasser blockaded the Straits of Tiran, effectively cutting off Israel from Africa and Asia and defying international law. His act of aggression also increased the peril of war between the Soviets and the Americans, who supported opposite sides in the conflict.

During the weeks of Arab military buildup and terrorist raids on Israel, a number of prominent Christians (e.g., Martin Luther King Jr., John Coleman Bennett, Robert McAfee Brown, Reinhold Niebuhr) signed an advertisement supporting the Jewish state and opposing the Arab blockade, which ran in the *New York Times* on Sunday, June 4, 1967. Headlined "The Moral Responsibility in the Middle East," the proclamation urged the U.S. government to "recall that Israel is a new nation whose people are still recovering from the horror of the European holocaust." But it was too late. The very next day, as Egypt, Syria, and Jordan prepared a devastating attack, the Israelis destroyed Egypt's entire air force and, with fierce fighting on all fronts, the West Bank. Captured as well were the Golan Heights and, most poignantly for religious Jews, the Old City of Jerusalem.

The Six-Day War (as Jews would subsequently call the victorious Israeli campaign of June 5–11) brought a sea change to Jews throughout the world. Suddenly, everywhere Jews rediscovered their identity. On the North American continent, in Europe, in North Africa, in Soviet Russia, even assimilated or nonobservant bystanders were seized by an unexpected, passionate identification with the Jewish state. Thousands of Jews, young and old, flew to Israel to help the Israelis or planned to settle in the Jewish homeland. Heschel, too, renewed his commitment to Zion, as he once again bore witness to Israel's miraculous survival.

Heschel spent the month of July in Jerusalem. He walked all around, but especially in the Old City, newly liberated by the Israeli army. As he touched the stones of the Western Wall, previously denied to Jews by the Jordanian authorities, he recovered concretely the Holy City of his daily prayers.

Heschel communicated these events using all the poetic instruments at his disposal. Speaking in Hebrew to a group of Conservative rabbis at Beit Berl, the teachers college near Tel Aviv, he expressed his amazement at what had occurred—not only the miraculous military victory, but also the worldwide renewal of Jewish identity.[19] The Six-Day War was "a time of a religious resurrection. . . . as if the Bible were continuing to be written." More analytically, Heschel attributed the Israeli victory to three factors: "the heroism of the Jews in Israel; the Jews in the Diaspora; and divine power. These three sources enabled the Jews to survive the Holocaust, the 1948 War of Independence, and the Six-Day War."

Heschel also declared that supporters of Israel have a moral obligation to the world at large: "Another part of this vision is a peaceful Jewish state, which should stand as a model to the Gentiles. This is why we should aspire toward peace. Now is the time to start negotiating with the Arabs; the God of Israel is the same as the God of the Arabs."[20]

Back in the United States, Heschel also prepared a poetic essay in English, "An Echo of Eternity," for *Hadassah* magazine's special issue on Jerusalem. In lyrical rhythms he voiced the yearning of Jews over the centuries: "The Wall. At first I faint. Then I see: a Wall of frozen tears, a cloud of sighs. The Wall. Palimpsests, hiding books, secret names. The stones are seals." The liberation of Jerusalem had inspired Heschel's liturgy of return.[21]

THE MOST ARDUOUS TEST

It was at this turning point in history that interfaith cooperation—coalitions supporting civil rights and the anti-war movement—faced, and failed, its most arduous test.

The swift Israeli victory aggravated existing disagreements. Almost immediately after the war's end, many Christians of good will expressed their sympathy for the newly occupied Palestinians while attempting, respectfully, to scrutinize the disparity of views among gentiles and Jews. *Christian Century* introduced its July 26, 1967, issue with an almost desperate humor: "It occurred to us as we planned this potentially incendiary issue on the Middle East crisis that it might be wise to have it printed on asbestine paper."[22]

In a scrupulous essay, "Urbis and Orbis: Jerusalem Today," James Sanders, Heschel's friend from Union Theological Seminary, sought to be impartial. Mindful of the fragility of interfaith dialogue, Sanders explained, "I am as 'pro-Jewish' as any Christian in print. Not only have I disavowed all forms of the Christian mission to the Jews; I have publicly defended the view that Christianity needs Judaism to perform and fulfill her 'Mission of Israel' to the world and to the church."[23] But he felt duty bound to reject the idea of a Palestinian state under Israeli domination. He opposed Israel's annexation of the Holy City, fearing "a more serious Arab crusade," and he called for the internationalization of Jerusalem, even urging that it revert to "Jordanian administration under massive UN presence."

The summer of 1967 was a low point in Heschel's Christian friendships. Sanders's article pained him, and the two did not speak for some time. Then, running into Sanders in the Union Theological Seminary's bookstore, Heschel brought up the issue. They took a walk, and as Sanders recalled, "I asked about the issue of holy space. He said that he knew I would ask, and we were back on track."[24] Avoidance was no longer necessary.

Trusting in the power of such candid communication, Sanders invited faculty from both the Jewish Theological Seminary and Union Theological Seminary to his apartment. But Heschel, overcome with distress, instead of building on their common devotion to one God, or on "the tragic insufficiency of human faith," discomfited his Christian colleagues by urging them to endorse a public statement of support for the Jewish state. As Sanders described it, "the Christians simply fell silent. They had not thought they would be asked to sign, as some later put it, a political document about Near Eastern foreign policy."[25] Heschel had once again foregone diplomacy to assert his prophetic devotion to truth and justice.

HALAKHAH AND INTERFAITH SPIRITUAL PROTEST

The anti-war movement continued to goad Heschel's preoccupation, almost obsession, with Vietnam. The second Clergy and Laymen Concerned about Vietnam national mobilization was scheduled for February 5–6, 1968, in Washington DC. The FBI domestic intelligence division carefully monitored the preparations, although details were readily available: Martin Luther King Jr. had announced them on January 12 at a press conference in New York City.

Right before the mobilization began, Heschel met with two prominent Reform rabbis—Maurice Eisendrath, president of the Union of American Hebrew Congregations (UAHC, the synagogue arm of the movement), and Balfour Brickner, co-director of the UAHC's National Commission on Social Action—at the Religious Action Center of Reform Judaism in Washington DC. They asked him why he was willing to join political coalitions associated with the New Left that opposed Israel, and Heschel responded with one of his favorite stories: "There was a Russian Jew whose son was drafted into the Czarist army, a tour of duty that might last 25 years. The father was alarmed. His son would be forced to eat *chazer* [pork, in Yiddish], since that was the only meat available to Russian soldiers. This would be an appalling desecration. He explained the situation to his rabbi: If his son didn't eat the pork he would starve to death. What did the rabbi decide?—He can eat the *chazer*, but he shouldn't lick his lips."

This forced eating of *treif* (ritually impure food) represented the compromises required by the Vietnam emergency. According to Jewish law, mitzvot such as kashrut and Sabbath observance were primary, but nonetheless had to be suspended for the sake of *pikuach nefesh*, saving a human life.[26]

After this visit to the Reform Religious Action Center (the RAC), Heschel then joined other Clergy and Laymen Concerned about Vietnam leaders for the opening plenary and interfaith worship service. There, after prayers of repentance, Heschel struck out at Americans' relative indifference to the sufferings in Vietnam: "The Lord roars like a lion. His word is like fire, like a hammer breaking rocks to pieces, and people go about unmoved, undisturbed, unaware. . . . A nation so rich in the appreciation of human dignity, in generosity and compassion, is destroying its own integrity in order to perform a game of power in the theater of absurdity."

Heschel's protest was deeply patriotic, and deeply spiritual, devoted to the ideal of America, intent on provoking the nation's conscience. In the typed manuscript of his speech, he added and underlined the final sentence: "*This is a war against America!*"[27]

The next morning, a memorial service at Arlington National Cemetery completed the liturgical protest. Forty chartered buses had brought people to honor the war dead—though they had to stand outside the cemetery walls, because Clergy and Laymen Concerned about Vietnam had been denied a permit to use the amphitheater. Heschel and other leaders then joined "a procession of agony" led by King. James Shannon, the auxiliary Roman Catholic bishop of Minneapolis, carried a cross; Rabbi Eisendrath carried a Torah scroll; Heschel, King, and others carried miniature American flags. It was an impressive, and photogenic, event.

The weather was beautiful, a crisp day, a clear and sunny sky. On the white steps before the Tomb of the Unknown Soldier, the only sounds were the slap of rifle butts and clicking of heels during the changing of the guard. Marching eight abreast half a mile down Arlington Ridge Road, the two thousand protestors passed row upon row of white tombstones, most bearing crosses but some showing Stars of David, all straight and orderly, but with mounds of fresh earth here and there.

The procession stopped. Dr. King intoned, "In this moment of complete silence, let us pray." All heads were bowed in soundless prayer for six minutes. Heschel broke the stillness with a lament in Hebrew from Psalm 22, which the Gospel of Mark also gave as the last words of Jesus: *Eli, Eli, lamah azavtani* (My God, my God, why hast Thou forsaken me?). Bishop Shannon closed the simple ceremony: "Let us go in peace. Amen."[28]

ALIENATION FROM WITHIN

As Heschel pushed forward with anti-war efforts, his alienation from his close Jewish associates increased. Soon after the mobilization, he signed two full-page advertisements in the *New York Times*, one supporting a negotiated settlement of the war and the other urging Americans to safeguard dissent and freedom of speech. Forthrightly pro-war, David C. Kogan, administrative vice chancellor of the Jewish Theological Seminary, and Wolfe Kelman, among others, signed a protest letter to the editor in the *New York Times*: "To point an accusing finger only at our armed forces and that of our allies creates the impression that all the evil is on one side. This lack of balance will no doubt serve the Communist cause well."[29]

Heschel was especially vulnerable to criticism from Orthodox Jews. When photographs of the interfaith mobilization appeared in newspapers around the world, angry letters poured into the Union of American Hebrew Congregations headquarters. Heschel was blamed for allowing Rabbi Eisendrath to desecrate a Torah scroll by carrying it into a cemetery, an act forbidden by Jewish law.

Leaders of Reform Judaism took this objection seriously. Eisendrath, post facto, consulted Solomon Freehof, the eminent Reform rabbi from Pittsburgh, and Heschel. Freehof cited the basic rule that "as long as you are not within four cubits of the dead (which is about three yards) you contravened no law. Besides, it is not sure that the Torah was kosher, not having [been examined] for errors in recent years. The Torah has to be regularly proofread."

Rallying his vast halakhic knowledge, Heschel telephoned his responsa (legal interpretations of *halakhah*) to Religious Action Center director Rabbi Richard Hirsch. Heschel drew six judgments from traditional sources:

1) In *Berachot* 18a, it says that "a man should not walk in a cemetery with tefillin on his head or a scroll of the Law in his arms and recite the *Shema*." [Heschel added:] "or read the Torah," but it does not say that it is prohibited to hold the Torah if a man does not read from it. 2) Maimonides maintains that even holding the Torah is prohibited. 3) The above applies to a Jewish cemetery, but in this instance, Arlington Cemetery is non-sectarian and obviously the same rules would not apply as in the instance of a Jewish cemetery. 4) The reciting of the *Shema* (and the reading of the Torah) is forbidden within four cubits of the dead, but in Arlington Cemetery, at no time was the Torah within four cubits of a grave. . . . 5) The noted Yechezkel Landau, in his commentary *Nodah bi-Yehuda* [a collection of more than 860 responsa, Prague, 1776] interpreted a passage in the Zohar to signify that at a time of great stress, the Torah should be taken by the community to the cemetery to pray, for example, for rain or to stop a plague. 6) In the 1956 Suez Campaign, Rabbi Shlomo Goren, chief chaplain of the Israeli army, was photographed taking the Torah in one hand and a rifle in the other to wage war. Is it not proper for us to use the Torah (without a rifle) to pray for peace? Heschel asked rhetorically.[30]

Heschel's mastery of *halakhah* demonstrated his life-affirming support for traditional (and Orthodox) Judaism. Rabbi Hirsch's memorandum to Eisendrath further exonerated Heschel for his part in the event.

Hirsch explained that the idea of using the Torah at Arlington Cemetery had first been introduced at a Clergy and Laymen Concerned about Vietnam board meeting, at which Heschel had opposed it on the grounds that the Torah was not a symbol for Jews in the sense that a cross was a symbol for Christians. But, shortly before the prayer service at Arlington Cemetery, when the Christians said that they were going to march behind a cross, Heschel, put on the spot, realized that for Jews to march behind a cross would represent a real *issur* (prohibition). He decided that in terms of public perception, it was better to march behind a Torah; the appearance of compromise was the lesser evil.

HONORED AS SCHOLAR AND ACTIVIST

Heschel turned sixty on January 11, 1967. By then he had achieved national, even international acclaim. Yet, he had not received esteemed recognition from the Conservative movement, for which he had worked and taught for decades. Eminent academics were usually honored at their fiftieth, jubilee birthday and given a Festschrift, a collection of essays in which colleagues and former students commented on the academic's work. In Heschel's case, no such Festschrift had been bestowed, and Heschel studies were far from becoming an established academic specialty.

Finally, in March 1968, rabbis of the Conservative movement attending the annual Rabbinical Assembly convention celebrated Heschel's sixtieth birthday (a year late), honoring his manifold contributions to Jewish scholarship and his social activism (most Conservative strongly supported the civil rights movement, and many still disapproved of America's intervention in Southeast Asia).

In the evening, the rabbis paid tribute to their keynote speaker, Dr. Martin Luther King Jr., by singing "We Shall Overcome" in Hebrew. Then Heschel introduced the prestigious guest, praising him as an authentic prophet: "Where in America do we hear a voice like the voice of the prophets of Israel? Martin Luther King is a sign that God has not forsaken the United States of America. God has sent him to us. His presence is the hope of America."

In his address, King reaffirmed the still positive alliance of African Americans and Jews, despite growing concerns about black antisemitism, the emerging issue of affirmative action, and divisive views on Israel and the Vietnam War. He spoke of being deeply moved by hearing the civil rights anthem sung in the language of the prophets. And he honored Heschel, acclaiming Heschel's speech at the 1963 Chicago Conference on Religion and Race and his participation in the Selma to Montgomery march. He considered Heschel "a truly great prophet"; he hoped to return to the Rabbinical Assembly to celebrate Heschel's hundredth birthday.[31]

After King's speech, the rabbis and pastor engaged in a frank exchange of views, characterized by candor and mutual respect. Most important, perhaps, was King's support for Israel: while peace was the issue, security came first. "We must stand with all our might to protect its right to exist, its territorial integrity," he proclaimed. For the Arabs, peace required another kind of security—basic economic stability: "These nations, as you know, are part of the third world of hunger, of disease, of illiteracy. I think that as long as these conditions exist there will be tensions, that there will be the endless quest to find scapegoats." King called for "a Marshall Plan for the Middle East" that would bring impoverished Arabs "into the mainstream of economic security."[32]

King urged the rabbis to support economic justice by opposing the Vietnam War, which was undermining the war on poverty, as well as by supporting, both financially and with their participation, the Poor People's Campaign that June: "We need a movement to transmute the rage of the ghetto into a positive constructive force."

The following day was devoted to Heschel. Formal papers by Edmond Cherbonnier, chairman of the Religion Department at

Trinity College in Hartford, Connecticut, and Fritz Rothschild and Seymour Siegel of the Jewish Theological Seminary explored Heschel's thought.

That afternoon Heschel gave the annual Rabbinical Assembly lecture. It was the first time in his twenty-three years on the JTS faculty that he had been accorded this honor (which was usually reserved for Mordecai Kaplan).

"The Theological Meaning of *Medinat Yisra'el* [the State of Israel]" asserted the meaning of the people, the land, and the state. Heschel opened by celebrating the Six-Day War as a vindication of an exiled people. The "existential fact" of being a Jew necessarily included "attachment to the land, waiting for the renewal of Jewish life in the land of Israel." Israel's astounding victory inspired a revival of religious faith, even "a new certainty." Israel's survival was providential; "Bible lives on, always being written, continuously proclaimed." Again Heschel disputed the (mostly Christian) "death of God" theologians, who blamed the Nazi extermination on divine absence: "We all died in Auschwitz, yet our faith survived. . . . At that moment in history we saw the beginning of a new awakening, the emergence of a new concern for a living God theology."[33]

Quite explicitly, Heschel rejected the perilous notion that the State of Israel was God's "atonement" for not intervening to stop Hitler and his murderers: "It would be blasphemy to regard [Israel] as a compensation. However, the existence of Israel reborn makes life in the West less unendurable."

The warring extremes of Heschel's personality—melancholy and awe, dismay and exaltation—found a discordant unity in these reflections. From one perspective, Hitler darkened the world irremediably, wounding Heschel's heart forever: "If I should go to Poland or to Germany, every stone, every tree, would remind me of contempt, hatred, murder, of children killed, of mothers burned alive, of human beings asphyxiated." From the other, the rebirth of Israel offered a counterpoise: "When I go to Israel, every stone, every tree is a reminder of hard labor and glory, of prophets and psalmists, of loyalty and holiness. . . . Jews go to Israel for renewal, for the experience of resurrection." Heschel thus revitalized his Zionism while remaining true to the Diaspora.

In the discussion that followed, sharp questions took aim at the advisability of challenging the U.S. government on Vietnam and Heschel's grim view of the twentieth century "in terms of horror and destruction." Heschel pointed out that his research on members of the State Department and the Pentagon had convinced him that their decision to persist in Vietnam was a "perfect example of dehumanization of judgment." Today, America was known around the world as "the largest purveyor of violence. . . . America doesn't have a single ally." Coming close to endorsing pacifism, he recalled how, as a child, he had felt contaminated by being in a room with a man suspected of murder: "I have to be afraid of God. I don't want to be responsible for murder, for the killing of innocent people." At the same time, he reassured his critics in the room that he was "rather careful and moderate in my protest work in the peace movement." He concluded with the idea he had made the center of his mission: faith in the living God. "Without God man is a lost soul, and it is in a lost soul that the demonic comes to life."[34]

Then catastrophe struck. Two weeks after Martin Luther King Jr. saluted Heschel at the Rabbinical Assembly, the thirty-nine-year-old King was gunned down in Memphis. As riots, destruction, and looting erupted in more than a hundred American cities, the nation prepared to honor its fallen prophet.

Mrs. Coretta Scott King asked Heschel to participate in her husband's funeral. On Tuesday, April 9, Heschel flew to Atlanta and went to King's house, meeting with the bereaved family, Robert Kennedy, Jacqueline Kennedy Onassis, and other national leaders. Two services were to be given that day, and Heschel attended both—a morning service at the Ebenezer Baptist Church, where King was co-pastor with his father, and an afternoon service at Morehouse College, where King had been an undergraduate. King's widow invited Heschel to read from the Old Testament at the Morehouse service.

The passage she chose, on the Suffering Servant from Second Isaiah (53:3–5), was dear to both Jews and Christians. Christians interpreted its stirring portrait of Israel, the afflicted beloved of God, as a prefiguration of the betrayal of Christ. Dramatically, in his melancholic, singsong voice, Heschel paid a final tribute to his friend and ally.[35] The widow of Dr. King appreciated Heschel's spiritual authenticity, beyond sectarian principles, Jewish or Christian.

Nine months later, Heschel's national stature as theologian of the spiritual dimension was further recognized in the year-end issue of *Newsweek*. In a comprehensive article on prayer that cited the archbishop of Canterbury Michael Ramsey, the Greek Orthodox archbishop Iakovos, and the bishop of Rochester Fulton J. Sheen, Heschel was described as "perhaps the most knowledgeable theologian on the meaning of prayer."[36]

REFLECTIONS ON DEATH AND WAR

In mid-January 1969 Heschel embarked upon a speaking tour of Italy at the invitation of the prolific writer Elémire Zolla. The vibrant professor of Anglo-American literature was well admired for his vast knowledge of Hinduism and Buddhism, literature, and the arts. He was also a broad-minded Christian who had published Italian translations of Heschel's work in his journal *Conoscenza religiosa* (Religious knowledge).[37]

The two had first met in Rome during Vatican II, at Heschel's favorite kosher restaurant, Tenenbaum's, on via Cavour. Zolla often went there to discuss Kabbalah with a mysterious, erudite man who was doing research at the Vatican Library, whose name he never learned. One evening as he was sitting with Cristina Campo, a poet and critic interested in mysticism, the strange man announced that he would not discuss Kabbalah that evening, as someone with superior knowledge was present. He silently pointed to Heschel, who was having a drink "in the Polish manner" (straight up) with Zachariah Shuster of the American Jewish Committee. Heschel and Zolla were introduced, and Heschel asked, "Why are you interested in the Kabbalah?" Zolla answered, "It is the Kabbalah that is interested in me." Heschel responded, "Fine, that's something like the title of one of my books." Thus began many conversations and a lasting friendship.[38]

Zolla was attuned to Heschel's intuitive personality and felt "a flow of sympathy that made conversation intoxicating." The men shared similar perceptions of art. Also they both appreciated thinkers such as Henry Corbin, the French scholar of Islamic mysticism whom Heschel had first met in prewar Berlin. Later on, the two would appear together on an Italian television program about prayer.

The culmination of Heschel's trip to Italy was the First International Conference on the Genesis of Sudden Death and Reanimation. Held in Florence, it was a wide-ranging interdisciplinary meeting that included physicians, medical researchers, philosophers, and religious thinkers from Italy, France, Russia, Japan, South Africa, and the United States. On the last day, January 14, 1969, Heschel addressed the "religious-philosophical" session.

Heschel's talk, "Reflections on Death," delivered in the Sala Bianca of the ornate Pitti Palace, developed the idea that death was an essential component of human life. He had surveyed attitudes toward death in biblical, talmudic, and Hasidic sources, he explained to the audience (yet again, his lecture was refocusing material drawn from his previous writings), and this in turn had led him to his God-centered thinking: "Man's being is rooted in his being known about. It is the creation of man that opens a glimpse into the thought of God, into the meaning beyond the mystery." According to Heschel, there was no one doctrine of death in Jewish tradition; rather, the varied beliefs were less significant than their ethical value.[39]

Soon after Heschel's return from Italy, he played a major role in the third Clergy and Laymen Concerned about Vietnam mobilization, February 3–5, 1969, in Washington. This time he was cautious in his endorsement of the radical theme announced for the gathering, "Vietnam and the Future of the American Empire." But he did agree with other leaders of the now twenty-five-thousand-member group that "Americans cannot be the policeman of the world nor impose [America's] social system on other nations."[40]

Heschel also opposed the draft: "Conscription is a form of involuntary servitude. As such it is incompatible with the democracy for which we hope."[41] He stood for the new emphasis on healing America's social wounds.

Clergy and Laymen Concerned about Vietnam tried to arrange meetings with government officials. Heschel looked forward to a meeting with Henry Kissinger, President Richard Nixon's new national security adviser, scheduled for the mobilization's final day. At the last moment, Kissinger had agreed to meet with a group comprising Coretta Scott King, Heschel, Neuhaus, Fernandez, and Coffin (who was appealing his recent federal conviction for counseling young men against the draft). The *New York Times* reported the next day: "Leaders of a group that has supported defiance and evasion of the draft as a form of protest against the war in Vietnam said they were given a 'very respectful hearing' at the White House today when they pleaded for amnesty for draft resisters." The visit appeared to be a public relations success for both sides.[42]

As with the McNamara visit, the inside story revealed greater tension. The group met with Kissinger in his White House basement office. During a discussion in which Kissinger expressed frustration with the bureaucracy he had inherited, Heschel broke in, again goaded by emotion: "How could you as a good Jew prosecute a war like this?" Kissinger was tongue-tied but remained respectful toward Heschel, whose tone was more pastoral than accusatory, and muttered something in return. The visit ended in a stalemate.[43]

Clergy and Laymen Concerned about Vietnam's final interfaith worship at the Metropolitan African Methodist Episcopal Church was a fitting climax to the lobbying, crowned by a symbolic media event in which Heschel and Coretta Scott King led a solemn procession of hundreds of people out of the church and to the Constitution Avenue entrance of the Justice Department. In his brief speech, Heschel asked President Nixon to pardon all those who had refused induction. Then he, Mrs. King, and Pastor Neuhaus placed their hands on the head of Thomas Lee Hayes, a young cleric working with American draft resistors in Sweden, as the group recited, "I pledge myself to the ministry of reconciliation. To seek the release of those in prison for conscience's sake, the return in freedom of those in hiding and abroad, and to work for the rebuilding of America in a world of enduring peace."[44]

INTERPRETING ISRAEL FOR CHRISTIANS, MUSLIMS, AND JEWS

As the Vietnam protests continued, Jewish-Christian relations were increasingly undermined by conflicting views of the Jewish state, the Six-Day War, and the occupation of Arab territories. Heschel persisted in his support of the State of Israel along with his ongoing domestic protests.

Soon after the June 1967 war, recognizing his scholarly credentials and renown in the civil rights and anti-war movements, the Anti-Defamation League of the B'nai B'rith (ADL) commissioned Heschel to write a book explaining to Christians the passionate attachment of Jews to Israel. Heschel agreed to undertake this sensitive educational task after the ADL sent him a dynamic helper, Judith Herschlag. She spent late afternoons and early evenings in Heschel's Jewish Theological Seminary office being his "ear."

Israel: An Echo of Eternity, published by Farrar, Straus, was officially launched on February 20, 1969, at the ADL's Lexington Avenue headquarters. Seventy-five Christian leaders in addition to Jewish dignitaries attended the newsworthy interfaith event. The publishers and B'nai B'rith had hoped for widespread appreciation of the book's artistic quality as well. It had been illustrated by the American expressionist artist Abraham Rattner, a strongly identified Jew who worked in both Paris and New York. Israel's victory in the Six-Day War had inspired Rattner to create vivid line drawings in honor of Jerusalem, which corresponded brilliantly to Heschel's lyrical celebration of the Holy Land.

Heschel's apparent support for Israel's war, even for its defense, aroused public debate. A perceptive essay in *Time* magazine, unsigned but probably written by the religion editor, John Elson, attempted to reconcile Heschel's anti–Vietnam War stand with his justification of Israel's attack the preceding June. "Jews: A Plea for Love without Cause" opened with an anecdote taken from *Israel: An Echo of Eternity* about "a Christian friend" who had asked Heschel why he was so "dreadfully upset" during the months before the Six-Day War. "Heschel thought for a moment. Then he replied gently: 'Imagine that in the entire world there remains one copy of the Bible, and suddenly you see a brutal hand seize this copy, the only one in the world, and prepare to cast it into the flames.'" For Heschel the Jewish state was not the spiritual equivalent of the Jewish people; the State of Israel carried a universal responsibility. The article concluded, "Heschel insists that Israel must be more than usually benevolent for a secular nation, and should extend an open hand of friendship to its Arab neighbors."[45]

For some, Heschel's moral positions on war (Israel or Vietnam) were contradictory and incompatible. The reality was that Heschel subordinated ideological considerations (for example, political rights to captured territory) to the defense of human life and eternal values.

Another reality was that Heschel emphasized his commitment to the reconciliation of Jews and Arabs while he clearly favored the Jewish perspective—placing blame for the June war and the Palestinian refugee problem exclusively on the Arabs. And yet, while stressing the Jewish historical and theological claim to the Land of Israel, he was convinced that his book would promote peace. Employing what could be called ethical acrobatics, he directed *Israel: An Echo of Eternity* at readers of every background; transcending his bias, he was moved to have it translated into Arabic.

Ultimately, Heschel continued to demand that Israel measure itself according to prophetic standards. And he reaffirmed his view—first expressed in *The Sabbath*—that "we meet God in time rather than in space, in moments of faith rather than in a piece of space." It was another effort to prove his lifelong claim that the Hebrew Bible was a sacred source, and a moral challenge, to all people.[46]

NEAR-DEATH EXPERIENCE

The Vietnam War showed no sign of ending. It remained a constant source of anguish to Heschel even as he persisted in dispersing his energies among several projects.

In August 1969 Heschel was the sole Jew invited to address a mass meeting of the National Liturgical Conference (an unofficial Catholic organization) in Milwaukee. The agenda called for a fusion of inwardness and action: political change, social justice, and the virtues of prayer. Most of the attendees were young, progressive Catholics.

Heschel's meditation, a condensation of his theology and ethics of prayer, glowed with intensity. In rhythmical cadences, the rabbi offered "hope in the midst of alienation, chaos, and destruction." How could this be found? Through prayer. Prayer was a sanctuary for the "weary, sobbing soul." Prayer was—or could be—one's home, he exclaimed: "How marvelous is my home. I enter as a suppliant and emerge as a witness; I enter as a stranger and emerge as next of kin. . . . I pray because God, the *Shekhinah*, is an outcast. I pray because God is in exile, because we all conspire to blur all signs of His presence in the present or in the past. I pray because I refuse to despair. . . . *I pray because I am unable to pray.*"[47]

Heschel's outlook on prayer even explained his political dissent: "Religion as an establishment must remain separated from the government. Yet prayer as a voice of mercy, as a cry for justice, as a plea for gentleness, must not be kept apart." Religious observance, he insisted, braces us to reject the status quo, even if it means toppling the authorities: "Prayer is meaningless unless it is subversive, unless it seeks to overthrow and to ruin the pyramids of callousness, hatred, opportunism, falsehoods. The liturgical movement must become a revolutionary movement, seeking to overthrow the forces that continue to destroy the promise, the hope, the vision." Thrilled at Heschel's "terse, proverbial insights," the audience gave him a standing ovation.

But for Heschel, the strain of so much intense activity and emotion was too much. On the airplane back to New York, he suffered a massive heart attack. Upon landing he was rushed to intensive care at New York University Hospital. For several days he remained close to death. Sylvia and Susannah, now a senior at the Dalton School, kept vigil with Wolfe Kelman.

There were moments when the doctors lost hope. At one point a young intern reported to Mrs. Heschel that the monitors had briefly gone flat; her husband had been clinically dead for some minutes, but the doctors were able to revive him. The physician did not expect Heschel to survive. Sylvia answered that they must save him; thousands of people depended on him. The next day Heschel improved slightly.[48]

Kelman spent his waking hours at the hospital. When he and Heschel were alone together, they shared moments of delicate tenderness. Unable to speak and hardly able to hold a pencil, Heschel, in a shaky script, wrote this note: "I love you Wolfe. Kiss Me."[49]

Heschel remained in serious condition. On September 13, 1969, at Kelman's request, Rabbi Joshua Shmidman, who lived within walking distance of NYU Hospital, invited Sylvia and Susannah to stay at his apartment over the forthcoming High Holy Days, during which Jewish law would prohibit them from riding to the hospital.

On Rosh Hashanah, Shmidman visited Heschel, shofar in hand. Heschel looked frightening, gray-faced and hooked up to monitors and medication drips. Shmidman was afraid to speak, but he began to address Heschel in Yiddish—not the formal Lithuanian Yiddish of the Yidisher Visnshaftlekher Institut, but the earthy Yiddish of Warsaw.[50] Heschel stirred and awakened. He asked his visitor to blow the shofar, which Jews are commanded to hear when Rosh Hashanah does not fall on Shabbat. Heschel was extremely feeble, but he whispered the blessings, and as Shmidman prepared to blow, Heschel softly named the first blast: *tekiah*. . . . And then each of the others: *shevarim* . . . (Shmidman blew) *teruah* . . . *tekiah*. . . . Heschel called and Shmidman sounded all thirty blasts. Now he was sitting up, growing stronger.

As the invocation ended, Heschel "received" his visitor. Still speaking Yiddish, he asked, "Who are you?"

Shmidman explained that he was teaching Jewish philosophy at Stern College, the women's branch of Yeshiva University. They spoke about the *Akedah* (the Binding of Isaac, read on Yom Kippur) as interpreted by Kierkegaard in *Fear and Trembling*. His intellectual energy restored, Heschel described his writing projects in which the Christian existentialist played a large part.

By September 15, Heschel had recovered enough to be transferred from the intensive care unit to a private room. Still, some days his condition worsened. When his cousin Rabbi Jacob Perlow, son of the Novominsker rebbe of Williamsburg and a leader of the Agudah, came to see him, Heschel was unable to speak, so he wrote a note in Hebrew with a quotation from Psalm 22:7, *Anokhi tolaat v'lo ish* (I am a worm, less than human). Rabbi Perlow removed the "worm" reference. Heschel then wrote, *Kasheh lichyot* (It is difficult to live), and finally, *Im kitzi b'Nu York, ani rotzeh lalun etzel dodi* (If my end is to be in New York, I want to rest next to my uncle). In choosing his final resting place, Heschel was reaffirming his Hasidic roots.[51]

Heschel correctly sensed that his years were limited. His heart had been irreparably damaged, and a tremendous amount of scar tissue remained. He had been prone to heart disease for most of his life. His mother's twin brother, the Novominsker rebbe of Warsaw, had died of an aneurysm at age fifty-eight; his mother had died of a heart attack in the Warsaw Ghetto. Heschel himself suffered from high blood pressure, was somewhat overweight, and had long avoided salted food because of his heart condition.

Heschel was able to return home by early October but could no longer resume his teaching duties. Meanwhile, many in the Jewish Theological Seminary community—especially the young rabbinical students—had joined the anti-war movement. On October 15, they organized a Moratorium Day "in protest of the war in Vietnam," endorsed by the Student-Faculty Committee of the Rabbinical School and the Teachers Institute. Although Heschel applauded this stance, a momentous change from the earlier faculty opposition to anti-war protest, he was too weak to attend.

For the winter Heschel and Sylvia rented a furnished hotel apartment in Miami, while Susannah entered Trinity College in Hartford, Connecticut. Friends brought the Heschels meals, drove them to market, took them for rides or to the library. Sylvia practiced the piano every morning at a local synagogue. In early March, Heschel was hospitalized with hepatitis, further delaying his recovery.

Yet Heschel did recover. Afterward, he gave up smoking cigars. He was ordered to moderate his liquor intake, to have only a single glass of alcohol before dinner, yet he continued to drink two or three. When his wife complained, his sense of humor came to the rescue. "But Sylvia, after I drink one glass, I become another man!"[52]

CHAPTER 13

Summation of a Life, 1970–1972

Heschel turned sixty-five on January 11, 1972, but he appeared far older than his years. He contended with illness. His face was deeply furrowed and his walk had lost vigor; he shuffled, slightly dragging his feet. Still, he was now maintaining his full teaching load at the Jewish Theological Seminary, struggling to complete two books on the Kotzker rebbe—and, on top of all that, despite his recent brush with death, accepting many invitations to travel and to speak. Through it all, he remained forceful as a public orator.

His resilience, however, was weakened by the massive human suffering inflicted by the U.S. bombings in Southeast Asia, reported in the *New York Times* in gruesome detail. People close to Heschel noticed that he appeared to be lonely and sad.[1]

Meanwhile, in an almost uncanny way, during what would turn out to be his final year, month by month, sometimes week by week, he would give closure to major areas of his calling, putting the last touches on his spiritual legacy.

THE RADICAL OF KOTZK

For several years now, Heschel had been engrossed, obsessed even, with completing two books, one in Yiddish, the other in English—both of them on the life, personality, and teachings of Menahem Mendl Morgenstern (1787–1859), known as the rebbe of Kotzk.

The two books had emerged from previous essays and lectures in Yiddish and Hebrew. In 1959 Heschel had commemorated the Kotzker rebbe's hundredth yahrzeit (death anniversary) with a lecture in Yiddish to the Rabbinical Assembly entitled "A Dissenter in Hasidism." His language itself was dissent; the fact that Heschel had used Yiddish, the language of the common people of Eastern Europe, rather than English or even Hebrew, the learned (or holy) language of the educated élite, created a small tempest among the American rabbis who might have preferred a language the majority could understand. For his part, Heschel had been deliberate in his choice of language, perhaps, if only to bear witness to his essential identity as a Warsaw Jew. The cultural wars of the American survivors burned eternal.

Soon afterward, Heschel's essay on the Baal Shem Tov and the Kotzker rebbe, in Hebrew for Jewish readers not necessarily religiously committed, appeared in *Hadoar*, the widely circulated Hebrew weekly in which he often published. There he contrasted the benevolence of Medzibozh with the brutal demands of Kotzk. The Kotzker's teachings had created a revolution in the Hasidic world, stirring unrest in the Jewish soul.[2]

Several years later Heschel was invited to contribute an article on the Kotzker for an English-language foundational reference work, the *Encyclopaedia Judaica*. Again, Heschel highlighted the cultural conflict: "While [the Baal Shem Tov] emphasized love, joy, and compassion for this world, Kotzk demanded constant tension and an unmitigated militancy in combating this egocentricity." The Kotzker's banner was *emet* (truth).

From there, Heschel penned essays in Hebrew and in English. Directing his commentary at a broader, even interfaith readership, he compared the Kotzker rebbe with Søren Kierkegaard, the Christian father of existentialism, another "tormented master."[3] Sensing, probably, that the Yiddish and English books on the Kotzker rebbe would be his final works, Heschel reframed his earlier essays to display his inner psychological, cultural, even theological struggles.

For the first time in his life, in the final books—*A Passion for Truth* (New York, 1973) and *Kotsk: In gerangl far emesdikayt* (*Kotzk: The struggle for integrity;* two volumes, Tel Aviv, 1973)—Heschel wrote directly of his Hasidic ancestry, revealing the most intimate and the least known dimensions of his life—his thirty-three years in Europe, from birth to escape.[4] He explained how forces had battled in his personality since age nine, when his father suddenly died and his uncle the Novominsker rebbe had found a preceptor who instilled in him the relentless demands of Kotzk.

The autobiographical preface to the English volume would recapitulate the astounding tensions that allowed him to embody a productive synthesis: "I was taught about inexhaustible mines of meaning by the Baal Shem; from the Kotzker I learned to detect immense mountains of absurdity standing in the way."[5] Heschel's sensibility came to encompass a constant battle between the kindness of the Baal Shem Tov and the harshness of the Kotzker rebbe. As he would write in the preface to the Yiddish volume: "I am the last of a generation, perhaps the last Jew of Warsaw, whose soul lives in Medzibozh [the final home of the Baal Shem Tov] and whose mind lives in Kotzk."[6]

The Kotzker and Kierkegaard were Heschel's model extremists, radical "outsiders" who had "little compassionate consideration for the human condition and its natural limitations." Both were alienated from normal society, subject to depression, and "haunted by mysterious states of anguish, the price they had to pay for their penetrating insights."[7] Heschel shared their "predilection for sarcasm, irony, satire, and polemic. No one in the history of Jewish piety was more biting [than the Kotzker] in exposing the subterfuges of man." Heschel, too, had been reproached for his demeaning sarcasm, such as condemning the suburban synagogue as "a graveyard where prayer is buried."[8]

The Kotzker's battle with metaphysical absurdity unveiled the fragility of Heschel's own faith: The two final chapters of *A Passion for Truth*—"The Kotzker and Job" and "The Kotzker Today"—map out his spiritual legacy of dissent. He recognized the absurdity of human existence as he denounced its horrors: "The Kotzker, a soul living in dissent, was all protest against the trivialization and externalization of Judaism. Rejecting half-truths, mediocrity, compromise, he challenged even the Lord."

Through all this, completing his two final books, Heschel intrepidly took measure of his life, repaying his debts. He dedicated the Kotzker book in Yiddish to six men who had saved him at crucial stages of life: Bezalel Levy, his tutor in Warsaw; Yitzhak Levin, follower of Kotzk, who supported Heschel's secular studies; Leo Hirsch, literary critic in Berlin; David Koigen, who inspired Heschel to interpret Hasidism for moderns; Erich Reiss, who subsidized his dissertation on the prophets; and, finally, Levi (Louis) Ginzberg, who brought Heschel to the Jewish Theological Seminary and helped promote his first American books.

In an incandescent paragraph Heschel asserted that people must trust in God in spite of God: "The agony of our problem foments like a volcano, and it is foolish to seek finite answers to infinite agony. . . . The pain is strong as death, cruel as the grave. But perhaps it will be in the grave, the dwelling place of Truth, that our own death will somewhat hasten its resurrection."[9]

REWARDS AND RECOGNITION

The political climate in which Heschel had developed these daunting reflections had become increasingly contentious. On March 10, 1970, five American soldiers were court-martialed for war crimes committed at the village of My Lai in Vietnam. On April 30, the United States invaded Cambodia. Barely a week later, the National Guard killed and wounded American student protesters at Kent State University. Responding to the Cambodian invasion and the Kent State massacre, Clergy and Laymen Concerned about Vietnam co-sponsored a mobilization in Washington on May 9. Still recuperating from his heart attack and hepatitis, Heschel was not able to attend.

Heschel's consecration by the secular mainstream came that spring. He was among 107 new members elected to the American Academy of Arts and Sciences. The other honorees included theology professor H. Richard Niebuhr (brother of Reinhold), CBS news commentator Eric Sevareid, Norman Mailer, Günter Grass, Duke Ellington, and Charlie Chaplin.

Within the interfaith community, Heschel was invited to contribute to a Festschrift honoring John Coleman Bennett, the former Union Seminary president and Heschel's partner in opposing the Vietnam War. Heschel's essay, "God, Torah, and Israel," was the only Jewish reflection in the volume, which was balanced toward liberal Protestant and Catholic theology. Abstracting from the uncompleted third volume of his Hebrew study of the Talmud, he drew a parallel between the trinity of God, Christ, and the Holy Spirit and the Jewish hierarchy of God, Torah, and the Jewish people, giving priority to the Divine.[10]

Meanwhile, at the Jewish Theological Seminary, Heschel was receiving long-overdue recognition. Despite the denigration of his personal approach to scholarship by the institution's powers that be, Heschel had brought distinction to the seminary. He was finally allowed to offer a course on Hasidism as part of the Rabbinical School curriculum. Finkelstein had at long last given his unacknowledged rival this measure of trust.

Heschel's teaching as well was no longer perceived in a negative light. During the 1970–1971 academic year, JTS students embraced

Heschel as a celebrity—and, even more important, as a great Jew, a model of what they themselves wanted to become.

Many students who had avoided his classes on Maimonides and Yehuda Halevi registered for his course on Hasidism. When it opened, Heschel read from his manuscript on the Kotzker rebbe. In the past this had been a bad sign. Now students were thrilled. Heschel also presented the ethical and religious treatises *Menorat ha-Maor* (Candlestick of light; fourteenth century), *Orchot Tzadikim* (*The Ways of the Righteous*; fifteenth century), and Bahya Ibn Paquda's classical work *Chovot ha-Levavot* (*Duties of the Heart*; eleventh century) as literary efforts to transform souls.

A second generation of Heschel followers emerged. They appreciated, even revered Heschel as a religious philosopher capable of fostering life-transforming insights.

He was pleased—and flattered—that he had suddenly become popular at the seminary. He became more responsive to classroom questions than he ever had been. When pressed to explain something, he would back up his philosophical arguments with his enormous knowledge of classic Jewish texts. In all likelihood, he would have produced many more followers had he taught as effectively earlier in his career.

Heschel remained at his best with seekers. In the fall of 1970, a Japanese Christian, Jacob Yuroh Teshima, entered the Jewish Theological Seminary after completing advanced Judaic studies at the Hebrew University in Jerusalem. His attraction to Judaism had been inspired by his father, Ikuroh A. Teshima, the charismatic founder of the Original Gospel Movement, or Makuya (Non-church, or Tabernacle), a Japanese Christian sect whose followers revered the Hebrew Bible and the State of Israel. Their symbol was the menorah, signifying worship, rather than the cross, which signified suffering.[11] Teshima had heard Heschel speak in Israel in 1965, and he entered the JTS graduate program to study philosophy with Heschel (as well as Bible with H. L. Ginsburg).

Teshima became Heschel's closest student in the two years before his death. At first Teshima was disappointed by Heschel's class on Rabbinic theology, since Heschel simply read from the Hebrew original of *Heavenly Torah* and asked students to summarize its contents without correcting and returning their papers. But Heschel's class on the Kotzker rebbe made up for the other class's shortcomings. Here, students read original Hasidic texts and wrote a research paper on one of them. All discussions were in Hebrew. Heschel stressed the conflict between *ahavah* (love), represented by his ancestor the Apter Rav, and criticism, represented by the Kotzker.

Heschel was impressed by the Japanese student's paper in fluent Hebrew, and he took a liking to his devout and original personality, combining a sense of humor, thoughtful independence, and reverence for his teacher. The Heschels became close to Jacob and his wife, Tamiko (Tammy), a concert pianist like Sylvia, and their baby daughter. Teshima often accompanied Heschel home from his office late at night.

After earning a DHL (doctor of Hebrew letters) with a thesis on Zen Buddhism and Hasidism, Teshima returned to Japan with his family. He stopped working for the Makuya movement and earned a living in business, with a mission to "convey the message of Judaism to secular Japanese society." Along with his own teachings, Teshima translated Heschel's works into Japanese.

Toward the end of his own life, Heschel experienced another deep personal loss. Right before the New Year, on Thursday, December 31, 1970, Heschel's older sixty-seven-year-old brother, Jacob, died of a heart attack. He was buried in London a few hours after death, following Orthodox custom and because of the coming Sabbath. Heschel remained in New York for the memorial week of shivah, holding services every day at his apartment.

Jacob had long served as the rabbi of an Orthodox congregation, where he was known to introduce ancestral stories into his sermons,

and as headmaster of a religious school in London. He had also published one scholarly article, "The History of Hasidism in Austria."[12]

Heschel and Yankele (as Heschel called his brother in Yiddish)
had been close and affectionate. Jacob was not an intellectual like
Heschel, but he was beloved as a sweet, generous, and devout Jew.

PUBLIC AUDIENCE WITH THE POPE

Still grappling with his loss, and despite his still fragile health,
Heschel returned to Italy in March 1971, accompanied by Sylvia,
for a lecture tour arranged by the Italian Cultural Association. He also
scheduled a public audience with Pope Paul VI, in order to reinforce
his symbolic authority at the Vatican, having significantly contributed
to *Nostra Aetate*, opening a new era in Jewish-Christian relations.

Heschel gave lectures in several cities using material from *Who
Is Man?* which had been recently published in Italian translation.
His lectures in English were simultaneously translated into Italian
by Elèna Mortara, a young professor of American Jewish literature,
who quickly formed a friendship with the Heschels. Heschel's listeners were enthusiastic, and he relished the stimulating European
environment.[13]

As he spoke in Rome at the Eliseo Theater, for example, Heschel's
slow, impassioned manner struck the imagination of a writer for
Shalom, the Jewish community magazine. The listener imagined that
Heschel looked "as though he had hurled himself into a mytholog-
ical challenge with Titans. . . . So fragile, so vulnerable behind his
beard, eyes shining, intent on making us aware, making us expand
that inner light."[14]

On March 17 (a Wednesday), the Heschels were received ceremo-
niously by Pope Paul VI. Heschel wrote a memorandum to himself
afterward that appeared to emphasize his central role in the ritualized
meeting. The theme, Heschel wrote, was set by the pontiff's warm
greeting: "When he saw me he smiled joyously, with a radiant face,

shook my hand cordially with both his hands—he did so several times during the audience. He opened the conversation by telling me that he was reading my books, that my books are very spiritual and very beautiful, and that Catholics should read my books." Heschel gave him a signed copy of *Who Is Man?* in Italian.[15]

After Heschel thanked the pope "for what he had done for the Jewish people through the Ecumenical Council," he underscored the importance of Jerusalem to Jews everywhere: "'All of Jewish history is a pilgrimage to Jerusalem, and the union of the Jewish people and the city of Jerusalem we regard as a sign of divine grace and providence in this age of darkness.' The pope then said: 'I will remember your words,' and added: 'I hope that you and I will meet together in Jerusalem.'"

The pope commemorated the occasion with photographs. Heschel continued in his memorandum: "Mrs. Heschel started to move away, the Pope took her hand and then my hand, placed them on the arms of his chair, and a picture was taken." Heschel thus successfully completed the "summit meeting" he had arguably mishandled in secret six years earlier.

This photograph and another one showing only Heschel and the pope were distributed to Jewish and Catholic publications around the country. Both communities used it to advance interfaith relationships carefully built up since the promulgation of *Nostra Aetate* in 1965. The image of the Heschels standing on either side of the pope was interpreted in *The Pilot*, the official paper of the Boston Archdiocese, as symbolizing the pontiff's high regard for the Jewish people in general and for Rabbi and Mrs. Heschel in particular. Heschel and the pope were featured on the cover of *United Synagogue Review* (Fall 1971, the High Holy Day issue), distributed to members of all Conservative Jewish congregations throughout North America.[16]

When Heschel returned to the United States, the Jewish Theological Seminary's media relations office began to promote him as a celebrity. In May, he did a radio interview with the novelist and television writer Harold Flender. (Transcripts were available from JTS for fifty cents.) Recapping his recent trip to Italy, Heschel touched on his relationships with Christians, the Middle East situation, and his friendships with Martin Luther King Jr. and the controversial Jesuit priest Daniel Berrigan. He went on to reassert his own patriotism: "Most Americans have by now forgotten what was so vital to me as a youngster, namely America as the great hope in a dark world and a reactionary world."[17]

Then, answering a question about Soviet Jewry, Heschel pointed to his central role in historic events: "I believe I was the very first man who . . . initiated the movement for the Jews in Soviet Russia. At the beginning there were very few individuals who responded to my appeal, and it took several years finally to awaken the organized Jewish community." In part, taking credit was Heschel's indirect way of expressing anger at American Jews for their apathy toward Vietnam, Israel, civil rights, and other calls to personal or community responsibility.

HONORING HIS ELDERS

One of Heschel's most important friendships came to an end when Reinhold Niebuhr died on June 2, 1971, at age seventy-eight. After moving from New York into a retirement home in Stockbridge, Massachusetts, Niebuhr and his wife, Ursula, had begun planning his funeral. They decided to invite Heschel to give the only eulogy. Heschel's participation would reaffirm Niebuhr's closeness to prophetic Judaism as well as his love for the Hebrew Bible and the Jewish people.

Addressing two hundred mourners at the First Congregational Church in Stockbridge, Heschel spoke from the heart: "This is a critical moment in the lives of many of us, in the history of religion in America: to say farewell to the physical existence of the master and to pray: Abide, continue to dwell in our midst, spirit of Reinhold Niebuhr." Niebuhr "combined heaven and earth," said Heschel, referring to the theologian's synthesis of spirituality and activism. After remembering him as "a staunch friend of the Jewish people and the State of Israel, of the poor and the down-trodden everywhere," Heschel concluded by celebrating Niebuhr's life as "a song in the form of deeds, a song that will go on forever."[18]

The following week Heschel was to pay tribute to another giant of American religious life—Mordecai Menahem Kaplan, a theological rival but also a respected friend. It had become customary to honor each decade of the Reconstructionist patriarch's life with a gala dinner and speeches. Kaplan was ninety years of age and still very much alive. For the first time Kaplan invited Heschel to speak. Heschel had to deal with his ambivalent feelings: he loved Kaplan the man but repudiated his ideas.

Present at the gala were the Jewish élite, most of whom approved Kaplan's religious naturalism. Heschel had not prepared a speech; he rarely did for such occasions. Now, worried about what to say, Heschel sought advice from Wolfe Kelman while they had a few drinks. By the time the master of ceremonies, former B'nai B'rith president Philip Klutznik, called on Heschel to give remarks before the dinner, he was already a bit tipsy.

Heschel's spontaneous performance that evening revealed his tension, illustrating Freud's theory that wit (especially aided by alcohol) can liberate forbidden thoughts and feelings.[19] With a string of witticisms intended to relax the audience, and himself, Heschel teased Kaplan, playing on his key ideas.

Under Kaplan's direction, the Reconstructionist movement had inaugurated the bat mitzvah ceremony (the first bat mitzvah being Kaplan's own daughter, Judith) and had been first to ordain female rabbis. Humorously, Heschel now chided Reconstructionism for abandoning its feminist principles. "Kaplan is the founder of 'Women's Lib' in Jewish life," quipped Heschel, "but there is a major inconsistency: there are so few 'ladies' seated at the head table!" He went on in this vein. Kaplan's life at ninety years was like that of Sarah the matriarch, pregnant with meaning. There was uncontrolled laughter at certain points, uncomfortably shared by audience and speaker. It was obvious that Heschel had been drinking and that he was improvising, brilliantly.

Yet his joking was also sincerely intended as praise. He knew Kaplan took his religion personally and seriously, like Jewish mystics who remain awake for *tikkun chatzot* (all-night study sessions). "Kaplan stays up past midnight worrying about the Jewish people," he told the crowd. Such was Kaplan's "magnificent obsession," which he himself shared. In the end, Heschel's wit had successfully tamed his ambivalence toward Kaplan.

Heschel himself was receiving numerous honors. Early in November, he became the first rabbi to receive the Anti-Defamation League's prestigious Democratic Legacy Award. Previous recipients included former Chief Justice Earl Warren and Presidents Truman, Eisenhower, Kennedy, and Johnson.[20]

The award ceremony featured Heschel's interfaith contributions. Eugene Carson Blake, general secretary of the World Council of Churches (which had more than four hundred million members), described Heschel as "an authentic saint" who was helping to achieve "the miracle of mutual understanding and greater cooperation which is bridging religious differences."

Father Edward H. Flannery, executive secretary of the Secretariat for Catholic-Jewish Relations of the Bishops' Committee for Ecumenical and Interreligious Affairs and author of an influential book on antisemitism, *The Anguish of the Jews* (1965), praised Heschel's ability to expound the Jewish view of Israel and the Hebrew Bible.[21]

Heschel's prestige at the Vatican was proclaimed by a message (received as a telegram) from Pope Paul VI, who praised the "sometimes lonely witness of the great and wise rabbi scholar."

Still the spiritual radical, Heschel responded to this acclaim by criticizing "do-gooders," Jews who were beginning to withdraw from the civil rights movement. The antisemitism of some black militants could not excuse this, admonished Heschel. As a child in Poland he knew "what it means to live in a country where you are despised. Blacks have the same feelings here."

Referring to the Knapp Commission's inquiry into police brutality and corruption, Heschel warned his audience, "If a few filthy guttersnipes put a fire to a synagogue, we all feel alarmed, and rightly so. But when we are told that police serve as patrons of deadly crimes, the community remains unconcerned." As Jews, he insisted, we must "keep our tongues and souls clean." Both Christian and Jewish listeners were moved by the half-hour talk.

The intense year was coming to an end. Rabbi and Mrs. Heschel were given a surprise party at their Riverside Drive apartment on Saturday evening, December 11, 1971, after Shabbat, to honor their twenty-fifth wedding anniversary. The embossed invitation cited the Song of Songs (4:1–8, 5:10–16, 6:3): "Behold, thou art fair, my love; behold thou art fair; / Thine eyes are as doves behind thy veil; / Thy hair is as a flock of goats. . . . / His head is as the most fine gold, His locks are curled, / And black as a raven."[22] Although Heschel's hair had by now become white, it retained its luxurious abundance.

TELLING TRUTH TO POWER

In part due to his bushy white hair and overall physical appearance, Heschel had become a valuable resource for the mass media. Such a role required him to travel frequently and apply his wisdom to events. On a national television program honoring the memory of Martin Luther King Jr. on January 9, 1972, he was the Jewish discussant along with two African American clergymen, the Protestant pastor

Jesse L. Jackson, a close associate of King's in the Southern Christian Leadership Conference, and a Catholic priest, George R. Clements. The moderator, ABC correspondent Frank Reynolds, had recently interviewed Heschel on national television, the day before Heschel received the Anti-Defamation League award.[23]

In a somber tone, Heschel praised King's nonviolence, keen intelligence, powerful presence, and grasp of complex sociological factors: "This combination of an inspired man and a sophisticated man is indeed unique." Heschel also asserted that the nation's spiritual health depended, to a large extent, on the quality of prayer he had experienced in African American religious services: "If there is an American Christianity, a living faith and a knowledge of the art of praying, it is still preserved in the black churches."

Elsewhere, Heschel focused his efforts on the anti-war movement's new goal of national reconciliation. Continuing to protest the U.S. bombings of Vietnam, Cambodia, and Laos, he contributed to an interfaith conference on peace held January 14–16 in Kansas City, Missouri, arranged by the National Council of Churches, Clergy and Laymen Concerned about Vietnam, and other religious organizations. The *New York Times* reported that the conference was "the most comprehensive religious gathering ever assembled in the United States over the peace issue." Heschel's statement on the necessity of truth was worthy of the Kotzker rebbe: "The cruelties committed by our armed forces in Southeast Asia were made possible by an unprecedented campaign of deceiving the American people. . . . The hour may have come to realize that falsehood, deception, is at the root of evil."[24]

The following week Heschel flew to Jerusalem for the Twenty-Eighth World Zionist Congress, an international gathering of Israel's active supporters. Nearly a thousand delegates and observers gathered on January 19 for the opening session.

In that vein, he insisted, Israel must uphold ethics over rigid legalism: "I am grateful to God that in the official establishments and hotels kashrut is observed. But what hurts is the question why it is only required for butcher-stores to be under religious supervision. Why not insist that banks, factories, and those who deal in real estate should require a *heksher* [kosher certification] and be operated according to religious law?" His examples struck a raw nerve for Israelis recently alerted to scandals in their banking and construction industries: "When a drop of blood is found in an egg, we abhor eating the egg. But often there is more than one drop of blood in a dollar or a lira [Israeli pound], and we fail to remind the people constantly of the teachings of our tradition."[25] The Jewish state, he proclaimed, must be a light unto the nations: "[For] the sake of God, for the sake of Israel and the world, the people Israel and the State of Israel must emerge as religious witnesses, to keep the consciousness of the God of Abraham and the reverence for the Bible alive in the world."

That same month, on March 26–27, Heschel joined other dissenters in Washington DC in calling for a general amnesty for all draft resistors. The U.S. government needed to liberate the more than one hundred thousand young Americans who had been exiled or imprisoned for obeying their moral judgment: "They are guilty of seeing earlier what all honest men should now see [when it is rather late]: that the war in Vietnam was a stupid, immoral, absurd adventure for which it is not worthwhile shedding the blood of a single soldier." Using religious law to justify the resistors' civil disobedience, he cited the Talmud: "The law of the secular government must be strictly obeyed in civil affairs (*Babba Kamma* 113A). . . . However, if the law of the state is in conflict with the religious and moral laws, one must obey the Master of all of us and disobey the state."[26] His final Jewish authority on the subject was Rashi, who had forbidden a man to murder another, even if the town governor had ordered him to do so: "How could you say that your life is dearer to God than his?"

Heschel's carefully documented paper, "The Theological, Biblical, and Ethical Considerations of Amnesty," was never published, but it circulated widely in anti-war and civil liberties communities.[27]

On June 4, another of Heschel's conflicts was resolved—his strained relationship with Hebrew Union College. After his departure from Cincinnati in 1945, he had made no secret of his disdain for some basic Reform "customs and ceremonies," as he urged Reform Jews to take *halakhah* seriously. By the 1960s the Reform movement had recognized Heschel's value for all Jews. In 1971, in one of his first acts as the new Hebrew Union College president, Rabbi Alfred Gottschalk (formerly a German student whose life had also been saved by President Morgenstern) invited Heschel to receive an honorary doctorate of humane letters at ordination exercises at its New York branch. A delighted Heschel accepted immediately: "Becoming an honorary alumnus will only deepen my relationship to the College."[28]

Addressing the newly ordained Reform rabbis after their graduation ceremony at Temple Emanu-El of New York, Heschel challenged their conscience to confront the crisis in America's cities. At the luncheon that followed, he continued to encourage Jewish activism, dealing cautiously with the contentious issue of affirmative action, which was leading many Jewish liberals to abandon their support for the civil rights movement. He urged Jews to continue fighting for the rights of blacks and other minority groups, but "not by gimmickry and quotas." He urged the new Reform rabbis to confront the self-interest of white liberals and those who suffer with courage and nobility.

RECONCILIATION OF THE CHILDREN OF ABRAHAM

Heschel's vigorous schedule was interrupted by an extraordinary invitation. For the first time in his life, he was invited to participate in an interfaith conference that included Muslims. Sponsored by the

American Friends Service Committee (Quakers) in the Middle East, with tacit Vatican support,[29] this unpublicized four-day meeting on "A Spiritual Charter for Jerusalem" would take place at the Center for Mediterranean Studies in Rome August 29–September 1, 1972.

Until then, Heschel had had little contact with Muslims. He publicly supported Israel's occupation of Arab territories conquered in 1967, though privately he shared some reservations with his daughter and a few others. This was a chance to speak directly with Arabs. Above all, Heschel hoped that sharing "spiritual anxiety" about Jerusalem would open hearts: "It is important for me to remember now that while I have prayed from the heart for the Muslims all my life . . . I have never been face-to-face with them to talk about God! This is *very* important. We must go further."[30] So, Heschel made his final trip to Rome.

The twenty-five participants represented eight nationalities and included nine Christians, four Muslims (no Arab Muslims), and six Jews; there were also several observers, some from the Vatican. No reporters were present, no formal report was produced, and brief summaries released to the press did not name the participants. This was a spiritual, not public, event.

To disarm potential disputes, the convener, the Jerusalem metropolitan archbishop George Appleton, developed a contemplative focus. "Each session began with a few moments of meditation, a reading from the Bible or the Qur'an, and existential, often unspoken reminders of the chairman that there was some transcendental value to the search for all present." Each session ended with a period of silence.[31]

Pleased that the conference surpassed "religious politics," Heschel was charming and at ease, especially in individual conversations. For most of the sessions, he was seated next to Seyyed Hossein Nasr (a Shia or Sufi), vice chancellor and dean of faculties at Aryamehr University. Heschel was familiar with Nasr's books on Sufism and Islamic mysticism; Nasr knew Heschel's writings from the time he and Henry Corbin had taught them at Tehran University. In discussions, the two faith leaders developed a common understanding. In the future, they agreed, Jews and Muslims should develop their dialogue separately from Christians. Judaism and Islam had a spiritual continuity in common, while Christianity, imbued with Greek thought and Western secularism, had lost much of its Semitic character over the centuries. Jews and Muslims might begin with the patriarch Abraham, who in the Qur'an is called *chalil allah*, "God's friend."

Leading the opening devotions at the fourth and final session, on Friday, September 1, Heschel took the opportunity to dramatize the Jews' attachment to Jerusalem. Stating that the haftarah portion from Isaiah would be read that Sabbath by Jews throughout the world, he recited the English text, which begins, "I will greatly rejoice in the Lord" (61:10), softly underscoring the final verses: "For Zion's sake, I will not hold my peace, and for Jerusalem's sake, I will not rest, until her triumph go forth as brightness and her salvation as a torch that burneth!" (62:1). He concluded with the passage on the Suffering Servant, which he had presented at the funeral of Martin Luther King Jr.: "So He was their Savior. In all their affliction, He was afflicted, and the angel of His presence saved Him; in His love and His pity, He redeemed them" (63:8–9). Simply by reciting the sacred text, Heschel evoked his people's millennial exile from Jerusalem and their hope for its redemption.[32]

The prayers ended, Heschel sat down without another word. The room was silent. In this contemplative atmosphere Archbishop Appleton closed the conference with a magnanimous summary: "Whatever may be the political settlement finally agreed, the pluralistic nature of Jerusalem will continue. The challenge is to have a love for the city and also a possibility of embracing all who love her."[33]

As Heschel slowly shuffled out, most of the others had already left, but Serif Mardin (a Sunni), professor of political science at the Bogazici University in Istanbul and visiting professor at Princeton

University, and Seyyed Hossein Nasr remained. Mardin pressed Heschel's hand and walked away without saying a word. Nasr, now alone with Heschel, took his hand and said, "This is an unforgettable moment for me. I have read everything you have written I could find. God give you strength."[34]

Returning to New York, Heschel shared his enthusiasm for the conference with his students. He asked his assistant Judith Herschlag at the Anti-Defamation League to airmail a copy of *Israel: An Echo of Eternity* to Nasr in Tehran. Heschel then wrote to Archbishop Appleton, saying that he hoped to have the book translated into Arabic. Heschel soon found translators in Israel and immediately sent Appleton a $250 check to help him pay them.[35]

Heschel believed he was a step closer to his lifelong dream of ultimate reconciliation: "The God of Israel is also the God of Syria, the God of Egypt. The enmity between the nations will turn into friendship."[36] Beyond this, Heschel remained a staunch supporter of the State of Israel, while maintaining his spiritually radical perspective. Sadly to say, the hope he shared with Henry Corbin in Nazi Berlin and with Archbishop Appleton in occupied Jerusalem has yet to bear new fruit.

JEWISH INFIGHTING

At the same time, Heschel remained a controversial figure for many Jews. While more appreciated in the classroom, he became further alienated from the Jewish Theological Seminary, this time quite openly, because of his support for presidential candidate George McGovern. Heschel believed that McGovern, a man of moral integrity, would be more beneficial to Americans—and to the Jews, as the saying goes—than the crafty Nixon and his adviser Henry Kissinger. Heschel's advocacy of the liberal senator even put him at odds with his inner circle—Seymour Siegel, Fritz Rothschild, and Wolfe Kelman.

Jewish internal conflicts were national news. On October 9, 1972, several articles in the *New York Times* focused on the division. Page I reported, "GOP Intensifies Drive to Attract Jews to Nixon," while the headline banner of the op-ed section announced the day's topic in bold type: "The Question of the Jewish Vote." Among the interviewees, Eugene Borowitz at Hebrew Union College and Seymour Siegel at the Jewish Theological Seminary were quoted as choosing Nixon.

Heschel was dismayed. As he saw it, Nixon's commitment to a negotiated peace in Vietnam was questionable, as was his support for the Democratic social programs fostered by Lyndon Johnson. His indignant letter to the *Times*, which appeared on October 27, stated that the views expressed by his "former students" Borowitz and Siegel "depressed me deeply by the absence of any reference to the war in Vietnam, by the highly exaggerated claim of 'pressure the Israelis have put on U.S. Jewry,' and above all, by the lack of any reference to the fundamental commitments that characterize Jewishness." Religious thinking must inform politics, he insisted. Would Isaiah and Amos, he asked rhetorically, "accept the corruption in high places, the indifferent way in which the sick, the poor, and the old are treated?" The Hebrew prophets, Heschel claimed, would support gun-control legislation and oppose the Vietnam War. "God's law" was a higher authority than nationalism, and McGovern was the candidate most likely to confront the violence of American society. Heschel mailed out dozens of copies of his statement.

A rebuttal by Isaac Lewin, professor of history at Yeshiva University, appeared on November 5, right before the election. Lewin praised Nixon for making "heroic efforts . . . to reach an agreement on Vietnam and to stop the violence." He deplored Heschel's contention that "Isaiah and Amos might be campaigning against the re-election of President Nixon and would be 'standing amidst those who protest against the violence of the war in Vietnam, the decay of our cities, the hypocrisy and falsehood that surround our present Administration.'" The professor concluded with a severe reprimand: "To accuse him [Nixon] of hypocrisy and falsehood is unfair and certainly not in the spirit of the Jewish sages who said (Talmud, tractate *Berachot* 31a): 'One who suspects his neighbor of a fault which he has not committed must beg his pardon, nay more, he must bless him.'"[37]

The conservatives had the last word. On November 7, 1972, President Richard Nixon won a landslide victory over George McGovern, who carried only Massachusetts and the District of Columbia. Ironically, at Nixon's inauguration on January 20, 1973, Heschel's protégé Rabbi Seymour Siegel pronounced a blessing in Hebrew and in English. (Siegel chose the blessing that the Talmud prescribes for the appearance of a king and his court. He did alter the prayer slightly but was still criticized for his choice.) Heschel would not be alive to witness it.[38]

The opprobrium of many Jews was somewhat soothed for Heschel by the admiration of Christians, among whom he had achieved iconic stature. The day before the election, the College of Saint Scholastica, a coeducational Benedictine institution in Minnesota, awarded Heschel, the "Rabbi to the World," with an honorary doctorate of humane letters. Six colleges and universities were represented by their presidents, chancellors, and other officers at the impressive ceremony held at the University of Wisconsin, Superior. This would be one of Heschel's last public appearances.[39]

Heschel's last public act was a symbolic gesture of solidarity with Daniel and Philip Berrigan, an association that Heschel's critics deplored. Heschel's long-standing, though not uncritical, friendship with Daniel Berrigan had endured even after their ways had diverged. A founding member of Committee of Clergy Concerned about Vietnam, Daniel, along with his brother Philip, had soon moved beyond lobbying and mobilizations. The two launched a campaign of symbolic "crimes," such as splattering blood on selective service files, damaging missiles or airplanes at military bases, and burning draft cards with napalm. After their highly politicized trials, Philip was sent to prison and Daniel went "underground" to defy government authority. He was finally captured in August 1970.

Heschel and other mainstream clergy admired the Berrigans' spirit of resistance without condoning their ideology and tactics. After they began to serve sentences in the Danbury Correctional Institution for destroying draft records, a group that included Heschel and other prominent clergy appealed to authorities to allow the imprisoned clerics to distribute written or taped sermons to the outside—although Heschel strongly disagreed with Daniel Berrigan that serving time in prison was an effective way to bear witness. Better to work on the outside, he reasoned. In this respect, Heschel was a moderate who respected the rule of law and practical action. (As such, years earlier he'd arranged for Daniel Berrigan to come to his class at the Jewish Theological Seminary to debate these issues.)[40]

On Wednesday morning, December 20, Philip Berrigan would complete his thirty-nine-month sentence and be released from the Danbury prison. Heschel wanted to be at the rally of his supporters. Well before dawn on a cold and snowy Wednesday, Daniel Berrigan (who had already been released), and Tom Lewis, an artist and Catholic activist, picked up Heschel at his apartment. Heschel asked permission to say his morning prayers in the car. His worship moved these pacifists, who listened respectfully.[41]

At Danbury, Philip Berrigan emerged from the prison, giving a clenched-fist salute to the inmates at the windows. Then he and Daniel waved to the more than three hundred followers who had come to greet him, among them Heschel's daughter, Susannah, who had arrived from Trinity College in Hartford. Pete Seeger sang protest songs, and with other notables, Heschel and the Berrigans walked about a mile to the Amber Room restaurant, where they held a religious service and a news conference in the ballroom. As Heschel left, he invited the brothers to tea at his apartment on Shabbat, December 23.[42]

On Friday, Jacob Teshima met Heschel in a JTS hallway. Heschel was ecstatic; he had just finished correcting and mailing the proofs of his Yiddish book *Kotsk: In gerangl far emesdikayt* (Kotzk: A struggle for integrity) to the publisher in Tel Aviv. In addition, he had completed the manuscript of the English-language version, *A Passion for Sincerity*—whose title he had discussed with several people, hesitating between *Sincerity* and *Truth*—and delivered that manuscript to Farrar, Straus. (Heschel had brought Roger Straus the manuscript, which would still require considerable editing. After consulting several people on Heschel's list, including this author, the publisher would eventually decide on *A Passion for Truth*.)[43] That afternoon, Heschel told Fritz Rothschild about his plans to leave that Sunday for a two-week winter vacation with Sylvia and Susannah in Los Angeles. On the way to California, Heschel would stop in Chicago to officiate at the marriage of his former student Byron Sherwin. He had told Teshima that he expected to visit Japan after February.[44]

The Heschels had invited several guests for Shabbat dinner. The list included a not unusual mixture: the family dentist Stanley Batkin and his wife, who were active in their Conservative synagogue in New Rochelle; the actor Joseph Wiseman and his wife, the dancer and choreographer Pearl Lang, who was a good friend from the Yiddish-speaking and artistic worlds; and their daughter, Susannah, with a friend from Trinity College.

After dinner, Heschel, in a pensive mood, took out his book of Yiddish poetry from a shelf and asked Joseph Wiseman to read "God Follows Me Everywhere" (*Got geht mir nokh umetum*), which included these mystical lines: "I go with my reveries as with a secret . . . and sometimes I glimpse high above me, the faceless face of God." Eventually the guests left and Heschel, sixty-five years of age, went to bed.

He did not wake up. He left this world peacefully, a sanctified departure, on the Sabbath, between darkness and dawn. Like Moses, Heschel died with the kiss of God.[45]

Epilogue

On Shabbat morning. December 23, 1972, Sylvia and Susannah discovered Heschel's lifeless body.[1]

Immediately, they started contacting family, friends, and colleagues.[2] Two young faculty, Neil Gillman and Seymour Siegel, were in services at the Jewish Theological Seminary chapel when they were asked to fetch Wolfe Kelman, who was attending a bar mitzvah at the Spanish and Portuguese Synagogue on Central Park West. After services they met Kelman on the sidewalk and told him of Heschel's death. Despite the Sabbath prohibition against traveling in a car, the three jumped into a cab and raced to the Heschel apartment, where Sylvia and Susannah were distraught. Pastor Richard John Neuhaus was kneeling in prayer beside Heschel's bed. The Berrigan brothers arrived soon thereafter; they too prayed at the bedside.

As soon as evening fell—early, it was midwinter—the family called Heschel's Hasidic relatives in Brooklyn (who would not answer the telephone on Shabbat). Soon afterward Rabbi Moses (Moyshe) Heschel, the young Kopitzhinitzer rebbe and a son of Heschel's first cousin, arrived with other men to prepare the body for burial. The Hasidim arranged everything according to the strictest laws and customs. The body was removed from the apartment carefully, to be returned to his ancestors.

It was soon reported (although Susannah denies the entirety of the incident) that Heschel's last reading material, remaining in the bedroom, consisted of David Halberstam's exposé of Nixon's war cabinet, *The Best and the Brightest*, and the *Keter Shem Tov*, a Hasidic classic.[3] These two books symbolized the dynamic coexistence of Heschel's two main spheres of action: piety and political responsibility. And yet, the morning after Heschel's death, Sylvia Heschel confided to Pastor Richard John Neuhaus that she had deliberately positioned the books, replacing the *Newsweek* of December 25, 1972, which Heschel had been reading.[4] The widow felt that the books would be more appropriate. The mythologizing of Heschel had thus begun.

Heschel's funeral brought into sharp relief the tensions of his life. Jews are usually buried within twenty-four hours of their death, but Heschel had made no specific arrangements for his funeral. Saul Lieberman remembered that Heschel had once expressed the hope to be buried in Israel, but there were no documents verifying this. Wolfe Kelman soon learned that Heschel had told his cousin Jacob Perlow that he wished to be buried near his uncle Yehuda Aryeh Leib Perlow, the Novominsker rebbe of Brooklyn.[5] Perlow had been buried in Beth David Cemetery in Elmont, Long Island.

The family decided to hold the funeral on neutral territory, at Park West Memorial Chapel on Seventy-Ninth Street. The service began at 1:45 p.m. on Sunday, December 24. New York mayor John Lindsay had made the exceptional decision to close the street to traffic. According to the *New York Times*, five hundred people were present, including Mayor Lindsay; Christopher Mooney, president of the Jesuit Woodstock College; Samuel Belkin, president of Yeshiva University; Louis Finkelstein, chancellor emeritus of the Jewish Theological Seminary; Alfred Gottschalk, president of Hebrew Union College; J. Brooke Mosley, president of Union Theological Seminary; and numerous colleagues, friends, and students.[6] Many people had to remain outside the packed chapel.

The coffin was placed in a small side room, where black-suited Hasidim were chanting *tehillim* (psalms) over the body, according to Jewish custom and law. Fritz Rothschild, Yochanan Muffs (another former student now on the Jewish Theological Seminary faculty), and Samuel Dresner, who flew in from Chicago, met in the room to pay their last respects to their teacher, while Jacob Teshima checked to make sure that the white linen had been wrapped correctly to enshroud his beloved mentor.

It was a thoroughly traditional service. Susannah read from the book of Chronicles—the passage her father had cited in his dedication to her of *Who Is Man?*—in a trembling voice: "And thou Solomon, my son, know thou the God of thy father, and serve Him with a whole heart and a willing mind" (1 Chron. 28:9). Elie Wiesel recited Heschel's Yiddish poem "God Follows Me Everywhere," not knowing that this was the poem Heschel had asked Joseph Wiseman to read to him at his last Shabbat supper.[7]

Wolfe Kelman gave the eulogy.[8] As Heschel's closest friend and the executive vice president of the Rabbinical Assembly, he spoke of Heschel as both a person and a model Jew. Quoting selections from Heschel's own 1945 *hesped* (eulogy) "for the slaughtered Jews of Eastern Europe," Heschel's reflections on aging from his speech at the 1961 White House conference, and other talks, Kelman praised Heschel's participation in the Selma to Montgomery march, his "reaffirming the integrity of Jerusalem and the holiness of the land of Israel," and his witness for peace in Vietnam.

Heschel's personality was both benevolent and judgmental, Kelman explained: "Above all, he loved and lived passionately. He hated sham and hypocrisy. . . . He had an unsurpassed gift for friendship and we who were blessed and touched by it are bereft." Heschel's love for, even veneration of, all human beings was the most palpable motive of his impassioned social action: "Repeatedly, he would remind me, as he emphasized in his writing, that the one unforgivable sin is *halbanat panim*, to cause the face of another human being to blanch by humiliating him. To shame another person is like murder, for it drains blood from the face and heart of the shamed and the downtrodden. . . . He wept for the humiliated and the massacred in Treblinka, Alabama, Haiphong, everywhere." Kelman concluded with the three final paragraphs of *Man Is Not Alone*: "For this act of giving away is reciprocity on man's part for God's gift of life. For the pious man it is a privilege to die."

After the eulogy, Samuel Dresner, Heschel's closest disciple, read from Psalm 15 (which Heschel had planned to recite before the Selma to Montgomery march, but, after his arrival in Selma, he chose Psalm 27[9]):

> Lord, who shall sojourn in Thy tabernacle?
> Who shall dwell upon Thy holy mountain?
> He that walketh uprightly, and worketh righteousness,
> And speaketh truth in his heart;
> That hath no slander upon his tongue,
> Nor doeth evil to his fellow.

Fritz Rothschild, Heschel's foremost interpreter and close colleague, recited Psalm 42, a song of mystical longing, in both Hebrew and English:

> As the hart panteth after the water brooks,
> So panteth my soul after Thee, O God.
> My soul thirsteth for God, for the living God:
> "When shall I come and appear before God?"

To close, one of the Kopitzhinitzer Hasidim chanted in Hebrew *El Malei Rachamim*, the plaintive petition of Jewish funeral services: "Lord of mercy, bring him under the cover of Thy wings, and let his soul be bound up in the bond of eternal life. Be Thou his possession, and may his repose be peace. Amen."[10]

When the service was over, according to custom, the coffin was carried for two blocks down the middle of Seventy-Ninth Street to the waiting hearse. The cortège to Beth David Cemetery in Elmont was slowed by heavy traffic and perhaps also because of the police escort. The trip took a full hour, and many people were lost along the way. The gravediggers were on strike, and it was feared that the burial place would not be ready.

The scene at the cemetery was pitiful and grotesque. It was raining and cold; the ground was muddy and slippery; mounds of wet dirt were scattered around. The burial pit was so large that some Hasidim worried "their rebbe's grave" (the grave of Heschel's uncle) had been disturbed. As the black-suited pallbearers—among them a tall, thin Hasid who resembled Heschel, with white hair and goatee—lowered the coffin into the ground, someone slipped, the straps twisted, and the coffin fell to the bottom of the pit, opening up and exposing the white shrouds (*tachrikhin*) and tallit in which Heschel was wrapped. Heschel's ultimate helplessness was appalling.

In the ensuing consternation, Jacob Teshima realized that as a gentile he could close the coffin (strictly Orthodox Jews considered it a defilement to touch an open coffin). He leapt into the open grave and closed the lid. Although one of the young Hasidim yelled in Yiddish, "Get the '*orel*' [gentile] out of the grave," Reb Moses told him that the Japanese Christian was worthy to restore the dignity of his teacher.

The sorrow was unspeakable. The coffin was secured, and the widow and daughter, sobbing, sheltered from the rain by Elie Wiesel holding an umbrella, and other family members, friends, and colleagues, in turn shoveled dirt into the pit, until it was completely filled. Seymour Siegel led the graveside service, and a Kopitzhinitzer Hasid slowly recited the *Kaddish* one more time. Many cars returned to the city, while for those remaining there was a *Mincha* (afternoon) prayer service at the cemetery administrative building.[11]

It was now time to sit shivah. In accordance with Jewish tradition, the family remained at home for a week, receiving visits from friends and family. At the Heschel apartment on Riverside Drive, there were three prayer services a day.

At the end of shivah, Sylvia and Susannah took Jacob Teshima to another room to speak with Reb Moses Heschel. Teshima was afraid that he might have done something to offend the Orthodox Jews. Instead, the rebbe praised his spiritual sensitivity: "I have observed you for the entire week of shivah, and no one else has shown as much *kavanah*. I name you Reb Yaacov, and you are one of us, part of our family." This strictly Orthodox leader was at one with his modern uncle's generous heart.[12]

HESCHEL FOR POSTERITY

An obituary in the *New York Times* appeared on the day of the funeral, along with a long article by the *Times* journalist Robert D. McFadden and excerpts from Heschel's writings. The *Jerusalem Post* of December 29 carried a life summary by the Israeli teacher Pinchas Peli, accompanied by Heschel's preface to his books on the Kotzker rebbe, which were about to appear in Israel and New York. Heschel was also celebrated in the *Wall Street Journal*, *Time*, and *Newsweek*. Martin Marty, an eminent professor of American religion at the University of Chicago, announced in the *Christian Century*, "A Giant Has Fallen."[13]

In New York, a traditional memorial gathering took place at the Park Avenue Synagogue on January 21, 1973, the thirtieth day since the funeral (*sheloshim*), in the presence of Heschel's widow and daughter. Rabbi Judah Nadich, a friend and the leader of the Conservative synagogue, led the proceedings, which brought together Jewish and Christian speakers: Jewish Theological Seminary chancellor Gerson Cohen; Fritz Rothschild; W. D. Davies, now professor at Duke

University, who recalled Heschel's year at Union Seminary; and Coretta Scott King, who spoke of Heschel's partnership with her late husband. The Israeli consul read a message from Israel's president Zalman Shazar, a youthful friend from Warsaw who praised Heschel's forthcoming books on the Kotzker rebbe.

In Rome, the pope confirmed Heschel's spiritual stature for people of all faiths. A Vatican communiqué printed in the *New York Times* on February 2 explained that "in an address to pilgrims attending the weekly general audience in the Vatican, Pope Paul VI quoted a Jewish theologian, the late Rabbi Abraham J. Heschel of New York. The pontiff, who rarely quoted non-Christian writers, used the words, 'before we have moved to seek for God, God has come in search of us' from the French translation of Rabbi Heschel's book *God in Search of Man.*" Whatever Heschel's struggles during Vatican II, his final legacy was revered.[14]

Longer essays honoring Heschel soon appeared. The first was in the Jesuit weekly *America*, whose editor, Donald R. Campion, stressed that this was the first time a Christian magazine had devoted an entire issue "to contemporary Jewish religious thought and life." A dramatic drawing of Heschel (taken from a Lotte Jacobi photograph) graced the red and black cover.[15] A commemorative issue of *Conservative Judaism* included Heschel's essay on death and the first English translation of one of his German articles on the metaphysics of Solomon Ibn Gabirol. The written expressions of grief and admiration bore witness to the transformed lives of Heschel's disciples of the present and future.[16]

Two weeks before Heschel's death, on December 10, the Jewish Theological Seminary and NBC had recorded an hour-long interview with him, conducted by U.S. Supreme Court correspondent Carl Stern.[17] Now, in February, the finished interview, "Conversation with Doctor Abraham Joshua Heschel," was broadcast nationally on NBC television, as part of the network's *The Eternal Light* series. The conversation summarized Heschel's life and legacy. After surveying Heschel's Hasidic childhood, his openness to surprise, the paradox of God in search of man, and the centrality of the Bible, Stern asked Heschel whether he was a prophet. Heschel demurred: "I won't accept this praise. . . . It is a claim almost arrogant enough to say that I'm a descendant of the prophets, what is called *B'nai Nevi'im*. So let us hope and pray that I am worthy of being a descendant of the prophets."[18]

Heschel and Stern spoke about civil rights, the dehumanization of politics, the demands God makes on human beings, and religious pluralism as the will of God. Heschel explained that he believed himself to be accountable to God: he "could not always control my mean leanings" without belief in God. When asked about life after death, Heschel answered curtly: "We believe in an afterlife. But we have no information about it. . . . I think that's God's business— what to do with me after life."

When Stern broached Heschel's role in the Second Vatican Council, Heschel proudly recalled his "very strong rebuke" about choosing death in Auschwitz over conversion to Christianity. Then he proclaimed, "And I succeeded in persuading even the Pope, the head of the Church, you realize; he personally crossed out a paragraph in which there was a reference to conversion or mission to the Jews. The Pope himself. And the declaration published by the Ecumenical Council—if you study it carefully, you will notice the impact of my effort."

As the hour came to an end, Heschel addressed a message to the youth of America that he had prepared in advance. Telling young people, "There is a meaning beyond absurdity," he identified the current trend of "drug addiction" as evidence of a widely felt search for exultation. "Above all," he urged, "remember that the meaning of life is to build a life as if it were a work of art."

Thus Heschel was canonized by national television. The Jewish Theological Seminary made mimeographed transcripts—and, eventually, videotapes—of the program available for sale to the public.

It is customary to let nearly a year pass before a headstone is placed on the grave of a Jew, but Heschel's grieving widow and daughter took longer. Jacob Teshima visited the unadorned burial place of his mentor about a year after his death; he constructed a temporary memorial out of clay, which stated simply: "Abraham Joshua Heschel (1907–1972)." He drove to the cemetery with Morton Leifman, dean of the Jewish Theological Seminary cantorial school, Wolfe Kelman, and Kelman's son Levi, and the four men said *Kaddish* over the makeshift tomb.[19]

Some time later, with the help of Heschel's Hasidic family, a traditional headstone was erected that listed his illustrious ancestry (*yichus*) in Hebrew.

Here is buried
Abraham Joshua Heschel
the son of sainted Master
Our Rabbi Moshe Mordecai and Reizel Heschel
the grandson of the holy Rabbi
Baal Ohev Yisrael
and the holy Rabbi of Ruzhin
and the holy Rabbi of Berditchev
and of great sanctity
the Maggid of Mezritch
Who left this life on
18 Tevet 5733
May his soul be bound up
in the bond of everlasting life

Heschel joined his Hasidic ancestors, embodying in death as in life their efforts to sanctify the world.

NOTES

1. HASIDIC WARSAW

1. Materials housed at AJH Archive/JTS. For the best account of Heschel's self-knowledge, see Dresner, "Introduction: Heschel as a Hasidic Scholar," vii–xlv.

2. Heschel, *Passion for Truth*, xiii.

3. Moshe Mordecai Heschel had three brothers: Israel Sholem Joseph (1852–1911), rebbe of Zinkov; Yitzhak Meir (1861–1936), rebbe of Kopitzhinitz; and Meshullam Zusya (1871–1920), rebbe of Medzibozh. (Dates vary in different sources.) Their sisters—Gittel, Chava, and Devorah (whose birth dates were not preserved)—all married rabbis.

4. T. Rabinowicz, *Chassidic Rebbes*, 161–66.

5. H. Rabinowicz, *Hasidism*, 269–70; cf. H. Rabinowicz, *Hasidism*, 289–95.

6. Dresner, *Levi Yitzhak of Berditchev*; Buber, *Tales of the Hasidim*, vol. 1, 203–34.

7. Kendall, Interview, AJH Archive/JTS.

8. Hofer, "Milkhome—1914," 381–87.

9. Heschel, *A Passion for Truth*.

10. Hofer, Interview, AJH Archive/JTS.

11. Heschel, "Hasidism as a New Approach to Torah," 21; cf. Heschel, *Moral Grandeur*, 38.

12. Singer, *Love and Exile*, 6.

13. Dresner Diary, AJH Archive/JTS; T. Rabinowicz, *Chassidic Rebbes*, 138.

14. Heschel, *The Earth Is the Lord's*, 89.

15. Zemba, "Shtieblakh in Warsaw," 355–63.

16. Gold, "Religious Education in Poland," 272–82.

17. Heschel, *The Earth Is the Lord's*, 9.

18. These observations are from the Dresner Diary, 39, AJH Archive/JTS.

19. Hofer, "Milkhome—1914."
20. Bromberg, *Mi-gedolei Ha-Torah Ve-ha-hasidut*, 153; see Perlow, *Tiferet Ish*.
21. Israel Heschel, Interview, AJH Archive/JTS.
22. Kendall, Interview, AJH Archive/JTS.
23. Sarah Perlow (Mrs. Moses Eichenstein), Interview, AJH Archive/JTS.
24. Heschel, *A Passion for Truth*, xv.
25. Dresner Diary, 38–39, AJH Archive/JTS; confirmed by conversation with Heschel.
26. Leifman, Interview, AJH Archive/JTS; for more on Lieberman's dark side, see Schochet and Spiro, *Saul Lieberman*, 223–28.
27. Heschel, *A Passion for Truth*, xv.
28. Meyer, Interview, who heard it from Wolfe Kelman, AJH Archive/JTS; Twersky, Interview, AJH Archive/JTS.
29. Israel Heschel, Interview, AJH Archive/JTS.
30. Kendall, Papers, AJH Archive/JTS; Zemba, "Mesivta in Warsaw," 363–75.
31. Heschel, *The Earth Is the Lord's*, 53–54.
32. The *Bet Midrash* supplement was started in 1922 and edited by Rav R. Shlomo Altman, head of the *bet din* (rabbinical court) of Kikel, located in Warsaw.
33. Bernard Perlow, Interview, AJH Archive/JTS. Death certificate, "Madame Gitla Perlow," March 10, 1959; Archives of 5e Arrondissement, Paris, dossier décès no. 498. Excerpt from the death record: Married and divorced from Lucien Léon Wattécant, married to Paul Gaston Monthéard. Gitla Perlow, died March 10, 1959; 14, rue Henri-Barbusse, Paris 5th.
34. Heschel acknowledged Schneersohn's influence and remained in close touch with him for the remainder of his life. Sylvia Heschel, Conversation with Kaplan, n.d., AJH Archive/JTS.
35. Schneersohn, *Studies in Psycho-Expedition*, 168.
36. See Rosenstein, *The Unbroken Chain*; Bernard Perlow, Interview, AJH Archive/JTS.
37. USA Petition for Naturalization, no. 210036, dated November 29, 1935. His brother, Aaron Perlow (1902–1963), a close friend of Heschel's and also an ordained rabbi, eventually left for Antwerp and arrived in New York in 1930.
38. From a typewritten draft of a CV by Jacob Heshel, AJH Archive/JTS.
39. Nehama Perlow Teitelbaum (Mrs. Joel Teitelbaum), Interview, AJH Archive/JTS; H. Rabinowicz, *Hasidism*, 307–8.
40. As one participant described it: "Zeitlin was regarded as a heretic by the ultra-orthodox and a hypocrite by the *maskilim*. Yet to his home . . . flocked *hasidim*, *mitnagdim*, writers, politicians, Agudists, Bundists, and Zionists to

listen and to learn from this modern 'prophet.' He was no demagogue."
Klepfisz, *Culture of Compassion*, 30.

41. *Illustrirte Vokhe* 3, no. 20 (whole no. 73), erroneously dated "1924" in the *Leksikon fun der nayer yidisher literatur*. Ravitch was probably responsible for Heschel's first literary publication.

42. Heschel, "Se zilbert zin azoy loyter," trans. Sylvia Fuks Fried.

43. Dresner Diary, 40, AJH Archive/JTS.

44. Rabbi Mordecai Josef, a disciple of the Kotzker rebbe, wrote that under special circumstances one could violate the Torah. He based his interpretation on the Talmud's rendering of Psalm 119:126: "It is time to act for the Lord, for they have broken Thy Law," as "There are times when breaking Thy law is acting for the Lord" (B. *Berakhot* 54a and Rashi).

45. Dresner, "Introduction: Heschel as a Hasidic Scholar," xxxviii.

46. Towa (Gitla) Perlow, 1931. Thesis accepted by the dean, H. Delecroix, December 3, 1930, written under the direction of Professor Adolphe Lods of the Faculté des Lettres, Université de Paris, with the support of Professor A. Back of the École rabbinique de France.

47. Roskies, Interviews, AJH Archive/JTS; Sarah Perlow (Mrs. Moses Eichenstein), Interview, AJH Archive/JTS.

2. VILNA AND BERLIN

1. Pumpiansky, Interview, AJH Archive/JTS.

2. Dobruszkes, Interview, AJH Archive/JTS, citing Wojczyk, Lewin, and Dobruszkes. Conversations, AJH Archive/JTS.

3. Beilis, Interview, AJH Archive/JTS; Beilis, "Bei die Onheybn fun Yung Vilne," 18–19.

4. Heschel, "Se zilbert zin azoy loyter," 31–32.

5. Heschel, "Ikh nisht tragn mir mayn harts," 417.

6. Derszansky, Interview, AJH Archive/JTS.

7. Heschel, *Moral Grandeur*, x, dates June 24, 1927, for the final examination. Heschel's CV gives June 27 as his date of graduation. There is no copy of Heschel's Real-Gymnasium diploma in the Humboldt University Archives.

8. Heschel, preface to *Jerusalem of Lithuania*.

9. Heschel's university records state that he remained registered at the Philosophical Faculty from April 27, 1928 to January 24, 1931. Student number 5252/118. Humboldt University Archive, Heschel's *Matrikelbuch* (student registration book), now at DUA.

10. Eisner, "Reminiscences of the Berlin Rabbinical Seminary," 32–52.

11. Jung, *Guardians of Our Heritage*, 363–419; Marx (Hoffmann's son-in-law), *Essays in Jewish Biography*, 185–222.

12. *Jahresbericht des Rabbiner-Seminars zu Berlin.*

13. Wohlgemuth's paper on Scheler was published in the 1931 Festschrift in honor of Jakob Rosenheim, founder of the Agudat Israel.

14. For more on the university system, see Schnädelbach, *Philosophy in Germany 1831–1933*, 21–32.

15. Heschel, among other Liberal and Orthodox scholars, contributed a paper to the Festschrift published in Freimann's honor in 1937.

16. Heschel, "Toward an Understanding of Halacha," 389.

17. Maier published a three-volume study of Aristotle, *The Psychology of Emotional Thinking* (1908), and a three-volume *Philosophy of Reality* (1926–1935), which Heschel purchased in Berlin and preserved in his personal library after his immigration to the United States.

18. Schwab, *Chachme Ashkenaz*, 97–98.

19. Heschel, Conversation with Kaplan. Memory of author.

20. See Ismar Elbogen's encyclopedic study of Jewish liturgy, *Der jüdische Gottesdienst in seiner geschichtlichen Entwicklung*, first published in 1913, with additional notes in 1923.

21. See Guttmann, "Principles of Judaism."

22. "Educated" (*Hochgebildet*) to be distinguished from "cultured" (Cassirer), or "erudite" (Buber), Heschel's other (nonreligious) superlatives. Dresner et al., Roundtable, personal papers of the author. Heschel archive discussion organized by Wertheimer and Dresner, New York, August 1987, Transcript, 125, AJH Archive/JTS.

23. Heschel's candidacy book (Doktoranden-Buch) no. 68, journal no. 238, Humboldt University Archives, and Heschel's CV.

24. *Bericht der Hochschule*, 1931 (printed in 1932), 12.

25. Deutsch, *Larger Than Life*, vol. 2, 49, 124–34. For original sources, see *Leksikon fun der Nayer Yidisher Literatur* 8:755. Hofer, *Mit Yenem un mit Zikh.*

26. Koigen's typed academic résumé, Central Archives for the History of the Jewish People, Jerusalem, Hebrew University, Ramat Gan Campus, Box P196. Also, biographical essay by Hoffmann in Koigen, *Das Haus Israel*, 75–78. See Martine Urban, "Religion of Reason Revised: David Koigen on the Jewish Ethos," *Journal of Jewish Thought and Philosophy* 16, no. 1 (July 2008): 59–89.

27. Koigen, Hilker, and Schneersohn, *Ethos: vierteljahrsschrift für Soziologie, Geschicts und Kulturphilosophie.* Schneersohn's influence on Heschel, as part of the Koigen-Buber axis, cannot be overemphasized.

28. The poems appeared in this order in *Zukunft* 34: "God follows me every-where"; "Millions of eyes choke on one teardrop"; "Evening on the streets"; "I and Thou." See English trans. (with original) by Leifman in Heschel, *The Ineffable Name of God*.

29. New York YIVO Archives, Abraham Liessen Papers.

30. Bialik, *Igrot*.

3. PROPHETIC INSPIRATION, HITLER'S RISE

1. Heschel, "Toward an Understanding of Halacha," 386–87; cf. Heschel, *Moral Grandeur*, 127–45. The subsequent quotations are from his 1953 speech to the annual meeting of Reform rabbis in the United States.

2. Cassirer, *Philosophie der symbolischen Formen*; Muffs, Interview, AJH Archive/JTS.

3. Heschel, "Toward an Understanding of Halacha," 387–88, adapted in Heschel, *Man's Quest for God*, 96–98.

4. Heschel, "Toward an Understanding of Halacha," 389–90.

5. Heschel, "Toward an Understanding of Halacha," 391–93. The version included in Heschel, *Man's Quest for God*, 98, explains the reference: "How would I dare miss an evening prayer? Out of *eymah*, out of fear of God, do we read the Shema [*Me-eymah-tai*, the first word of the tractate Berachoth, Rabbi Levi Yizhak]."

6. Heschel, "Teaching Jewish Theology," 7; cf. Heschel, *Moral Grandeur*, 156.

7. Heschel, *Die Prophetie*, 127–83, section 1, "Knowing God and Comprehending God" ["Gotteserkenntnis und Gottesverständnis"] further specifies his phenomenological method, inspired, in large part, from Dilthey's hermeneutics and especially from Scheler's study of sympathy.

8. See Heschel, *The Prophets*, 319:22: "There is no fusion of being, *unio mystica*, but an intimate harmony in will and feeling, a state that may be called *unio sympathetica*," referring to Scheler's work on sympathy; see Heschel, *The Prophets*, 313:10. See Scheler, *The Nature and Forms of Sympathy*.

9. Heschel, *Die Prophetie*, 128–29, 129:2: Heschel followed phenomenological procedure by elaborating an intuitive method that allows the reader to grasp, through empathy, the prophets' experience of God: "*Verstehen* [comprehension] makes possible, as opposed to *Erkennen* [knowledge], a multiplicity of relationships with the 'comprehended' person. The prophet experiences emotional and intellectual situations, he makes demands, he prays."

10. Heschel, *Die Prophetie*, 53.

11. Heschel, *Die Prophetie*, 53–55.

12. Heschel, *Die Prophetie*, 143–45.

13. Heschel, *Die Prophetie*, 166; the following quotation: Heschel, *Die Prophetie*, 171.
14. "Im Erlebnis wird die transzendente Aufmerksamkeit erfahren, die Gottbesinnung ist Selbstbesinnung;" cf. Heschel, *The Prophets*, 488—the final sentence of the book.
15. Heschel to Liessen, December 5, 1932, New York YIVO Archives, Liessen Papers.
16. This and the following quotations: Humboldt University Archives.
17. As early as January 3, 1933, Koigen wrote to Buber, asking for financial help, MBA, Ms. Var. 350/379:22.
18. Rothschild, Interview, AJH Archive/JTS.
19. See especially AJC 1935, 38–46.
20. Elbogen, *Century of Jewish Life*, 642–43.
21. Heschel's first letter to the Polish Academy of Sciences was dated March 8, 1934; see Minutes of the Polish Academy, Jagiellonian University Archives, Kraków. See Henryk Halkowski, "A Branch Plucked from the Fire . . . ," 226.
22. Heschel first republished this piece in a commemorative brochure on the twenty-fifth anniversary of *Yung Vilne* (1955): 45–46, New York YIVO Archives. See Kaplan and Dresner, *Prophetic Witness*, 323:42–44.
23. Trans. by Shandler occasionally modified. AJH Archive/JTS; see Heschel, *Moral Grandeur*, 71–72.
24. Heschel, Conversation with Kaplan, 1971; see Heschel, *God in Search of Man*, 63–64:9, 70–71. According to the Bible (Gen. 1:26–27), humankind is God's only visible image; see Heschel, *Insecurity of Freedom*, 151–52. Also see Dresner, "Introduction: Heschel as a Hasidic Scholar," x:2, on the kabbalistic *gematria* of God's name being equivalent to humankind.
25. Heschel, *The Ineffable Name of God*, 31 and (the following quotation) 43.
26. Heschel, "David Koigen."
27. "Situational thinking is necessary when we are engaged in an effort to understand issues on which we stake our very existence"; Heschel, *God in Search of Man*, 5.
28. Guttmann states that he ordained Heschel in 1935. See Guttmann, "Hochschule Retrospective," 78.
29. Materials housed at the DUA.
30. Materials housed at Jagiellonian University, Archives of the Polish Academy of Sciences, Kraków.
31. Rothschild, Interview, AJH Archive/JTS.
32. To this author's knowledge, Heschel's letters to Tadeusz Kowalski are his only writings in Polish.
33. Heschel, *Maimonides*, 129; the following quotation: Heschel, *Maimonides*, 135.

34. Trans. in Heschel, *Insecurity of Freedom*, 289–90.
35. Heschel, *Maimonides*, 243; see Heschel, *Insecurity of Freedom*, 290.
36. Heschel, *Insecurity of Freedom*, 293.
37. The May–June 1935 publication of the B'nai B'rith.
38. Bernard Chapira, preface to Heschel, *Maïmonide*, 12.
39. Fraiman, "Transformation of Jewish Consciousness," 41–59.
40. See Hirsch, "Der Dreitage-Jude: Kritik eines Übergangs."
41. See Mendes-Flohr, *Divided Passions*, 77–132.
42. *Der Morgen* 10 (1934–1935), 570.
43. The poem appeared in *Der Morgen* 11 (1935–1936), 127.

4. SYMBOLIC OR SACRED RELIGION

1. Rothschild, Interview, AJH Archive/JTS.
2. See Mendes-Flohr, *Martin Buber*; and Mendes-Flohr, "Martin Buber's Conception of God," in *Divided Passions*, 237–82.
3. Buber, "Sinnbildliche und sakramentale Existenz im Judentum," 339–67. Heschel's letter cites pages from the German publication, originally presented in August 1934 in Ascona, Switzerland.
4. From Heschel to Buber, July 24, 1935, published in Buber, *Briefwechsel aus Sieben Jahrzehnten*, vol. 2, letter no. 510, 568–69; original in MBA, Ms. Var. 290:2. For the fuller context of these fundamental issues, see Mendes-Flohr, *Divided Passions*.
5. Buber, *Prophetic Faith*, 96–109; the footnote reads: "Cf. especially Heschel, *Die Prophetie* (1936), 76ff."
6. Heschel's opposition to Buber's exegesis of God's word as symbol advanced an older debate with Buber, when Franz Rosenzweig, in "Atheistic Theology," criticized Buber's early romantic approach to the biblical God. (Heschel recommended Rosenzweig's essay to students as a useful critique of contemporary religion.) See E. Kaplan, *Holiness in Words*, 75–89.
7. Buber, *Hasidism and the Modern Man*, 52–53.
8. Buber, *Hasidism and the Modern Man*, 54–55.
9. Heschel, *Moral Grandeur*, 385.
10. This and all letters to Kowalski are preserved at the Jagiellonian University Archives, Kraków.
11. Letter in Archives Diplomatiques de Nantes, Berlin fonds C: no. 121, dossier lettre H. See also Jambet, *L'Herne Henry Corbin*.
12. May 7, 1936, copy from the personal library of Henry Corbin.
13. It had a circulation of fifty-two thousand. Strauss, *Jewish Immigrants of the Nazi Period*, 99.

14. See Simon, "Jewish Adult Education in Nazi Germany as Spiritual Resistance," 68–104.
15. Rosh Hashanah, Tishri 1, 1936, files of Rabbi Meir Wunder, Jerusalem.
16. Not to be confused with the medieval scholar Ernst Hartwig Kantorowicz (1895–1963).
17. Kantorowicz took over in March 1938, right after Buber emigrated. Buber, *Letters of Martin Buber*, 466:1; also Simon, "Martin Buber and German Jewry," 80.
18. Heschel to Buber, March 2, 1937, MBA, Ms. Var. 290:6.
19. Heschel's letter of March 26, 1937; see Heschel, *Moral Grandeur*, xv–xvi.
20. Friedman, *Martin Buber: Middle Years*, 256; see also Rothschild, Interview, AJH Archive/JTS; Heschel, Conversation with Kaplan, AJH Archive/JTS.
21. Hertz (née Simon), Interview and Letters, 1978–1979, AJH Archive/JTS.
22. For the titles of courses Heschel offered, see *Israelitische Gemeinde (Frankfurt, Main)* (Frankfurt am Main: Gemeinde, 1929–1937).
23. Heschel, "Teaching Jewish Theology," 32–33.
24. See Heschel, "Abravanel," 5, 8–12. Quotation translated from the German original, Heschel, *Don Jizhak Abravanel*, 5.
25. Heschel, *Don Jizhak Abravanel*, 5.
26. Heschel, *Don Jizhak Abravanel*, 5–6.
27. Heschel, *Don Jizhak Abravanel*, 30; Heschel, "Abravanel," 12; cf. Heschel, *Israel: An Echo of Eternity*, 114.
28. Rothschild read Heschel's essay as an eighteen-year-old in Germany and never forgot being impressed by this insightful twist at the end.
29. Translated into Polish by Ozjasz Tilleman, Lwow, 1938.
30. Heschel gave a list of reviews with brief excerpts (all dated 1936) to Corbin in Paris.
31. Heschel to Corbin, January 18, 1938, AJH Archive/JTS.
32. Heschel's first article in English, "An Analysis of Piety," published in 1942, was an amalgam of two articles from 1939, one in German ("Das Gebet als Äusserung und Einfühlung") and the other in Hebrew ("'Al Mahut Ha-tefillah").
33. Heschel to Corbin, January 18, 1938, AJH Archive/JTS.
34. Buber, *Letters of Martin Buber*, 467, letter no. 516.
35. Lachmund, introduction to *Begegnung mit dem Judentum*; Heschel, "Versuch einer Deutung," 11–13.
36. Heschel published a revised translation of this speech in the United States, first in the *Hebrew Union College Bulletin* (March 1943). A slightly revised version, with specific references to the war, appeared in *Liberal Judaism*

(February 1944). The final chapter of *Man's Quest for God* reproduces the *Liberal Judaism* version, with an incorrect indication of date (March instead of February 1938).

37. This and the following quotations: Heschel, *Pikuach Neshama*; translated in Heschel, *Moral Grandeur*, 54–67.

38. Heschel, *Moral Grandeur*, xvii.

39. On March 13, the Bubers left for Zurich and Italy, sailing for Palestine on March 19.

40. Finkelstein to Heschel, n.d., GF/JTS.

41. Heschel, *Moral Grandeur*, xvii.

42. Zusya Heschel, in Mintz, *Hasidic People*, 72–73.

43. Rosenstein, *Unbroken Chain*, vol. 2, 937–38.

44. Quoted without date by Heschel, *Moral Grandeur*, xix.

5. STRUGGLING TO ESCAPE

1. See Buber, *Pointing the Way*, 177–91.

2. Heschel to Buber, April 25, 1938, MBA, Ms. Var. 290:12.

3. Heschel to Buber, May 21, 1938, MBA, Ms. Var. 290:13.

4. Heschel to Buber, May 21, 1938, with postscript dated May 22, MBA, Ms. Var. 290:13–14.

5. Heschel to Buber, October 24, 1938, MBA, Ms. Var. 290:22.

6. A graphic account of the expulsion of Polish Jews from Germany appeared in a front-page article in the *New York Times*, October 29, 1938.

7. Rothschild, Interview, AJH Archive/JTS.

8. *Contemporary Jewish Record* 2, no. 1 (January 1939): 102–3.

9. *Contemporary Jewish Record* 1 (November 1938): 56a–b; see "Digest of Public Opinion," *Contemporary Jewish Record* (January 1939): 41–50.

10. "From 10 November 1938 to 15 December 1938, Reiss was captive in Ora-nienburg, then allowed to emigrate to Sweden where he lived for a year. . . . In 1939 he emigrated to the United States, where his brother had been living since 1928. In 1940 Reiss married the photographer Lotte Jacobi, who fled Germany in 1935." Halbey, *Der Erich Reiss Verlag*, 1145.

11. Tartakover, "Institute for Jewish Studies in Warsaw," 163–76; Eden, "Institute for Jewish Studies and Research in Warsaw," 561–84.

12. Heschel's appointment as *Dozent* at the Institute for Jewish Studies was registered with the Polish Ministry of Education. See Heschel to Morgenstern from London, July 28, 1939, AJA.

13. Heschel was invited to contribute to the volume sponsored by the Warsaw Institute to honor Mayer Balaban's sixtieth birthday. The first part of the

Mayer Balaban Jubilee Volume appeared the next year (Biderman, *Mayer Balaban*, 78, 83:20). Heschel's essay for the second volume, "The Essence of Prayer," was written in crisp Modern Hebrew. The Nazis destroyed the volume before its publication.

14. See Meyer, "Refugee Scholars Project of the Hebrew Union College." After the Kristallnacht pogrom, Morgenstern asked Elbogen to draw up a list of scholars who might be brought to the Reform rabbinical institution. Among the many names, Morgenstern chose the following: Julius Guttmann, Franz Landsberger, Albert Lewkowitz, Isaiah Sonne, Eugen Täubler, Max Weiner, Alfred Gottschalk, Franz Rosenthal, and of course Abraham Heschel. Official invitations were sent to them on April 6, 1939. Such was Morgenstern's "College in Exile."

15. Heschel to Buber, March 20, 1939, Frankfurt poste restante (general delivery), MBA, Ms. Var. 290:30.

16. AJA, file Morgenstern; see Meyer, "Refugee Scholars Project of the Hebrew Union College," 363–64.

17. Heschel to Morgenstern, n.d., AJA.

18. Heschel to Buber, July 13, 1939; Jacob Heshel's apartment was the return address: 70 Highbury New Park, London N5. MBA, Ms. Var. 290:33.

19. Kendall, Interview, AJH Archive/JTS.

20. Heschel, "No Religion Is an Island," cf. Heschel, *Moral Grandeur*, 235.

21. Heschel, *A Passion for Truth*, 301.

22. Morgenstern to the American Consul, Dublin, Ireland, September 25, 1939.

23. Kendall, Interview, AJH Archive/JTS.

24. A dispatch of December 29 from Geneva reported, however, that the typhus epidemic had been stamped out. This and the following information is from the *Contemporary Jewish Record* (January–February 1940): 68–69.

25. *Jewish Chronicle*, February 2, 1940, 21.

26. "Die Idee der jüdischen Bildung." The event took place at Maccabi House, 73 Compagne Gardens.

27. Heschel to Morgenstern, January 31, 1940, AJA.

28. This and the following quotations are from Heschel to Buber, February 7, 1940, MBA, Ms. Var. 290:37.

29. Heschel to Buber, February 7, 1940, Ms. Var. 290:37.

30. According to Corbin, the philosophical method of phenomenology could become a spiritual discipline: "To save the phenomenon by demonstrating its hidden meaning is expressed by the Arabic term *kashf al-mahjub* . . . unveiling, uncovering of that which was hidden. . . . [The term *ta'wî* signifies] the hermeneutic practiced by Iranian thinkers, whose technical designation

means 'to lead back something to its source.'" Corbin, *En Islam iranien: Aspects spirituels et philosophiques*, vol. 1, xix–xx, translated by Kaplan.

31. Heschel translated this essay and published it in revised form in *Man's Quest for God*, chapter 2, "The Person and the Word." For the earliest version see Heschel, "Prayer."

32. Petuchowski and Spicehandler, *Perakim Ba-yahadut*, 37–49; Heschel, "'Al Mahut Ha-tefillah" [The essence of prayer].

33. Passenger List no. 7, United States National Archives. The document from the British Home Office notes that the departure was registered on March 15, 1940. For an account of the crossing, see the *New York Times*, March 22, 1940.

34. Wolf, Interview, AJH Archive/JTS. Wolf witnessed Heschel's conversation, in Yiddish, with Borowitz's father.

35. Heschel to Morgenstern, March 21, 1940; see letter to Finkelstein, March 24, 1940, GF/JTS.

36. *New York Times*, July 26, 1940, 1–2; military censors concealed the event for three months.

37. T. Rabinowicz, *Chassidic Rebbes*, 336–37.

38. Heschel, *Torah Min Ha-shamayim*, vol. 1. For the English translation, see Heschel, *Heavenly Torah*.

39. Heschel, *A Passion for Truth*, viii.

6. BECOMING AN AMERICAN

1. Borowitz, Interview, AJH Archive/JTS; Plotkin, Interview, AJH Archive/JTS.

2. Heschel to Buber, April 16, 1940, MBA, Ms. Var. 290:38.

3. This and the following quotations: Temkin, "Century of Reform Judaism," 60.

4. Plotkin, Interview, AJH Archive/JTS.

5. The Hebrew Union College catalog of 1940–1941 praised the library's important collection as its greatest resource after the faculty.

6. Declaration of intention to become a United States citizen, Certification no. 9–24996, May 15, 1940: Petition for Naturalization, no. 17894, May 28, 1945. The witnesses were Amy Blank and Bertha Feinberg. Signed on April 17, 1945, United States District Court.

7. Stenographic transcript of "Proceedings: Conference on Science, Philosophy and Religion in Their Relation to the Democratic Way of Life," microfilm, GF/JTS, September 9–11, 1940.

8. Albert Einstein, "God's Religion or Religion of the Good?," *Aufbau* (September 13, 1940), published by the German-Jewish Club. Heschel's essay appeared in *Aufbau* the following week, September 20, 1940. Einstein's essay: *Science, Philosophy and Religion: A Symposium*, 209–14.

9. Einstein, "God's Religion or Religion of the Good?," cited in Heschel, "Antwort an Einstein"; further quotations are from this source.

10. Lewy, "Hitler's Contribution to the Teaching Staff of HUC, Part 2," 8–10.

11. Plotkin, Interview, AJH Archive/JTS; Silberman, in Karff, *Hebrew Union College–Jewish Institute of Religion at 100 Years*, 415–17.

12. Marcus, Interview, AJH Archive/JTS; Sylvia Heschel, Conversations, AJH Archive/JTS.

13. Dreyfus, Interview, AJH Archive/JTS; Wolf, Interview, AJH Archive/JTS; Davis, Interview, AJH Archive/JTS; Dresner memorandum, August 31, 1999, AJH Archive/JTS.

14. Davis, Interview, AJH Archive/JTS.

15. Eden, Interview, AJH Archive/JTS.

16. Heschel to Strauss, March 30, 1941, Leo Baeck Archives.

17. Heschel, "Das Gebet als Äusserung und Einfühlung," and Heschel, "'Al Mahut ha-Tefillah"; both articles appeared the following spring; Heschel, "Analysis of Piety"; Heschel, review of Baron, *Essays on Maimonides*.

18. Heschel, "Analysis of Piety," 298; see E. Kaplan, *Holiness in Words*, 33–43.

19. Heschel, "Analysis of Piety," 307–9.

20. Heschel to Buber, March 1, 1942, MBA, Ms. Var. 290:39.

21. Heschel to Buber, June 2, 1942, MBA, Ms. Var. 290:40.

22. Hebrew Union College catalog, 1942–1943.

23. Dresner and Ruth Dresner, Conversations; also, Dresner, memoranda, AJH Archive/JTS.

24. Gertel, "Remembering Rabbi Samuel H. Dresner," 12; see E. Kaplan, introduction to *Heschel, Hasidism, and Halakha*, ix–x.

25. Wolf, Interviews, AJH Archive/JTS.

26. Penkower, "American Jewry and the Holocaust," 97–98; see also Medoff, "New Perspectives."

27. *Contemporary Jewish Record*, July 1942.

28. Penkower, "American Jewry and the Holocaust," 98; Faierstein, "Abraham Joshua Heschel and the Holocaust," 272.

29. Jacobson, Interview, AJH Archive/JTS; Heschel, *Circle of Baal Shem Tov*.

30. From the cover of *The Reconstructionist* (November 3, 1944), in which part 1 of Heschel's article "Faith" appeared; Eisenstein, Interview, AJH Archive/JTS. See Scult, "Kaplan's Heschel."

31. Heschel to Kaplan, February 3, 1943, AJH Archive/JTS.

32. Heschel, "Meaning of This War," *Hebrew Union College Bulletin*, 2. Unless otherwise indicated, future quotations are from this version.

33. Heschel, "Meaning of This War," 20.

34. *Jewish Currents* (April 1991): 4.
35. Heschel, *Moral Grandeur*, xix.
36. Heschel, "Holy Dimension," 117; the following quotation is from Heschel, "Holy Dimension," 120–21.
37. Hebrew Union College faculty minutes, April 11, 1943, AJA; Hebrew Union College faculty minutes, April 23, 1943, AJA; Hebrew Union College, Minutes of the Board of Governors, May 12, 1943, AJA.
38. Rakeffet-Rothkoff, *Silver Era*, 217 ff. The following year, Silver admonished President Roosevelt about the Auschwitz concentration camp; Rakeffet-Rothkoff, *Silver Era*, 223. See Zuroff, *Response of Orthodox Jewry*, for a more complex view.
39. See "Rabbis Present Plea to Wallace," *New York Times*, October 7, 1943, 7; Sarna, *American Judaism*, 263–64; Medoff, "The Day the Rabbis Marched."
40. Finkelstein to Heschel, March 23, 1942, and June 27, 1943, GF/JTS.
41. Heschel's two foundational monographs, published in Hebrew in 1945 and 1950, did not appear in English translation until 1996, in *Prophetic Inspiration after the Prophets*.
42. Idel, "Ramon Lull and Ecstatic Kabbalah," 171:11.
43. Heschel, review of *Major Trends in Jewish Mysticism*, 140–41.
44. See E. Kaplan, *Holiness in Words*, 133–46.
45. These quotations are from Heschel, "Faith."
46. Heschel to Finkelstein, January 30, 1945, GF/JTS; *Newsletter of the YIVO* (February 1945): 5. For the best analysis of this episode with precise bibliographical references, see Shandler, "Heschel and Yiddish," 268–84; see also Neusner, *Stranger at Home*, 82–96. About fourteen hundred people were in attendance. *Newsletter of the YIVO* (December 1944 and February 1945).
47. Heschel, "Eastern European Era in Jewish History," 89, 105–6.
48. See Shandler, "Heschel and Yiddish," 275:60; and Alstat, review of "The East European Era in Jewish History." It is likely that memories of Heschel's first speech were confused with impressions surrounding the address he gave two years later, at the twenty-first annual YIVO meeting. Nearly three thousand people heard Heschel consider the "Meaning of Jewish Existence" at the Hunter College Assembly Hall on January 18, 1947.
49. This and the following quotations: Heschel, "Prayer," 158, 164, 168.
50. Hartstein to Heschel, February 15, 1945, Hartstein Administrative Files, Yeshiva University, NY.
51. Finkelstein, "Louis Ginzberg," 573–79; Parzen, "Louis Ginzberg, the Proponent of *Halakhah*," 128–54; Ginzberg, "Address in Honor of L.G.," 109–19; Ginzberg, Interview, AJH Archive/JTS.

52. Heschel's letter of resignation to Morgenstern, dated May 3, 1945, is reproduced in HUC's Minutes of the Board of Governors, May 9, 1945, 6–7, AJA.

53. Certificate of Arrival no. 9–24996c. Documents from District Court of the United States, Cincinnati, Ohio, Southern District of Ohio.

7. RESCUING THE AMERICAN SOUL

1. For the most complete history of the Jewish Theological Seminary, see Wertheimer, *Tradition Renewed*.

2. Finkelstein to Heschel, September 27, 1940, GF/JTS.

3. Statement by the Jewish Theological Seminary faculty, marked in pencil: "Confidential, Draft subject to revision, not for pub. or dist.," GF/JTS, IC-47-6: 1945–1946 Faculty Folder; further quotations are from this source.

4. Cf. Heschel, "Meaning of This War": "Let us forever remember that the sense for the sacred is as vital to us as the light of the sun. There can be no nature without spirit, no world without the Torah, no brotherhood without a father, no humanity without God"; cf. Heschel, *Moral Grandeur*, 211.

5. Bernard Perlow, Interview, AJH Archive/JTS; Rabbi Jacob Perlow, Interview, AJH Archive/JTS.

6. See Mintz, *Hasidic People*, 13–20.

7. Ravitch to Heschel, February 18, 1946; Heschel to Ravitch, January 31, 1947; Ravitch Archive, Jerusalem.

8. Translated by Yossel Birstein from Ravitch, *Mayn Leksikon*, vol. 2, 21–23; further quotations from the conversation are from this source.

9. Heschel, *Moral Grandeur*, xx; Sylvia Heschel, Conversations.

10. The Heschels were married by Rabbi Eliezer Adler at 556 N. Flores Street, Los Angeles, California, December 10, 1946. The marriage certificate read: "Abraham Heschel, age last birthday: 39; birthplace: Poland; occupation: teacher; father: Moses Heschel, born Russia; mother: Reisel Perlow, born Poland. Sylvia Straus, age last birthday: 29; occupation: pianist; father: Samuel Straus, born Russia; mother: Anna Hoffman, born Poland." Certificate No. 3984 on file, County of Los Angeles, Registrar-Recorder, County Clerk. Sylvia Straus was really thirty-three years old; cf. obituary, *New York Times*, March 27, 2007.

11. Heschel, "To Be a Jew: What Is It?"; four years later, the piece was translated in the inaugural issue of *Zionist Quarterly*, 78–84; cf. Heschel, *Moral Grandeur*, 3–11.

12. This and the following quotations: Heschel, "After Majdanek," *Modern Judaism*, 264–71.

13. See Dresner et al., Roundtable discussion organized by Wertheimer and Dresner, New York, August 1987, Transcript, AJH Archive/JTS.

14. Kelman, Interview, AJH Archive/JTS; Szoni, Interview, AJH Archive/JTS; Leifman, Interview, AJH Archive/JTS; see also Dresner et al., Roundtable discussion organized by Wertheimer and Dresner, New York, August 1987, Transcript, AJH Archive/JTS.

15. Tanenbaum, Interviews, AJH Archive/JTS; see Tanenbaum, *Prophet for Our Times*.

16. Rothschild, Interviews, AJH Archive/JTS; Rothschild to Buber, October 18, 1943; Buber to Rothschild, November 21, 1943, in Buber, *Letters of Martin Buber*, 500–504.

17. Dresner et al., Roundtable discussion organized by Wertheimer and Dresner, New York, August 1987, Transcript, Novak, 69–70, who originally heard it from Kelman, AJH Archive/JTS. See Baker, *Days of Sorrow and Pain*.

18. Baronial Press published Heschel's booklet. The quotation is from Heschel, *"Pikuach Neshama,"* 54–67.

19. Heschel, *"Pikuach Neshama,"* 55, 58–60; the following quotation: Heschel, *"Pikuach Neshama,"* 66.

20. Jacobson, "Interview, Prof. Heschel about Russian Jewry," 272–74.

21. *Commentary* evolved from the AJC's wartime news digest *Contemporary Jewish Record*, which excerpted detailed information from the world press.

22. This and the following quotations: Heschel, "Two Great Traditions," 416–22.

23. Heschel, "Two Great Traditions," 420–21; Elbogen, *Der jüdische Gottesdienst*.

24. Heschel, *The Earth Is the Lord's*, 10.

25. Heschel, *The Earth Is the Lord's*, 14.

26. Heschel, *The Earth Is the Lord's*, 19.

27. Heschel, *The Earth Is the Lord's*, 75.

28. Heschel, *The Earth Is the Lord's*, 98, 103–4, 108.

29. Kristol, "Elegy for a Lost World," 490–91.

30. Samuel, Review of *The Earth Is the Lord's*, 7–9. Kristol dismissed Samuel as another idealizer in Kristol, "Elegy for a Lost World," 491.

31. Friedman, *Abraham Joshua Heschel and Elie Wiesel*; see also Friedman to Heschel, August 2, 1950, GF/JTS.

32. This and the following quotations: Friedman, *Abraham Joshua Heschel and Elie Wiesel*, 7–8.

33. Marshall Meyer, Interview, AJH Archive/JTS. See Marshall Meyer Archive at Duke University, which also holds Abraham Joshua Heschel papers.

34. Will Herberg, "From Marxism to Judaism"; Herberg, "Has Judaism Still Power to Speak?," 455. See Dalin, "Will Herberg," in Katz, *Interpreters of Judaism in the Late Twentieth Century*, 113–30.

35. Schochet and Spiro, *Saul Lieberman*; Spiro, "The Moral Vision of Saul Lieberman," 64–84; Greenbaum, "The Finkelstein Era," in Wertheimer, *Tradition Renewed*, vol. 1, 161–232. Golinkin, "The Influence of Seminary Professors," 450–52, 472–74, notes 35–37.

36. Kelman, Interview, AJH Archive/JTS; see Sarna, "Two Traditions of Seminary Scholarship," 53–80. Lieberman once introduced Scholem to a Jewish Theological Seminary audience with the words, "Nonsense (*narishkeit*) is nonsense, but the history of nonsense can be great scholarship," Novak, Interview, Roundtable discussion organized by Wertheimer and Dresner, New York, August 1987, Transcript, AJH Archive/JTS.

37. Jacobs to Heschel, July 19, 1948; Heschel to Grayzel, July 28, 1948, JPS Archives.

38. See Sarna, *JPS: The Americanization of Jewish Culture*, and especially Sarna, *American Judaism*.

39. Grayzel to Heschel, November 15, 1948, JPS Archives.

40. Straus to Grayzel, June 30, 1950, JPS Archives.

41. *New York Times*, February 26, 1951, 20.

42. Finkelstein to Heschel, October 9, 1950; see Heschel to Finkelstein, October 11, 1950, GF/JTS.

43. Heschel, *Man Is Not Alone*, 67–79; see E. Kaplan, "Mysticism and Despair in Abraham J. Heschel's Religious Thought."

44. Niebuhr, "Masterly Analysis of Faith"; Dresner et al., Roundtable discussion organized by Wertheimer and Dresner, New York, August 1987, Transcript, Novak, 12, AJH Archive/JTS; see Goldy, *The Emergence of Jewish Theology in America*.

45. Niebuhr, "Masterly Analysis of Faith."

46. Agus, review of *Man Is Not Alone*, 12–13.

47. Gordis, "The Genesis of *Judaism*," 390–95.

48. Fackenheim, review of *Man Is Not Alone*, 85–89; further quotations are from this source.

49. Heschel, *Man Is Not Alone*, 151.

50. Bergman was a librarian at the University of Prague, where Buber later delivered his famous *Drei Reden über des Judentum*. Bergman, "Der Mensch ist nicht allein"; further quotations are from this source.

8. THEOLOGICAL REVOLUTION

1. Heschel, "Between Civilization and Eternity," 378.
2. Heschel, *The Sabbath*, 6.
3. Heschel, "Architecture of Time."
4. Herberg's lead article, "Prophetic Faith in an Age of Crisis," implicitly supported Heschel's mission to import Jewish holiness into American culture. Herberg's subtitle defined their common perspective: "God-Centered Religion Meets the Challenge of Our Time." See Heschel, "Space, Time, and Reality"; cf. Heschel, *To Grow in Wisdom*, 83–95.
5. Heschel, "Space, Time, and Reality," 277–78.
6. Glatzer, review of *The Sabbath*, 283–86.
7. "A Trumpet for All Israel," *Time*, October 15, 1951, 52–59.
8. Rosenberg, quoted in "Reminiscences by Heschel's Former Students," 175; Holtz, Interview, AJH Archive/JTS.
9. Gillman, Interview, AJH Archive/JTS; "Abraham Joshua Heschel: Twenty-Fifth Yahrzeit Tribute."
10. For the speech, "Hope for This Hour," see Friedman, *Martin Buber: Later Years*, 303–6; the quotation is from Buber, *Pointing the Way*, 222. In 1952 Buber collected his American lectures into a powerful book, *Eclipse of God: Studies in the Relation Between Religion and Philosophy*.
11. Heschel to Finkelstein, May 19, 1952, GF/JTS; Heschel to Meyer, May 15, 1952, Meyer, personal papers; Susannah Heschel, email to Kaplan, January 2001, AJH Archive/JTS.
12. Heschel, "Symbolism and Jewish Faith," 53, 59–60.
13. Reprinted in Heschel, *Man's Quest for God*, "Symbolism," 117–44; cf. Heschel, *Moral Grandeur*, 80–99. Quotations are from Heschel, "Symbolism and Jewish Faith."
14. Heschel, "Symbolism and Jewish Faith," 62–63; the following quotation: Heschel, "Symbolism and Jewish Faith," 70, 72.
15. Heschel, "Symbolism and Jewish Faith," 55–56.
16. See Johnson, *Religious Symbolism*, 204.
17. Heschel, "The Divine Pathos," 64.
18. Heschel, "The Moment at Sinai"; cf. Heschel, *Moral Grandeur*, 13. In America, the Zionist Organization of America sponsored secular or denominational Jewish summer camps, as well as the Young Judaea youth movement; in Israel the ZOA funded Zionist education.
19. Heschel, "Preface to the Understanding of Revelation," 28, 33.

20. Cohen to Heschel, March 5, 1953, AJH Archive/JTS. The expression for God as "the most moved mover" came originally from Rothschild.

21. Heschel, "Spirit of Jewish Education," 11–12, 15–17.

22. Heschel, "Spirit of Jewish Education," 62.

23. Heschel, "Spirit of Jewish Prayer," 151. Heschel incorporated a revised version of the speech into chapter 3 of *Man's Quest for God*, "Spontaneity Is the Goal," 49–89. All quotations are from the original *Proceedings* version, which contains a number of Hebrew words, phrases, and quotations.

24. In the printed version, Heschel referred in a footnote (*Proceedings* 1953, 156:3) to Josiah Royce's *The Problem of Christianity* (1913), rather than to Mordecai Kaplan's *Judaism as a Civilization* (1934), when citing a Kaplanian axiom: God is a symbol of social action, "the spirit of the beloved community."

25. Joseph Segond, *La prière, étude de psychologie religieuse* (Paris: F. Alcan, 1911), 52; *Proceedings* 1953, 158:7a.

26. Heschel is referring to Joseph Zeitlin, *Disciples of the Wise: The Religious and Social Opinions of American Rabbis* (New York: Teachers Institute, Columbia University Press, 1945).

27. Kohn, "Prayer and the Modern Jew," 184–85; the following quotation: Kohn, "Prayer and the Modern Jew," 187–88.

28. Lehrman's remarks, *Proceedings* 1953, 192–93; further quotations from the audience discussion are from this source, 194–217.

29. Heschel to Meyer, undated (June 1953), Meyer, personal papers; Irving Spiegel, *New York Times*, June 24, 1953, 26.

30. Cohon, "The Existentialist Trend in Theology," 348–85. Especially useful was Rosenzweig's "new thinking," as found in *The Star of Redemption* and the example of the man's final years, in which he continued to teach and write despite his debilitating terminal illness.

31. Polish, "Current Trends in Jewish Theology," 420–30. Polish quoted a passage from Heschel, *Quest for Certainty*.

32. Heschel, "Toward an Understanding of Halacha," 387. This was revised, with significant deletions, in *Man's Quest for God*, "Continuity Is the Way," 93–114; cf. Heschel, *Moral Grandeur*, 127–45.

33. Heschel, "Toward an Understanding of Halacha," 389.

34. Heschel, "Toward an Understanding of Halacha," 393–96, 399. Heschel's religious standards were practical: "The highest peak of spiritual living is not necessarily reached in rare moments of ecstasy; the highest peak lies wherever we are and may be ascended in a common deed" (404). The following quote: Heschel, "Toward an Understanding of Halacha," 390.

35. Heschel, "Toward an Understanding of Halacha," 407–9.

36. Al-Yahud, *Jewish Forum*, 1952–1953. Heschel, *A Passion for Truth*, 1, 137, 139. The following quotations: Heschel, *A Passion for Truth*, 141; Al-Yahud, *Jewish Forum*, 1952–1953; Heschel, *A Passion for Truth*, 2, 48–49. Al-Yahud's identity has remained a mystery, but he was formed in Orthodox Judaism, involved in contemporary debates, and probably an immigrant. Lawrence Kaplan (McGill University) most plausibly points to Rabbi Israel Elfenbein (1810–1964) as the man behind the pseudonym.

37. Heschel, "Umbakante Dokumentn tsu der Geshikhte fun Khasidus."

38. Heschel rejected the hypothesis of Gershom Scholem and Joseph Weiss that Hasidism originated in the Sabbatean heresy of the false messiah. See Faierstein, "Gershom Scholem and Hasidism," 221–33; Faierstein, review of *Circle of the Baal Shem Tov*.

39. In 1985, Dresner gathered translations of Heschel's articles in *Circle of the Baal Shem Tov*.

40. See Heschel, *God in Search of Man*, 181–83; E. Kaplan, "Language and Reality," 94–113; E. Kaplan, *Holiness in Words*, 45–59; Heschel, *Man's Quest for God*, 25–27.

41. *Man's Quest for God*, 39–40.

42. *Man's Quest for God*, 150. Heschel used a slightly revised version of his 1943–1944 essay on World War II as this final chapter of *Man's Quest for God* (now entitled "The Meaning of This Hour").

43. Herberg, review of *Man's Quest for God*, 404–6.

44. Synan, "Abraham Heschel and Prayer," 256–65. Having been inspired by the words of Pope Pius XI, "Spiritually We Are Semites," the Institute of Judeo-Christian Studies launched *The Bridge*.

45. Eisenstein, "Book Notes," 24–26.

46. See Marmur, "Heschel's Rhetoric of Citation."

47. Heschel, *God in Search of Man*, 138, 143:5. See E. Kaplan, *Holiness in Words*, 133–45; Heschel, "Ha-he'emin Ha-rambam Shezakhah L'anevuah?"

48. Heschel, *God in Search of Man*, 258–59.

49. Heschel, *God in Search of Man*, 317–19:3.

50. Heschel, *God in Search of Man*, 369.

51. Heschel, *God in Search of Man*, 425; the following quotations: Heschel, *God in Search of Man*, 421, 425–26.

52. *Time*, March 19, 1956, 64.

53. Herberg, "Converging Trails," 486.

54. Lookstein, "The Neo-Hasidism of Abraham J. Heschel," 248.

55. Rackman, "Can We Moderns Keep the Sabbath?," 211–20; Rackman, "Dr. Heschel's Answer," 16.

9. BIBLICAL PROPHECY, CURRENT EVENTS

1. See Heschel, *God in Search of Man*, 367–68, 382–86; references to R. Niebuhr, *Nature and Destiny of Man* (380:5), and *Interpretation of Christian Ethics* (381:19).
2. Heschel, *The Insecurity of Freedom*, "Confusion of Good and Evil."
3. R. Niebuhr's address, "The Relations of Christians and Jews in Western Civilization," was incorporated into his *Pious and Secular America*.
4. U. Niebuhr, "Notes on a Friendship," 35–43.
5. See Heschel, "Sacred Images of Man"; cf. *Religious Education* (March–April 1958), 97.
6. *Religious Education* (March–April 1958), 102, the final lines. Heschel often quoted this passage in subsequent speeches, and he repeated it in his 1969 book on Israel.
7. Heschel, "Religious Message," 252.
8. Heschel, "Religious Message," 264. Packard had addressed the 1957 Religious Education Association convention at which Heschel spoke on "Sacred Images of Man."
9. Heschel, "Religious Message," 270.
10. Heschel, "Some Basic Issues of Jewish Education," 3–12; further quotations are from this source.
11. Heschel "Relevance of Prophecy," 13–19.
12. See the final paragraph of Heschel, "'Al Ruah Ha-kodesh Bimey Ha-beynayim," trans. in Heschel, *Prophetic Inspiration after the Prophets*, 67. See Heschel, *God in Search of Man*, 138.
13. Heschel, "To Be a Jew," *Zionist Quarterly*, 81; cf. Heschel, *Moral Grandeur*, 7. The Yiddish original of Heschel's article appeared in 1947 in the *Yidisher Kemfer*.
14. Kelman, Interview, AJH Archive/JTS.
15. Heschel to Kelman, August 4, 1957; Kelman to Heschel, August 7, 1957; Kelman personal files, JTS.
16. Eva Grunebaum, "Jewish Mystic, Modern Scholar," *Jerusalem Post*, August 15, 1957.
17. Heschel, "Individual Jew and His Obligations," 10. The original Hebrew speech, Heschel, "Nation and the Individual," was repeated in various forms, including an English translation.

18. This and the following quotations: Heschel, "Individual Jew and His Obligations," 12–13, 16, 17–18; Heschel, *Insecurity of Freedom*, 189, 191 (passage revised), 198, 199–200.

19. This and the following quotations: Heschel, "Yisrael: *Am, Eretz, Medinah*," 118–19.

20. Heschel, "Yisrael: *Am, Eretz, Medinah*," 118–19. This was Heschel's second public condemnation of racism in America.

21. Heschel, "Yisrael: *Am, Eretz, Medinah*," 126, 136.

22. Ben-Gurion's letter and most of the replies were originally in Hebrew. The following quotations: Hoenig and Litvin, *Jewish Identity*. Heschel's answer, dated December 18, 1958 (Tevet 7, 5719), is repeated as "Answer to Ben Gurion" in Hoenig and Litvin, *Jewish Identity*, 229–31. See Heschel, "Answer to Ben Gurion," for repetitions in both English and Hebrew.

23. Heschel, "Should the United Synagogue of America Join the World Zionist Organization? No," 77. The meeting took place on November 15–19, 1959. See "Jewish Split over Zionist Ties," *New York Times*, November 18, 1959.

24. "Jewish Split over Zionist Ties," *New York Times*, November 18, 1959. The paper featured a photograph of a younger, beardless Heschel and identified him as the instigator of the split.

25. This and the following quotation: Rothschild, introduction to *Between God and Man*, 22, 24.

26. Rothschild, introduction to *Between God and Man*, 30; Rothschild, Interview, AJH Archive/JTS.

27. After 1961 Tanenbaum headed interreligious affairs at the AJC, a position from which he helped Heschel extend his international presence. See Tanenbaum, *Prophet for Our Times*.

28. Memorandum dated April 6, 1960 from Morris Fine and Samuel Fishzohn (director of AJC's youth division), re. conference program, AJC/NY Archives; Heschel's untitled address is quoted from a mimeographed copy dated March 27, 1960, AJC/NY Archives.

29. *New York Times*, March 28, 1960, 1, 23.

30. Memoranda and other preparatory materials for the 1960 "White House Conference" from AJC/NY; Heschel, "Call of the Hour."

31. *Washington Post*, March 29, 1960, A1. Heschel also suggested that the government supplement compulsory military service in peacetime with "compulsory adult education for leisure time for the sake of spiritual security." See *New York Times*, March 31, 1960, 27; April 1, 1960, 25; April 2, 1960, 25.

32. Heschel to Finkelstein, May 1, 1959, GF/JTS.

33. Heschel, "Depth Theology." Quotations: Heschel, *Insecurity of Freedom*, 121–26.
34. Heschel, "To Grow in Wisdom"; cf. Heschel, *To Grow in Wisdom*, 179–80. The speech was considerably revised for Heschel, *Insecurity of Freedom*, 70–84.
35. Heschel, *To Grow in Wisdom*, 181. Heschel set the emphasized phrase at the end of the essay when he revised it for Heschel, *The Insecurity of Freedom*, 84.
36. *Congressional Record*, March 21, 1961; it also reappeared in the same publication on June 14, 1961.
37. Remarks, Greenberg, Kelman, Schafler, *Proceedings* 1962.
38. Heschel, "Values of Jewish Education," 83–85; comments by Simcha Kling and David Lieber, *Proceedings* 1962, 101–9.
39. Heschel, "Values of Jewish Education," 86; the following quotations: Heschel, "Values of Jewish Education," 93, 98.
40. Heschel, "Idols in the Temples," 127–37; repeated in Heschel, *Insecurity of Freedom*, 52–69.
41. Heschel, *Heavenly Torah*, 255.
42. From the Hebrew volume, Heschel, *Torah Min Ha-shamayim*," as cited by Levin, "*Torah Min Hashamayim.*" Heschel summarized these contrasts in Heschel, *Heavenly Torah*, 1–46, 47–64.
43. The discussion in this paragraph was inspired by Eisen, "Abraham Joshua Heschel's Rabbinic Theology." Tucker translated the last phrase as "May their Souls be bound up in the bond of life." See Kaplan and Dresner, *Prophetic Witness*, 306; and Eisen, "Abraham Joshua Heschel's Rabbinic Theology," 217.
44. This and the following quotations: Heschel, *The Prophets*, xii.
45. Cf. Heschel, "The Hiding God," in *Man Is Not Alone*, 151–57.
46. Heschel, *The Prophets*, 14–16.
47. Heschel, *The Prophets*, 90; the following quotation: Heschel, *The Prophets*, 126.
48. Heschel, *The Prophets*, 143, 151. Heschel also defined a biblical equivalent of a post-Holocaust theology of God's absence: "Out of despair, out of total inability to believe, prayer bursts forth" (191–92).
49. Terrien, "The Divine Pathos," 482–88, 485.
50. Daiches, "Doom and Love," 537–40. Daiches apparently ignored Heschel's citation of Psalm 44 and the chapter "Chastisement," which raised the question of undeserved suffering.
51. Daiches, "Doom and Love," 539–40; Berkovits, "Dr. A. J. Heschel's Theology of Pathos," 70. Heschel's discussion of metaphorical language in

Heschel, *God in Search of Man* and Heschel, *The Prophets* should have eliminated these erroneous charges of literalism. See E. Kaplan "Language and Reality"; E. Kaplan, *Holiness in Words*, 176:19.

52. David Shlomo Shapiro, "Haneviim" ["The Prophets"], *Hadoar*, September 4, 1964, 665–67; David Shlomo Shapiro, "A New View on the System of Rabbis Akiva and Ishmael," *Hadoar*, September 27, 1963, 769–72. See Rotenstreich, "On Prophetic Consciousness," 185–98.

10. A SACRED HUMANISM

1. Heschel, "White Man on Trial"; cf. Heschel, *The Insecurity of Freedom*, 107. In 1963 *Time* magazine named Martin Luther King Jr. "Man of the Year."

2. Heschel, "Yisrael: *Am, Eretz, Medinah*," 118. This line was not included in the edited version of "Israel and the Diaspora," that Heschel published in *The Insecurity of Freedom*.

3. Minutes of Program Committee Meeting, August 7, 1962, 1–3, AJC/NY, folder "Conf. on Religion and Race."

4. Program, "National Conference on Religion and Race," Chicago, January 14–17, 1963.

5. This and the following quotations: Heschel, unpublished manuscript, 5a, AJC/NY; see also Heschel, "Religious Basis of Equality of Opportunity," 58–59.

6. Mimeographed copy of King's speech "A Challenge to the Churches and Synagogues," from files of Taylor Branch, personal communication. The quotation is from the published version in Ahmann, *Race*, 155, 157–58.

7. *Time*, January 23, 1963, 66.

8. This telegram was not made public until Heschel's daughter Susannah reproduced it in her introduction to Heschel, *Moral Grandeur*. Photographs and a transcript are available at the JFK Library/Boston.

9. *New York Times*, February 22, 1964, 24.

10. Heschel, "White Man on Trial"; cf. Heschel, *The Insecurity of Freedom*, 101–2; the following quotation: Heschel, *The Insecurity of Freedom*, 105–6.

11. John C. Bennett, Abraham J. Heschel, and Gregory L. Mooney, "Crisis in Education" [letter to the editor dated January 29, 1965], *New York Times*, February 2, 1965, 32.

12. *New York Times*, March 10, 1965, 23; see also Garrow, *Bearing the Cross*, 396–400.

13. Information on the demonstration from FBI files, memorandum, NYO 100–153735, March 9, 1965, Subject: Freedom March Sponsored by Student Non-Violent Coordinating Committee to FBI: Racial Matters; memorandum (100–442529) to FBI director J. Edgar Hoover.

14. The advertisement was dated March 10, 1965; FBI files, memorandum from SAC, WFO (100–231150), to SAC, Chicago, dated May 18, 1965.
15. Lewis, *Walking with the Wind*, 341–47.
16. Lewis, *Walking with the Wind*, 345–47; an unpublished memoir cited by Heschel, *Moral Grandeur*, xxiii.
17. Wolfe Kelman, "Report of the Executive Vice-President," *Proceedings* 1961, 124–25.
18. See Jewish Theological Seminary news release of October 6, 1963, Jewish Theological Seminary Public Affairs files; Heschel, "Momentous Emergency." A French version appeared in *L'Arche* (August–September 1964): 23–29.
19. This and the following quotation: Heschel, "Momentous Emergency"; the biblical quotations are from Lev. 21:1–9 and Deut. 21:1–9.
20. Heschel, "Call to Conscience"; cf. Heschel, *The Insecurity of Freedom*, 278.
21. *Jewish Times* (Baltimore), June 17, 1966.
22. Elie Wiesel, "World Jewry and Russian Jewry: A Paradox," *Proceedings* 1966, 44; Irving Spiegel, "Inaction Charged to Western Jews on Soviet Issue," *New York Times*, May 17, 1966.
23. See, e.g., *Long Island Jewish Press*, June 1966.
24. See also *Jewish Telegraph Agency News Bulletin*, May 17, 1966 and May 27, 1966. Wiesel visited the Soviet Union during the High Holy Days, September–October 1965. See Wiesel, *The Jews of Silence*.
25. Editorial, *Jewish Week*, June 23, 1966; Lyndhurst to the editor of *Jewish News* (Cleveland), July 8, 1966.
26. Clipping from *New York Times*, December 8, 1966, 30, and in FBI files, SAC, Newark (100–42359), Subject: CP, USA, Counterintelligence Program, IS-C.
27. Documents on the Raymond Fred West Memorial Lectures from the Department of Special Collections, Stanford University Libraries.
28. *Stanford Daily*, May 6, 1963; May 8, 1963; May 9, 1963.
29. Heschel, *Who Is Man?*, vii. The chapters devoted to the Shoah in *Man is Not Alone* and *God in Search of Man* recognize the power of evil.
30. Heschel, *Who Is Man?*, 27; the following quotation: Heschel, *Who Is Man?*, 33.
31. Heschel, *Who Is Man?*, 97.
32. Heschel, *Who Is Man?*, 111, 119.
33. "The Last Years of Maimonides" was first published in June 1955 in the *National Jewish Monthly*; cf., Heschel, *The Insecurity of Freedom*.

11. APOSTLE TO THE GENTILES

1. Tobias, *Jewish Conscience of the Church*, 307.
2. Zachariah Shuster obituary, *New York Times*, February 16, 1986, 44.

3. Shuster to Slawson, October 28, 1960, AJC/NY.
4. Gerald Nachman, "Vatican Liberal," *New York Post*, November 1964; see the symposium in Bea's honor: *Simposio Card. Agostino Bea (16–19 dicembre 1981)*, 1983.
5. This narrative is drawn primarily from unpublished documents preserved in the AJC archives, in particular, a ninety-five-page draft of an in-house white paper entitled "The Vatican Decree on Jews and Judaism and the American Jewish Committee: A Historical Record" (marked "strictly confidential"), August 28, 1964. The present author has supplemented the AJC institutional narrative with the raw data of numerous memoranda and letters. For the official AJC narrative, see the two-part article by Hershcopf, "The Church and the Jews." For complete documentation from the AJC Archives, see E. Kaplan, *Spiritual Radical*, 235–76.
6. Tanenbaum memorandum, "Zachariah Shuster's request for AJC Policy re Ecumenical Council, Pro Deo, etc.," to Slawson, Danzig, et al., December 29, 1961; Shuster to Tanenbaum and Heschel, February 27, 1962; Heschel to Shuster, March 2, 1962, dictated by telephone; Tenenbaum to Slawson et al., March 8, 1962; Hershcopf memorandum to Tanenbaum, March 9, 1962; draft outline, March 2, 1962; Tanenbaum to Shuster, April 13, 1962, on Finkelstein and Soloveitchik (they spoke about the memorandum), AJC/NY.
7. Tanenbaum, draft memorandum, August 6, 1962, 23–25, AJC/NY.
8. Unless noted, quotations from Heschel's typed five-page memorandum, "On Improving Catholic-Jewish Relations: A Memorandum to His Eminence Agostino Cardinal Bea, President, the Secretariat for Christian Unity," May 22, 1962, Tanenbaum, personal papers; AJA and AJC/NY.
9. Susannah Heschel, "Out of the Mystery Comes the Bond: The Role of Rabbi Abraham Joshua Heschel in Shaping Nostra Aetate," in *Righting Relations after the Holocaust and Vatican II: A Festschrift Honoring John Pawlikowski*, edited by Elena Procario-Foley (New Jersey: Paulist Press, 2018), 199–225.
10. Ten-page outline of Heschel's introductions and discussion; twelve-page "Conversation of Cardinal Bea with Jewish Scholars and Theologians, Summary of the Main Ideas," AJC/NY.
11. Copy of Cardinal Bea's statement, 2, AJC/NY.
12. Heschel's speech was reprinted as "Ecumenical Movement," in Heschel, *The Insecurity of Freedom*, 179–83; cf. Heschel, "Jewish Response," 4. For the address on April 1, 1963 to Cardinal Bea, see *Jewish Chronicle* (London), April 5, 1963; and Milton Bracker, *New York Times*, n.d., collected in a folder at AJC/NY.

13. Heschel to Shuster, September 16, 1963, AJC/NY; Milton Bracker, *New York Times*, October 17, 1963, 1. See Hershcopf, "The Church and the Jews," 114–23.

14. Shuster, letter to Tanenbaum, December 12, 1963, AJC/Paris.

15. Seven-page confidential account of the audience, dated June 4, 1964, from Slawson's office, AJC/NY. The conversation was publicized the next day in *L'osservatore romano*, the quasi-official Vatican newspaper.

16. Merton, *Dancing in the Water of Life*, 126–27.

17. Burns, Interview, AJH Archive/JTS; Hart, Interview, AJH Archive/JTS; see Merton, *Dancing in the Water of Life*, 126–27, 142–43; E. Kaplan, "'Under My Catholic Skin,'" 109–25; Heschel and Merton, letters; Bruteau, *Merton and Judaism*, 217–31, 269–81.

18. Merton to Cardinal Bea, July 14, 1964; Merton to Heschel, July 27, 1964, quoted in Fairaday, "Merton's Prophetic Voice," 221–22.

19. *New York Herald Tribune*, September 3, 1964; Irving Spiegel, "Jewish Group Concerned," *New York Times*, September 4, 1964, 2. Spiegel cites Heschel's acerbic response to the draft.

20. This and the following quotations: Bruteau, *Merton and Judaism*, 223–24. Professor R. L. Zwi Werblowsky of the Hebrew University reported a conversation with Cardinal Willebrands about Judaism as *preparatio evangelica*, to which Heschel retorted, "If this is going to be in the Vatican document, I prefer going to Auschwitz"; Werblowsky to Kaplan, 1994, AJH/NY.

21. Merton to Heschel, September 9, 1964, Merton Archive, Bellarmine University; Bruteau, *Merton and Judaism*, 225.

22. Paul Marcinkus was known for his bluntness and skill in organization; he became Pope Paul's advance man in his various travels and was promoted to bishop in 1969. Eventually appointed head of the Vatican Bank, he resigned in 1982 under shadow of scandal. See *New York Times*, January 4, 1969, 19, and July 8, 1982, A4; obituary, *Boston Globe*, February 22, 2006.

23. This considerably abridged presentation of Heschel's audience with the pope is based on the following archival documents: Four-page Shuster Report 1: "Audience with the Pope of Dr. Heschel and Mr. Shuster on September 14, 1964," unsigned, included in Slawson to Rabb, September 18, 1964; a draft of that same report, typed in italics, by Heschel and Shuster; log of a telephone call from Shuster to Slawson, September 14, 1964; Shuster to Slawson, September 15, 1964; "Addendum to White Paper Pamphlet," September 22, 1964; all in folders Documents, Chronological, AJC/NY. Five-page, single-spaced Shuster Report 2: "Notes on Audience with Paul VI, September 14, 1964; Shuster to Tanenbaum, September 10, 1964; Shuster

to Slawson and Heschel, September 15, 1964, both with official report; Morlion to Slawson, September 18, 1964; AJC/Paris. This author found Shuster's highly confidential, candid account only in the files of the AJC Paris office conserved at New York YIVO Archives.

24. The following, official version of the meeting is from Shuster Report 1, "Audience with the Pope," AJC/NY.

25. The following version of the meeting is from Shuster Report 2, "Notes on Audience with Pope Paul VI," AJC/Paris.

26. Martin, Interview, AJH Archive/JTS.

27. Reported by the *Jewish Telegraph Agency* on September 15, 1964, quoting Rabbi Soloveitchik, AJC/NY.

28. *Day-Morning Journal*, October 2, 1964, 1, 9.

29. *Jewish Chronicle* (London), October 9, 1964.

30. Shuster memorandum to Slawson, October 9, 1964, AJC/Paris.

31. This and following quotation, "Audience That Was," 23–24, 68.

32. Hershcopf, "The Church and the Jews," 99. The larger declaration on non-Christian religions passed by 1,651 to 99, with 242 in favor with reservations: Hershcopf, "The Church and the Jews," 46–47, 126–27. For details see Rynne, *Vatican Council II*, 303–5, 415–25.

33. Shuster to Tanenbaum, December 7, 1964, AJC/Paris.

34. "Unyielding Israeli Warrior," *New York Times*, July 31, 1980, A8. See Cohen, *Woman of Violence*, 275.

35. AJC translation of *Ma'ariv* interview, dated January 4, 1965, 3. Also consulted were the three-page "Report on Vatican Reactions to Heschel Interview, *Ma'ariv*," January 4, 1965, sent by Shuster only to Slawson; Shuster, "Dr. Heschel's Interview in *Ma'ariv*," "strictly confidential" memorandum to Tanenbaum, January 4, 1965; original clipping of published interview; Shuster to Slawson, "personal and confidential," January 5, 1965; and others. None of the AJC documents mentions Cohen by name, only as "journalist" or "she." All are from AJC/Paris.

36. This and the following quotations: five-page American Jewish Committee translation of *Ma'ariv* interview, AJC/Paris.

37. Shuster, "comments concerning Dr. Heschel's Interview with *Ma'ariv*," memorandum to Slawson; Shuster, letter to Slawson, personal and confidential, January 5, 1965; Shuster, "Dr. Heschel's Interview in *Ma'ariv*," memorandum to Tanenbaum, AJC/Paris. Following quotation, "Report on Vatican Reactions," 1, 2, AJC/Paris.

38. The author spent several hours of multiple days making copies of the internal, mostly secret, Vatican dossiers stored either at AJC/NY or YIVO.

39. Heschel, unsigned memorandum, AJC/NY, quoted in *New York Herald Tribune*, October 1, 1965. For the entire text, "Declaration on the Relation of the Church to Non-Christian Religions," see Hershcopf, "The Church and the Jews," 75–77. For comparison of the versions of *Nostra Aetate* in English and in Latin, see Somerville, "Successive Versions of *Nostra Aetate*," 341–71.

40. Pope Paul VI himself publicly received Rabbi and Mrs. Heschel at the Vatican in 1971; later, he became the first pope to officially cite a Jewish thinker when he quoted from a French translation of *God in Search of Man*. See *America* 128 (March 10, 1973): 202.

41. Heschel, "Protestant Renewal," 1501–2; Niebuhr, "Crisis in American Protestantism," 1498–1501.

42. Handy, *History of Union Theological Seminary*, 260–69; Bennett to Heschel, November 5, 1964, BL/UTC.

43. Jessica Feingold to Heschel, December 9, 1964, GF/JTS.

44. Minutes of the Meeting of the Board of Directors, March 9, 1965, BL/UTC.

45. News release, March 10, 1965; Bennett to Heschel, March 22, 1965; Heschel to Bennett, March 24, 1965; Memorandum, "Provisional Schedule for Dr. Abraham Heschel," dated July 30, 1965, BL/UTC.

46. Susannah Heschel to E. Kaplan, January 2001.

47. This and the following quotations: Heschel, "No Religion Is an Island;" cf. Heschel, *Moral Grandeur*, 235–50.

48. Muffs, Interview, AJH Archive/JTS; Harlow, Interview, AJH Archive/JTS.

49. This and the following quotation: Dring Jr. to Dresner, 1988, AJH Archive/JTS.

50. Davies, Interview, AJH Archive/JTS. For the commemorative essay on Heschel, see W. D. Davies, "Conscience, Scholar, Witness," *America* 128, no. 9 (March 10, 1973): 213–15.

51. Sanders, Interviews, AJH Archive/JTS; also see Sanders, "An Apostle to the Gentiles."

52. Kenneth L. Woodward's admiring unsigned essay, "What God Thinks of Man," was accompanied by a photograph captioned "Heschel: A Radical Judaism," *Newsweek*, January 31, 1966, 57.

53. Program of special academic convocation, Saint Michael's College, March 1–8, 1966; see especially Thurin, "Vatican II Epilogue," 8–19.

54. The conference was sponsored by the Canadian Catholic Bishops and organized by the Pontifical Institute of Saint Michael's College. See Heschel, "Jewish Notion of God," 379–80; French translation, "La notion judaïque de Dieu et le renouveau chrétien," vol. 1, 111–31; Shook to Heschel, May 19, 1966, Farrar, Straus & Giroux Archives.

55. Heschel, "Jewish Notion of God," 110.

1. This and the following quotations, unless noted: Heschel, "Reason for My Involvement in the Peace Movement"; cf. Heschel, *Moral Grandeur*, 224–26.
2. Heschel, *The Prophets*, 4–5.
3. Heschel, *The Prophets*, xvi. The following quotation: Heschel, *The Prophets*, xvii.
4. This and the following quotations: Heschel, quoted in "Battle of Conscience," *Newsweek*, November 15, 1965, 78, quoted in Hall, *Because of Their Faith*, 15; John Sibley, "Clergymen Defend Right to Protest Vietnam Policy," *New York Times*, October 26, 1965, 10; Hall, *Because of Their Faith*, 14–15; Neuhaus, Interview, AJH Archive/JTS; Hall, *Because of Their Faith*, 14:40.
5. *New York Times*, November 28, 1965. See also FBI files, FBI/NYO 100–154786 4076, DHL; quotation from 100. This packet of more than two hundred pages contains clippings of anti-war activities from both the leftist and the mainstream press, in addition to reports from informants. See *New York Times* advertisement, December 12, 1965, "protesting the reassignment of Father Daniel Berrigan, a Jesuit priest, poet, and opponent of the Vietnam war, to South America."
6. The present account of Clergy and Laymen Concerned about Vietnam follows Hall, *Because of Their Faith*, often using the same primary sources, such as newspaper articles, FBI reports, and archival documents. For a detailed chronology see Hall, *The Vietnam War*.
7. Clergy and Laymen Concerned about Vietnam records, series 2, box 2, SPC.
8. This first meeting and the Sabbath dinner in Coffin, *Once to Every Man*, 217–23.
9. This and the following quotations: Heschel, "The Moral Outrage of Vietnam," 24–26; reprinted in *Vietnam: Crisis of Conscience*, 48–61.
10. Mimeographed report written by Kaplan in February 1967, when the author was a graduate student at Columbia University, Edward Kaplan personal papers, now AJH Archive/JTS; cf. Coffin, *Once to Every Man*, 224–29.
11. Heschel's speech quoted from a pamphlet entitled "Vietnam: The Clergymen's Dilemma," printed and distributed by Clergy and Laymen Concerned about Vietnam and published in Heschel, "Moral Outrage of Vietnam," in *Vietnam*, 51–52.
12. *New York Times*, February 2, 1967.
13. Coffin, *Once to Every Man*, 229.
14. This and the following quotation: Hall, *Because of Their Faith*, 40–45.
15. For King's entry into the anti-war movement, see Garrow, *Bearing the Cross*, 449–557.
16. King, "Beyond Vietnam," in *Dr. Martin Luther King, Jr., Dr. John Bennett, Dr. Henry Steele Commager, Rabbi Abraham Heschel Speak on the War in Vietnam*, 10–11.

17. This and the following quotation: Heschel, "Moral Outrage of Vietnam"; cf. Heschel, *Vietnam*, 52, 56–57. The important paragraph on "engaged Buddhism" was omitted from this reprint. *Vietnam* also contained a bibliography, official statements from the Synagogue Council of America and the Central Committee of the World Council of Churches, excerpts from the Encyclical *Christi Matri* of Pope Paul VI, a statement by the American Roman Catholic bishops, and an appeal from the General Assembly of the National Council of Churches. See Hall, *Because of Their Faith*, 47.

18. Wiesel, Bulletin of the Jewish Peace Fellowship, 1987, 5–6; Brickner, Interview, AJH Archive/JTS; Kelman (who was present at the meeting with the Israeli delegate), Interview, AJH Archive/JTS.

19. Later published as Heschel, "Ginzey Ha-yesha" [The hidden sources of redemption], *Hadoar*, August 11, 1967, 643–45; further quotations are from this source.

20. See Isa. 19:23–24 on the reconciliation of Egypt, Assyria, and Israel: "All three will be equally God's chosen people"; Heschel, "Sacred Images of Man"; cf. *Religious Education* (March–April 1958), 102. Heschel quotes this passage with references to a myriad of biblical sources in Heschel, *The Prophets*, 185–86.

21. Heschel, "An Echo of Eternity," 4–6.

22. Note from the editors, *Christian Century*, July 26, 1967, 955.

23. This and the following quotation: Sanders, "Urbis and Orbis: Jerusalem Today," 967–70. Sanders took his title from *Urbis et Orbis* [To the city and to the world], the pope's annual Easter homily to world Christians.

24. Sanders, Interview, AJH Archive/JTS.

25. Description of meeting in his apartment, Sanders email to Kaplan, 2004, AJH Archive/JTS.

26. Richard Hirsch memorandum to Eisendrath, Heschel, Brickner, January 30, 1968, SPC; Kaplan, mimeographed report, February 1968, Edward Kaplan personal papers.

27. Heschel gave a photocopy of his speech to Kaplan, reprinted in the brochure "In Whose Name?" distributed by CALCAV, Edward Kaplan personal papers.

28. Heschel's interfaith gesture was criticized after the *New York Times* mistakenly transcribed the words from Psalm 22 in the Aramaic of Jesus; see *New York Times*, February 7, 1968, and the correction in *New York Times*, February 16, 1968, 18.

29. "A Turning Point, Peace or War?" and "How Much Do You Value Free Speech?" *New York Times*, February 11, 1968, E5, E7. Kogan, Kelman,

Siegel, Hertzberg, "Clergyman's War Protest" letter to the editor, *New York Times*, February 11, 1968, E13.

30. Richard Hirsch to Eisendrath, February 20, 1968, notes of a telephone conversation with Heschel, Edward Kaplan personal papers. Rabbi Alexander M. Schindler, vice president of the Union of American Hebrew Congregations, memorandum to members of the Union of American Hebrew Congregations Board of Directors, April 4, 1968; attached were Freehof to Eisendrath, February 23, 1968. Ezekiel ben Judah Landau (1713–1793), born in Opatow, Poland, was rabbi of Prague and the whole of Bohemia and the author of numerous responsa.

31. Heschel, "Conversation with Martin Luther King," 1. King, quoted in Heschel, "Conversation with Martin Luther King," 2. Four years earlier, the Jewish Theological Seminary had conferred an honorary doctor of laws on King.

32. King, quoted in Heschel, "Conversation with Martin Luther King," 12; the following quotation: Heschel, "Conversation with Martin Luther King," 15.

33. Heschel, "Theological Dimensions," 93, 96; the following quotations: Heschel, "Theological Dimensions," 97, 101–2.

34. *Proceedings* 1968, 104–9, 106–7, 107–8. Heschel also reminded the rabbis of German Catholics who did not want to oppose Hitler in order to protect the church.

35. A description of King's funeral can be found in the *New York Times*, April 9–10, 1968, which includes transcriptions of the eulogies; King, *My Life with Martin Luther King, Jr.*, 328–30 ff.; Oates, *Let the Trumpet Sound*, 493–96; and Lewis, *Walking with the Wind*, 390–94.

36. Kenneth L. Woodward, *Newsweek*, December 30, 1968, 38.

37. In 1969, Elémire Zolla published an Italian translation (by Elèna Mortara) of Heschel, *God in Search of Man*, chap. 4, "La meraviglia" [Wonder], in *Conoscenza religiosa* 1 (1969): 4–18, with a "Note on Heschel." In 1971 Zolla published a translation excerpt from the manuscript of Heschel, *Passion for Truth: Conoscenza religiosa* 4 (1971): 337–53, "Il chassidismo e Kierkegaard."

38. Zolla, Interview, AJH Archive/JTS. Zolla to Dresner, 1979, AJH Archive/JTS. See also Zolla, Untitled, *Corriere della sera*, April 14, 1986.

39. Heschel, "Reflections on Death," 534, 542.

40. As usual the FBI and related agencies kept themselves informed, mainly through public documents and direct observation. FBI documents 121362–63 and others. All in MIKL/UK.

41. The 1969 Position Paper of CALCAV, "The Reconciliation We Seek: Consequences and Lessons of the Vietnam War," from FBI files, 121277–80, MIKL/UK.

42. *New York Times*, February 5, 1969, 10; FBI file, 124339, MIKL/UK; Ben A. Franklin, "Opponents of Vietnam War Meet with Kissinger," *New York Times*, February 6, 1969, 17; Coffin, *Once to Every Man*, 294–98.

43. Fernandez, Interviews, AJH Archive/JTS; Neuhaus, Interview, AJH Archive/ JTS. Henry Kissinger was a literate Jew who was reared in an observant family. His father was a Hebrew teacher.

44. FBI report, 121261, 6; FBI report, 124275, MIKL/UK.

45. *Time*, March 14, 1969. See also Eckardt, review of Heschel, *Israel: Echo of Eternity*, 70–73; Zvi Zinger, "Humanize the Sacred, Sanctify the Secular," *Jerusalem Post*, August 8, 1969, 14. A Hebrew translation of Heschel's book was published soon after the author's death: see review by Pinchas Lapide, *Jerusalem Post*, January 11, 1974.

46. Heschel, *Israel: Echo of Eternity*, 14. See also "Jerusalem is not divine, her life depends on our presence. Alone she is desolate and silent, with Israel she is a witness, a proclamation"; Heschel, *Israel: Echo of Eternity*, 14.

47. Heschel, "On Prayer," 2–3, 4; the following quotation: Heschel, "On Prayer," 5, 7; Ethel Gintoft, "Rabbi Reminds Conference of Need for Prayer," AJH Archive/JTS.

48. Rothschild to his sister, December 31, 1972, AJH Archive/JTS; Kelman, Interview, AJH Archive/JTS; Sylvia Heschel, Conversations, AJH Archive/JTS.

49. Kelman gave the present author a photocopy of Heschel's note.

50. Shmidman, Interview, AJH Archive/JTS.

51. Rabbi Jacob Perlow, Interview, AJH Archive/JTS.

52. Sylvia Heschel, Conversation, AJH Archive/JTS.

13. SUMMATION OF A LIFE

1. Kronholtz, Interview, December 24, 1989, AJH Archive/JTS.

2. Heschel's talk, May 20, 1959, at a session in honor of Boaz Cohen, Jewish Theological Seminary professor of rabbinics, *Proceedings*, 1959, 23; Kalman A. Siegel, "Jewish Scholars Sift Man's Role," *New York Times*, May 21, 1959, 18.

3. In 1968 Heschel placed a short piece in Hebrew in the Israeli quarterly *Sedemot* and another one in Pinhas Peli's weekly journal *Panim el Panim*. The next year, he contributed a two-part essay in Yiddish to Abraham Sutzkever's *Di goldene Keyt*. For Heschel's articles, "Rabbi Mendel mi-Kotzk," "Kotzk," and "Der Kotsker Rebbe," see Heschel to Sutzkever, YIVO Archives, New York; also see Green, *Tormented Master*.

4. Heschel, *A Passion for Truth*. Heschel completed both the 694-page Yiddish book (two vols.), and the 323-page English volume before he died; both appeared posthumously.

5. Heschel, *Kotsk*, manuscript of the translation by Jonathan Boyarin, 3. Not in circulation.

6. Heschel, *A Passion for Truth*, 204.

7. Heschel's article in the *Encyclopaedia Judaica* glossed over the most controversial event of the Kotzker's life: the so-called Friday Night Incident, in which the rebbe was said to have committed an act of blasphemy that led to his withdrawal from his community for the last twenty years of his life. See Faierstein, "The Friday Night Incident in Kotzk," 179–80; also Faierstein, review of *Kotsk: In gerangl far emesdikayt*, 211–14.

8. Heschel, *A Passion for Truth*, 210; the following quotations: Heschel, *A Passion for Truth*, 307; and Heschel, "The Spirit of Jewish Prayer," *Proceedings* 1953, 151.

9. Heschel, *A Passion for Truth*, 301.

10. Heschel, "God, Torah, and Israel."

11. Teshima, Interviews, AJH Archive/JTS; Israel Shenker, "Japanese Christian Is Awarded a Doctorate by Jewish Seminary," *New York Times*, May 31, 1977, 25.

12. Memoir by Felice Morgenstern, niece of Jacob Heshel; this and the other documents are from Thena Heshel Kendall, daughter of Heschel's brother Jacob. See also Heshel, "The History of Hasidism in Austria," 347–60.

13. Mortara to Dresner, 1987, AJH Archive/JTS.

14. Marcello Molinari, "Spazio interiore" [Interior space], *Shalom*, March 1971, quoted in Mortara, "Ricordi di Heschel"; Mortara, translation of Mortara, "Ricordi di Heschel," AJH Archive/JTS.

15. *United Synagogue Review* 24, no. 3 (Fall 1971). The account is taken from a three-page Heschel memorandum, AJH Archive/JTS, cited in part in Heschel, *Moral Grandeur*, xxvi–xxvii.

16. *The Pilot*, May 29, 1971, 3, Religious News Service photo. As a reminder of Heschel's moral authority, the *United Synagogue Review* also included his essay on Captain William Calley, whom a military tribunal had condemned for his responsibility for the My Lai massacre: Heschel, "Required: A Moral Ombudsman."

17. The Jewish Theological Seminary sponsored Flender's weekly program. See Heschel, "Two Conversations with Abraham Joshua Heschel," *parts 1 and 2*. The quotations are from Heschel, *A Passion for Truth*, 1, 3, 5–6, 7.

18. "Friends Officiate at Service for Niebuhr," *Berkshire Eagle*, June 5, 1971; Heschel, "Reinhold Niebuhr: A Last Farewell"; Siegel, *New York Times*, June 3, 1971, 42.

19. Eisenstein, Interview, AJH Archive/JTS; Kelman, Interview, AJH Archive/JTS; the quotations are from the audiotape of Heschel's speech, AJH Archive/JTS.

20. Jewish Theological Seminary publicity file; *Anti-Defamation League Bulletin*, December 1971; Edward Kaplan's personal papers; letters and Anti-Defamation League press release, November 4, 1971; Anti-Defamation League files.

21. *Anti-Defamation League Bulletin*, December 1971; Anti-Defamation League press release; Anti-Defamation League files.

22. Invitation, AJH Archive/JTS.

23. The following quotations are from "Heritage of Martin Luther King, Jr.," ABC, January 9, 1972; Frank Reynolds interview, "Conversation with Rabbi Abraham J. Heschel," ABC, November 21, 1971.

24. Edward B. Fiske, "Religious Assembly Terms Vietnam Policy Immoral," *New York Times*, January 17, 1972, 35; Heschel, "The Reason for My Involvement in the Peace Movement."

25. This and the following quotations: Heschel, "A Time for Renewal," 50–51.

26. Heschel cited Maimonides, *Laws Concerning Kings* (III, 8, 9) as a basic authority. The Rashi citation is *Pesachim* 25A; see *Sanhedrin* 74A.

27. Ronald Taylor, "Group of Clergy Supports Amnesty for Everyone but War Criminals," *Washington Post*, March 28, 1972, A8; Eleanor Blau, "Amnesty for Dissenters on War Is Backed by Religious Leaders," *New York Times*, March 28, 1972, 16; see Hall, *Because of Their Faith*, 161–65. Provided by Henry Schwarzschild.

28. Gottschalk to Heschel, March 20, 1972; Heschel to Gottschalk, March 24, 1972; AJA.

29. Original documents at the AFSC Archive; Mardin, Interview, AJH Archive/JTS; Bayne, Kollek, Appleton, letters, AJH Archive/JTS; Heschel, *Moral Grandeur*, xxviii: "Only later, in the few years before his sudden death in December, 1972, did my father begin to speak out on behalf of the Palestinians and with great criticism of certain Israeli government actions"; Melman, Interview, AJH Archive/JTS.

30. E. A. Bayne, "Heschel," *Mediterranean Report, Bulletin of the Center for Mediterranean Studies of the American Universities Field Staff in Rome, Italy* (Spring–Summer 1973), 8.

31. Bayne, "Staff Memorandum," September 8, 1972; Johnson memorandum, summary of seminar, 3. George Appleton's assessment, "The Spiritual Nature of Jerusalem," undated, marked confidential, all AFSC Archive. Werblowsky to Kaplan, 1991.

32. Appleton to Dresner, 1982; and Bayne to Dresner, 1982, 1983, AJH Archive/JTS.

33. Appleton, summary of meeting, 1972, 3, AFSC Archive.

34. Goodhill to Dresner, 1982; Dresner, unpublished note, April 27, 1982, AJH Archive/JTS.

35. Heschel to Herschlag Muffs, September 13, 1972; Appleton to Heschel, October 19, 1972; Herschlag Muffs to Foxman, January 22, 1973; Appleton to Heschel, October 19, 1972: the archbishop suggested some revisions, "a paragraph put here and there in a slightly different way so as not to hurt the sensitivity of Arabs."

36. Heschel, *Israel: Echo of Eternity*, 218.

37. Letter of Isaac Lewin, *New York Times*, November 5, 1972.

38. Israel Shenker, "Rabbi to Give Nixon a Kingly Blessing," *New York Times*, January 19, 1973, 16.

39. Press releases from Jewish Theological Seminary publicity files; *Superior Evening Telegram*, November 7, 1972, 16. Audiotape of Heschel's speech, AJH Archive/JTS.

40. Peter Kihiss, "Religious Leaders Back Berrigans on Sermons," *New York Times*, November 11, 1970, 16. See Berrigan, *To Dwell in Peace*, 179; Berrigan, "My Friend" [on Heschel], in *No Religion Is an Island*, ed. Kasimow and Sherwin, 68–75.

41. Berrigan, Interview, AJH Archive/JTS; Lewis, Interview, AJH Archive/JTS.

42. Susannah Heschel, communication, AJH Archive/JTS.

43. Straus wrote to Edmond Fuller, the author of an important essay on Heschel in the *Wall Street Journal*, that Heschel had turned in the manuscript "the morning of the day he died." (Heschel died after midnight on Saturday morning, December 23.) Straus to Fuller, February 2, 1973. The book was officially published in October 1973.

44. Teshima, "In Memory of My Teacher," 52–53; Rothschild to his sister, December 31, 1972, AJH Archive/JTS.

45. Batkin to Dresner, 1978; Batkin, Interview, AJH Archive/JTS; Wiseman, Interview, AJH Archive/JTS; Lang, Interview, AJH Archive/JTS; Heschel, *The Ineffable Name of God*, 57: poem dedicated "to my teacher David Koigen, May his soul be in paradise."

1. As a final irony, Heschel's death was accompanied by Nixon's "Christmas bombings" of North Vietnam. That very morning, December 23, 1972, page 1 of the *New York Times* announced: "U.S. to Continue Bombing; Says Next Move is Hanoi's."

2. The account of Heschel's death and funeral preparations is from interviews and Rothschild to his sister, December 31, 1972, AJH Archive/JTS.

3. Peli, *Jerusalem Post*, December 29, 1972. See Dresner to Peli, January 15, 1973: "He died with two books at his side, one lying by his side was David Halberstam's bestseller on Viet Nam, and the other in his hand was the Keter Shem Tov. Who else combined these two worlds as he?"

4. Neuhaus shared his conversation with Sylvia Heschel during Dresner et al., Roundtable discussion organized by Wertheimer and Dresner, New York, August 1987, Transcript, AJH Archive/JTS.

5. Heschel, last will and testament, dated May 21, 1965, with Proskauer Rose Goetz & Mendelsohn, Counselors at Law, contains no mention of his burial.

6. The present author attended the funeral and rode in the limousine with Kelman and others to the cemetery.

7. *New York Times*, December 25, 1972, 20.

8. The eulogy was published later: Kelman, "Abraham Joshua Heschel: In Memoriam," 2–3.

9. Heschel, *Moral Grandeur*, 223; E. Kaplan, *Spiritual Radical*, 434:2.

10. Park West Memorial Chapel provided the English translation of the Hebrew in the booklet.

11. Teshima, Interview, AJH Archive/JTS; Zusya Heschel, Interview, AJH Archive/JTS.

12. Teshima, Conversation.

13. Marty, "A Giant Has Fallen," 87; Robert D. McFadden, *New York Times*, December 24, 1972, 40; the funeral described the following day: "Homage Paid to Rabbi by 500 at Traditional Service," *New York Times*, December 25, 1972, 20; Pinchas Peli, *Jerusalem Post*, December 29, 1972; "A Militant Mystic," *Time*, January 8, 1973, 43; Kenneth L. Woodward, "A Foretaste of Eternity," *Newsweek*, January 8, 1973, 50; Robert Fuller, "Rabbi Heschel's Heritage of Wonder and Awe," *Wall Street Journal*, February 2, 1973, 8.

14. James F. Clarity, "Notes on People," *New York Times*, February 2, 1973, 37.

15. *America*, March 10, 1973.

16. *Conservative Judaism* 28, no. 1 (Fall 1973).

17. In the program, Heschel, with bags under his eyes, sat stiffly on the edge of his chair, shuffling his file cards. For those who knew Heschel, it was an

awkward performance. At one point his black yarmulke fell off his head; he didn't retrieve it until later.

18. The following quotations: Heschel, *Moral Grandeur*, 395–412.

19. Leifman, Interview, AJH Archive/JTS; Teshima, email, 2005, AJH Archive/JTS.

NOTE ON SOURCES

For a more complete listing of archival materials than found in the bibliography, see:

Kaplan, Edward K., and Samuel H. Dresner. *Abraham Joshua Heschel: Prophetic Witness*. New Haven and London: Yale University Press, 1998.

Kaplan, Edward K. *Spiritual Radical: Abraham Joshua Heschel in America, 1940–1972*. New Haven and London: Yale University Press, 2007.

Marmur, Michael. "In Search of Heschel." *Shofar* 26, no. 1 (2007): 9–40.

Heschel studies have not yet received the sustained and cooperative attention they deserve. (My model would be the International Thomas Merton Society, ITMS.) For the most comprehensive overview of Heschel's works and critical responses to them, see Joseph Harp Britton's book *Abraham Heschel and the Phenomenon of Piety* (London and New York: Bloomsbury T&T Clark, 2013). John C. Merkle has summarized Heschel's theological system in *Approaching God: The Way of Abraham Joshua Heschel* (Collegeville MN: Liturgical Press, 2009), a handy introduction.

Four recent books demonstrate that the time is ripe for developing academically rigorous approaches to Heschel's insights. See Alexander Even-Chen and Ephraim Meir's *Between Heschel and Buber: A Comparative Study* (Boston: Academic Studies Press, 2012), for a useful overview. More specialized is Shai Held's *Abraham Joshua Heschel: The Call of Transcendence* (Bloomington IN: University of Indiana Press, 2013), a revised doctoral dissertation with close readings, scrutiny of Heschel's contradictions or ambiguities, and comparisons with Jewish or Christian thinkers. Michael Marmur's elegant approach in *Abraham Joshua Heschel and the Sources of Wonder* (Toronto, Buffalo, and London: University of Toronto Press, 2016), focused on *God in Search of Man*, provides a glimpse of Heschel's Jewish sources. For a rigorous analytical approach, see Lawrence Perlman's *The Eclipse of Humanity: Heschel's Critique of Heidegger* (Berlin and Boston: Walter de Gruyter, 2016).

In addition, two important books have been published in Israel in Hebrew: Dror Bondi's *Where Art Thou? God's Question and the Translation of Tradition in the Thought of Abraham Joshua Heschel* (Jerusalem: Shalem Press, 2008); and Alexander Even-Chen's *The Ineffable Name of God: Man, Analysis of Abraham Joshua Heschel Songs* (New York and Jerusalem: Jewish Theological Seminary of America, 2017).

Transcripts and/or original recordings of the interviews and correspondence are preserved at the Abraham Joshua Heschel Archive/ Jewish Theological Seminary, as are most items in the author's personal papers.

SELECTED BIBLIOGRAPHY

ARCHIVES/MANUSCRIPT MATERIALS

ADL. Anti-Defamation League files, B'nai B'rith, New York.

AFSC. American Friends Service Committee Archives, Philadelphia.

AJA/HUC. American Jewish Archives, Hebrew Union College, Cincinnati OH.

AJC/NY. American Jewish Committee Archives, New York (AJC/New York).

AJC/Paris. American Jewish Committee Archives, Paris.

AJH Archive/JTS. Abraham Joshua Heschel Archive/Jewish Theological Seminary, New York.

AJSG. Archives of the John Simon Guggenheim Memorial Foundation, New York.

Archives nationales, Paris.

Archives of 5e Arrondissement, Paris.

Archives of the Rectorat de Paris.

Bibliothèque nationale, Paris.

BL/UTC. Burke Library, Union Theological Seminary, New York.

Central Archives for the History of the Jewish People, Hebrew University, Ramat Gan, Jerusalem.

David S. Wyman Institute for Holocaust Studies.

DUA. Duke University Archives, Durham NC.

Farrar, Straus & Giroux Archives, New York Public Library, New York.

FBI files at MIKL/UK, Margaret I. King Library, Special Collections, University of Kentucky, Lexington.

GF/JTS. Jewish Theological Seminary General Files, New York.

Heschel, Abraham Joshua. "Das Gebet" ["Prayer"]. *Bulletin of Congregation Habonim at Central Synagogue* (September 1941): 2–3.

———. *Der Shem Hameforash: Mentsh* [*The Ineffable Name of God: Man*]. Freely trans. by Zalman Schachter-Shalomi. Winnipeg, Canada: distributed privately, 1973. Author's collection.

———. "Dr. Martin Luther King, Jr., Dr. John Bennett, Dr. Henry Steele Commager, Rabbi Abraham Heschel Speak on the War in Vietnam." Remarks given at Riverside Church on the Vietnam War. New York: Clergy and Laymen Concerned about Vietnam, April 4, 1967.

———. "Heschel's Last Words." *Jerusalem Post Weekly* (January 1, 1973): 14. Excerpt and introduction from *A Passion for Truth*, by Abraham Joshua Heschel. New York: Farrar, Straus & Giroux, 1973.

———. Letter to Hofer's widow. "Lider fun shpisal, Lider fun nacht" [A song of the game, a song of the night]. Tel Aviv: n.p., 1972.

———. "The Meaning of the Spirit." *The Clarement Church Lectures* (February 2, 1964). Claremont CA: Claremont Community Church of Seventh-day Adventists.

———. "The Patient as a Person." American Medical Association's 113th Convention, June 21, 1964: 23–41. Chicago: Department of Medicine and Religion, American Medical Association, 1964. Reprinted in *Conservative Judaism* 19, no. 1 (Fall 1964): 1–10. Reprinted, abridged, as "The Sisyphus Complex." *Ramparts* (October 1964): 45–49. Reprinted as "The Patient as a Person," in *The Insecurity of Freedom: Essays on Human Existence*, by Abraham Joshua Heschel, 24–38. New York: Farrar, Straus & Giroux, 1966.

———. "Some Basic Issues of Jewish Education" and "The Relevance of Prophecy." Fifth Annual Pedagogic Conference, Institute of Jewish Studies, February 9, 1958. Reprinted in mimeographed booklet. Cleveland Bureau of Jewish Education: n.p.: 3–19.

———. "The Theological, Biblical, and Ethical Considerations of Amnesty" (unpublished manuscript). Abraham Joshua Heschel Archive/Jewish Theological Seminary, 1972.

———. "A Time for Renewal." Meeting of the 28th World Zionist Congress, Jerusalem, January 19, 1972.

Heschel, Susannah. Correspondence with Edward Kaplan. N.d.

Heschel, Sylvia Straus. Several conversations with Edward Kaplan, 1990–2005.

Humboldt University Archives, Berlin.

Jagiellonian University, Archives of the Polish Academy of Sciences, Kraków.

John F. Kennedy Presidential Library and Museum, Boston.

JPS. Jewish Publication Society of America Archives, Balch Institute for Ethnic Studies, Philadelphia Jewish Archives Center.

Leo Baeck Institute, New York.

Marshall Meyer Archive at Duke University, Durham NC.

MBA. Martin Buber Archives, National Jewish Library and Hebrew University, Ramat Gan,

Melekh Ravitch Archive, National Jewish Library and Hebrew University, Ramat Gan, Jerusalem.

SPC. Swarthmore College Peace Collection, Swarthmore PA.

Teshima, Jacob Yuroh, Japan. Correspondence with Edward Kaplan, April 1988 and later.

Thena Heshel Kendall, London. Family papers and several conversations.

Thomas Merton Archive, Bellarmine University, Louisville KY.

United States National Archives, Washington DC

University of Iowa Archives, Iowa City.

University of Minnesota Archives, Minneapolis.

University of Notre Dame Archives, South Bend IN.

Yeshiva University Archives, New York.

YIVO. Yidisher Visnshaftlekher Institut Archives, New York.

PUBLISHED WORKS

"Abraham Joshua Heschel: Twenty-Fifth Yahrzeit Tribute." Special issue, *Conservative Judaism* 50, no. 2–3 (Winter–Spring 1998).

"Abraham Joshua Heschel: A Yahrzeit Tribute." Special issue, *Conservative Judaism* 28, no. 1 (Fall 1973).

Abraham Weiss Jubilee Volume. New York: Yeshiva University, 1964.

Abramowicz, Dina. "My School Years in the Real-Gymnasium." *Dorem Afrike* (May 27, 1946).

Agus, Jacob B. *Modern Philosophies of Judaism: A Study of Recent Jewish Philosophies of Religion.* New York: Behrman Jewish Book House, 1941.

———. Review of *Man Is Not Alone*, by Abraham Joshua Heschel. *Congress Weekly* (April 16, 1951): 12–13.

Ahmann, Mathew, ed. *Race: Challenge to Religion.* Chicago: Henry Regnery 1963.

Al-Yahud, Dayyan. "Professor Heschel, the Creative Thinker: A Critical Study of His Works." 4 parts. *Jewish Forum* (September 1952): 137–41; (November 1952): 189–90; (January 1953): 16–18; (March 1953): 48–49.

Alstat, Philip R. Review of "The East European Era in Jewish History." *Jewish Examiner* (March 24, 1950).

America. Special issue of *America* 128, no. 9 (March 10, 1973).

"Audience That Was." *Jewish World* (October 1964): 23–24, 68.

Baker, Leonard. *Days of Sorrow and Pain: Leo Baeck and the Berlin Jews.* New York: Oxford University Press, 1978.

Baumgardt, David. "Looking Back on a German University Career." *Leo Baeck Institute Yearbook* 10 (1965): 239–65.

Beilis, Shlomo. "Bei die Onheybn fun Yung Vilne." *Di Goldene Keyt* 101 (1980): 11–65.

Bergman, Shmuel Hugo. "Der Mensch ist nicht allein." *Mitteilungsblatt der Hebräschen Universität* (May 18, 1951), n.p. Translated by Stephanie Wollny, n.d., AJH Archive/JTS.

Bericht der Hochschule für die Wissenschaft des Judentums in Berlin. 1928–1939.

Berkovits, Eliezer. "Dr. A. J. Heschel's Theology of Pathos." *Tradition* 6 no. 2 (Spring–Summer 1964): 70.

Berrigan, Daniel. *To Dwell in Peace: An Autobiography.* New York: Harper & Row, 1987.

Bialik, Haim Nahman. *Igrot* [*Correspondence*]. Vol. 5. Tel Aviv: Dvir, 1939.

Biderman, I. M. *Mayer Balaban: Historian of Polish Jewry.* New York: I. M. Biderman Book Committee, 1976.

Brenner, Michael. *The Renaissance of Jewish Culture in Weimar Germany.* New Haven CT: Yale University Press, 1996.

Bromberg, Abraham. *Mi-gedolei Ha-Torah Ve-ha-hasidut* [Masters of Torah and Hasidism]. Vol. 20. Jerusalem: Ha-techiya Publishers, 1963.

Bruteau, Beatrice, ed. *Merton and Judaism: Recognition, Repentance, and Renewal; Holiness in Words.* Louisville KY: Fons Vitae, 2004.

Buber, Martin. *Briefwechsel aus Sieben Jahrzehnten. Band ii: 1918–1938; Band iii: 1938–1965.* Heidelberg: Verlag Lambert Schneider, 1973, 1975.

———. *Hasidism and the Modern Man.* Translated by Maurice Friedman. New York: Horizon Press, 1958.

———. *The Letters of Martin Buber: A Life of Dialogue.* Edited by Nahum Glatzer and Paul Mendes-Flohr. New York: Schocken, 1991.

———. *Pointing the Way: Collected Essays* [*Mein Weg zum Chassidismus: Erinnerungen*]. Translated and edited by Maurice Friedman. New York: Harper Torchbook, 1957.

———. *The Prophetic Faith.* Translated by Carlyle Witton-Davies. New York: Macmillan, 1949.

———. "Sinnbildliche und sakramentale Existenz im Judentum." Translated by Maurice Friedman as "The Origin and Meaning of Hasidism," in *Hasidism and the Modern Man,* 152–81. New York: Horizon Press, 1958.

————. *Tales of the Hasidim: Early Masters.* Vol. 1. New York: Schocken Books, 1947.

————. *Tales of the Hasidim: Later Masters.* Vol. 2. New York: Schocken Books, 1948.

Cassirer, Ernst. *Philosophie der symbolischen Formen.* 3 vols. Berlin: n.p., 1923, 1925, 1929.

Central Conference of American Rabbis. *Yearbook of the Central Conference of American Rabbis: Sixty-Fourth Annual Convention* 63 (1953).

Coffin, William Sloane, Jr. *Once to Every Man.* New York: Atheneum, 1977.

Cohen, Geula. *Woman of Violence: Memoirs of a Young Terrorist, 1943–48.* New York: Holt, Rinehart and Winston, 1966.

Cohon, Samuel S. "The Existentialist Trend in Theology." *Yearbook of Central Conference of American Rabbis* 63 (1953): 348–85.

Contemporary Jewish Record: A Review of Events and a Digest of Opinion. New York: American Jewish Committee, 1938, 1939, 1940, 1942.

Corbin, Henry. *En Islam iranien: Aspects spirituels et philosophiques.* Vol. 1. Paris: Gallimard, 1971.

Daiches, David. "Doom and Love." *Commentary* (June 1963): 537–40.

Dalin, David. "Will Herberg." In *Interpreters of Judaism in the Late Twentieth Century,* edited by Steven T. Katz, 113–30. Washington DC: B'nai B'rith Books, 1993.

Der Morgen [The morning]. Berlin, 1934–1938.

Deutsch, Shaul Shimon. *Larger Than Life: The Life and Times of the Lubavitcher Rebbe, Rabbi Menachem Mendel Schneerson.* 2 vols. New York: Chassidic Historical Productions, 1995, 1997.

Dr. Martin Luther King, Jr., Dr. John Bennett, Dr. Henry Steele Commager, Rabbi Abraham Joshua Heschel Speak on the War in Vietnam. New York: Clergy and Laymen Concerned about Vietnam, 1967.

Dresner, Samuel H. "Hasidism and Its Opponents." In *Great Schisms in Jewish History,* edited by Raphael Jospe and Stanley Wagner, 119–75. New York: KTAV, 1981.

————. *Heschel, Hasidism, and Halakha.* New York: Fordham University Press, 2002.

————. "Introduction: Heschel as a Hasidic Scholar." In *The Circle of the Baal Shem Tov,* by Abraham Joshua Heschel. Chicago: University of Chicago Press, 1985.

————. *Levi Yitzhak of Berditchev: Portrait of a Hasidic Master.* New York: Hartmore House, 1974.

————. *Prayer, Humility, and Compassion.* Philadelphia: Jewish Publication Society of America, 1957.

————. *The Sabbath.* New York: Burning Bush, 1970.

————. *The Zaddik.* Northvale NJ: Jason Aronson, 1994.

————, ed. *I Asked for Wonder: A Spiritual Anthology*. New York: Crossroad, 1983.

Eckardt, A. Roy. Review of *Israel: Echo of Eternity*, by Abraham Joshua Heschel. *Conservative Judaism* 23, no. 4 (Summer 1968): 70–73.

Eden, Shevach. "The Institute for Jewish Studies and Research in Warsaw." In *Mosdot Torah Be-Eropah Be-vinyanam Uve-hurbanam* [Jewish institutions of higher learning in Europe: Their development and destruction], 689–714. New York: Ogen, 1956.

Einstein, Albert. "God's Religion or Religion of the Good?" *Aufbau* (September 13, 1940). Reprinted in *Science, Philosophy and Religion: A Symposium*, 209–14. New York: Kraus, 1940.

Eisen, Robert. "Abraham Joshua Heschel's Rabbinic Theology as a Response to the Holocaust." *Modern Judaism* 23, no. 3 (October 2003): 211–25.

Eisenstein, Ira. "Book Notes." *The Reconstructionist* (December 30, 1955): 24–26.

Eisner, Isi Jacob. "Reminiscences of the Berlin Rabbinical Seminary." *Leo Baeck Institute Yearbook* 12 (1967): 322–52.

Elbogen, Ismar. *A Century of Jewish Life*. Philadelphia: Jewish Publication Society of America, 1944.

————. *Der jüdische Gottesdienst in seiner geschichtlichen Entwicklung* [*Jewish Liturgy: A Comprehensive History*]. Leipzig: Fock, 1913.

Fackenheim Emil L. "Can We Believe in Judaism Religiously? An Ethical Faith Is Not Enough." *Commentary* (November 1948): 521–27.

————. Review of *Man Is Not Alone*, by Abraham Joshua Heschel. *Judaism* 1, no. 1 (January 1952): 85–89.

Faierstein, Morris. "Abraham Joshua Heschel and the Holocaust." *Modern Judaism* 19 (1999): 255–75.

————. "The Friday Night Incident in Kotsk: History of a Legend." *Journal of Jewish Studies* 34, no. 2 (1983): 179–89.

————. "Gershom Scholem and Hasidism." *Journal of Jewish Studies* (Oxford) 37, no. 2 (Autumn 1987): 221–33.

————. Review of *The Circle of the Baal Shem Tov: Studies in Hasidism*, by Abraham Joshua Heschel. *Judaism* 39, no. 2 (Spring 1990): 250–51.

————. Review of *Kotsk: In gerangl far emesdikayt* [The struggle for integrity], by Abraham Joshua Heschel. *Shofar* 26 (2007): 211–14.

Fairaday, Brenda Fitch. "Merton's Prophetic Voice." In *Merton and Judaism: Recognition, Repentance, and Renewal; Holiness in Words*, edited by Beatrice Bruteau, 221–22. Louisville KY: Fons Vitae, 2004.

Finkelstein, Louis. "Three Meetings with Abraham Heschel." *Conservative Judaism* 28, no. 1 (Fall 1973): 19–22.

————. "Louis Ginzberg." *American Jewish Year Book* (1955): 573–79.

————, ed. *The Jews: Their History, Culture, and Religion.* 2 vols. New York: Harper & Brothers; Philadelphia: Jewish Publication Society of America, 1949.

Fraiman, Sarah. "The Transformation of Jewish Consciousness in Nazi Germany as Reflected in the German Jewish Journal *Der Morgen*, 1925–1938." *Modern Judaism* 20, no. 1 (2000): 41–59.

Friedman, Maurice. *Abraham Joshua Heschel and Elie Wiesel: You Are My Witnesses.* New York: Farrar, Straus & Giroux, 1987.

————. *Martin Buber: His Life and Work. The Middle Years, 1923–1945.* New York: E. P. Dutton, 1983.

————. *Martin Buber: His Life and Work: The Later Years, 1945–1965.* Detroit: Wayne State University Press, 1983.

————. *Martin Buber: The Life of Dialogue.* New York: Harper, 1960.

————. "The Thought of Abraham Heschel." *Congress Weekly* (14 November 1955): 18–20.

Garrow, David J. *Bearing the Cross: Martin Luther King, Jr., and the Southern Christian Leadership Conference.* New York: Random House, 1986.

Gertel, Elliot. "Remembering Rabbi Samuel H. Dresner." *National Jewish Post and Opinion* (May 24, 2000): 12.

Ginzberg, Eli. "Address in Honor of L.G." *Proceedings* 28 (1964): 109–19.

————. *Keeper of the Law: Louis Ginzberg, a Personal Memoir.* Philadelphia: Jewish Publication Society of America, 1966.

Glatzer, Nahum. "The Frankfort Lehrhaus." *Leo Baeck Institute Yearbook* 1 (1956): 109–18, 122.

————. Review of *Sabbath*, by Abraham Joshua Heschel. *Judaism* 1, no. 3 (July 1952): 283–86.

Gold, Ben-Zion. "Religious Education in Poland: A Personal Perspective." In *The Jews of Poland Between Two World Wars*, edited by Yisrael Gutman, Ezra Mendelsohn, Jehuda Reinharz, and Chone Shmeruk, 272–82. Hanover NH: University Press of New England, 1989.

Goldberg, Hillel. *Between Berlin and Slobodka: Jewish Transition Figures from Eastern Europe.* Hoboken NJ: KTAV, 1989.

Goldy, Robert G. *The Emergence of Jewish Theology in America.* Bloomington: Indiana University Press, 1990.

Golinkin, David. "The Influence of Seminary Professors on *Halakhah* in the Conservative Movement, 1902–1968." In *Tradition Renewed: A History of the Jewish Theological Seminary*, edited by Jack Wertheimer, vol. 2, 450–74. New York: Jewish Theological Seminary, 1997.

Gordis, Robert. "The Genesis of *Judaism*: A Chapter in Jewish Cultural History." *Judaism* 30, no. 4 (Fall 1981): 390–95.

Gottschalk, Alfred. "Abraham Joshua Heschel, a Man of Dialogues." *Conservative Judaism* 28, no. 1 (Fall 1973): 23–26.

Grade, Chaim. *The Yeshiva.* Translated by Curt Leviant. Indianapolis IN: Bobbs-Merrill, 1976.

Green, Arthur. *Tormented Master: A Life of Rabbi Nahman of Bratslav.* New York: Schocken, 1979.

Greenbaum, Michael B. "The Finkelstein Era." In *Tradition Renewed: A History of the Jewish Theological Seminary*, edited by Jack Wertheimer, vol. 1, 162–232. New York: Jewish Theological Seminary, 1997.

Greenberg, Hayim. "Bankrupt." *Midstream* (March 1964): 5–10.

Guttmann, Julius. "Hochschule Retrospective." *Central Conference of American Rabbis Journal*, Autumn 1972, 73–79.

———. *Philosophies of Judaism: The History of Jewish Philosophy from Biblical Times to Franz Rosenzweig.* Translated by David W. Silverman. New York: Holt, Rinehart & Winston, 1964.

———. "Principles of Judaism." Translated by David Wolf Silverman. *Conservative Judaism* 14, no. 1 (Fall 1959): 1–16.

Halbey, Hans Adolf. *Der Erich Reiss Verlag, 1908–1936: Versuch eines Porträts.* Frankfurt am Main: Buchhändler-Vereinigung, 1980–81.

Halkowski, Henryk. "'A Branch Plucked from the Fire . . .'" In *The Jews of Poland*, edited by Andrzej K. Paluck, vol. 1, 223–34. Kraków: Jagiellonian University, 1992.

Hall, Mitchell K. *Because of Their Faith: CALCAV and Religious Opposition to the Vietnam War.* New York: Columbia University Press, 1990.

———. *The Vietnam War.* New York: Longman, 2000.

Handy, Robert T. *A History of Union Theological Seminary in New York.* New York: Columbia University Press, 1987.

Herberg, Will. "Converging Trails." *Christian Century* (April 18, 1956): 486.

———. "From Marxism to Judaism." *Commentary* (January 1947): 25–32.

———. "Has Judaism Still Power to Speak? A Religion for an Age of Crisis." *Commentary* (May 1949): 447–57.

———. "Prophetic Faith in an Age of Crisis: God-Centered Religion Meets the Challenge of Our Time." *Judaism* 1, no. 3 (July 1952): 198.

———. Review of *Man's Quest for God: Studies in Prayer and Symbolism*, by Abraham Joshua Heschel. *Theology Today* (January 12, 1956): 404–6.

Hershcopf, Judith. "The Church and the Jews: The Struggle at Vatican Council II." *American Jewish Year Book* 66 (1965): 99–136.

————. "The Church and the Jews: The Struggle at Vatican Council II." *American Jewish Year Book* 67 (1966): 45–77.

Heschel, Abraham Joshua. "Abraham Joshua Heschel." Interview by Patrick Granfield, OSB. In *Theologians at Work*, edited by Patrick Granfield, 69–85. New York: Macmillan, 1967. Reprinted as "Interview at Notre Dame," in *Moral Grandeur and Spiritual Audacity*, edited by Susannah Heschel, 381–93. New York: Farrar, Straus & Giroux, 1996.

————. "Abschied von der Bockenheimer Synagoge" [Farewell to the Bockenheimer Synagogue]. *Jüdisches Gemeindeblatt für Frankfurt* 16, no. 12 (September 1938): 17.

————. "After Majdanek: On Aaron Zeitlin's Poetry." Translated by Morris Faierstein. *Modern Judaism* 19 (1999): 264–71.

————. "After Majdanek: On the Poetry of Aaron Zeitlin." *Yidisher Kemfer* (October 1, 1948): 28–30.

————. "'Al Mahut Ha-tefillah" [The essence of prayer]. Prepared for the *Mayer Balaban Jubilee Volume* (Warsaw, 1939), but confiscated by the Nazis; first published in *Bitzaron* 3, no. 5 (February 1941): 346–53.

————. "'Al Ruah Ha-kodesh Bimey Ha-beynayim" [Prophetic inspiration in the Middle Ages]. In *Alexander Marx Jubilee Volume*, 175–208. New York: Jewish Theological Seminary, 1950. Translated as "Prophetic Inspiration in the Middle Ages" by David Wolf Silverman and David Shapiro, in *Prophetic Inspiration after the Prophets: Maimonides and Other Medieval Authorities*, edited by Morris Faierstein, 1–67. Hoboken NJ: KTAV, 1996.

————. "An Analysis of Piety." *Review of Religion* 6, no. 3 (March 1942): 293–307. Reprinted in *Moral Grandeur and Spiritual Audacity*, edited by Susannah Heschel, 305–17. New York: Farrar, Straus & Giroux, 1996.

————. "Answer to Einstein." Translated by Susannah Buschmeyer. *Conservative Judaism* 35, no. 4 (Summer 2003): 39–41.

————. "Antwort an Einstein" [Reply to Einstein]. *Aufbau* (September 20, 1940): 3.

————. "'Arakhim Ba-hinukh Hayehudi" [Values in Jewish education]. *Gesher* 8, no. 1–2 (30–32) (n.d.): 54–60.

————. "Architecture of Time." *Judaism* 1, no. 1 (January 1952): 44–51.

————. "Auswanderungsprobleme" [Emigration problems]. *Gemeindeblatt der jüdischen Gemeinde zu Berlin* 28, no. 31 (July 31, 1938): 4–5.

————. "Bet Midrash (Part 1, no. 4, sect. 78 [on Bava Kama 62]), Hidushei Torah" [Notes on points of Rabbinic law]. *Sha'arey Torah* 13, no. 1 (1922, Tishri–Kislev 5683).

———. "Bet Midrash (Part 1, no. 5, sect. 98 [yishuv divrey R. Aharon Halevi on 'kinyan de'orayta'])." *Sha'arey Torah* 13, no. 2 (1922–23, Tevet–Adar 5683).
———. "Bet Midrash (Part 1, no. 6, sect. 108 [on Rashi and Bava Kama 28])." *Sha'arey Torah* 13, no. 3 (1923, Nissan–Iyar 5683).
———. "Between Civilization and Eternity." *Commentary* (October 1951): 375–78.
———. *Between God and Man.* Edited by Fritz A. Rothschild. New York: Free Press, 1959. Review bibliography: 1975.
———. "The Biblical View of Reality." In *Contemporary Problems in Religion*, edited by Harold A. Basilius, 57–76. Detroit: Wayne State University Press, 1956. Reprinted in *Moral Grandeur and Spiritual Audacity*, edited by Susannah Heschel, 354–65. New York: Farrar, Straus & Giroux, 1996.
———. "A Brokhe Dem Nosi" [Greetings to President Zalman Shazar on his eightieth birthday]. *Di goldene Keyt: Periodical for Literature and Social Problems* 68 (1968): 26.
———. "A Cabbalistic Commentary to the Prayerbook" [Text of Abulafia]. In *Kovetz Madda'i le-Zekher Moshe Schorr* [Studies in memory of Moses Schorr, 1874–1941], edited by Louis Ginzberg and Abraham Weiss, 113–26. New York: Professor Moses Schorr Memorial Committee, 1944.
———. "Call of the Hour." *Law and Order: The Independent Magazine for the Police Profession* (May 1960): 14–15, 18–22, 25. Reprinted as "Children and Youth," in *The Insecurity of Freedom: Essays on Human Existence*, by Abraham Joshua Heschel, 39–51. New York: Farrar, Straus & Giroux, 1966.
———. "Call to Conscience." Paper presented at the New York Conference on Soviet Jewry, Hunter College, October 28, 1964. Reprinted as "A Declaration of Conscience," in *The Insecurity of Freedom: Essays on Human Existence*, by Abraham Joshua Heschel, 274–84. New York: Farrar, Straus & Giroux, 1966.
———. "Celebration and Exaltation." *Jewish Heritage* (Summer 1972): 5–10.
———. "Choose Life!" *Jubilee* (January 1966): 37–39. Reprinted as "Choose Life!" in *Moral Grandeur and Spiritual Audacity*, edited by Susannah Heschel, 251–56. New York: Farrar, Straus & Giroux, 1996.
———. "Christian-Jewish Dialogue and the Meaning of the State of Israel." *CrossCurrents* (Fall 1969): 409–25. Reprinted as "Dialogue in the Judaic-Christian Community," in *Theology and the City of Man: A Sesquicentennial Conference*, edited by John W. Padberg. West Nyack NY: CrossCurrents, 1970.
———. *The Circle of the Baal Shem Tov: Studies in Hasidism.* Edited by Samuel Dresner. Chicago: University of Chicago Press, 1985.
———. "The Concept of Man in Jewish Thought." In *The Concept of Man*, edited by S. Radhakrishnan and P. T. Raju, 108–57. London: Allen & Unwin, 1960.

———. "A Concise Dictionary of Hebrew Terms." Mimeograph. Cincinnati: Hebrew Union College Press, October 1941.

———. "A Conversation with Doctor Abraham Joshua Heschel." Interview by Carl Stern. New York: National Broadcasting Company, February 4, 1973. Reprinted in *Moral Grandeur and Spiritual Audacity*, edited by Susannah Heschel, 395–412. New York: Farrar, Straus & Giroux, 1996.

———. "Conversation with Martin Luther King." *Conservative Judaism* 22, no. 3 (Spring 1968): 1–19.

———. "A Conversation with Rabbi Abraham J. Heschel." Interview by Frank Reynolds. New York: American Broadcasting Company, November 21, 1971.

———. "Das Gebet als Äusserung und Einfühlung" [Prayer as expression and empathy]. *Monatsschrift für die Geschichte und Wissenschaft des Judentums* 83 (1939): 562–67.

———. "Das Wesen der Dinge nach der Lehre Gabirols" [The status of the thing in Gabirol's teaching]. *Hebrew Union College Annual* 14 (1939): 359–85.

———. "David Koigen." *Jüdische Rundschau* (February 27, 1934): 5.

———. "David Koigens Sinndeutung der jüdischen Geschichte" [David Koigen's interpretation of Jewish history]. *Jüdische Rundschau* 80–81 (October 7, 1938): 4.

———. "Death as Homecoming." In *Jewish Reflections on Death*, edited by Jack Riemer, 58–73. New York: Schocken, 1974.

———. "Depth Theology." *CrossCurrents* (Fall 1960): 317–25. Reprinted in *The Insecurity of Freedom: Essays on Human Existence*, by Abraham Joshua Heschel, 115–26. New York: Farrar, Straus & Giroux, 1966.

———. "Der Begriff der Einheit in der Philosophie Gabirols" [The concept of unity in Gabirol's philosophy]. *Monatsschrift für die Geschichte und Wissenschaft des Judentums* 82 (March/April 1938): 89–111.

———. "Der Begriff des Seins in der Philosophie Gabirols." In *Festschrift Jakob Freimann zum 70*, 68–77. Berlin: Geburtstag, 1937. Translated by David Wolf Silverman as "The Concept of Being in Gabirol's Philosophy," *Conservative Judaism* 28, no. 1 (Fall 1973): 89–95.

———. "Der Kotsker Rebbe." *Di goldene Keyt: Periodical for Literature and Social Problems* 65 (1969): 138–56; 71 (1970): 60–70.

———. *Der mizrekh-Eyropeyisher Yid* [The Eastern-European Jew]. New York: Schocken, 1946.

———. *Der Shem Hameforash: Mentsh* [*The Ineffable Name of God: Man*]. Warsaw: Farlag Indzl, 1933.

———. "Der Zaddik fun Freyd" [The zaddik of joy]. *Illustrirte Vokh* 3, no. 20 (whole no. 73) (May 21, 1925).

————. "Die Gewaltigen Dinge" [The powerful things]. *Gemeindeblatt der jüdischen Gemeinde zu Berlin* 26, no. 47 (November 22, 1936): 4.

————. "Die Kraft der Buße" [The power of repentance]. *Gemeindeblatt der jüdischen Gemeinde zu Berlin* 26, no. 37 (September 13, 1936): 4.

————. "Die Marranen von Heute" [The Marranos of today]. *Gemeindeblatt der jüdischen Gemeinde zu Berlin* 26, no. 38 (September 16, 1936): 2. Translated and reprinted as "The Meaning of Repentance," in *Moral Grandeur and Spiritual Audacity*, edited by Susannah Heschel, 68–70. New York: Farrar, Straus & Giroux, 1996.

————. *Die Prophetie*. Kraków: Polish Academy of Sciences, 1936.

————. "Die Verdienste Abrahams" [The merits of Abraham]. *Gemeindeblatt der jüdischen Gemeinde zu Berlin* 26, no. 47 (November 22, 1936): 17.

————. "Die Wirtschaftswerte der Gemeinden" [The economic values of the communities]. *Gemeindeblatt der jüdischen Gemeinde zu Berlin* 27, no. 9 (February 28, 1937): 9.

————. "Di Mizrekh-eyropeishe Tkufe in der Yidisher Geshikte" [The Eastern European era in Jewish history). *YIVO Bleter* 25, no. 2 (March–April 1945): 163–83. Reprinted and translated as "The Eastern European Era in Jewish History," probably translated by Shlomo Noble, *YIVO Annual of Jewish Social Science* 1 (1946): 86–106.

————. "The Divine Pathos: The Basic Category of Prophetic Theology." Translated by William Wolf. *Judaism* 2, no. 1 (January 1953): 61–67. Excerpt (part 3, chapter 1) from *Die Prophetie*, by Abraham Joshua Heschel. Kraków: Polish Academy of Sciences, 1936.

————. *Don Jizhak Abravanel*. Berlin: Erich Reiss Verlag, 1937. Translated into Polish by Ozjasz Tilleman. Lwow: Towa przjacio universytetu hebrajskiego w jerozolimie, 1938. Slightly abridged and translated into English as "Abravanel" by William Wolf, *Intermountain Jewish News* (December 19, 1986): 5, 8–12.

————. *The Earth Is the Lord's: The Inner World of the Jew in East Europe*. New York: Henry Schuman, 1950.

————. "The Eastern European Era in Jewish History." Probably translated by Shlomo Noble. *YIVO Annual of Jewish Social Science* 1 (1946): 86–106.

————. "The Eastern European Jew." Translated from English by Ovadiah Margaliot. In *Sheviley Ha-emunah Ba-dor Ha-aharon* [The paths of faith in the last generation], 328–426. Tel Aviv: Mahbarot Lesifrut, 1964.

————. "An Echo of Eternity." *Hadassah Magazine* (September 1967): 4–6.

————. "Eine Fabel Rabbi Meirs" [A story from Rabbi Meir]. *Gemeindeblatt der jüdischen Gemeinde zu Berlin* 26, no. 19 (May 10, 1936): 5.

————. "Eine Festschrift für Samuel Krauss" [A Festschrift for Samuel Krauss]. *Gemeindeblatt der jüdischen Gemeinde zu Berlin* 26, no. 14 (April 4, 1936): 18.

————. "Elischa ben Abuja." *Gemeindeblatt der jüdischen Gemeinde zu Berlin* 26, no. 17 (April 26, 1936): 16.

————. *Essential Writings*. Edited by Susannah Heschel. Maryknoll NY: Orbis Books, 2011.

————. "Existence and Celebration." New York: Council of Jewish Federations and Welfare Funds, 1965. Reprinted in *Moral Grandeur and Spiritual Audacity*, edited by Susannah Heschel, 18–31. New York: Farrar, Straus & Giroux, 1996.

————. "Faith." Part 1, *The Reconstructionist* 10, no. 13 (November 3, 1944): 10–14; part 2, *The Reconstructionist* 10, no. 14 (November 17, 1944): 12–16. Reprinted in *Moral Grandeur and Spiritual Audacity*, edited by Susannah Heschel, 328–39. New York: Farrar, Straus & Giroux, 1996.

————. Foreword to *A Hero for Our Time: The Trial and Fate of Boris Kochubi-yevsky*, edited by Moshe Decter, 3. New York: Academic Committee on Soviet Jewry, Conference on the Status of Soviet Jews, 1970.

————. Foreword to *Prelude to Dialogue: Jewish-Christian Relationships*, by James Parkes, vii. London: Vallentine Mitchell, 1969.

————. Foreword to *The Unredeemed: Antisemitism in the Soviet Union*, edited by Ronald I. Rubin, 13–16. Chicago: Quadrangle, 1968.

————. "From Mission to Dialogue." *Conservative Judaism* 21, no. 3 (Spring 1967): 1–11.

————. *God in Search of Man: A Philosophy of Judaism*. New York: Farrar, Straus & Cudahy; Philadelphia: Jewish Publication Society of America, 1955.

————. "God, Torah, and Israel." Translated by Byron L. Sherwin. In *Theology and Church in Times of Change: Essays in Honor of John Coleman Bennett*, edited by Edward Long and Robert Handy, 71–90. Philadelphia: Westminster, 1970. Reprinted in *Moral Grandeur and Spiritual Audacity*, edited by Susannah Heschel, 191–208. New York: Farrar, Straus & Giroux, 1996.

————. "Ha-he'emin Ha-rambam Shezakhah L'anevuah?" [Did Maimonides strive for prophetic inspiration?]. In *Louis Ginzberg Jubilee Volume*, 159–88. New York: American Academy for Jewish Research, 1945. Translated by David Wolf Silverman and David Shapiro as "Did Maimonides Believe That He Had Attained the Rank of Prophet?" in *Prophetic Inspiration after the Prophets: Maimonides and Other Medieval Authorities*, edited by Morris Faierstein, 69–139. Hoboken NJ: KTAV, 1996.

————. "Hasidism as a New Approach to Torah." *Jewish Heritage* 14, no. 3 (Fall–Winter 1972): 4–21. Reprinted in *Moral Grandeur and Spiritual*

Audacity, edited by Susannah Heschel, 33–39. New York: Farrar, Straus & Giroux, 1996.

———. "Ha-Yehudi shel Mizrah Eropa" [The Eastern European Jew]. Translated by Yehudah Yaari. In *Luah ha-Aretz 1947–1948*, 98–124. Tel Aviv: Haim, 1947.

———. *Heavenly Torah as Refracted through the Generations* [*Torah Min Hashamayim Be-aspaklaryah Shel Ha-dorot*] (1962, 1965, 1990). Edited and translated by Gordon Tucker, with Leonard Levin. New York: Continuum, 2005.

———. "Hebräische Lesestücke" [review of essays from the Hebrew supplement to the *Jüdische Rundschau*]. *Gemeindeblatt der jüdischen Gemeinde zu Berlin* 26, no. 20 (May 17, 1936): 15.

———. "A Hebrew Evaluation of Reinhold Niebuhr." In *Reinhold Niebuhr: His Religious, Social, and Political Thought*, edited by Charles Kegley and Robert Bretall, 391–410. The Library of Living Theology 2. New York: Macmillan, 1956. Reprinted as "Confusion of God and Evil," in *The Insecurity of Freedom: Essays on Human Existence*, by Abraham Joshua Heschel, 127–49. New York: Farrar, Straus & Giroux, 1966.

———. "The Hebrew Prophet in Relation to God and Man." In *The Old Testament Conception of God, Man and the World*, edited by Zevi Adar, 215–24. Tel Aviv: Massadah, 1957.

———. "The Heritage of Martin Luther King, Jr." Interview with Frank Reynolds, Jesse Jackson, and George Clements. New York: American Broadcasting Company, January 9, 1972.

———. "Hillel Bavli: In Memoriam." *Conservative Judaism* 17, no. 1–2 (Fall–Winter 1962–1963): 70–71.

———. "The Holy Dimension." *Journal of Religion* 23, no. 2 (April 1943): 117–24.

———. *I Asked for Wonder: A Spiritual Anthology*. Edited by Samuel Dresner. New York: Crossroad, 1987.

———. "Idols in the Temples." *Religious Education* (March–April 1963): 127–37. Reprinted as "Idols in the Temple," in *The Insecurity of Freedom: Essays on Human Existence*, by Abraham Joshua Heschel, 52–69. New York: Farrar, Straus & Giroux, 1966.

———. "Ikh nisht tragn mir mayn harts" [I can no longer carry my heart] (untitled poem). *Literarishe Bleter* 22 (June 3, 1927): 417.

———. "Il chassidismo e Kierkegaard." *Conoscenza religiosa* [Religious knowledge] 4 (1971): 337–53.

———. "Ilya Schor." *Conservative Judaism* 16, no. 1 (Fall 1961): 20–21.

———. "The Individual Jew and His Obligations." Translated by Simha Kling and Samuel Dresner. *Conservative Judaism* 15, no. 3 (Spring 1961): 10–26. English translation in *The Insecurity of Freedom: Essays on Human Existence*, by Abraham Joshua Heschel, 187–211. New York: Farrar, Straus & Giroux, 1966.

———. *The Ineffable Name of God: Man; Poems* [*Der Shem Hameforash: Mentsh*]. Translated by Morton Leifman. New York: Continuum, 2005.

———. "In Search of Exaltation." *Jewish Heritage* (Fall 1971): 29, 30, 35. Reprinted in *Moral Grandeur and Spiritual Audacity*, edited by Susannah Heschel, 227–29. New York: Farrar, Straus & Giroux, 1996.

———. *The Insecurity of Freedom: Essays on Human Existence*. New York: Farrar, Straus & Giroux, 1966.

———. *In This Hour: Heschel's Writings in Nazi Germany and London Exile*. Translated by Marion Faber and Stephen Lehmann. Notes by Helen Plotkin. Philadelphia: Jewish Publication Society, 2019.

———. *Israel: An Echo of Eternity*. New York: Farrar, Straus & Giroux, 1969.

———. "The Israelite Prophet in His Relation to God and the People." *Davke* (*Precisamente*) 50 (Buenos Aires) (July–December 1963): 203–16.

———. [Itzhik, pseud.] "In tog fun has" [Day of hate]. *Haynt* (May 10, 1933). Reprinted in commemorative brochure on the twenty-fifth anniversary of *Yung Vilne*, 45–46.

———. "I will give you—O world." *Naye Folks-Tsaytung* (April 25, 1930). Reprinted in *Unzer Zeit* (1973): 46. Reprinted in *Moral Grandeur and Spiritual Audacity*, edited by Susannah Heschel, 318–27. New York: Farrar, Straus & Giroux, 1996.

———. "*Iyunim Ba-midrash*" [Studies in midrashic literature"]. In *The Abraham Weiss Jubilee Volume*, edited by Samuel Belkin, 349–60. New York: n.p., 1964.

———. "Jehuda Ha-Nassi." *Gemeindeblatt der jüdischen Gemeinde zu Berlin* 26, no. 22 (May 31, 1936): 16.

———. "The Jewish Notion of God and Christian Renewal." In *Renewal of Religious Thought: Proceedings of the Congress on the Theology of the Church Centenary of Canada, 1867–1967*, edited by L. K. Shook, CSB, 105–29. Montreal: Palm, 1968. Reprinted in French, as "La notion judaïque de Dieu et le renouveau chrétien," in *La théologie du renouveau*, edited by Laurence K. Shook, C.S.B., and Guy-M. Bertrand, C.S.C., vol. 1, 131. Montréal: Les Éditions Fides, Paris: Les Éditions du Cerf, 1968. Reprinted as "The God of Israel and Christian Renewal," in *Moral Grandeur and Spiritual Audacity*, edited by Susannah Heschel, 268–85. New York: Farrar, Straus & Giroux, 1996.

————. "A Jewish Response." *Catholic News* (April 4, 1963): 4. Remarks to Cardinal Bea, April 1, 1963. Reprinted as "The Ecumenical Movement," in *The Insecurity of Freedom: Essays on Human Existence*, by Abraham Joshua Heschel, 179–83. New York: Farrar, Straus & Giroux, 1966.

————. "Kinder in Luft und Sonne" [Children outside in the sun: About an orphan home]. *Gemeindeblatt der jüdischen Gemeinde zu Berlin* 28, no. 21 (May 22, 1938): 5

————. *Kotsk: In gerangl far emesdikayt* [*Kotzk: The struggle for integrity*]. 2 vols. Tel Aviv: Hamenorah, 1973.

————. "Kotzk." *Panim el Panim* (Jerusalem) 507 (February 7, 1969): 10–11, 18.

————. "Kotzk, Menahem Mendel of." In *Encyclopaedia Judaica*, vol. 10. Jerusalem: Keter, 1971.

————. "The Last Years of Maimonides." Translation of chapter 25, *Maimonides: Eine Biographie*. *National Jewish Monthly* (June 1955): 7, 27–28.

————. "Le Judaïsme concerne-t-il l'homme américain?" *L'Arche* (August–September 1962): 64–67.

————. "Letoldot R. Pinhas mi-Koretz" [The history of R. Pinhas of Koretz]. In *'Alei 'Ayin: The Salman Schocken Jubilee Volume*, 213–44. Jerusalem: n.p., 1951–1952. Translated as "Rabbi Pinhas of Lorzec," in *The Circle of the Baal Shem Tov: Studies in Hasidism*, edited by Samuel Dresner, 1–43. Chicago: University of Chicago Press, 1985.

————. "Lichter über dem Meer" [Lights over the sea, a parable]. *Gemeindeblatt der jüdischen Gemeinde zu Berlin* 27, no. 48 (November 29, 1937): 4.

————. "Lider" (poems): "Got geht mir nokh umetum," "In ovent oyf gasn, milionen oygen shtiken zikh," "Ikh un du" ["God follows me everywhere," "Evening in the streets, Millions of eyes choke," "I and Thou"]. *Zukunft* 34 (December 1929): 825. Reprinted in *Der Shem Hameforash: Mentsh*, by Abraham Joshua Heschel. Warsaw: Farlag Indzl, 1933.

————. "Lider" (poems): "Zumer," "Ikh volt azoy velen zayn farlibt: aydeler fraynd," "Ruf durkh di nekht" ["Summer," "O how I want to be in love, gentle friend," "Call through the nights"). *Zukunft* 35 (August 1930): 576

————. *Maïmonide* [Maimonides]. Paris: Payot, 1936.

————. *Maimonides: A Biography*. Translated by Joachim Neugroschel. New York: Farrar, Straus & Giroux, 1982.

————. *Man Is Not Alone: A Philosophy of Religion*. New York: Farrar, Straus & Young; Philadelphia: Jewish Publication Society of America, 1951.

————. *Man's Quest for God: Studies in Prayer and Symbolism*. New York: Charles Scribner's Sons, 1954.

―――. "Man's Search for Faith." *United Synagogue Review* (Spring 1971): 14, 15, 24.

―――. "Man—Who Is He?" In *Today's Changing Society: A Challenge to Individual Identity*, edited by Clarence Walton, 50–56. New York: Institute of Life Insurance, 1967.

―――. "The Meaning of This War." *Hebrew Union College Bulletin* (March 1943): 1–2, 18. Revised ed. in *Liberal Judaism* 11, no. 10 (February 1944): 18–21. Revised ed. "Versuch einer Deutung" [Search for a meaning], in *Begegnung mit dem Judentum: Ein Gedenkbuch* [Encounter with Jewry: A memorial book, voices of [the Society of] Friends in Germany], edited by Margarethe Lachmund, vol. 2, 11–13. Bad Pyrmont: Auslieferung, 1962.

―――. "The Meaning of This War." *Liberal Judaism* 11, no. 10 (February 1944): 18–21. Reprinted as "The Meaning of This Hour," in *Man's Quest for God: Studies in Prayer and Symbolism*, by Abraham Joshua Heschel, 147–51. New York: Charles Scribner's Sons, 1954. Reprinted in *Moral Grandeur and Spiritual Audacity*, edited by Susannah Heschel, 209–12. New York: Farrar, Straus & Giroux, 1996.

―――. "Modern Man." In *Sheviley Ha-emunah Ba-dor Ha-aharon* [The paths of faith in the last generation], translated from English by Ovadiah Margaliot, 11–15. Tel Aviv: Mahbarot Lesifrut, 1964.

―――. "The Moment at Sinai." *American Zionist* 43, no. 7 (February 5, 1953): 18–20. Reprinted in *Moral Grandeur and Spiritual Audacity*, edited by Susannah Heschel, 12–17. New York: Farrar, Straus & Giroux, 1996.

―――. "A Momentous Emergency—The Russian Jewry." *Day-Morning Journal* 12 (September 13 and October 12, 1963). Reprinted as broadside. Synagogue Council of America, n.p.: n.d. Reprinted in *The Insecurity of Freedom: Essays on Human Existence*, by Abraham Joshua Heschel, 262–73. New York: Farrar, Straus & Giroux, 1966.

―――. "The Moral Dilemma of the Space Age." In *Space: Its Impact on Man and Society*, edited by Lilian Levy, 176–79. New York: Norton, 1964. Reprinted in *Moral Grandeur and Spiritual Audacity*, edited by Susannah Heschel, 216–18. New York: Farrar, Straus & Giroux, 1996.

―――. *Moral Grandeur and Spiritual Audacity: Essays by Abraham Joshua Heschel.* Edited by Susannah Heschel. New York: Farrar, Straus & Giroux, 1996.

―――. "The Moral Outrage of Vietnam." *Fellowship* (September 1966): 24–26. Reprinted in *Vietnam: Crisis of Conscience*, by Abraham Joshua Heschel, Robert McAfee Brown, and Michael Novak, 48–61. New York: Association Press, Behrman House, Herder & Herder, 1967.

————. "Moses Maimonides." *Jubilee* (January 1966): 36–41. Excerpt (chapter 20) from *The Insecurity of Freedom: Essays on Human Existence*, by Abraham Joshua Heschel. New York: Farrar, Straus & Giroux, 1966.

————. "The Mystical Element in Judaism." In *The Jews: Their History, Culture, and Religion*, edited by Louis Finkelstein, vol. 1, 602–23. New York: Harper and Brothers; Philadelphia: Jewish Publication Society of America, 1949. Reprinted in *Moral Grandeur and Spiritual Audacity*, edited by Susannah Heschel, 164–84. New York: Farrar, Straus & Giroux, 1996.

————. "No Religion Is an Island." *Union Seminary Quarterly Review* 21, no. 2, part 1 (January 1966): 117–34. Reprinted in *The Graduate Journal: The University of Texas* 7 (1966), supplement: 65–82. Reprinted in *No Religion Is an Island: Abraham Joshua Heschel and Interreligious Dialogue*, edited by Harold Kasimow and Byron Sherwin, 3–22. Maryknoll NY: Orbis, 1991. Reprinted in *Moral Grandeur and Spiritual Audacity*, edited by Susannah Heschel, 235–50. New York: Farrar, Straus & Giroux, 1996.

————. "On Prayer." *Conservative Judaism* 25, no. 1 (Fall 1970): 1–12. Excerpts reprinted in *Tempo* (October 15, 1969): 8, 11. Reprinted in *Understanding Jewish Prayer*, edited by Jakob Petuchowski, 69–83. New York: KTAV, 1972. Reprinted in *Moral Grandeur and Spiritual Audacity*, edited by Susannah Heschel, 257–67. New York: Farrar, Straus & Giroux, 1996.

————. "Our Heritage from Eastern Europe." In *Roads to Jewish Survival*, edited by Milton Berger, Joel Geffen, and M. David Hoffman, 390–95. New York: Bloch, 1967.

————. "Pachad Jizchak." Review of the second edition of the Talmud encyclopedia of that name. *Gemeindeblatt der jüdischen Gemeinde zu Berlin* 26, no. 20 (May 17, 1936): 16.

————. *A Passion for Truth*. New York: Farrar, Straus & Giroux, 1973.

————. "'Perakim Le-'inyan 'Torah mi-sinay'" ["Did Moses incorporate into the Pentateuch pre-Sinaitic Laws?"]. In *Hagut Ivrit Ba-Amerika* [Studies on Jewish themes by contemporary American scholars], edited by Menahem Zohori, Arie Tartakover, and Haim Ormian, vol. 1, 308–17. Tel Aviv: Yavneh-Brit Ivrit Olamit, 1972. Excerpts of *Torah Min Ha-shamayim Be-aspaklaryah Shel Ha-dorot* [*Theology of Ancient Judaism*], by Abraham Joshua Heschel. Vol. 1: London: Soncino, 1962. Vol. 2: London: Soncino, 1965. Vol. 3: Jerusalem: Jewish Theological Seminary, 1990.

————. "Persönlichkeiten der jüdischen Geschichte: Jochanan ben Zakkai." *Gemeindeblatt der jüdischen Gemeinde zu Berlin* 26, no. 8 (February 23, 1936): 14.

————. "Persönlichkeiten der jüdischen Geschichte: Rabbi Akiba." *Jüdisches Gemeindeblatt für Frankfurt* 16, no. 5 (February 1938): 21–22.

————. "Piety." *Hamigdal* (September–October, 1946): 12–13.

————. "*Pikuach Neshama*: To Save a Soul." Translated by Aryeh Cohen and Samuel Dresner in *Moral Grandeur and Spiritual Audacity*, edited by Susannah Heschel, 54–67. New York: Farrar, Straus & Giroux, 1996.

————. "The Plight of Russian Jews." *United Synagogue Review* (Winter 1964): 14–15, 26–27. Reprinted in *Moral Grandeur and Spiritual Audacity*, edited by Susannah Heschel, 213–15. New York: Farrar, Straus & Giroux, 1996.

————. "Prayer." *Review of Religion* 9, no. 2 (January 1945): 153–68. Reprinted in *Moral Grandeur and Spiritual Audacity*, edited by Susannah Heschel, 340–53. New York: Farrar, Straus & Giroux, 1996.

————. "Prayer and Theological Discipline." *Union Seminary Quarterly Review* (May 1959): 3–8.

————. "A Prayer for Peace." *Jewish Heritage* (Spring–Summer 1971): 7–11. Excerpt from *Vietnam: Crisis of Conscience*, by Abraham Joshua Heschel, Robert McAfee Brown, and Michael Novak, 48–61. New York: Association Press, Behrman House, Herder & Herder, 1967. Reprinted in *Moral Grandeur and Spiritual Audacity*, edited by Susannah Heschel, 230–34. New York: Farrar, Straus & Giroux, 1996.

————. Preface to *Jerusalem of Lithuania*. Edited by Layzer Ran. Translated by Shlomo Noble. New York: Vilner albom komitet, 1974.

————. "A Preface to the Understanding of Revelation." In *Essays Presented to Leo Baeck on the Occasion of His Eightieth Birthday*, 28–35. London: East and West Library, 1954. Reprinted in *Moral Grandeur and Spiritual Audacity*, edited by Susannah Heschel, 185–90. New York: Farrar, Straus & Giroux, 1996.

————. "The Problem of the Individual" ["Yihudo shel Ha-kiyyum Ha-Yehudi"]. In "Sefer Ha-kinnus Ha-iyyuni Ha-olami Ha-rishon Bi-Yerushalayim" [Proceedings of the Ideological Conference in Jerusalem], edited by N. Rotenstreich and Z. Shazar, *Hazut* 4 (1958): 312–19.

————. "Prophetic Inspiration." *Judaism* 11, no. 1 (Winter 1962): 3–13.

————. *Prophetic Inspiration after the Prophets: Maimonides and Other Medieval Authorities*. Translated by David Wolf Silverman and David Shapiro. Edited by Morris Faierstein. Hoboken NJ: KTAV, 1996. "Did Maimonides Believe That He Had Attained the Rank of Prophet?" by Abraham Joshua Heschel, originally published as "Ha-he'emin Ha-rambam Shezakhah L'anevuah?" in *Louis Ginzberg Jubilee Volume*, 159–88. New York: American Academy for Jewish Research, 1945. "Prophetic Inspiration in the Middle Ages," by Abraham Joshua Heschel, originally published as "'Al Ruah Ha-kodesh Bimey Ha-beynayim," in *Alexander Marx Jubilee Volume*, 175–208. New York: Jewish Theological Seminary, 1950.

————. "Prophétie et poésie." *Evidences* (January–February 1963): 45–50. French translation of excerpts (chapter 22) of *The Prophets*, by Abraham Joshua Heschel. New York: Harper & Row; Philadelphia: Jewish Publication Society of America, 1962.

————. *The Prophets*. New York: Harper & Row; Philadelphia: Jewish Publication Society of America, 1962.

————. "Protestant Renewal: A Jewish View." *Christian Century* (December 4, 1963): 1501–4. Reprinted in *The Insecurity of Freedom: Essays on Human Existence*, by Abraham Joshua Heschel, 168–78. New York: Farrar, Straus & Giroux, 1966.

————. *The Quest for Certainty in Saadia's Philosophy*. New York: Philip Feldheim, 1944.

————. "The Quest for Certainty in Saadia's Philosophy. Part 1," *Jewish Quarterly Review* 33, no. 2–3 (1943): 263–313; part 2, *Jewish Quarterly Review* 34, no. 4 (1944): 391–408.

————. "Rabbi Akiba." *Gemeindeblatt der jüdischen Gemeinde zu Berlin* 26, no. 13 (March 29, 1936): 16.

————. "Rabbi Chiya." *Gemeindeblatt der jüdischen Gemeinde zu Berlin* 26, no. 33 (August 16, 1936): 15.

————. "Rabbi Gamliel II." *Gemeindeblatt der jüdischen Gemeinde zu Berlin* 26, no. 10 (March 8, 1936): 15.

————. "Rabbi Gershon of Kuty." *Hebrew Union College Annual* 23, no. 2 (1950–51): 17–71. English translation in *The Circle of the Baal Shem Tov: Studies in Hasidism*, edited by Samuel Dresner, 44–112. Chicago: University of Chicago Press, 1985.

————. "Rabbi Meir." *Gemeindeblatt der jüdischen Gemeinde zu Berlin* 26, no. 20 (May 17, 1936): 16.

————. "Rabbi Mendel mi-Kotzk." *Shedemot* 29 (Spring 1968): 87–94.

————. "Rabbi Nahman of Kossov, Companion of the Baal Shem." In *The Harry A. Wolfson Jubilee Volume*, edited by Saul Lieberman et al., 113–41. New York: American Academy for Jewish Research, 1965. English translation in *The Circle of the Baal Shem Tov: Studies in Hasidism*, edited by Samuel Dresner, 113–51. Chicago: University of Chicago Press, 1985.

————. "Rabbi Pinhas of Koretz and the Maggid of Meseritz." In *Hadoar: Thirtieth Anniversary Jubilee Volume*, 279–85. New York: Histadruth Ivrith of America, 1952.

————. "Rabbi Schimon ben Gamliel II." *Gemeindeblatt der jüdischen Gemeinde zu Berlin* 26, no. 15 (April 12, 1936): 15.

————. "Rabbi Schimon ben Gamliel II." *Jüdisches Gemeindeblatt für Frankfurt* 16, no. 6 (March 1938): 5–6.

————. "Rabbi Yitzhak of Drohobitsh." *Hadoar Jubilee Volume* 37, no. 28 (May 31, 1957): 86–94. English translation in *The Circle of the Baal Shem Tov: Studies in Hasidism*, edited by Samuel Dresner, 152–81. Chicago: University of Chicago Press, 1985.

————. "Reason and Revelation in Saadia's Philosophy." *Jewish Quarterly Review* 34, no. 4 (1944): 391–408.

————. "The Reason for My Involvement in the Peace Movement." *Journal of Social Philosophy* 4 (January 1973): 7–8. Reprinted in *Moral Grandeur and Spiritual Audacity*, edited by Susannah Heschel, 224–26. New York: Farrar, Straus & Giroux, 1996.

————. "Reb Pinkhes Koritser" [Reb Pinchas of Koretz]. *YIVO Bleter* 33 (1949): 9–48.

————. "Reflections on Death." *Proceedings of the First International Congress on Genesis of Sudden Death and Reanimation: Clinical and Moral Problems Connected* [*Genesi della morte improvisa e rianimazione*] (January 10–14, 1969), edited by Vincenzo Lapiccirellam 522–33, 533–42. Florence: Marchi and Bertolli, 1970. Abridged in *Conservative Judaism* 28, no. 1 (Fall 1973): 3–9. Reprinted as "Death as Homecoming," in *Jewish Reflections on Death*, edited by Jack Riemer, 58–73. New York: Schocken, 1974. Reprinted in *Moral Grandeur and Spiritual Audacity*, edited by Susannah Heschel, 366–78. New York: Farrar, Straus & Giroux, 1996.

————. "Reinhold Niebuhr: A Last Farewell." *Conservative Judaism* 24, no. 4 (Summer 1971): 62–63. Reprinted in *Moral Grandeur and Spiritual Audacity*, edited by Susannah Heschel, 301–2. New York: Farrar, Straus & Giroux, 1996.

————. "The Religion of Sympathy." *The Leo Jung Jubilee Volume: Essays in His Honor on the Occasion of his Seventieth Birthday*, edited by Menahem Kasher, Norman Lamm, and Leonard Rosenfeld, 105–13. New York: n.p., 1962.

————. "The Religious Basis of Equality of Opportunity: The Segregation of God." In *Race: Challenge to Religion*, edited by Mathew Ahmann, 55–71. Chicago: Henry Regnery, 1963. Abridged in *United Synagogue Review* (Spring 1963). Reprinted as "Religion and Race," in *The Insecurity of Freedom: Essays on Human Existence*, by Abraham Joshua Heschel, 85–100. New York: Farrar, Straus & Giroux, 1966.

————. "The Religious Message." *Religion in America: Original Essays on Religion in a Free Society*, edited by John Cogley, 244–71. New York: Meridian, 1958. Reprinted as "Religion in a Free Society," in *The Insecurity of Freedom:*

Essays on Human Existence, by Abraham Joshua Heschel, 3–23. New York: Farrar, Straus & Giroux, 1966.

————. "Required: A Moral Ombudsman." *United Synagogue Review* (Fall 1971): 2, 4, 5, 28, 30. Reprinted in *Moral Grandeur and Spiritual Audacity*, edited by Susannah Heschel, 219–23. New York: Farrar, Straus & Giroux, 1996.

————. "The Restoration of Israel." *Catholic Digest* (May 1969): 21–23.

————. Review of "Abraham Danzig." *Gemeindeblatt der jüdischen Gemeinde zu Berlin* 26, no. 19 (May 10, 1936): 5.

————. Review of *Von den höchsten Tagen*, by Agnon. *Gemeindeblatt der jüdischen Gemeinde zu Berlin* 28, no. 21 (May 22, 1938): 6.

————. Review of *Aus der Wissenschaft des Judentums*. *Gemeindeblatt der jüdischen Gemeinde zu Berlin* 26, no. 48 (November 29, 1936): 16.

————. Review of *Chaje Adam*, a compendium of the *Shulhan Arukh*. *Gemeindeblatt der jüdischen Gemeinde zu Berlin* 26, no. 19 (May 10, 1936): 5.

————. Review of *Chassidische Erzählungen* [Yiddish stories by I. L. Perets. Berlin: Schocken, 1936]. *Gemeindeblatt der jüdischen Gemeinde zu Berlin* 26, no. 40 (September 30, 1936): 10.

————. Review of *Das Achtzehngebet* [Prayers of the eighteen benedictions]. *Gemeindeblatt der jüdischen Gemeinde zu Berlin* 27, no. 3 (January 17, 1937): 4.

————. Review of *Der Hebräische Lehrer* [The Hebrew teacher]. *Gemeindeblatt der jüdischen Gemeinde zu Berlin* 26, no. 18 (May 3, 1936): 22.

————. Review of *Der Sinn der Lehre* [The meaning of the teaching]. *Gemeindeblatt der jüdischen Gemeinde zu Berlin* 27, no. 5 (January 31, 1937): 4.

————. Review of *Die Tora* [The Torah]. *Gemeindeblatt der jüdischen Gemeinde zu Berlin* 27, no. 20 (May 16, 1937): 8.

————. Review of *Ein Dichterjubiläum* [A poet's anniversary: Tribute to the Yiddish poet David Einhorn on his fiftieth birthday]. *Gemeindeblatt der jüdischen Gemeinde zu Berlin* 27, no. 2 (January 10, 1937): 17.

————. Review of *Eine Bibelkonkordanz* [A Bible concordance]. *Gemeindeblatt der jüdischen Gemeinde zu Berlin* 27, no. 26 (June 27, 1937): 3.

————. Review of *Ein jüdischer Bibelkommentar* [A Jewish Bible commentary]. *Gemeindeblatt der jüdischen Gemeinde zu Berlin* 26, no. 43 (October 25, 1936): 9.

————. Review of *Einleitung zum Talmudstudium* [A guide for studying the Talmud], by Naftali Cohen. *Gemeindeblatt der jüdischen Gemeinde zu Berlin* 27, no. 1 (January 10, 1937): 3.

————. Review of *Ein Mischnatraktat* [A Mishnah tractate]. *Gemeindeblatt der jüdischen Gemeinde zu Berlin* 28, no. 21 (May 22, 1938): 6.

————. Review of *Ein neues Gebetbuch* [*Seder Avodat Israel*]. *Gemeindeblatt der jüdischen Gemeinde zu Berlin* 27, no. 21 (May 23, 1937): 5.

————. Review of *Epochen jüdischer Geschichte: Ein Pessach-Rückblick in Bildern* [Epochs of Jewish history: A Pesach review in pictures]. *Gemeindeblatt der jüdischen Gemeinde zu Berlin* 26, no. 14 (April 4, 1936): 5.

————. Review of *Essays on Maimonides: An Octocentennial Volume*, edited by Salo Wittmayer Baron. *Review of Religion* 6, no. 3 (March 1942): 315.

————. Review of *Hamore Haiwri* [The Hebrew teacher]. *Gemeindeblatt der jüdischen Gemeinde zu Berlin* 26, no. 40 (September 30, 1936): 10.

————. Review of *Hebräische Dichtung: Anthologie der hebräischen Dichtung in Italien* [Hebrew poems: An anthology of Hebrew poetry in Italian]. *Gemeindeblatt der jüdischen Gemeinde zu Berlin* 27, no. 2 (January 10, 1937): 17.

————. Review of *Hebräische Dichtung* [Hebrew poems: piyyutim], by Jannai. *Gemeindeblatt der jüdischen Gemeinde zu Berlin* 27, no. 1 (10 January 1937): 3.

————. Review of *Hebräische Redewendungen* [Hebrew idiomatic expressions], by A. Abraham, Frankfurt, 1936. *Gemeindeblatt der jüdischen Gemeinde zu Berlin* 26, no. 48 (November 29, 1936): 16.

————. Review of *Jiddische Gedishte* [Yiddish poetry]. *Gemeindeblatt der jüdischen Gemeinde zu Berlin* 26, no. 51 (December 20, 1936): 15.

————. Review of *Jüdische Erzählungen* [Jewish stories]. *Gemeindeblatt der jüdischen Gemeinde zu Berlin* 27, no. 46 (November 14, 1937): 5.

————. Review of *Jüdische Lesehefte* [Jewish booklets]. *Gemeindeblatt der jüdischen Gemeinde zu Berlin* 27, no. 46 (November 14, 1937): 5.

————. Review of *Major Trends in Jewish Mysticism*, by Gershom Scholem. *Journal of Religion* 24 (1944): 140–41.

————. Review of *Meine Lebensjahre* [Years of my life], by J. H. Weiss. *Gemeindeblatt der jüdischen Gemeinde zu Berlin* 26, no. 39 (September 27, 1936): 9.

————. Review of *Personality and Community in Judaism*, by Chaim W. Reines. *Historia Judaica* 4: 115–16.

————. Review of *Rashi Anniversary Volume. Review of Religion* 7, no. 1 (November 1942): 105.

————. Review of *Vom Forschungsinstitut für Hebräische Dichtung* [From the research institute of Hebrew poetry]. *Gemeindeblatt der jüdischen Gemeinde zu Berlin* 26, no. 48 (November 29, 1936): 16.

————. Review of *Zur Kunde der biblischen Eigennamen* [On biblical proper names]. *Gemeindeblatt der jüdischen Gemeinde zu Berlin* 27, no. 19 (May 9, 1937): 5.

————. Review of *Zur Literatur Martin Bubers* [The literary writings of Martin Buber]. *Gemeindeblatt der jüdischen Gemeinde zu Berlin* 28, no. 21 (May 22, 1938): 6.

————. *The Sabbath: Its Meaning for Modern Man.* New York: Farrar, Straus & Young, 1951.

———. "The Sabbath: Its Meaning for Modern Man." *Petahim* 15 (November 1970): 307. Excerpts from *The Sabbath: Its Meaning for Modern Man*.

———. "Sacred Images of Man." *Christian Century* (December 11, 1957): 1473–75. Reprinted in *Religious Education* (March–April 1958): 97–102. Reprinted in *The Insecurity of Freedom: Essays on Human Existence*, by Abraham Joshua Heschel, 150–67. New York: Farrar, Straus & Giroux, 1966.

———. Selections of *Die Prophetie*. Translated by Henry Corbin. *Hermès. Mystique—Poésie—Philosophie* III (November 1939): 78–110.

———. "Se zilbert zin azoy loyter" [The womanly skin silvers so purely] (untitled poem). *Varshaver Shriftn*. Warsaw Writers and Journalists Association, 1926–1927.

———. "Should the United Synagogue of America Join the World Zionist Organization? No." In *Proceedings of the 1959 Biennial Convention of the United Synagogue of America*, 76–85. New York: United Synagogue of America, 1960. Reprinted as "The Great Debate," in *The Torch* (Winter 1960). Philadelphia: National Federation of Jewish Men's Clubs, Inc. Reprinted as "Should the United Synagogue of America Join the World Zionist Organization? No, Says Rabbi Abraham Joshua Heschel," in *Roads to Jewish Survival*, edited by Milton Berger, Joel Geffen, and M. David Hoffman, 330–42. New York: Bloch, 1967.

———. "Søren Kierkegaard and the Rabbi of Kotzk." *Monastic Studies* 8 (Mount Savior Monastery, Pine City NY; Spring 1972): 147–51.

———. "Space, Time, and Reality: The Centrality of Time in the Biblical World View." *Judaism* 1, no. 3 (July 1952): 262–69.

———. "The Spirit of Jewish Education." *Jewish Education* (Fall 1953), 9–20. Reprinted as "Jewish Education," in *The Insecurity of Freedom: Essays on Human Existence*, by Abraham Joshua Heschel, 223–41. New York: Farrar, Straus & Giroux, 1966.

———. "The Spirit of Jewish Prayer." *Proceedings of the Rabbinical Assembly of America* 17 (1953): 151–77 (without discussion). Reprinted as "The Spirit of Jewish Prayer," translated by "Alef Lamed" (A. L.). *Megillot* (New York) 15 (March 1954): 3–24.

———. "S. R. Hirsch und unsere Zeit" [Samson Raphael Hirsch and our times]. *Gemeindeblatt der jüdischen Gemeinde zu Berlin* 26, no. 47 (November 22, 1936): 4.

———. "Staatsmann und Theologe" [Statesman and theologian: Biographical sketch of Don Isaac Abravanel]. *Gemeindeblatt der jüdischen Gemeinde zu Berlin* 27, no. 6 (February 7, 1937): 9.

———. "Symbolism and Jewish Faith." In *Religious Symbolism*, edited by F. Ernest Johnson, 53–79. New York: Institute for Religious and Social Studies, Harper & Brothers, 1955. Reprinted as "Symbolism," in *Man's Quest for God: Studies in Prayer and Symbolism*, by Abraham Joshua Heschel, 117–44. New York: Charles Scribner's Sons, 1954. Reprinted in *Moral Grandeur and Spiritual Audacity*, edited by Susannah Heschel, 80–100. New York: Farrar, Straus & Giroux, 1996.

———. "The Task of the Hazzan." *Conservative Judaism* 12, no. 2 (Winter 1958): 1–8. Reprinted in *The Insecurity of Freedom: Essays on Human Existence*, by Abraham Joshua Heschel, 242–53. New York: Farrar, Straus & Giroux, 1966.

———. "Teaching Jewish Theology in the Solomon Schechter Day School." Transcribed and edited by Pesach Schindler. *Synagogue School* (Fall 1969): 1–33. Reprinted as "Jewish Theology" and without the discussion, in *Moral Grandeur and Spiritual Audacity*, edited by Susannah Heschel, 154–63. New York: Farrar, Straus & Giroux, 1996.

———. "Teaching Religion to American Jews." *Adult Jewish Education* (Fall 1956): 3–6. Reprinted in *Moral Grandeur and Spiritual Audacity*, edited by Susannah Heschel, 148–53. New York: Farrar, Straus & Giroux, 1996.

———. "The Theological Dimensions of Medinat Yisrael." *Proceedings* (1968): 91–103; discussion, 104–9.

———. "The Theology of Pathos." In *The Sense of the Sixties*, edited by Edward Quinn and Paul Dolan, 297–310. New York: Free Press, 1968.

———. "A Time for Renewal." Meeting of the Twenty-Eighth World Zionist Congress, Jerusalem, January 19, 1972. English translation reprinted in *Midstream* 18, no. 5 (May 1972): 46–51. Reprinted in *Moral Grandeur and Spiritual Audacity*, edited by Susannah Heschel, 47–53. New York: Farrar, Straus & Giroux, 1996.

———. "To Be a Jew: What Is It?" *Yidisher Kemfer* (September 12, 1947): 25–28.

———. "To Be a Jew: What Is It?" *Zionist Quarterly* 1, no. 1 (Summer 1951): 78–84. Reprinted in *Moral Grandeur and Spiritual Audacity*, edited by Susannah Heschel, 3–11. New York: Farrar, Straus & Giroux, 1996.

———. "To Grow in Wisdom." *New York American Examiner* (February 1961). Reprinted in *Congressional Record: Proceedings and Debates of the 87th Congress, First Session* (March 21, n.d.): appendix A; 1973–75; and June 14, n.d., appendix A: 4364–67. Extracts reprinted in the Jewish Theological Seminary's *The Beacon* (June 1961): 5, 19–20. Reprinted with significant revisions in *The Insecurity of Freedom: Essays on Human Existence*, by Abraham Joshua Heschel, 70–84. New York: Farrar, Straus & Giroux, 1966.

———. *To Grow in Wisdom: An Anthology of Abraham Joshua Heschel*. Edited by Jacob Neusner and Noam Neusner. Lanham MD: Madison, 1990.

———. *Torah Min Ha-shamayim Be-aspaklaryah Shel Ha-dorot* [*Theology of Ancient Judaism*]. Vol. 1: London: Soncino, 1962. Vol. 2: London: Soncino, 1965. Vol. 3: Jerusalem: Jewish Theological Seminary, 1990.

———. "Toward an Understanding of Halacha." *Yearbook of the Central Conference of American Rabbis* 63 (1953): 386–409. Reprinted in part in *Jewish Frontier* (April 1954): 22–28. Reprinted in *Moral Grandeur and Spiritual Audacity*, edited by Susannah Heschel, 127–45. New York: Farrar, Straus & Giroux, 1996.

———. "Two Conversations with Abraham Joshua Heschel, Part 1." *The Eternal Light*. Radio interview by Harold Flender, May 9, 1971.

———. "Two Conversations with Abraham Joshua Heschel, Part 2." *The Eternal Light*. Radio interview by Harold Flender, May 16, 1971. Excerpts in *Women's American ORT Reporter* (January–February 1971): 7, 8, 11.

———. "The Two Great Traditions." *Commentary* (May 1948): 416–22.

———. "Umbakante Dokumentn tsu der Geshikhte fun Khasidus" [Unknown documents in the history of Hasidism]. *YIVO Bleter* 36 (1952): 113–35.

———. "The Values of Jewish Education." *Proceedings of the Rabbinical Assembly of America* 26 (1962): 83–100.

———. "Versuch einer Deutung" [Search for a meaning]. In *Begegnung mit dem Judentum: Ein Gedenkbuch* [Encounter with Jewry: A memorial book, voices of [the Society of] Friends in Germany], edited by Margarethe Lachmund, vol. 2, 11–13. Bad Pyrmont: Auslieferung, 1962.

———. "A Visit with Rabbi Heschel." Interview by Arthur Herzog, *Think* (January–February 1964): 16–19. Abridged version in *Jewish Digest* (December 1968): 15–19.

———. "What Ecumenism Is." In *Face to Face: A Primer in Dialogue*, edited by Lily Edelman. Washington DC: B'nai B'rith Adult Jewish Education, 1967.

———. "What Ecumenism Is." *Jewish Heritage* (Spring 1967): 1–4. Reprinted in *Moral Grandeur and Spiritual Audacity*, edited by Susannah Heschel, 286–89. New York: Farrar, Straus & Giroux, 1996.

———. "What Scripture Really Says About Jewish Restoration in Israel." *Jewish Digest* 15, no. 5 (February 1970): 19–21.

———. "What We Might Do Together." *Religious Education* (March–April 1967): 133–40. Reprinted in *Moral Grandeur and Spiritual Audacity*, edited by Susannah Heschel, 290–300. New York: Farrar, Straus & Giroux, 1996.

———. "The White Man on Trial." In *Proceedings of the Metropolitan New York Conference on Religion and Race*, 100–110. New York: New York City

Youth Board, 1964. Reprinted in *The Insecurity of Freedom: Essays on Human Existence*, by Abraham Joshua Heschel, 101–11. New York: Farrar, Straus & Giroux, 1966.

———. *Who Is Man?* Stanford: Stanford University Press, 1965. Revision of Fred West Lectures delivered at Stanford University, 1963.

———. "Who Is Man?" *Stanford Today* (July 1965): 12–16.

———. "Wie man den Seder hält" [How to perform the seder]. *Gemeindeblatt der jüdischen Gemeinde zu Berlin* 26, no.14 (April 4, 1936): 6.

———. "Why Not Choose Life?" *Dominion* (October 1966): 9–16.

———. "Yir'at shamayim" ["God-fearing-ness"]. In *Sefer Hashnah L'yhudey Amerikah*, 61–72. New York: Histadruth Ivrith, 1942.

———. "Yisrael: *Am, Eretz, Medinah*: Ideological Evaluation of Israel and the Diaspora." *Proceedings* (1958): 118–36. Reprinted as "Israel and the Diaspora," in *The Insecurity of Freedom: Essays on Human Existence*, by Abraham Joshua Heschel, 212–22. New York: Farrar, Straus & Giroux, 1966.

———. "Yom Kippur." *Mas'at Rav* (professional supplement to *Conservative Judaism*) (August 1965): 13–14. Reprinted in *Moral Grandeur and Spiritual Audacity*, edited by Susannah Heschel, 146–47. New York: Farrar, Straus & Giroux, 1996.

———. "Zevi Diesendruck." *American Jewish Year Book* 43 (1941–1942): 391–98.

———. "Zionismus und Überseewanderung" [Zionism and emigration overseas]. *Gemeindeblatt der jüdischen Gemeinde zu Berlin* 28, no. 21 (May 22, 1938): 4.

———. "Zum Eintritt in den Ruhestand." *Jüdisches Gemeindeblatt für Frankfurt* 16, no. 7 (April 1938): 22.

Heschel, Abraham Joshua, Robert McAfee Brown, and Michael Novak. *Vietnam: Crisis of Conscience*. New York: Association Press, Behrman House, Herder & Herder, 1967.

Heschel, Susannah. Introduction to *Israel: An Echo of Eternity*, by Abraham Joshua Heschel, xvii–xxix. Woodstock VT: Jewish Lights Publishing, 1997.

———. "Judaism." In *Her Voice, Her Faith*, edited by Arvind Sharma and Katherine Young, 145–67. Cambridge: Westview, 2003.

———. Preface to *Moral Grandeur and Spiritual Audacity*, by Abraham Joshua Heschel, vii–xxix. New York: Farrar, Straus & Giroux, 1996.

———. "Theological Affinities in the Writings of Abraham Joshua Heschel and Martin Luther King, Jr." In *Black Zion: African American Religious Encounters with Judaism*, edited by Yvonne Chireau and Nathaniel Deutsch, 168–86. New York: Oxford University Press, 2000.

———, ed. *On Being a Jewish Feminist: A Reader*. New York: Shocken, 1983.

Heshel, Jacob. "The History of Hasidism in Austria." In *The Jews of Austria: Essays on Their Life, History and Destruction*, edited by Josef Fraenkel, 347–60. London: Vallentine Mitchell, 1967.

Hirsch, Leo. "Der Dreitage-Jude: Kritik eines Übergangs" [Three-day Jews: criticism of a change]. *Der Morgen* 10 (1934–1935): 295–98.

———. "Pathos und Sympathie. Über Heschels *Die Prophetie*." *Der Morgen* 12 (February 1937): 514–17.

Hoenig, Sidney B., and Baruch Litvin, eds. *Jewish Identity: Modern Responsa and Opinions on the Registration of Children of Mixed Marriages; David Ben-Gurion's Query to Leaders of World Jewry*. New York: Feldheim, 1965.

Hofer, Yehiel. *A Hoyf af Maranow*. 2 vols. Tel Aviv: Farlag Y. L. Perets, 1962.

———. "Milkhome—1914." *Zukunft* (October 1967): 381–87.

———. *Mit Yenem un mit Zikh*. Tel Aviv: Hamenorah, 1976.

Hoffmann, Ernst. 1934. "Koigens Kampf um die Geschichte" [Koigen's battle with history]. *Jüdische Rundschau* (February 27, 1934): 5–6.

Idel, Moshe. "Abraham Heschel on Mysticism and Hasidism." In *Old Worlds, New Mirrors. On Jewish Mysticism and Twentieth-Century Thought*, 217–33. Philadelphia: University of Pennsylvania Press, 2010.

———. *Kabbalah: New Perspectives*. New Haven CT: Yale University Press, 1988.

———. "Ramon Lull and Ecstatic Kabbalah: A Preliminary Observation." *Journal of the Warburg and Courtauld Institutes* 51 (1988): 171:11.

Jacobson, Gershon. "Interview, Prof. Heschel about Russian Jewry." Translated by Morris Faierstein as "Abraham Joshua Heschel and the Holocaust." *Modern Judaism* 19 (1999): 72–74.

Jahresbericht des Rabbiner-Seminars zu Berlin für 1925, 1926, 1927 (5686–88). Berlin: n.p., 1928.

Jambet, Christian, ed. *L'Herne Henry Corbin*. Paris: Cahiers de l'Herne, 1981.

Johnson, F. Ernest, ed. *Religious Symbolism*. Religion and Civilization Series. New York: Institute for Religious & Social Studies, Harper & Brothers, 1955.

Jung, Leo, ed. *Guardians of Our Heritage*. New York: Bloch, 1958.

Kaplan, Edward K. "Heschel as Philosopher: Phenomenology and the Rhetoric of Revelation." *Modern Judaism* 21, no. 1 (February 2001): 1–14.

———. *Holiness in Words: Abraham Joshua Heschel's Poetics of Piety*. Albany NY: SUNY Press, 1996.

———. Introduction to *Heschel, Hasidism, and Halakha*, by Samuel Dresner, ix–xiii. New York: Fordham University Press, 2002.

———. Introduction to *The Ineffable Name of God: Man, Poems*, by Abraham Joshua Heschel. 7–18. New York: Continuum, 2005.

———. *La Sainteté en paroles, Abraham Heschel: piété, poétique, action.* Translated by Paul Kessler. Paris: Les Éditions du Cerf, 1999.

———. *La santità nelle parole. Abraham Joshua Heschel: Poetica, devozione, azione.* Translated by Anna Lissa. Naples: Giannini Editiore, 2009.

———. "Language and Reality in Abraham J. Heschel's Philosophy of Religion." *Journal of the American Academy of Religion* 41, no. 1 (March 1973): 94–113.

———. "Metaphor and Miracle: A. J. Heschel and the Holy Spirit." *Conservative Judaism* 46, no. 2 (Winter 1994): 3–18.

———. "Mysticism and Despair in Abraham J. Heschel's Religious Thought." *Journal of Religion* 57 (January 1977): 33–47.

———. "Revelation and Commitment: Abraham Joshua Heschel's Situational Philosophy." In *Filosofia e critica della filosofia nel pensiero ebraico,* edited by P. Amodio, G. Giannani, and G. Lissa, 199–222. Naples: Giannini Editore, 2004.

———. "Sacred versus Symbolic Religion: Abraham Joshua Heschel and Martin Buber." *Modern Judaism* 14, no. 3 (October 1994): 213–31.

———. *Spiritual Radical, Abraham Joshua Heschel in America, 1940–1972.* New Haven and London: Yale University Press, 2007.

———. "'Under My Catholic Skin': Thomas Merton's Opening to Judaism and to the World." In *Merton and Judaism: Recognition, Repentance, and Renewal; Holiness in Words,* edited by Beatrice Bruteau, 109–25. Louisville KY: Fons Vitae, 2004.

Kaplan, Edward K., and Samuel H. Dresner. *Abraham Joshua Heschel: Prophetic Witness.* New Haven CT: Yale University Press, 1998.

Kaplan, Edward K., and Shaul Magid, eds. *Pushing the Boundaries: Brandeis Centenary Conference on Abraham Joshua Heschel.* Special issue of *Modern Judaism* 29, no. 1 (February 2009): 1–160.

Kaplan, Mordecai M. *Judaism as a Civilization: Toward a Reconstruction of American-Jewish Life.* New York: Macmillan, 1934.

Karff, Samuel, ed. *Hebrew Union College–Jewish Institute of Religion at 100 Years.* Cincinnati: Hebrew Union College Press, 1976.

Kasimow, Harold, and Byron L. Sherwin, eds. *No Religion Is an Island: Abraham Joshua Heschel and Interreligious Dialogue.* Maryknoll NY: Orbis, 1991.

Katz, Steven T. "Abraham Joshua Heschel and Hasidism." *Journal of Jewish Studies* 31 (Spring 1980): 82–104.

———, ed. *Interpreters of Judaism in the Late Twentieth Century.* Washington DC: B'nai B'rith Books, 1993.

Kelman, Wolfe. "Abraham Joshua Heschel: In Memoriam." *Congress Bi-Weekly* (January 12, 1973): 2–3.

King, Coretta Scott. *My Life with Martin Luther King, Jr.* New York: Holt, Rhinehart and Winston, 1969.

Klein, Zanvel. "Heschel as a Hasidic Scholar." *Journal of Jewish Studies* 31 (Spring 1980): 212–14.

Klepfisz, Heszel. *Culture of Compassion: The Spirit of Polish Jewry from Hasidism to the Holocaust.* Hoboken NJ: KTAV, 1983.

Kohn, Eugene. "Prayer and the Modern Jew." *Proceedings of the Rabbinical Assembly of America* 17 (1953): 184–85.

Koigen, David. *Apokalyptische Reiter* [Horsemen of the apocalypse]. Berlin: Erich Reiss Verlag, 1925.

———. *Das Haus Israel: Aus den Schriften von David Koigen.* Edited by Ernst Hoffmann. Berlin: Schocken Verlag, 1934.

Koigen, David, Franz Hilker, and Fishl Schneersohn, eds. *Ethos: vierteljahrsschrift für Soziologie, Geschicts und Kulturphilosophie* [Ethos: Quarterly journal of sociology, history and philosophy of culture]. 2 vols. Karlsruhe: Verlag G. Braun, 1925–26, 1928.

Krajewski, Stanislaw, and Adam Lipszyc, eds. *Abraham Joshua Heschel: Philosophy, Theology, and Interfaith Dialogue.* Wiesbaden: Harrassowitz Verlag, 2009.

Kristol, Irving. "Elegy for a Lost World." *Commentary* (May 1950): 490–91.

Krome, Frederic. "Correspondence between Martin Buber, Hans Kohn, Abraham Joshua Heschel, and Adolph Oko." *Jewish Culture and History* 5, no. 1 (Summer 2002): 121–34.

Lachmund, Margarethe, ed. *Begegnung mit dem Judentum: Ein Gedenkbuch* [Encounter with Jewry: A memorial book, voices of [the Society of] Friends in Germany]. 2 vols. Bad Pyrmont: Auslieferung, 1962.

Leksikon fun der Nayer Yidisher Literatur. 8 vols., various eds. New York: Altveltlekhn Yidishn Kultur-Kongres, 1956–1981.

Levin, Leonard. "Heschel's Homage to the Rabbis: *Torah Min Ha-shamayim* as Historical Theology." *Conservative Judaism* 50, no. 2–3 (Winter–Spring 1998): 56–66.

Lewis, John. *Walking with the Wind: A Memoir of the Movement.* New York: Simon & Schuster, 1998.

Lewy, Julius. "Hitler's Contribution to the Teaching Staff of HUC, Part 2." *Hebrew Union College Bulletin* (April 1945): 8–10.

Lookstein, Joseph H. "The Neo-Hasidism of Abraham J. Heschel," *Judaism* 5, no. 3 (Summer 1956): 248.

Magid, Shaul. "Abraham Joshua Heschel and Thomas Merton: Heretics of Modernity." *Conservative Judaism* 1, no. 2–3 (Winter–Spring 1998): 445–61.

————. "A Monk, a Rabbi, and 'The Meaning of This Hour': War and Non-Violence in Abraham Joshua Heschel and Thomas Merton." *CrossCurrents* (Summer 2005): 184–213.

Marmur, Michael. "Abraham Joshua Heschel, Teenage Halakhist." In *Abraham Joshua Heschel: Philosophy, Theology and Interreligious Dialogue*, edited by Stanislaw Krajewski and Adam Lipszyc, 89–101. Wiesbaden: Harrassowitz Verlag, 2009.

————. "Heschel's Rhetoric of Citation: The Use of Sources in *God in Search of Man*." PhD dissertation, Hebrew University, Jerusalem, 2005.

————. "In Search of Heschel." *Shofar* 26, no. 1 (2007): 9–40.

Marty, Martin. "A Giant Has Fallen." *Christian Century* (January 17, 1973): 87.

Marx, Alexander. *Essays in Jewish Biography*. Philadelphia: Jewish Publication Society of America, 1947.

McNamara, Robert S. *In Retrospect: The Tragedy and Lessons of Vietnam*. New York: Random House, 1995.

Medoff, Rafael. "The Day the Rabbis Marched." David S. Wyman Institute for Holocaust Studies, nd. http://new.wymaninstitute.org/2017/01/the-day -the-rabbis-marched-history-and-impact-of-the-march/.

————. "New Perspectives on How America, and American Jewry, Responded to the Holocaust." *American Jewish History* 84, no. 3 (1996): 253–66.

Mendelsohn, Ezra. *The Jews of Poland between the World Wars*. Bloomington: Indiana University Press, 1983.

Mendes-Flohr, Paul. *Divided Passions: Jewish Intellectuals and the Experience of Modernity*. Detroit MI: Wayne State University Press, 1991.

————. *Martin Buber: From Mysticism to Dialogue: Martin Buber's Transformation of German Social Thought*. Detroit MI: Wayne State University Press, 1989.

————. "Theologian before the Abyss." Introduction to *The Meaning of Jewish Existence: Theological Essays, 1930–1939*, by Alexander Altmann. Hanover NH: University Press of New England for Brandeis University Press, 1991.

Merkle, John C., ed. *Abraham Joshua Heschel: Exploring His Life and Thought*. New York: Macmillan, 1985.

————. *The Genesis of Faith: The Depth Theology of Abraham Joshua Heschel*. New York: Macmillan, 1985.

Merton, Thomas. *Dancing in the Water of Life: Seeking Peace in the Hermitage; The Journals of Thomas Merton*. Vol. 5. Ed. Walter E. Daggy. San Francisco: HarperSanFrancisco, 1997.

Meyer, Michael. "The Refugee Scholars Project of the Hebrew Union College." In *A Bicentennial Festschrift for Jacob Rader Marcus*, edited by Bertram Korn, 359–75. New York: KTAV, 1976.

Milton, Sybil. "The Expulsion of Polish Jews from Germany, October 1938 to July 1939." *Leo Baeck Institute Yearbook* 29 (1984): 169–99.

Minczeles, Henri. *Vilna—Wilno—Vilnius. Le Jérusalem de la Lithuanie*. Paris: La Découverte, 1993.

Mintz, Jerome. *Hasidic People: A Place in the New World*. Cambridge MA: Harvard University Press, 1992.

Mirsky, Samuel K., ed. *Mosdot Torah Be-Eropah Be-vinyanam Uve-hurbanam* [Jewish institutions of ligher Learning in Europe: Their development and destruction]. New York: Ogen, 1956.

Monatsschrift für Geschichte und Wissenschaft des Judentums [Monthly journal for science and history of Judaism]. 1928–1939.

Mortara di Veroli, Elèna. "Ricordi di Heschel" [Memories of Heschel]. *Rassegna mensile di Israel* [Monthly review of Israel] (February 1973): 3–11.

Neusner, Jacob. "Abraham Joshua Heschel: The Man." In *To Grow in Wisdom: An Anthology of Abraham Joshua Heschel*, edited by Jacob Neusner and Noam Neusner, 3–22. Lanham MD: Madison Books, 1990.

———. "The Intellectual Achievement of Abraham Joshua Heschel." In *To Grow in Wisdom: An Anthology of Abraham Joshua Heschel*, edited by Jacob Neusner and Noam Neusner, 3–22. Lanham MD: Madison Books, 1990.

———. Review of *Torah Min Ha-shamayim Be-aspaklaryah Shel Ha-dorot*, by Abraham Joshua Heschel. *Conservative Judaism* 20, no. 3 (Spring 1966): 66–73.

———. *Stranger at Home: "The Holocaust," Zionism, and American Judaism*. Chicago: University of Chicago Press, 1981.

Niebuhr, Reinhold. "The Crisis in American Protestantism." *Christian Century* (December 4, 1963): 1498–1501.

———. "Masterly Analysis of Faith." *New York Herald Tribune Book Review* 1 (April 1951): 12.

———. *Pious and Secular America*. New York: Scribner's, 1958.

Niebuhr, Ursula. "Notes on a Friendship: Heschel and Reinhold Niebuhr." In *Abraham Joshua Heschel: Exploring His Life and Thought*, edited by John C. Merkle, 35–43. New York: Macmillan, 1985.

Oates, Stephen B. *Let the Trumpet Sound: The Life of Martin Luther King, Jr.* New York: Harper and Row, 1982.

Oesterreicher, John M. 1967. "Declaration on the Relationship of the Church to Non-Christian Religions: Introduction and Commentary." In *Commentary on the Documents of Vatican II*, edited by Herbert Vorgrimler, 1–136. New York: Herder & Herder, 1967.

Parzen, Herbert. "Louis Ginzberg, the Proponent of *Halakhah*." In *Architects of Conservative Judaism*, 128–54. New York: Jonathan David, 1964.

Penkower, Monty. "American Jewry and the Holocaust: From Biltmore to the American Jewish Conference." *Jewish Social Studies* 47, no. 2 (1985): 95–114.

Perlow, Alter Israel Shimon. *Tiferet Ish*. Edited by Nahum Mordecai Perlow. Jerusalem, n.p: 1968.

Perlow, Towa (Gitla). *L'Education et l'enseignement chez les Juifs à l'époque talmudique*. Paris: Librairie Ernest Leroux, 1931.

Petuchowski, Jakob J., and Ezra Spicehandler, eds. *Perakim Ba-yahadut* [Essays on Judaism]. Cincinnati: Hebrew Union College Press; Jerusalem: M. Newman, 1963.

Polish, David. "Current Trends in Jewish Theology." *Yearbook of the Central Conference of American Rabbis* 63 (1953): 420–30.

Proceedings of the Rabbinical Assembly of America. New York: Rabbinical Assembly of America, 1953, 1958, 1959, 1961, 1962, 1964, 1966, 1968.

Rabinovitch, Gérard, ed. *Abraham J. Heschel. Un tsaddiq dans la cité*. Paris: Alliance israélite universelle, 2004.

Rabinowicz, Harry M. *Hasidism: The Movement and Its Masters*. Northvale NJ: Jason Aronson, 1988.

Rabinowicz, Tzvi. *Chassidic Rebbes, From the Baal Shem Tov to Modern Times*. Southfield MI: Targam Press; Spring Valley NY: Feldheim, 1989.

Rabinowitsch, Wolf Zeev. *Lithuanian Hasidism from Its Beginnings to the Present Day*. London: Vallentine, Mitchell, 1970.

Rackman, Emanuel. "Can We Moderns Keep the Sabbath?" *Commentary* (September 1954): 211–20.

———. "Dr. Heschel's Answer." *Jewish Horizon* (October 1956): 16.

Rakeffet-Rothkoff, Aaron. *The Silver Era in American Jewish Orthodoxy: Rabbi Eliezer Silver and His Generation*. Jerusalem: Feldheim, 1981.

Ran, Leyzer, ed. *Jerusalem of Lithuania: Illustrated and Documented*. 3 vols. New York: privately printed, 1974.

Ravitch, Melekh. *Mayn Leksikon* [My lexicon]. 2 vols. Montreal: Aroysgegeben fun A Komitet, 1945, 1947.

"Reminiscences by Heschel's Former Students." *Conservative Judaism* 50, no. 2–3 (Winter–Spring 1998): 175.

Rosenstein, Neil, ed. *The Unbroken Chain: Biographical Sketches and Genealogy of Illustrious Jewish Families from the 15th–20th Centuries*. 2 vols. 2nd ed. New York, London, and Jerusalem: CIS Publishers, 1990.

Rosenzweig, Franz. *F. R. His Life and Thought*. Edited by Nahum Glatzer. New York: Schocken, 1953.

———. *On Jewish Learning*. Edited by Nahum Glatzer. New York: Schocken, 1965.

————. *The Star of Redemption*. Translated by Barbara E. Galli. Madison: University of Wisconsin Press, 2005.

Rotenstreich, Nathan. "On Prophetic Consciousness." *Journal of Religion* 54 (1974): 185–98.

Rothschild, Fritz A. "Architect and Herald of a New Theology." *Conservative Judaism* 28, no. 1 (Fall 1973): 55–60.

————. "God and Modern Man: The Approach of Abraham J. Heschel." *Judaism* 8, no. 2 (Spring 1959): 112–20.

————. "Conservative Judaism Faces the Need for Change." *Commentary* (November 1953): 447–55.

————, ed. Introduction to *Between God and Man*, by Abraham Joshua Heschel, 7–32. 3rd ed. New York: Free Press, 1975.

Rubenstein, Richard L. *After Auschwitz: Radical Theology and Contemporary Judaism*. Indianapolis IN: Bobbs-Merrill, 1966.

Rynne, Xavier (Fr. Francis Xavier Murphy, CSSR). *Vatican Council II*. Maryknoll NY: Orbis, 1999.

Samuel, Maurice. Review of *The Earth Is the Lord's*, by Abraham Joshua Heschel. *Congress Weekly* (1950): 7–9.

Sanders, James. "An Apostle to the Gentiles." *Conservative Judaism* 28, no. 1 (Fall 1973): 61–63.

————. "Urbis and Orbis: Jerusalem Today." *Christian Century* 84, no. 30 (July 26, 1967): 967–70.

Sarna, Jonathan. *American Judaism: A History*. New Haven CT: Yale University Press, 2004.

————. *JPS: The Americanization of Jewish Culture, 1888–1988; A Centennial History of the Jewish Publication Society*. Philadelphia: Jewish Publication Society, 1989.

————. "Two Traditions of Seminary Scholarship." In *A History of the Jewish Theological Seminary*, vol. 2, 53–80. Edited by Jack Wertheimer. New York: Jewish Theological Seminary, 1997.

Schachter-Shalomi, Zalman. *Spiritual Intimacy: A Study of Counseling in Hasidism*. Northvale NJ: Jason Aronson, 1991.

Scheler, Max. *The Nature and Forms of Sympathy*. London: Routledge & K. Paul, 1954.

Schnädelbach, Herbert. *Philosophy in Germany 1831–1933*. Translated by Eric Matthews. Cambridge: Cambridge University Press, 1984.

Schneersohn, Fishl. *Der Weg tsum Mentsh* [The way to humanity]. Vilna, 1928.

————. *Studies in Psycho-Expedition: Fundamentals of the Psychological Science of Man and a Theory of Nervousness*. New York: Science of Man Press, 1929.

Schochet, Elijah Judah, and Solomon Spiro. *Saul Lieberman: The Man and His Work*. New York: Jewish Theological Seminary, 2005, 1993.

Scholem, Gershom. *Major Trends in Jewish Mysticism*. 3rd ed. New York: Schocken, 1991.

Schorsch, Rebecca. "The Hermeneutics of Heschel in *Torah min Hashamayim*." *Judaism* 43, no. 3 (Summer 1991): 301–8.

Schwab, Hermann. *Chachme Ashkenaz*. London: Mitre Press, 1964.

Scult, Mel. "Kaplan's Heschel: A View from the Kaplan Diary." *Conservative Judaism* 54, no. 4 (Summer 2002): 3–14.

Shandler, Jeffrey. "Heschel and Yiddish: A Struggle with Signification." *Journal of Jewish Thought and Philosophy* 2 (1993): 245–99.

Shulvass, Moses. "The Rabbiner-Seminar in Berlin." In *Mosdot Torah Be-Eropah Be-vinyanam Uve-hurbanam* [Jewish institutions of higher learning in Europe: Their development and destruction], 689–714. New York: Ogen, 1956.

Simon, Ernst. "Jewish Adult Education in Nazi Germany as Spiritual Resistance." *Leo Baeck Institute Yearbook* 1 (1956): 68–104.

————. "Martin Buber and German Jewry." *Leo Baeck Institute Yearbook* 3 (1958): 3–39.

Simposio Cardinal Agostino Bea (16–19 dicembre 1981). Rome: Pontificia Università Lateranense, 1983.

Singer, Isaac Bashevis. *Love and Exile*. Garden City NY: Doubleday, 1984.

Soloveitchik, Joseph Baer. *Halakhic Man*. Translated by Lawrence Kaplan. Philadelphia: Jewish Publication Society, 1983.

Somerville, James M. "Successive Versions of *Nostra Aetate*." In *Merton and Judaism: Recognition, Repentance, and Renewal; Holiness in Words*, edited by Beatrice Bruteau, 341–71. Louisville KY: Fons Vitae, 2004.

Spiro, Solomon. "The Moral Vision of Saul Lieberman: A Historiographic Approach to Normative Jewish Ethics." *Conservative Judaism* 46, no. 4 (Summer 1994): 64–84.

Staub, Michael E. *Torn at the Roots: The Crisis of Jewish Liberalism in Postwar America*. New York: Columbia University Press, 2002.

Stern, Harold. "A. J. Heschel, Irenic Polemicist." *Proceedings of the Rabbinical Assembly of America* 45 (1983): 169–77.

Strauss, Herbert A., ed. *Jewish Immigrants of the Nazi Period*. Vol. 6. New York, Munich, London, and Paris: K. G. Saur, 1987.

Synan, SJ, Edward A. "Abraham Heschel and Prayer." In *The Bridge: A Yearbook of Judeo-Christian Studies*, edited by John M. Oesterreicher, 256–65. New York: Pantheon, 1955.

Tanenbaum, Marc H. "A Jewish View on *Nostra Aetate*." In *Twenty Years of Jewish-Catholic Relations*, edited by Eugene J. Fisher, James Rudin, and Marc Tanenbaum, 39–60. New York: Paulist. 1986.

———. *A Prophet for Our Times: An Anthology of the Writings of Rabbi Marc H. Tanenbaum*. Edited by Judith H. Banki and Eugene J. Fisher. New York: Fordham University Press, 2002.

Tartakover, Abraham. "The Institute for Jewish Studies in Warsaw." In *Kovetz Madda'i le-Zekher Moshe Schorr* [Studies in memory of Moses Schorr, 1874–1941], edited by Louis Ginzberg and Abraham Weiss. New York: Professor Moses Schorr Memorial Committee, 1944.

Temkin, Sefton D. "A Century of Reform Judaism in America." *American Jewish Year Book* (1973): 3–75.

Terrien, Samuel. "The Divine Pathos." *Interpretation* 17 (1963): 482–88.

Teshima, Jacob Yuroh. "In Memory of My Teacher." *Light of Life* (1973): 49–55.

Thurin, John P. "Vatican II Epilogue." *Insight: Notre Dame* (Summer 1966): 8–19.

Tikkun. Special issue on Abraham Joshua Heschel. January–February 1998.

Tobias, Norman C. *Jewish Conscience of the Church: Jules Isaac and the Second Vatican Council*. Cham, Switzerland: Palgrave Macmillan, 2017.

Weltsch, Robert. "David Koigen." *Jüdische Rundschau* (March 6, 1933): 1.

———. "Tragt ihn mit Stolz, den gelben Fleck!" *Jüdische Rundschau* (April 4, 1933).

Wertheimer, Jack, ed. *Tradition Renewed: A History of the Jewish Theological Seminary*. 2 vols. New York: Jewish Theological Seminary, 1997.

Wiesel, Elie. *The Jews of Silence: A Personal Report on Soviet Jewry*. Translated by Neil Kozodoy. New York: Holt, Rinehart & Winston, 1966.

Wohlgemuth, Josef. "Tschuvah" [Repentance]. In *Grundgedanken der Religionsphilosophie, Max Schelers im jüdischer Beleuchtung: Festgabe für Jakob Rosenheim* [Principles of the philosophy of religion, Max Scheler in Jewish light: Festschrift for Jacob Rosenheim], edited by Heinrich Elsemann, 19–76. Frankfurt am Main: J. Kaufmann, 1931.

Zemba, Abraham. "The Mesivta in Warsaw." In *Mosdot Torah Be-Eropah Be-vinyanam Uve-hurbanam* [Jewish institutions of higher learning in Europe: Their development and destruction], edited by Samuel K. Mirsky, 363–75. New York: Ogen, 1956.

————. "Shtieblakh in Warsaw." In *Mosdot Torah Be-Eropah Be-vinyanam Uve-hurbanam* [Jewish institutions of higher learning in Europe: Their development and destruction], edited by Samuel K. Mirsky, 355–63. New York: Ogen, 1956.

Zuroff, Efraim. *The Response of Orthodox Jewry in the United States to the Holocaust: The Activities of the Vaad Ha-Hatzala Rescue Committee, 1939–1945.* New York: KTAV, 2000.

INDEX OF NAMES

212, 257, 259, 287, 289, 329, 350, 367n40, 369n35, 371n40, 371n46, 371n51, 372n2

Flannery, Edward H., 336

Flender, Harold, 334, 391n17

Fosdick, Harry Emerson, 286, 290, 296

Freehof, Solomon, 310, 389n30

Freimann, Jakob, 37, 361n15

Friedman, Dovid Moshe (Heschel's grandfather), 6, 77

Friedman, Israel (1797–1850), 5

Friedman, Israel (1854–1934, Heschel's first cousin), 107

Friedman, Maurice, 166–67, 366n20, 373nn31–32, 375n10

Friedman, Mordecai Shlomo, 107, 135

Friedman, Ralph, 257, 261

Friedman, Sarah, 14

Gendler, Everett, 243

Gillman, Neil, 349, 375n9

Ginsburg, Harold Louis, 330

Ginzberg, Louis (Levi), 137, 142–43, 146, 153, 168–70, 328, 371n51

Glatzer, Nahum Norbert, 178–79, 374n6

Goethe, Johann Wolfgang von, 53

Goldmann, Nahum, 222, 261

Gordis, Robert, 175, 374n47

Gottschalk, Alfred, 115, 340, 350, 368n14, 392n28

Grayzel, Solomon, xv, 170, 374n37, 374nn39–40

Green, Arthur, 198, 390n3

Greenberg, Hayim, 131, 154, 245, 379n37

Greenberg, Moshe, 159

Greenberg, Simon, 180, 223

Guttmann, Alexander, 67, 115

Guttmann, Julius, 40–41, 55, 362n21, 364n28, 368n14

Hartstein, Jacob I., 142, 371n50

Heidegger, Martin, 80, 86, 194, 250

Heller, Haim, 37

Herberg, Will, 167, 194, 200, 204, 213, 374n34, 375n4, 377n43, 377n53

Hershcopf, Judith (Banki), 259, 383nn5–6, 384n13, 385n32, 386n39

Hershlag, Judith (Yocheved Muffs), 319, 343, 393n35

Hertz, Joseph Herman, 101

Hertzberg, Arthur E., 388–89n29

Heschel, Abraham Joshua (1832–1881, Heschel's grandfather), 5

Heschel, Abraham Joshua (1888–1967, Heschel's first cousin and brother-in-law), 14, 82, 90–91, 107, 151

Heschel, Devorah Miriam. *See* Dermer, Devorah Miriam Heschel (Heschel's sister)

Heschel, Esther Sima (Heschel's sister), 7, 103, 107, 109, 230

Heschel, Gittel (Heschel's sister), 7, 14, 92, 107, 109, 134, 230

Heschel, Hannah Susannah (daughter), P8, xvi, xviii, 182, 218, 225, 242, 251, 260, 287, 298, 322–24, 346, 347, 349–451, 354, 375n11, 381n8, 383n9, 386n46, 393n42

Heschel, Israel (Heschel's first cousin and nephew), 360n21, 360n29

Heschel, Moses (Moyshe) (Heschel's first cousin), 349, 353–54

Heschel, Moshe Mordecai (Heschel's father), P1, 5–8, 13, 15, 21, 357, 359n3, 372n10

Morgenstern, Menahem Mendl, 16–18, 26–27, 109, 141, 194, 325–28, 330–31, 338, 354–55, 361n44, 390n3, 391n7

Morlion, Felix, 332, 389n37, 391nn13–14

Mortara, Elèna (di Veroli), 332, 389n37, 391nn13–14

Muffs, Yochanan, 351, 362n2, 386n48

Muilenburg, James, 212

Nahman, Rabbi of Bratslav, 18, 296

Nadich, Judah, 354

Nasr, Seyyed Hossein, 341–43

Nasser, Gamal Abdel, 304–5

Neusner, Jacob, 371n46

Niebuhr, H. Richard, 329

Niebuhr, Reinhold, 167, 174, 197–98, 204, 210–12, 238, 249, 251, 285–86, 297, 305, 329, 334–35, 374n45, 378n1, 378n3, 385n41, 391n18

Niebuhr, Ursula, 212, 334, 378n4

Nixon, Richard Milhous, 318–19, 343–45, 350, 393n38, 394n1

Pacelli, Eugenio. See Pope Pius XII (Eugenio Pacelli)

Packard, Vance, 214, 378n8

Pappenheim, Bertha, 67

Peli, Pinchas, 354, 390n3, 394n3, 394n13

Perlow, Aaron (Heschel's first cousin), 27, 150

Perlow, Alter Israel Shimon (Heschel's uncle), 6, 7, 9, 15–16, 18–19, 21–23, 27, 60, 126, 323–24, 327, 360n20

Perlow, Chaya (Heschel's maternal grandmother), 6

Perlow, Tova Gittel (Towa Gitla) (Heschel's first cousin), 21, 27, 150, 218, 360n33, 361n46

Perlow, Jacob (Heschel's maternal grandfather), 6–7

Perlow, Jacob (son of Yehuda Aryeh Perlow), 323, 350, 372n5, 390n51

Perlow, Nahum Mordecai, 23

Perlow, Rivka Reizel. See Heschel, Rivka Reizel Perlow (Heschel's mother)

Perlow, Yehuda Aryeh Leib, 16, 23, 350

Philipson, David, 116, 122, 135

Pope John XXIII (Angelo Roncalli), 235, 237, 253–55, 261, 262–63, 265

Pope Paul VI (Giovanni Montini), 266, 269, 272, 277–79, 283–84, 289, 332, 337, 355, 384n22, 384n25, 386n40, 388n17

Pope Pius XII (Eugenio Pacelli), 253, 256, 377n44

Prinz, Joachim, 248

Rackman, Emanuel, 204–5, 378n55

Radhakrishnan, Sarvepalli, 213

Raju, P. T., 213

Ran, Leyzer, 34

Randall, John Herman, 224

Rashi (Rabbi Shlomo Itzhaki), 11, 128, 137, 155, 202, 339, 361n44, 392n26

Rattner, Abraham, 320

Ravitch, Melekh, 25, 33, 44, 97, 151–52, 361n41, 372nn7–8

Reiss, Erich, 68–69, 71, 78, 86, 97, 172, 328, 367n10

Reynolds, Frank, 338, 392n23

Rilke, Rainer Maria, 45–46

Roncalli, Angelo Giuseppe. See Pope John XXIII (Angelo Roncalli)

Roosevelt, Franklin Delano, 130, 136, 142, 146, 371n38

Roosevelt, Theodore, 224

Rosenthal, Franz, 102, 115, 368n14

Rosenstock-Huessy, Eugen, 167

Rosenzweig, Franz, 71, 82, 84, 167, 172, 174, 179, 185, 194–95, 204, 365n6, 376n30

Rothschild, Fritz Alexander, 158–59, 223–24, 294, 314, 343, 347, 351–52, 354, 364n18, 364n31, 365n1, 366n20, 366n28, 367n7, 373n16, 376n20, 379nn25–26, 390n48, 393n44, 394n2

Rubinstein, Arthur, 152, 298

Saadia Gaon (Saadia ben Joseph), 127–28, 163

Samuel, Maurice, 165–66, 373n30

Sanders, James Alvin, 290–91, 307, 386n51, 388nn23–25

Schechter, Solomon, 142, 145

Scheler, Max, 36, 55, 80, 362n13, 363n7, 363n8

Schlosser, Rudolph, 88–89

Schmidt, Stefan, 258, 262

Schneersohn, Fishl, 21–22, 24, 25–27, 30–31, 41–42, 150, 217, 360nn34–35, 362n27

Schneerson, Menahem Mendel, 37

Schocken, Shelomoh Salman, 62, 73

Scholem, Gershom Gerhard, 94, 138, 167, 198, 374n36, 377n38

Schonfeld, Solomon, 100

Schor, Ilya, 164, 178

Schorr, Moses, 98, 138

Schuman, Henry, 158, 164

Seeger, Pete, 346

Sellin, Ernst, 55

Shapiro, David Shlomo, 234, 380n52

Shazar, Zalman (Schneor, Rubashov), 217–18, 355

Sherwin, Byron L., 347, 393n40

Shmidman, Joshua, 323, 390n50

Shuster, Zachariah, 255, 257–59, 261, 265, 267, 269, 273–79, 282, 317, 382nn2–3, 383n6, 384nn13–14, 384nn23–25, 384n30, 384n33, 384n35, 384n37

Silver, Abba Hillel, 183

Silver, Eliezer, 123–24, 132, 135–36, 371n38

Simon, Ernst Akiba, 167, 366n14, 366n17

Simon, Jacob, 84–85

Singer, Isaac Bashevis, 9, 33, 359n12

Sister, Moses, 41

Slawson, John, 224, 269, 273, 275–77, 383n3, 383n6, 384n15, 384 85n23, 385n30, 385n35, 385n37

Soloveitchik, Joseph Baer, 37, 142, 189, 257, 259, 263, 268, 276, 280, 383n6, 385n27

Spellman, Francis Joseph, Cardinal, 239, 296

Stencl, Abraham Nochem, 46

Stern, Carl, 355–56

Steuermann, Edward, 152

Straus, Roger Williams, Jr., 171, 347, 374n40, 393n43

Straus, Anna (Sylvia's mother), 152–53, 372n10

Straus, Samuel (Sylvia's father), 152, 372n10

Straus, Sylvia. *See* Heschel, Sylvia Straus (wife)

Strauss, Eduard, 114, 125, 370n16

Sutzkever, Abraham, 390n3

Synan, Edward A., 200, 377n44

Tanenbaum, Marc Herman, P10,
    157–58, 164, 224, 236, 251, 254,
    255, 257, 259, 262–63, 267–68,
    273, 275–76, 279, 373n15, 379n27,
    383nn6–8, 384n14, 384–85n23,
    385n33, 385n35, 385n37
Terrien, Samuel, 233, 380n49
Teshima, Jacob Yuroh, P13, 330–31,
    347, 351, 353–54, 357, 391n11,
    393n44, 394nn11–12, 395n19
Tillich, Paul, 167, 182, 213
Tisserant, Eugene, Cardinal, 261, 279
Toaff, Elio, 256
Tucker, Gordon, 380n43

Vilna Gaon (Elijah ben Solomon
    Zalman), 143, 168

Wagner, Robert F., Jr., 239, 264
Warren, A. M., 103
Warren, Earl, 336
Weinreich, Max, 140
Weiss-Rosmarin, Trude, 178–79

Werblowsky, Raphael Juda Zwi,
    384n20, 392n31
Wiesel, Elie, 248, 304, 351, 353,
    373nn31–32, 382n22, 383n24,
    388n18
Willebrands, Johannes, Cardinal, 258,
    262, 267, 269, 384n20
Wise, Isaac Mayer, 113
Wiseman, Joseph, 347, 351, 393n45
Wolfson, Harry Austryn, 257
Wohlgemuth, Josef, 36, 362n13
Woodward, Kenneth L., 291, 386n52,
    389n36, 394n13

Yehuda Halevi 148, 289, 330
Yitzhak, Levi, of Berditchev, 6, 19,
    359n6
Young, Andrew Jackson, Jr., 243–44

Zeitlin, Aaron, 149
Zeitlin, Hillel, 24, 109, 149
Zemba, Menahem, 19, 109, 359n15,
    360n30
Zolla, Ellémire, 316–17, 389nn37–38